CREATING AN
OPPORTUNITY
SOCIETY

CREATING AN
OPPORTUNITY
SOCIETY

RON HASKINS
ISABEL SAWHILL

BROOKINGS INSTITUTION PRESS
Washington, D.C.

Library of Congress Cataloging-in-Publication data
Haskins, Ron.
    Creating an opportunity society / Ron Haskins and Isabel Sawhill.
        p.   cm.
    Includes bibliographical references and index.
    Summary: "Presents facts and factors that contribute to economic opportunity, looking at how poor, middle class, and rich have fared in recent decades. Proposes a cost-effective agenda for increasing opportunity, consistent with American values, and focuses on improving lives of the young and disadvantaged, emphasizing individual responsibility as indispensable for success"—Provided by publisher.
        ISBN 978-0-8157-0322-8 (pbk. : alk. paper)
    1. Social mobility—United States.   2. Social classes—Economic aspects—United States.   3. United States—Economic policy—21st century.   4. United States—Social policy—21st century. I. Sawhill, Isabel V.   II. Title.
        HN90.S65H35 2009
        305.5'13—dc22   2009026627

9 8 7 6 5 4 3 2

Printed on acid-free paper

Typeset in Minion and Univers Condensed

Composition by R. Lynn Rivenbark
Macon, Georgia

Printed by R. R. Donnelley
Harrisonburg, Virginia

Contents

Foreword

Think tanks make their mark by applying reason and evidence to the choices facing policymakers. At Brookings, we summarize that mission in three words: quality, independence, impact. This book, written by Ron Haskins and Belle Sawhill—two colleagues with extensive experience in government and the NGO world—is an example of how the think-tank formula for producing usable knowledge can lead to imaginative, pragmatic public policy proposals.

For those of us who are not experts in social policy, it often seems that government programs designed to fight poverty and increase economic opportunity have enjoyed little success. This impression seemed to be confirmed by the pictures of destitution on our TV screens following Katrina and by scores of headlines over the years telling of the failure of yet another government social program. Against this bleak backdrop, Ron and Belle's work in the pages that follow is especially welcome. They describe the problem of poverty and circumscribed opportunity in detail while examining the values Americans bring to thinking about what they owe to the disadvantaged. They also provide interesting and even provocative analyses of the role of family background and other factors in accounting for poverty and intergenerational mobility.

Ron and Belle leave little doubt that Americans, broadly speaking, want to help those on the bottom; that government has already responded generously; that social science knowledge about both the problems and solutions is robust and growing; and that further progress in reducing poverty and increasing opportunity is possible. They lay out an agenda for reforms designed to strengthen education at all levels, to increase both work and government supports for low-income working families, and to reduce nonmarital births and encourage marriage. Taken together, these reforms, if aggressively implemented, would almost certainly promote opportunity and reduce poverty. A notable feature of the reforms proposed here is the extent to which they entail policies that are explicitly designed to encourage personal responsibility.

Arriving at a moment of economic peril, especially for those dealing with poverty, this book establishes the basis for believing that when the worst recession since the Great Depression passes, as it must, wise policy choices and widespread insistence on personal responsibility by all our institutions and leaders will give more people a shot at moving up the economic ladder.

So not only is the optimism that infuses this book striking—there's good reason to hope it might be catching, including among those who face tough policy choices in the years ahead.

STROBE TALBOTT
President
Brookings Institution

Washington, D.C.
July 2009

Preface

In mid-2009 as this book went to press, the economy was in a deep recession. Recessions are not equal opportunity disemployers. Hardest hit are people and families with the least skills and the fewest assets to fall back on in hard times. The safety net in the United States provides some cushion but less than in other advanced countries. Because the annual poverty rate is released by the Census Bureau only with a long lag, we don't yet know exactly how the recession is affecting the poor. Still, we know enough to predict that the story will be a depressing one for those at the bottom of the income scale. The number of people receiving food stamps increased by about 2.4 million or 25 percent between April 2007 and February 2009, and the unemployment rate had more than doubled between 2007 and the summer of 2009. Based on historical evidence, analysts are predicting that the poverty rate in 2009 and 2010 will be in the neighborhood of 15 percent and that unemployment will exceed 10 percent for the first time since the early 1980s. However, at some point the economy will recover, and as a nation, we will still face the question of what the most advantaged owe to the least advantaged—and what the least advantaged should do to deserve it. This book is about that more fundamental question and especially about how we create greater opportunity for those in less advantaged families to climb the economic ladder.

Not only was the nation fighting the biggest economic collapse since the Great Depression in 2009, but a new administration took office and began rapidly changing the policy landscape it had inherited. The social policy reforms contained in the $787 billion stimulus package enacted by Congress in February and the budget proposal unveiled by President Obama in April would, if all the reforms were enacted, constitute something of a domestic policy revolution. In addition to significant moves toward universal health coverage, Obama's reforms included major expansions of preschool programs, huge new spending on the public schools, a substantial retooling of and increased funding for postsecondary education, a new home-visiting program for poor families that would grow to nearly $2 billion annually, expansions of tax provisions that provide cash to working families, expansions of the unemployment insurance program, reform and growth of emergency cash welfare benefits, a major expansion of food stamps, and many others. It will be at least two years before it becomes clear which of these changes will become temporary responses to the recession and which permanent law, but the clues provided by the president's 2010 budget indicate that many of the programs may continue.

Several of the legislative actions taken or proposed by the Obama administration mirror the proposals in this book. Where possible we note these similarities in chapters 8, 9, and 10. We wish we could report that all of our proposals have been enacted or proposed, but we take considerable satisfaction from knowing that many of them—perhaps in a slightly different form— have already found their way into law or into President Obama's 2010 budget proposal. At the very least, we think the actual and proposed Obama legislation shows that nearly all our proposals are politically feasible.

We sketch out the major themes of the volume in the first chapter. Two of them grow out of our earlier work. The first is the theme of opportunity. Sawhill began work on this topic in the late 1990s and published an earlier book (coauthored with Daniel McMurrer) called *Getting Ahead: Economic and Social Mobility in America*. With generous support from the Pew Charitable Trusts, the two of us, along with our Brookings colleague Julia Isaacs, collaborated on a more recent volume summarizing what is known about economic inequality and opportunity called *Getting Ahead or Losing Ground: Economic Mobility in America*. The second theme is personal responsibility— a concept which now seems to have broad backing from policymakers from both parties but which was still controversial as recently as the 1990s. As a senior staffer with the Ways and Means Committee and as a senior adviser to President George W. Bush, Haskins has worked on several pieces of federal legislation, notably the 1996 welfare reform law, which embodied the concepts of personal responsibility so central to this book. His book, *Work over Welfare*, published by Brookings in 2006, tells the story of how the 1995–96 welfare reform debate unfolded and describes the central role played by the bipartisan agreement that welfare policy had to be based squarely on personal responsibility.

When two people decide to collaborate on a book, it inevitably produces some disagreements but also great benefits. Haskins is a developmental psychologist by training and has worked with Republicans for nearly two decades. Sawhill is an economist and served in the Clinton White House from 1993 to 1995. Despite our different backgrounds and experience, we are able to find common ground on most issues, an outcome that is reflected in the pages that follow.

This volume grew out of many years of work the two of us have conducted in the course of running the Center on Children and Families at Brookings. Two projects were especially important. In the fall of 2007 we published a volume of the *Future of Children*, a journal we edit with our colleagues at Princeton, devoted to specific proposals for reducing poverty. Some of the top poverty experts in the country wrote chapters for the volume and we have been highly influenced by their ideas. These experts include Paul Amato, Gordon Berlin, Becky Blank, Greg Duncan, Mark Greenberg, Jens Ludwig, Katherine Magnuson, Rebecca Maynard, Larry Mead, Richard Murnane, and Alan Weil. We would also like to thank the discussants of the poverty volume— Gary Burtless, Robert Doar, Kathy Edin, Irv Garfinkel, Marva Hammons, Harry Holzer, Wade Horn, Melissa Kearney, Hugh Price, Craig Ramey, and Jesse Rothstein—for their helpful insights. The second project was the volume on mobility we wrote with our colleague Julia Isaacs; we have also drawn heavily from this volume. We are especially indebted to Julia for her work on economic mobility and opportunity and to our colleagues at Pew, especially John Morton and Ianna Kachoris, for their support.

We would like to thank several people and organizations for their invaluable support of the Center on Children and Families, as well as specific help with the book. Mark Steinmeyer of the Smith Richardson Foundation initially invited us to undertake a volume reviewing research on poverty to offer, in particular, new ideas on how poverty could be reduced, especially among children. We thank Mark and the foundation for this support. Thanks also to Mike Laracy and the Annie E. Casey Foundation for their financial support for our Center and for much of our work over the past eight years. Vicki and Roger Sant have been generous in their financial support for our Center while we were working on this volume. Benita Melton and the Charles Stewart Mott Foundation and Jennifer Phillips and the Joyce Foundation have provided valuable financial assistance as well. During this time our Center also received funding from the William and Flora Hewlett Foundation, the Pew Charitable Trusts, the Bill and Melinda Gates Foundation, the John D. and Catherine T. MacArthur Foundation, and the Doris Duke Charitable Foundation. Without the backing of these individuals and foundations we would not have been able to complete this book. None of them, of course, bears any responsibility for its content.

One of the most exhilarating parts of writing this book has been the advice and assistance given so generously by researchers, government officials, and foundation officers, some of them complete strangers. An especially notable instance of such advice occurred in December 2008 after we had finished the first draft of the book. We held a one-day conference at Brookings and asked our colleagues from around the country to comment on the volume. Nearly every person we invited attended, and, taken together, they provided us with the most penetrating criticism of the volume imaginable. We made changes to the text in response to nearly all the comments and criticisms of this august group, which included Gordon Berlin (MDRC), Becky Blank (Brookings, now with the Department of Commerce), Gary Burtless (Brookings), Stuart Butler (The Heritage Foundation), Greg Duncan (University of California–Irvine), Bill Galston (Brookings), Robert Haveman (University of Wisconsin–Madison), Harry Holzer (Urban Institute and Georgetown University), Wade Horn (Deloitte Consulting LLP), Jeffrey Kling (Brookings, now with the Congressional Budget Office), Bob Lerman (Urban Institute), Jens Ludwig (University of Chicago), Bhashkar Mazumder (Federal Reserve Bank of Chicago), Larry Mead (New York University), Charles Murray (American Enterprise Institute), Timothy Smeeding (University of Wisconsin–Madison), Gene Steuerle (Peter G. Peterson Foundation), and Russ Whitehurst (Brookings).

At Brookings, we were fortunate to have dedicated and exceptionally competent help from our assistants including Victoria ("Tori") Finkle, Mary Baugh, Emily Groves, and Julie Clover. Tori spent countless hours doing background research for this volume. Her meticulous attention to data analysis, the construction of charts and tables, preparation of literature reviews, and documentation of sources—all the while displaying great patience and perseverance—was simply extraordinary.

We have also received timely assistance on all aspects of publishing the volume from the Brookings Institution Press, especially Janet Walker and Chris Kelaher. Special thanks to our eagle-eyed editor Diane Hammond and to Rebecca Mintz for her careful verification.

Of the many others who helped in the research, writing, or production of the volume, too numerous to mention, we would especially thank Richard

Bavier, Sandy Baum, Len Berman, Alan Berube, Sarah Brown, Nancye Campbell, Sarah Chilton, Paul Cullinan, Gene Falk, Sabrina Fisher, Art Foley, Peter Germanis, Julia Isaacs, Pamela Jackson, Andrea Kane, Kelleen Kaye, Maggie McCarty, Sara McLanahan, Jonathan Morancy, Jenny Nagaoka, Ed Olsen, Theodora Ooms, James Riccio, Emily Roessel, Jeffrey Rohaly, Dottie Rosenbaum, Howard Rotston, Arloc Sherman, Dave Smole, Carmen Solomon-Fears, Karen Spar, Jeffrey Tebbs, Larry Temple, Adam Thomas, Matt Weidinger, James Weill, Brad Wilcox, Jim Ziliak, Nick Zill, and members of the Brookings Poverty and Inequality Seminar. In the end, the responsibility for any errors of judgment or fact belongs to the authors.

Ron Haskins
Isabel Sawhill

Washington, D.C.
July 2009

CREATING AN
OPPORTUNITY
SOCIETY

one
Our Vision

The test of our progress is not whether we add more to the abundance of those who have much; it is whether we provide enough for those who have too little.

FRANKLIN D. ROOSEVELT

No ancient king could have imagined the comforts and conveniences provided by houses, cars, computers, clothes, packaged foods, and various other amenities enjoyed by most Americans. As this book went to press, the economy was in a deep recession and could remain there for several years, but such temporary troubles should not detract from the fact that America is a very wealthy nation. If personal after-tax income in 2008 were divided equally among the population, every adult and child would have about $35,000 in goods and services each year—that's $140,000 for a family of four.[1] But the American economy is marked as much by the disparity between the top and the bottom as it is by its ability to generate income and wealth. Granted, some inequality in income and wealth is necessary to maintain the rewards for the planning, hard work, self-discipline, and risk taking that are the handmaidens of productivity. And productivity is the basis of America's wealth. But our society and political system seem to be more concerned with productivity and the generation of wealth than with inequality and those at the bottom of the heap.

That said, this book is not primarily about how to change the distribution of income per se. Nor is it only about the poor, although we do give them and their children special attention. Instead it is primarily about opportunity and how the nation can create more of it, especially for those at the bottom. We believe that everyone should have a shot at the American Dream and that too many people have been left behind. We focus more on opportunity than on inequality and poverty for two reasons. First, Americans believe in opportunity. They believe that anyone who works hard and has a certain amount of talent can get ahead. For this reason, they are more willing to support policies that reward personal responsibility and enhance mobility than policies that unconditionally redistribute income after the fact. They are far more interested in equal opportunity than in equal results. We argue that policies aligned with the value of helping people help themselves are likely to be politically acceptable as well as effective. Second, opportunity is a dynamic concept. It is about the process that lies behind where one ends up on the ladder of life. An individual or a family may be poor today and rich tomorrow, or vice versa. A middle-class family may fear that it is only one job away from being poor, and it may be right. A poor family may take great pride in the fact that, as a result of their own sacrifices, their children have entered the middle class. Like almost everyone else who has written about these topics, we rely heavily on data that measure the rich, the poor, and the middle class at one point in time. But too much focus on income at any one time may miss the more important fact that people's fortunes change over the course of their lives.

It is in this context that we examine the growing body of evidence on economic mobility. Mobility and the chance to move ahead in life depend in large part on the circumstances into which one is born. In a seminal address about poverty at Howard University in 1965, President Lyndon Johnson said that as a society we have a responsibility for bringing people to the "starting line" without significant disadvantages, because if we fail to do so they cannot fairly participate in the race.[2] The point is that people are not born equal. The genetic endowment passed to offspring by parents, which is an important influence on human development, is far from equally distributed. The plain fact, hard to admit in the land of opportunity, is that many children are already far behind at birth. Worse, children disadvantaged at birth have a high probability of being born into circumstances that are not conducive to their development. These include single-parent families, parents with low income and poor parenting skills, dangerous and crime-ridden neighborhoods, and lousy schools. In short, we are worried about the extent of opportunity in America, especially for those at the bottom and their children.

Since its founding, America has been an immensely successful nation. It has long been the world's most affluent society; it continues to be a bastion of individual freedom; and it has shown the way in using democratic government to solve a variety of problems thrown up by history. But now the country is confronted by economic and social disparities that have proven all but impervious to public and private efforts for nearly four decades. As detailed in subsequent chapters, income inequality is as high as it was in the roaring twenties, we have had few successes in fighting poverty, and the United States now offers less economic opportunity than some other countries. We believe that the lack of more significant progress signals that the country's efforts need to be expanded and retooled. In early 2009 a new administration and a new Congress took steps to address at least some of these problems in a so-called stimulus bill, which represents an almost unprecedented expansion of the role of government. However, little thought was given to the need to rethink and reform the social agenda. One problem with this approach is that a nation already failing to pay its bills cannot afford to permanently expand the size of government. Thus much of the spending in the stimulus bill will have to be stopped in two or three years. Programs that were temporarily expanded will have to contract, and many participants in these programs will lose benefits. This book provides a broader and longer-term look at how to think about social policy and about what needs to be done to create an opportunity society. And because we suggest ways of paying for any expansion of benefits, our proposals are fiscally responsible.

The authors of this book have been studying issues of poverty, inequality, and opportunity for more decades than we care to admit. This book is our attempt to synthesize much of what we have learned about the state of opportunity in America and to offer our views on what the next generation of social policies should look like. The two of us do not always agree. However, we have each benefited from our many debates; and we hope that our effort can serve as an example of what can happen when people from different perspectives seek to find solutions that command wider support than those favored by advocates on either side of the debate about what the more fortunate owe to the less fortunate in our society—and what the less fortunate must do to help themselves get ahead.

At the outset of our study, we want to clarify our general view of how the political system is dealing with the problem of opportunity. We do not side with those who think that the current distribution of income and wealth is just fine and that opportunities to get a firmer foot on the economic ladder cannot be improved. Nor do we side with those who say that all government needs to do is spend far more resources than it does at present on existing social programs. The federal government conducts literally hundreds of programs and spends billions of dollars on domestic social programs. One of our complaints is that the money is not being well spent. Too many programs are either poorly targeted (by age or income), ineffective, or inconsistent with widely held public values. And too many are also inconsistent with research on how people behave and the role that a little more paternalism or higher expectations might play in moving people up the ladder.

We wrote this book because we believe it is possible to do better by paying more attention to six criteria that should guide the nation's social policy. Our first criterion, policies consistent with public values (and thus politically sustainable), should be obvious in a democracy. Of course, political feasibility is also shaped by external events and changes in electoral fortunes. This shift was strikingly evident when Ronald Reagan took over the presidency in 1981 and Democrats won the White House and Congress in 2009. While we acknowledge the importance of elections, giving too much attention to these short-term political developments implies, in our view, insufficient attention to new ideas and expert opinion along with the need for consistent and coherent policymaking over the longer term. In short, policymakers ignore more durable public values at the risk of becoming irrelevant.

Our second criterion, policies that reward those who play by the rules or exercise personal responsibility, is more controversial. Personal responsibility means that individuals must make decisions and take actions that promote their own growth and well-being as well as that of their children. We place special emphasis in this book on the responsibility to get a good education, to work, and to marry before having children. We show that playing by these three rules would ensure almost everyone a middle-class income. We believe that social policy should encourage playing by this set of rules.

A third criterion is cost-effectiveness. Ideally, one would like to know both the costs and the benefits of a policy, but such information is often lacking. We rely on whatever information is available but do not shrink from making recommendations based on partial evidence when necessary.

A fourth criterion is targeting resources on disadvantaged families and especially on helping their children move up the economic ladder. Too many programs in the federal arsenal are poorly targeted or even perversely tilted toward the more advantaged, a fact that is inconsistent with creating a more equitable society. Many of the nation's most expensive programs, especially those for seniors, fail this test.

A fifth criterion is consistency of programs with new research on human behavior. This research suggests that people often engage in behavior that is shortsighted or even self-destructive but that they respond well when nudged to move in the right direction.

A final criterion is the need for greater simplicity. In some areas, the proliferation of programs has created a nightmare both for those receiving benefits and for those paying the bills. This alphabet soup of programs is unlikely to end any time soon, but we try to strain at least a few letters out of the broth.

In the end, we offer detailed recommendations about public policies that have a reasonable chance of helping those at the bottom move up. We argue for a three-front war: one front focused on improving educational outcomes for children and young adults, one focused on encouraging and supporting work among adults, and one focused on reducing the number of children being raised in single-parent families.

Like many others, we often focus on poor families or their children, but our attention is not confined solely to the bottom of the income distribution, for a number of reasons. First, we believe a case for action can best be constructed on knowledge of the entire income distribution. Poverty cannot be understood except in relation to how others in society live. The poor in the United States are quite well off by global standards but not in comparison to other Americans. Something is amiss with a society that pays its CEOs as much in a day as a low-wage worker makes in a year. Not only are these two people not in the same boat; they aren't even in the same sea. Second, large and growing differences in resources between the top and bottom may eventually lead to other kinds of stratification, including concentrations of political power, especially if they are combined with little opportunity for those at the bottom to move to the top. Third, the official poverty line of about $21,000 for a family of four is an arbitrary threshold and does not address the large number of Americans who, though not officially poor, are nonetheless far from financially comfortable. Finally, societies with large gaps between the haves and the have-nots produce less contentment among their populations than similar societies with less inequality.

We devote considerable attention to issues of public philosophy and to attitudes about poverty, inequality, and economic mobility. It turns out that Americans have a more optimistic vision of people's chances of success than the populations of other advanced countries. Moreover, although most Americans want to assist the less fortunate, their compassion is not unlimited and their confidence in government programs is not high. Complaints about "a lack of political will" to fight poverty and inequality need to be assessed against this more sober understanding of public attitudes and the extent to which they can be changed.

The political challenges of creating an opportunity society will intensify in the coming decades for reasons that have little to do with the design of antipoverty and opportunity policies themselves and a lot to do with other developments: the possibility of a prolonged and deep national or global recession, rapid changes in technology and international competition, a greater influx of poorly educated immigrants, the aging of the population along with rising health care costs, and enormous federal budget deficits. One of the most important changes produced by the technological revolution is the sharp decline in jobs that require little education yet pay well—jobs like those that used to be abundant in the manufacturing sector. We believe that, putting periods of recession aside, plenty of jobs will be available in the future. Anyone who needs evidence of the power of the American economy to create jobs need only consider the nation's ability to absorb 1.5 million immigrants every year for two decades (that's over 30 million people), while for most of this period unemployment rates remained low.

But we are greatly concerned about wages at the bottom of the distribution and the need to better prepare people for the kind of competition that will exist in the future. It is not just the unskilled high school dropout that will be affected; a broad swath of the population will be in competition with workers in newly developing countries such as India and China. In this context, how to balance assistance to the poor with assistance to middle-class workers, given the greater political clout of the latter, will be especially troublesome. And as if this political dilemma were not vexing enough, both groups will be competing with the growing number of elderly Americans, who have high and rapidly rising health care costs, for limited public resources. Either taxes are going to have to be raised to unprecedented levels for the United States, or promises to the elderly are going to have to be scaled back substantially.

Plan and Summary of the Book

The following chapters contain a wealth of research findings, some of them new, some of them old, and many of them based on the work of others, including our own colleagues at Brookings. Chapters 2 through 7 explore the lack of opportunity and the debates about its causes.

Public Values and Attitudes

Chapter 2 is about public values. It argues that a sense of compassion or fairness is deeply embedded in human nature, although compassion is stronger for those with whom the public shares common geography, race, or other ties and for those whom they perceive to be deserving of help. We review public attitudes toward poverty and inequality, concluding that they are almost entirely consistent with arguments that people are naturally sympathetic and value fairness but that their willingness to share with the less fortunate is highly dependent on their assumptions about why people are poor and about how much opportunity they believe exists for people to get ahead. The majority of the public is in favor of helping the disadvantaged, and this proportion has grown in recent years. The public believes that people are poor in part because of a lack of opportunity but in part because of their own failings or lack of personal responsibility. It follows that the public is less willing to provide unconditional assistance to the poor than they are to provide specific forms of assistance (such as food or housing) or to support programs that enable people to become more self-sufficient (such as education and training).

The chapter concludes that equal opportunity is a more widely held value than equal results but that the lottery of genes and early family environments complicates what is meant by opportunity. It further concludes that income is an imperfect if readily available measure of success. Finally, it concludes that the current way of measuring poverty in the United States does not capture the fact that a sense of well-being depends more on one's relative, than on one's absolute, position in society.

The Rich, the Poor, and the Middle Class

Chapter 3 presents the basic facts about how the rich, the poor, and the middle class have fared over the past four decades. The chapter concludes that inequality has risen dramatically and that there has been little overall progress in combating poverty except among the elderly and, more recently, among families headed by single mothers. The middle class may not have made much progress, especially of late, but is still extraordinarily well off by historical standards. The rich have garnered a huge share of the nation's income and wealth.

The lack of progress in combating poverty is especially surprising, given that poverty in the United States is measured by looking at the share of the overall population that falls below certain fixed thresholds. Economic growth should have automatically reduced the proportion of people falling below these thresholds. The primary reasons for this lack of progress are the stagnation of wages at the bottom of the skill ladder and changes in family composition. Although government spending on the poor has increased dramatically, much of the increase has gone to provide more access to health care and other noncash benefits, none of which shows up in the nation's official measure of poverty.

In the meantime, middle-class incomes have increased modestly, primarily because more of these families have two earners. Men in their thirties have lower wages than their fathers' generation did at the same age. The reasons for this lack of progress remain somewhat unclear but may relate to the ease with which many midlevel jobs can be outsourced to other countries or automated using new technologies. The rising tides of imports and immigration have played a smaller role. For whatever reasons, over the last two decades wages for middle-skilled jobs have lagged behind wages for both low-skilled and high-skilled jobs. So the middle class is not flourishing. This problem is compounded by rising expectations. Even those with incomes well over $100,000 a year consider themselves middle class, and most members of the middle class enjoy a standard of living that their parents would have envied.

While those at the bottom of the income scale have made no progress and those in the middle very little, those at the top of the income distribution have done spectacularly well. The share of total income going to the top 1 percent has more than doubled since 1980. The super rich have done even better. The median income of the nation's top executives went from 23 times the wages of an average worker in the 1970s to 120 times at its peak in 2000. Wealth is even more concentrated than income.

Opportunity

Chapter 4 picks up on the theme of opportunity. The chapter contains some surprising findings. First, Americans are convinced that they live in an opportunity-rich society. Almost 70 percent believe that people get rewarded for intelligence and skill, more than three times as many as those who believe that coming from a wealthy family is what helps people get ahead. This contrasts sharply with attitudes in other advanced countries, where people weight intelligence, skill, and effort much less heavily and family background more heavily. These disparate attitudes appear to be one reason that Americans are far less sympathetic to government efforts to reduce inequality than the citizens of other countries.

Second, despite its reputation as the land of opportunity, intergenerational mobility in the United States is actually lower for native-born Americans than it is for children in some other advanced nations.

Third, there are some indications that Americans have less mobility than they did in the 1960s or 1970s—that wider gaps between rich and poor make it more difficult to climb the ladder. Prospects for today's children may be constrained as a result.

Fourth, lack of mobility is especially evident in the tails of the income distribution. That is, if you are born into a poor family or a rich family your chances of moving up or down are lower than if you began life somewhere in the middle. That said, there is still plenty of mobility both over the life cycle and from one generation to the next. Children from middle-class families (defined as a family in the middle 20 percent of the income distribution) have about an equal chance of moving up or moving down the ladder by the time they are adults; and people at the start of their careers will typically move to a higher-income group over the course of their working lives. For example, about 60 percent of families in their prime working years will move up at least one quintile (20 percent) over a decade's time.

Fifth, those who finish high school, work full time, and marry before having children are virtually guaranteed a place in the middle class. Only about 2 percent of this group ends up in poverty. Conversely, about three-fourths of those who have done none of these three things are poor in any given year.

Family Background

Chapter 5 asks why it is that family background has a strong influence on where children end up. It explores four possible reasons: genes, parenting styles, material resources, and neighborhoods. It concludes that all four play some role and that they interact in complex ways, but the chapter raises questions about whether simply giving families more material resources would improve their children's life chances very much. Providing poor children and their families with the services of a visiting nurse followed by a high-quality preschool experience and better teachers using proven curricula during the elementary school years is likely to be a more cost-effective solution.

Perspectives on Poverty

Chapter 6 reviews the debates about the extent to which poverty is primarily cultural or structural, that is, related to the behavior of the poor or inherent in a market economy that pays low wages to a large segment of the labor force. Our sampling of the literature reveals no consensus on which is more important. The chapter explores the prevalence of dysfunctional behaviors such as dropping out of school, refusing to work, and having children outside of marriage. Research on the prevalence of such behaviors suggests that they are concentrated among a small segment of the poor living in neighborhoods characterized by the absence of good role models and good opportunities and that this group has been declining in numbers since the 1990s.

The chapter also reviews the extent to which lack of jobs, discrimination, and low wages condemn even those who play by the rules to living on the edge. With respect to jobs, although the economy usually produces enough jobs for all who want to work, jobs are obviously harder to find during periods of high unemployment and in local areas losing their economic base. As for discrimination against African Americans and women, it has declined sharply over the last four decades, although some convincing studies suggest that bias has not been eliminated from American life. Much more important than race or gender, however, are the wages available to those with little education or skills.

In the end, we conclude that both culture and structure keep people on the bottom rungs of the ladder—and that they feed on each other. Moreover, because the poor are a diverse group, any generalization about why they are poor makes little sense. Some of the poor are elderly or disabled and are not expected to work (or to marry). Among the nonelderly poor, many have simply lost a job, become ill, seen a business fail or a home foreclosed—and they will typically get back on their feet within a year or two. However, a small segment of the poverty population is chronically poor, sometimes across several generations, and if there is a culture of poverty in some urban or rural communities, it is found in this third group. Each group, indeed each individual case, needs to be viewed through a different lens.

These arguments about culture versus structure are also somewhat dated. They ignore the fact that it is not just the poor who make "bad decisions." New research in economics, psychology, and neuroscience suggest that most of us have a tendency to sabotage our own success. The difference is that the poor have fewer private safety nets upon which to rely when things go awry. This research points to the need for more paternalistic policies that nudge people in the right direction by rewarding them for actions that enhance their self-sufficiency.

Middle-Class Complaints

Chapter 7 addresses the politics of helping the poor during a period when even members of the middle class are anxious about their own and their children's prospects and when commitments to the elderly are absorbing a dramatically growing proportion of federal resources. The chapter notes that the middle class faces new insecurities that are not adequately addressed by current social insurance programs. Not only are young men earning less than their fathers did at the same age, but also the only reason family incomes have continued to grow is because more women are working. The time pressures faced by two-paycheck families have been much noted, but little has been done to relieve them through subsidized child care or other family-friendly policies. In addition, family income has become less stable, with a small but increasing share of households facing sharp drops in income from year to year.

The anxieties of the middle class are often attributed to globalization and its effects on trade and immigration. However, most evidence suggests that global trade has played only a small role in depressing domestic wages, although its effects, along with the increased offshoring of service sector jobs, could play a more important role in the future. Low-income workers may be less affected than those in the middle class by global trade and offshoring because of their concentration in personal service jobs that cannot, by definition, be done by workers in other countries. Immigration may have some depressing effects on the wages of the least skilled but not the terrible effects attributed to it by various talk show hosts.

Overall, evidence that the middle class faces greatly increased insecurity remains somewhat limited, leading us to conclude that the problem is at least partly one of rising expectations combined with modestly rising incomes. In the meantime, one group of middle-class citizens, the elderly, are costing the federal government a bundle, and we see no alternative to gradually shifting at least some resources from the more affluent elderly to both the poor and working-age families that are only a rung or two above poverty. Taxes are going to have to increase as well, but no feasible set of tax hikes will bring future federal spending on health programs and Social Security in line with costs. Tax increases will have to be accompanied by major reform of these programs that reduces their cost.

Policy Proposals

Chapters 8 through 10 present our policy proposals for helping those at the bottom achieve the American Dream. Chapter 11 details how we suggest paying for the proposals and argues for a broader, longer-term reallocation of resources from the more affluent elderly to less-advantaged younger families and their children. The three policy chapters address specific measures that could be taken to strengthen education, work, and the family, respectively. In all three cases our recommendations are based on the view—which pervades all the chapters—that government can help but that individuals and families must do their share.

We see the 1996 welfare reform law, which was based on the campaign promises of a Democratic president, written primarily by a Republican Congress, passed by a huge bipartisan vote in both Houses of Congress, and signed by that same Democratic president, as a turning point in the nation's social policy. We seem now to enjoy close to a national consensus that personal responsibility is as important as government policy in helping individuals take advantage of the opportunities offered by our economy and society. Policies that simply transfer money to able-bodied individuals who are not making healthy choices for themselves and their families are generally misdirected—and sometimes counterproductive.

Expanding Educational Opportunity. Chapter 8 argues for expanding educational opportunity at the preschool, K–12, and postsecondary levels. Education has always been the route to upward mobility, and in today's economy it is more important than ever. Economists estimate that the rate of return to education is on the order of 6 to 9 percent and perhaps twice as high if all the nonfinancial benefits, such as better parenting and lower rates of crime, are included. Despite these returns, rates of educational attainment have slowed, and large gaps by race and income in school achievement, high school graduation, and college enrollment and graduation have persisted or widened. While children from low-income families greatly enhance their chances of moving up the ladder by graduating from high school and obtaining a post-secondary degree, too few children from low-income families finish high school, fewer still enroll in college, and many of these college students drop out before obtaining a degree. Although math scores have improved somewhat, reading achievement at ages thirteen and seventeen has been virtually flat since the early 1990s.

With this as background, chapter 8 argues that we need to invest in education at every level, beginning in the preschool years. The foundation for later success in school is laid down early in life. Yet children from less-advantaged families begin school way behind their more advantaged peers. For this reason, we call for an expansion of home visiting and early education programs targeting disadvantaged children, including a high-quality preschool experience for every three- and four-year-old from a family with income below 150 percent of poverty. We recommend scaling up such programs gradually, and evaluating the results, to ensure that their quality is maintained.

We also call for better coordination of existing programs serving young children at the local level (the Child Care and Development Block Grant, Head Start, state pre-K programs) and preservation of choice for parents to enroll their children in any program that has a track record of successfully preparing children for school. Research shows that programs offered during infancy and preschool can produce significant impacts on development and be cost effective. Even so, implementation is the key, and our proposals are phased in so that only local programs that produce good outcomes would continue to receive funding or become the basis for expanded funding.

We also direct four recommendations to the public schools. First, although we applaud the emphasis on standards and improved accountability incorporated in the No Child Left Behind act, substituting national for state-based standards would avoid the tendency of states to set the bar too low. Not requiring schools to meet world-class standards is a losing strategy in a global economy.

Second, better teaching has to be at the core of any effort to improve education outcomes, so we call for the expansion of an existing federal program that encourages states to reform teacher hiring, retention, and compensation. Education researchers have clearly documented the gains in student achievement that good teaching can produce. They caution against putting too much weight on preservice credentials in selecting teachers and suggest instead putting more emphasis on nontraditional routes into teaching and on a teacher's ability to improve student achievements from year to year. These reforms should be accompanied by incentives for the best teachers to work in schools with high proportions of disadvantaged students.

Third, a major complaint of many teachers, especially those teaching in inner-city schools, is the difficulty of keeping children engaged and of maintaining order in the classroom. To combat this problem, some schools serving low-income communities are trying a new model that emphasizes high expectations, basic skills, good attendance, longer school hours, frequent assessments, and an insistence on orderly and respectful behavior in the classroom. Although more evaluation of these "paternalistic" schools is needed, they appear to have produced remarkable achievement gains for students in some inner-city schools. Their success is consistent with our view that a little more paternalism in working with disadvantaged youngsters might go a long way toward helping them obtain the education they need in today's economy.

Finally, we are encouraged by the new insights that more rigorous education research has produced in recent years and urge Congress to continue funding these efforts.

Poor preparation at the secondary level is a major reason for the low rates of college attendance among less-advantaged youth. For this reason we review federally funded programs designed to improve preparation for higher education among disadvantaged students. This review turned up little in the way of effective programs, so we do not recommend expanding such efforts; indeed, the current set of programs should be replaced with a new program driven by accountability for long-term results. However, we emphasize the importance of ensuring that disadvantaged students receive good college counseling in time to allow them to prepare for the rigors of college work.

In addition to poor preparation, another barrier to college for disadvantaged students and their families is the expense of going to college and the complexities involved in applying for financial aid. Here we recommend that the blizzard of financial aid programs be greatly simplified and that they more narrowly target the less advantaged. There are at least thirty-one federal provisions, including grants, loans, and tax breaks, many of them overlapping and redundant, with too much of the assistance going to students from more advantaged families. These programs greatly reduce the cost of attending college but have not kept pace with—and may even have contributed to—rising tuition levels at four-year public and private universities. We also recommend simplifying the application process, terminating some smaller aid programs, and reducing the burden of student debt by making repayment more contingent on income. We are also intrigued by a provocative proposal, put forward by Robert Haveman and Timothy Smeeding, to provide low-income students with vouchers to attend in-state colleges and universities, with the funding for the vouchers carved out of state grants to these same institutions.[3]

Because many low-income college students fail to graduate, we reviewed efforts to help them remain in college and turned up very few programs with even modest success in improving students' grades, rates of course completion, and persistence in school. Our conclusion is that, while more experimentation and evaluation of all of these efforts may be merited, without better preparation at the elementary and secondary level, efforts to help people move up the ladder through education will have limited effectiveness.

Supporting and Encouraging Work. Although education is an important route to upward mobility, not everyone will be successful in school. And those who are stuck in low-wage jobs as a result will often earn too little to support themselves and their families above the poverty line. For this reason, in chapter 9 we examine what the federal government currently does through the work support system both to encourage work and to provide assistance to those in low-wage jobs. The work support system is primarily composed of the following programs: the Earned Income Tax Credit, the Child Tax Credit, several benefit and tax programs that subsidize child care, food stamps (now called the Supplemental Nutrition Assistance Program, or SNAP), Medicaid, the State Children's Health Insurance Program, several housing programs, and several employment and training programs. This work-based system is now a critical and growing part of the social safety net. We propose that it be enhanced and reformed to encourage work, with more money for child care, a radical restructuring of housing assistance, and a permanently expanded Child Tax Credit (essentially a wage subsidy) for low-wage workers. We recognize that access to health care needs to be part of the work support package but believe it is best addressed as part of comprehensive health care reform.

With respect to disadvantaged men, many of whom are, or have been, in jail and most of whom receive few benefits, we recommend repeal of mandatory sentencing laws and the institution of demonstration programs to test three ideas that might encourage them to work more and contribute more to their families. One is a suspension of past-due child support payments conditional on fathers agreeing to stay current on their regular payments. Second is an expanded Earned Income Tax Credit (EITC) for childless individuals. Third is a new generation of career-oriented education and training programs. These programs would be based on the assumption that not everyone learns best in a traditional classroom. This assumption entails expanding apprenticeship programs for youth and creating a new competitive block grant to fund adult training and transitional jobs.

In addition to strengthening the work support system, we also argue for tightening work requirements, with the proviso that these should be liberalized rather than tightened during economic downturns. The history of the 1990s shows that a strong economy combined with welfare reform's tough love and an expansion of supports such as the EITC can do more than just one of these alone to move people into jobs and reduce child poverty. For this reason, we support a continuation of current welfare rules, with a few modifications such as adjusting program funding for inflation, providing contingency funding during economic downturns, allowing states to use more of the funds for education, and providing modest funding to expand services for the most troubled families. These modifications should be combined with a firm commitment to the goal of moving as many recipients as possible into jobs. To provide incentives for the recipients of subsidized housing to work, their rent would not be raised steeply or precipitously when they took a job. Fathers owing child support should be required to work, to look for work, or to get more training or education in order to participate in the program for suspending past-due child support.

Strengthening Families. If improving education and encouraging work are the first two legs of our policy stool, the final leg is the need to strengthen families.

As shown in chapter 4 and reinforced in chapter 6, opportunity would be greatly enhanced if the share of American children being reared by their own married parents were increased. For example, if the proportion of children living in female-headed families returned to its 1970 level, the child poverty rate would fall by 4 percentage points, and the proportion of people who could call themselves middle class would greatly expand. Our plan for working toward this goal is presented in chapter 10. In particular, we argue for reviving what some call the success sequence that describes what young people need to do and in what order they need to do it. First comes education (chapter 8). Then comes a stable job that pays a decent wage, made decent by the addition of wage supplements and work supports if necessary (chapter 9). Finally comes marriage, followed by children.

Not everyone will be able to achieve this ordering of life events, but we believe it should be the guide star that society sets for each new generation. The success sequence has fallen out of fashion in recent decades but is nonetheless still a tried and true means of ensuring that most children grow up in two-parent families. To those who argue that this goal is old-fashioned or inconsistent with modern culture, we argue that modern culture is inconsistent with the needs of children. Achieving this goal will require efforts on the part of many groups and individuals, both in and out of government, including elected officials, faith communities, teachers, and the media. Government's role may be limited, but it can help by funding effective programs and social marketing campaigns and by supporting nongovernmental organizations that are working toward these same goals.

Our specific suggestions for what government could do are organized around four goals: reducing teenage pregnancies, reducing nonmarital births, increasing marriage rates, and reviving the success sequence. To reduce teenage pregnancies, we call for an expanded block grant focused on prevention but with state flexibility to choose whatever approach is most consistent with local community values and with existing evidence on what works best to achieve this goal. In short, the federal government would no longer tell states how they can use their block grant funds, as it does now under the abstinence-only program. Because the most effective programs to date have been those that teach both the advantages of abstinence and the importance of contraception among those who are sexually active, most states would likely choose this broader approach. But if new research found that other approaches were more effective, states would be free to reallocate the funds.

We call for new efforts to reduce unplanned pregnancies, abortions, and unplanned births among unmarried adults, especially adults in their twenties. Today's twenty-somethings, as a group, are largely adrift, no longer moored to the success sequence, and increasingly at risk of having children outside marriage. Some of these children are born to cohabiting couples, but these relationships typically last for only a few years, thereby disrupting adult lives and depriving their children of the stable environment that research shows will best serve their interests. We suggest using community colleges to reach this group of young unmarried adults with additional education and services, including educating them about the benefits of shifting to more effective forms of contraception, such as long-acting methods. These methods are less subject to the problem of inconsistent use that plagues other methods. In addition, to make sure that reproductive health services are available, we also call for an expansion of Medicaid family planning services to more women, including those with higher incomes and those who have never had a child. Where states have been permitted to adopt this expansion under waivers from the federal government, good results have been achieved—and with savings to taxpayers to boot.

We recommend that some parts of the Bush marriage initiative be continued, especially demonstration programs that provide job search and job training, that help adults to strengthen their relationships, and that discourage marriage when it is not appropriate (such as in cases of domestic violence). Finally, we argue for marketing campaigns and educational programs to change social norms: to bring back the success sequence as the expected path for young Americans. Social marketing campaigns have proved quite successful in modifying behaviors that for many years were resistant to change (such as seat belt use and smoking cessation).

Paying the Bills. Chapter 11 addresses the question of how to pay for these initiatives. Taken together, all of our proposals would cost tens of billions of dollars, but because we call for scaling back other programs designed to achieve similar goals, the net cost of these proposals is reduced to around $20 billion a year. For example, we recommend reallocating Title I education funds to more effective programs, capping income eligibility for child care, and eliminating several major housing programs and some other smaller programs. Some readers will undoubtedly look at our proposed investments and view them as too small in comparison to the magnitude of the problem. These investments may also seem small in comparison to the funding provided by the nearly $800 billion stimulus package enacted at the beginning of the Obama administration. The stimulus funding, however, was intended to be temporary and thus was not paid for. Our proposals are meant to be permanent and thus must be properly financed.

Given the need to put the country on a more sustainable fiscal track over the longer term through enhanced revenues or reduced spending, we believe it would be irresponsible to continue to spend at current levels, much less add to this spending, unless a way can be found to do so in a fiscally responsible manner. Huge and growing deficits in the budget, and especially the growth of the three programs primarily responsible for the growing deficit (Medicaid, Medicare, and Social Security), threaten to crowd out spending on less-advantaged families and their children. As a vivid demonstration of this threat, budget projections show that by 2040 all federal revenues will be required just to pay for the three biggest programs, leaving no room for other spending or investments. We do not propose a detailed or comprehensive solution to the fiscal problem, but we do lay out a general strategy for making needed investments in working families and their children while simultaneously contributing something to reducing deficits. In common parlance, we propose not only to stop digging the budget hole but to actually begin filling up the hole, remembering that it is younger Americans, including the disadvantaged, who will end up paying the bill for our current profligacy.

We achieve these outcomes by proposing a new intergenerational contract in which the nation invests more in the young but then expects them to save more for retirement out of their higher incomes and, as a result, to be less dependent on public programs after retirement. We illustrate this general strategy by proposing several specific measures that save $46 billion by 2012, an amount that more than pays for the net new costs of our recommendations. Additional reforms in retirement programs are in order. They could be structured to preserve benefits for current retirees and those soon to retire, including preserving or enhancing benefits for low-income seniors, while gradually producing more resources for younger families and their children, especially the more disadvantaged.

Conclusion

This book offers a set of principles to guide social policy in the coming decades. The central principles are that government should endeavor to level the playing field for children from disadvantaged families and to provide extra help to those who play by the rules in their adolescent and adult years. This approach is consistent with public attitudes and also with new research on how people behave. Although broad in its reach, the book does not address every aspect of social policy. Instead it focuses on education, work, and stronger families as the most important elements for creating an opportunity society. In each of these areas the book lays out specific proposals that, based in most cases on solid evidence, would promote opportunity. The recommendations are by no means exhaustive, but we hope that both the principles and the specific recommendations will stimulate others to take action and that those actions will bring the United States a little closer to being the land of opportunity as celebrated in its history and public philosophy.

two
Public Values and Attitudes

How selfish soever man may be supposed, there are evidently some principles in his nature, which interest him in the fortune of others, and render their happiness necessary to him, though he derives nothing from it except the pleasure of seeing it.

ADAM SMITH

If America is going to address issues of poverty, inequality, and opportunity, policymakers need to understand the values and attitudes that underlie any set of chosen policies. In particular, if policies to fight poverty and promote opportunity are to be enacted and successfully maintained, they need to be consistent with the values of the American public. This chapter addresses the extent to which compassion is a universal sentiment, philosophical debates about what society's more advantaged members owe to its less-advantaged members, and the actual opinions of the public in the United States.

Drawing on this discussion, we come to five conclusions. First, there is a reservoir of good will toward the less fortunate. Most people are inherently compassionate, and public opinion polls show rising sympathy for the poor. Second, Americans believe more in equal opportunity than in equal results. As long as everyone has a shot at the American Dream, they believe the system is fair. Third, for opportunity to truly exist, there needs to be some compensation for the fact that not every child begins life at the same starting line. Fourth, compassion comes with strings attached. The public believes deeply in providing opportunity but wants to help those who help themselves, to provide a hand up, not a handout. They believe that government bears some responsibility to help the less advantaged, but not unconditionally. Fifth, the amount of assistance the advantaged owe to the disadvantaged cannot be divorced from social context. A society with a lot of wealth can afford to do more to redistribute that wealth than one in which everyone lives closer to the margin. The poor in the United States are well off in comparison to the poor in other parts of the world, but they have fallen further and further behind others in their own country.

A discussion of values is important for several reasons. Clarifying one's values is a prerequisite to designing policies consistent with one's goals, and policies that are not consistent with most people's values are not likely to be enacted—and even if they are, they are not likely to be politically sustainable. An example of unsustainable policy is the welfare system that prevailed before it was reformed in 1996. In the public's mind, this system came to be viewed as antiwork and antifamily. When most middle-class mothers were working to help support their families, and limiting the number of children they had to what they believed they could afford, it no longer made sense to ask them to pay taxes to support another group of women whose behavior was thought by many to be less responsible.

Conversely, if the public believes that most low-income families are working or are unable to work for reasons of poor health or disability, they are likely to be far more sympathetic. More broadly, the public's willingness to support policies may depend on its view of what caused poverty in the first place. When the public believes poverty is caused by a lack of opportunity or by disability rather than a failure on the part of some individuals to take advantage of the opportunities that already exist, its compassion is enhanced.

Compassion and Fairness

But where does such compassion come from? In his book *The Moral Sense*, James Q. Wilson argues that this sentiment grows out of our inherent sociability.[1] We react with sympathy to the misfortune of others, be it a soldier killed in war, an abused child, or an injured pet. We are even affected emotionally by fictionalized accounts of such events. It is hard to explain this kind of compassion as the result of pure self-interest. Indeed, even Adam Smith recognized such "moral sentiments." One of these principles, Smith writes, is "pity or compassion, the emotion which we feel for the misery of others, when we either see it, or are made to conceive it in a very lively manner."[2]

The Harvard professor Edward O. Wilson, a pioneer in the field of sociobiology, explains how evolutionary processes may have given way to these moral sentiments:

Now suppose that human propensities to cooperate or defect are heritable: some people are innately more cooperative, others less so. . . . To the heritability of moral aptitude add the abundant evidence of history that cooperative individuals generally survive longer and leave more offspring. Following that reasoning, in the course of evolutionary history genes predisposing people toward cooperative behavior would have come to predominate in the human population as a whole.[3]

Such a process repeated through thousands of generations inevitably gave rise to moral sentiments. The ability to feel compassion or sensitivity to the well-being of others is related to another widely observed phenomenon: a sense of fairness. According to James Q. Wilson, infants and toddlers may share their possessions, even when a parent is not insisting that they do so, and this tendency to share even when there is no obvious reason to do so grows stronger as children grow older. "By the time they are in elementary school, the idea of fairness has acquired a fairly definite meaning: people should have equal shares."[4] There are, however, many exceptions to this general principle. Most people, for example, believe that those who work harder should receive larger rewards. For this reason, the principle of equal shares eventually becomes understood as a principle of proportionality: that rewards should be commensurate with what the person deserves.[5]

Strong evidence for this sense of fairness comes from laboratory experiments with what economists call the ultimatum game.[6] The game begins with two players, the first of whom is given a sum of money to distribute between the two of them (both players know the amount of money). The rules of the game require that the first player make an offer to share the money with the second. If the offer is rejected, neither player gets anything. If it is accepted, they both get to keep their shares. The two players are strangers and are not expected to ever see each other again. Given this situation and set of rules, one might expect the first player to offer the second a trivial amount of money—say, $1 out of an initial sum of $100. Yet in repeated experiments with this game, using different amounts of money, different players, and different experimenters, most people offer either an equal share of the money to the second player or something that favors the first player only slightly (say, a $55–$45 split of $100). Other experiments show that, given a choice between receiving a large sum that is unevenly divided and a smaller sum that is more fairly shared, individuals prefer the latter.

Of course, feelings of compassion and fairness do not always lead to altruistic behavior. Much depends on the situation. People are more likely to behave in a benevolent fashion if the costs to them are small. In addition, willingness to help may depend on whether the recipient is perceived to be entirely innocent rather than partially responsible for his own fate. Willingness to offer assistance also depends on the extent to which one can remove oneself from confronting another's distress by putting it out of sight and out of mind and by the extent to which one believes that someone else—whether another individual or the government—is likely to take care of the problem.[7] Finally, people are more likely to play the Good Samaritan if the person or group in distress is similar to them or closely affiliated, as would be the case with members of one's family, one's community, or one's own racial, ethnic, or religious group. According to Edward O. Wilson, these variations may have evolutionary roots as well: "The dark side of the inborn propensity to moral behavior is xenophobia. Because personal familiarity and common interest are vital in social transactions, moral sentiments evolved to be selective. People give trust to strangers with effort, and true compassion is a commodity in chronically short supply."[8]

These observations help to explain why in a large and heterogeneous country, one in which rich and poor tend to live in different neighborhoods and where racial divisions run deep, the inclination to address poverty is relatively weak or diffuse, at least compared with the attitudes observed in more homogeneous societies.[9] They can also explain why impersonal mechanisms, such as relegating responsibility for the poor to government bureaucracies, can undermine people's charitable instincts and why a concrete and visible disaster such as Hurricane Katrina or the destitution of a person on the street can elicit sympathies that abstract discussions cannot. Finally, the principle of proportionality or of conditional judgment sheds light on why people may perceive a difference between the "deserving" and the "undeserving" poor. There will, of course, be disagreement about what *deserving* and *undeserving* mean, but that such judgments will be made cannot be in doubt. The same person who will help a man who has fallen down because he is lame may fail to come to the rescue of a man who has fallen down because he is drunk.[10]

Conceptions of Social Justice

The question of what more advantaged members of society owe to those who are less advantaged has been much debated by philosophers and public intellectuals of various stripes. Here we deal with just three subquestions that must be answered in analyzing how much the privileged owe to the poor and unfortunate: Do we care more about equal opportunity or about equal results? If the well-off are expected to provide for the poor, what are the poor expected to do in return (if anything)? How much assistance is enough?

Procedural Fairness versus Substantive Fairness

Many philosophers, such as Immanuel Kant, have emphasized what might be called procedural fairness in contrast to substantive fairness. Procedural fairness is the notion that what matters is fairness of process—how valued goods are acquired. Substantive fairness emphasizes end results, or the actual distribution of valued goods. To better understand what this means, imagine three societies, each with identical initial distributions of income or other goods but differing in the way in which people acquire their share of valuable goods. In the first society what people receive depends on the talent and effort they expend or their contributions to the general welfare. We call this a meritocracy. It may be procedurally fair but substantively unfair. In the second society, what people have is purely a matter of luck. We call this a fortune-cookie society. In the third society what people have depends on where they began, that is, on the economic or social status of their parents. We call this a class-stratified society.[11] Both of the latter societies may be viewed as less procedurally fair than a meritocratic society since the distribution of rewards depends respectively on randomly distributed opportunity and family position. The general point is that how people feel about the distribution of income in each case depends on which type of society they believe produced that distribution. Indeed, many people might prefer to live in a meritocratic society with a more unequal distribution of income than in a class-stratified society with a more equal distribution. Procedural fairness may trump substantive fairness and must be taken into account for this reason.

In the United States the public tends to believe strongly that the country's wealth distribution is fair and that all Americans can achieve a modicum of success if they work hard and play by the rules. This contrasts sharply with the views of people in other advanced countries, who are much more likely to say that luck or family background matter more and that the government has a role to play in reducing the gap between the rich and the poor. An emphasis on procedural justice leads to a focus on equal opportunity rather than equal results, a topic to which we return in chapter 4, in which we show that the United States is a more class-based society than many believe.

While procedural justice matters, it may be an incomplete criterion for judging the overall fairness of a society. Good rules can produce bad outcomes.[12] One reason that good rules may not produce good results is that they provide too little compensation for what we call the fundamental inequalities: the fact that people are born with different genetic endowments and into different environments. Assuming we are not prepared to engage in genetic engineering or to remove children from their families at an early age, these fundamental inequalities handicap some people at the very start of the race. Developmental psychologists and behavioral geneticists show that about half of the differences we observe between individuals in health, intelligence, sociability, and a variety of other traits are inherited.[13] Of course, these genetic proclivities or vulnerabilities interact with the environment after birth and are not immutable; nonetheless, they very much influence outcomes. Thus even in a society in which opportunities were open to all, we would still observe a great deal of inequality. This fact has led to the view that a just society provides extra help to those with such inherent disadvantages. John Rawls famously argues that a just society is one in which, assuming one knew nothing about the circumstances of one's own birth, one would still find the system a fair one—one in which even those handicapped from birth would not suffer unduly as a result.[14]

Most advanced societies deal somewhat inconsistently with inherited disadvantages. For example, they often compensate for physical disabilities by providing rather generous assistance to those born with such impairments. But problems that are more subtle, such as those involving a difficult-to-diagnose conduct disorder, a vulnerability to certain health conditions, or a below-average level of intelligence or stamina, are rarely considered in designing social policies even though they similarly affect success in life. Indeed, most people too readily attribute whatever success they have had to the way they played the game rather than to the hand they were dealt at the beginning. They may similarly attribute the failure of others to deficits of character, forgetting that some people start with bad cards. Once one recognizes the fundamental inequalities, however, one realizes that a fair process alone may not produce a just society. Starting lines matter.

Liberty, Equality, and Playing by the Rules

Assuming that procedural justice or equal opportunity is not sufficient, what then is the proper measure of compassion and fairness? There exists a spectrum of political beliefs about how to handle observed inequalities. Egalitarians argue that society should compensate in its education system, its labor market institutions, and its social safety net for existing inequalities. Because of their typically optimistic view of human nature, egalitarians believe that attempts to distinguish between the deserving and the undeserving poor are usually inappropriate. They believe that the primary reason that people fail to succeed or to escape poverty is external (structural) barriers, not deficits of capacity or of a motivation to succeed. They would come to the assistance of both the man who falls down because he is lame and the one who falls down because he is drunk, believing either that the latter is deserving (perhaps he just lost his job or is the helpless victim of alcoholism) or that making distinctions between the two is not worth the cost of stigmatizing various subgroups and, in any case, is inconsistent with an ethic of unconditional love and compassion for other human beings.

Libertarians reason that, whatever produces observed inequalities, any effort to tamper with them—for example, by using taxes to fund programs for the poor—is an infringement of the taxpayers' right to use their own resources as they see fit. This right to control one's own resources is fundamental, since liberty is a transcendent value in libertarian philosophy. It is not necessarily inconsistent with compassion, since those with the ability to do so can always provide voluntary assistance to the poor (ignoring the fact that their fellow libertarians may free ride on the generosity of others). Libertarians believe that the marketplace is better equipped to distribute resources than the government. The American libertarian philosopher Robert Nozick, for example, argues that Wilt Chamberlain deserves to keep all of his earnings since they are the legitimate consequence of people's willingness to pay for his extraordinary talents. The fact that not everyone is born tall enough and skilled enough to play basketball is an issue Nozick does not address.[15]

Still others, the contractarians, take a middle ground. They want to make the provision of extra help, especially to adults, conditional on their behavior—using public policy to encourage, or even require, people to act responsibly. This philosophy often finds its expression in the statement that government should help those who play by the rules. President Bill Clinton popularized this construct by saying that "those who work shouldn't be poor."[16] The basic idea is easy to extrapolate to other areas. For example, we might argue that those who perform well in school shouldn't be denied access to higher education and those who delay childbearing until they are ready to be good parents shouldn't be denied a decent income with which to raise their children.

Contractarians depart from libertarians in believing that public policy has a role to play in addressing fundamental inequalities. But they depart from egalitarians in giving more weight to individual responsibility in determining where people end up in society. If people often behave in ways that are not in their own long-run self-interest and if public policy is able to nudge them in a more constructive direction, it should do so; but public policy should not be a substitute for personal responsibility. We tend to favor the contractarian view and have more to say in chapter 6 about why we believe this is the most sensible and effective approach to combating poverty and inequality and to providing the opportunity for people to join the middle class.

Measures of Success

In thinking about how much the advantaged owe to the disadvantaged, two additional issues must be resolved. First, is individual or family income an adequate measure of success? And second, should we be more concerned with people's absolute incomes or their relative incomes?

Like many people writing about these issues, we focus on income and poverty, outcomes that can be readily measured in monetary terms. But few people, including us, would deny that other measures of well-being matter, measures such as health, physical security, political and civil liberties, and overall happiness. Most people would be willing to sacrifice additional income to secure these basic sources of individual well-being.

Even if we restrict our analysis to income, there is the issue of whether we are measuring someone's actual or potential income. A well-educated individual who chooses not to work or to devote his life to charitable causes may have a low income but should not be considered disadvantaged for this reason. In this vein, Amartya Sen argues that the major criterion for judging policies should not be the total income they produce, or even their fairness, but rather the extent to which they address the capabilities that enable individuals to function successfully in their society.[17] Sen argues that we have focused too heavily on narrow measures of income inequality or deprivation and not enough on outcomes that may matter as much or more: health, employment, education, and social integration.

Broader definitions of well-being have gained greater political traction outside the United States. The European Union, for example, has traded in a single poverty measure for a list of fourteen indicators that focus on broad national and multinational objectives, including social inclusion (defined as ensuring access for all the resources, rights, and services needed for participation in society). These overarching indicators include an at-risk-of-poverty rate set at 60 percent of national median income, an income inequality measure, and several measures relating to health, education, employment, and retirement readiness.[18] Moreover, since the 1990s the United Nations Development Program has produced a human development index that applies many of the same principles. The index combines life expectancy, literacy, school enrollment, and GDP data to compute an overall country score. The UN uses these scores to rank 175 member states, highlighting change over time. According to a 2007 report, the United States ranked twelfth. Iceland was first, followed by Norway, Australia, Canada, and Ireland.[19]

Assuming that we have an agreed-upon measure of well-being, however imperfect, an even more contentious issue is the extent to which policy should aim to lift people out of poverty, defined as some absolute level of income or material well-being, versus the extent to which it should aim to improve the relative status of the poor and reduce inequality in the process. Contemporary research on happiness suggests that, above some minimum, relative income is what matters. In any given year, more income does buy more happiness. Yet as

Figure 2-1. Happiness and Economic Growth, 1972–2006

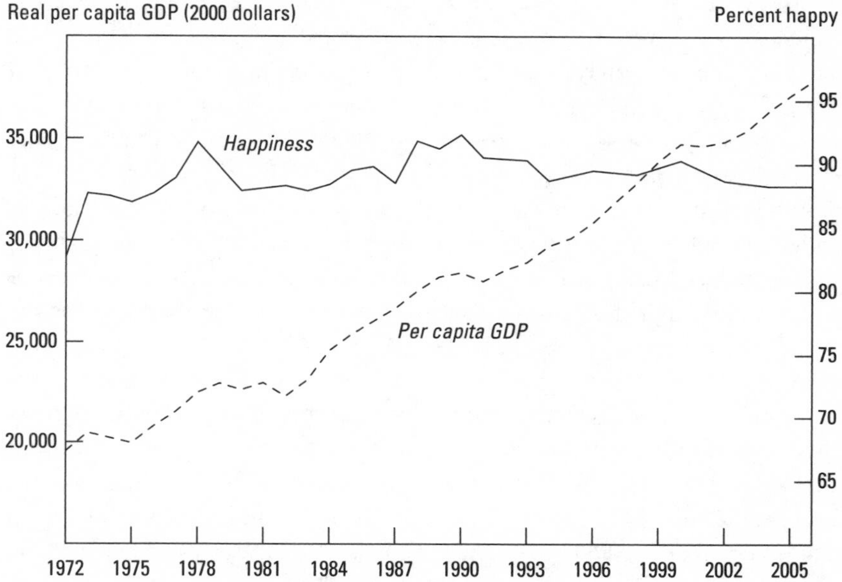

Real per capita GDP (2000 dollars)　　　　　　　　　　　　　　Percent happy

Source: General Social Survey, various years (www.norc.org/GSS+website); U.S. Census Bureau, *Statistical Abstract of the United States: 2009*, table 657.

a. Happiness data are taken from the General Social Survey question, "Taken all together, how would you say things are these days—would you say that you are very happy, pretty happy, or not too happy." Percent happy include the percentage sum of participants who responded very happy or pretty happy. Note that happiness data are missing for the following years: 1979, 1981, 1992, 1995, 1997, 1999, 2001, 2003, and 2005.

we might expect, the additional benefits diminish as incomes rise. For example, an index of people's reported happiness in 1994 rose sharply as per capita income rose from a few thousand dollars to about $15,000. It continued to increase beyond that point but more slowly.[20]

We might infer from the cross-sectional relationship between income and happiness that as economic growth moves people up the income ladder over time their sense of well-being should rise. Yet the evidence does not support this conclusion. In the United States, for example, per capita incomes have increased enormously over the past half century but measures of happiness have not (figure 2-1).

This finding—that income influences happiness at a point in time but not over time—is sometimes called the Easterlin paradox, after the economist who first called attention to the anomaly.[21] How can we explain the paradox? One explanation stresses the importance of relative income. At any point in time, people make comparisons with those around them; if they are doing relatively well, they feel a sense of well-being. Being poor in a rich society is much harder than being poor in a poor society.[22]

What does this literature imply about how to think about poverty and inequality? If the added benefit of extra income declines as income increases and if it is a person's relative position in the overall distribution that most affects his individual feeling of well-being, then a more equal distribution would produce an improvement in the overall welfare of the population. Indeed, people report less happiness in countries or states where inequality is higher than in those where it is lower, even after one controls for the level of income (although this finding is more robust for Europe than it is for the United States).[23]

Another reason to focus on relative rather than absolute income is that community norms or social context matter. Compared to most of those living in less-developed countries, the poor in the United States are very well off. In the United States 12.5 percent of the population—slightly more than 37 million people—live at or below the poverty line of around $10,500 a year for a single person or $16,500 for a family of three.[24] By contrast, 48 percent of the population of developing countries—around 2.5 billion people—live on approximately $2 or less a day ($786 a year). Almost 1 billion of these people live on approximately $1 a day ($393 a year).[25] The American poor are also as well off as the middle class was in the past. As recently as sixty years ago, the median income of a four-person family was $26,700 in 2007 dollars.[26] Today such a family would be considered just a little above the poverty line.

These comparisons dramatically underscore the importance of context and of relative measures of income. The social minimum cannot be defined without reference to how most people in a given society or country live. And as argued above, happiness depends more on people's relative position within their society than on absolute income.

If lower levels of inequality produce greater happiness, why not use government policy to reduce the gap between the rich and the poor? There are two complications. The first is what has been called loss aversion. People weight losses of income more heavily than potential gains.[27] Thus once a certain degree of inequality exists it is hard to reverse, because those who have benefited will resist losing what they have and will actually be made psychologically worse off in the process. If instead the inequality had never been allowed to occur in the first place, they wouldn't know what they were missing. This is an argument for preventing a high degree of inequality from emerging in any society and points to the difficulty of reversing it once it is embedded in the income structure.

Another complication is the fact that most redistributive schemes involve taxes and transfers that may affect incentives to work and save—and thus economic growth. However, in assessing the trade-off between greater equality and less growth one should keep in mind the historical relationship between per capita income and happiness: that is, well-being is not significantly affected by overall growth, at least for developed countries like the United States.[28] Thus even if some growth is forgone in the process of producing a somewhat more equal distribution of incomes, this outcome is not likely to adversely affect the overall well-being of the population. This is not an argument for a no-growth society or for ignoring the effects of badly designed policies on a nation's growth prospects. For one thing, in a stagnant economy, one person's gain is another person's loss, and there is no growth dividend to allocate to helping the less fortunate.[29] But from the perspective of human psychology, a little less potential growth as the price a society might pay for a little more equal division of the pie seems like a price that many would find worth paying.

Public Opinion

Despite a strong belief in meritocracy and a distaste for welfare, Americans do support programs that help those in need.[30] According to a 2007 poll by the Pew Research Center for the People and the Press, a majority of Americans has consistently been willing to spend on assistance to the poor.[31] What's more, this majority has grown over the last decade. The proportion of people who say government needs to "take care of people who can't take care of themselves" rose from 57 percent in 1994 to 69 percent in 2007. In addition, the proportion who agree that the government should help more needy people even if it means going deeper into debt was 54 percent in 2007, compared to 41 percent in 1994. While the percentage of people who support government aid to the poor seems to be growing, this majority is not overwhelming, and a substantial percentage of people do not believe that government intervention is the answer to concerns over poverty and inequality.

Further, the public maintains decidedly mixed views on why people are poor and on how to achieve the right balance between government action and greater personal responsibility. According to the 2007 Pew study, 62 percent of people disagree with the idea that success is largely determined by forces outside of one's control, indicating that individual responsibility remains a strong American value. A 2001 poll by National Public Radio, the Kaiser Family Foundation, and Harvard University Kennedy School found that people are about evenly divided in ranking lack of personal effort or outside circumstances as the bigger cause of poverty. When asked to elaborate on the root causes of poverty, some popular answers—drug abuse, medical bills, too few jobs, too many single-parent families, and too many immigrants—further illustrate the conflicted American attitudes toward poverty.[32]

Given their mixed views about why people are poor, it is not surprising that the public prefers opportunity-enhancing programs to those that simply provide income or other resources to low-income families. The public also prefers earmarked forms of assistance to simple cash. For example, more than nine of ten adults support expanding job training and improved education in low-income areas. Eight of ten support subsidized day care, tax credits for low-income workers, and medical care for the poor. By contrast, just over half of adults support more cash assistance for poor families.[33] And even though most people would like the government to do more about poverty and inequality, they are somewhat skeptical about government's ability to get it right. They do not believe that most efforts have been successful. Only 34 percent responded that government programs make things better, 48 percent said that government programs do not have much impact, and 13 percent thought they make things worse. Public opinion around welfare remains equally mixed. Only half of the population knows that significant welfare legislation has been passed in the last five years (as of 2001); however, 61 percent of those who know about changes in the law report that the new law is working well.

In sum, popular opinion is consistent with the view that people are naturally sympathetic and value fairness and that they are willing to be generous, at least when those receiving aid are perceived to be deserving and the assistance perceived to be enhancing their opportunities. Nevertheless, the public remains skeptical about government's ability to eliminate poverty entirely and believes that personal responsibility is as important as government intervention in working toward this goal.

Conclusion

As countless philosophers, researchers, and politicians have discovered, the study of poverty and inequality often raises as many questions as it answers. We argue that humanity is endowed with an innate sense of compassion and fairness; however, these moral sentiments merely serve as the starting point for a more substantive discussion of aid to the disadvantaged. The policy recommendations we make in this volume are founded on four values-based premises about the appropriate role of government.

First, fairness of the process matters. Equal opportunity for all to succeed on the basis of hard work and talent is a core American value.

Second, society should compensate for the fundamental inequalities of genetic inheritance and family background. Some people are blessed with multiple advantages from the start; others with very few. These fundamental inequalities constitute a lottery of inherited talents and resources. We believe that those who have won the lottery should share something with those who didn't.

Third, we believe the provision of extra help, especially to adults, should be made conditional on their circumstances or behavior. We should use public policy to encourage, or even require, people to do what is in their own self-interest. Most of the public prefers opportunity-enhancing and conditional forms of assistance. Americans are more willing to provide education and job training than direct assistance and much more willing to provide earmarked forms of aid such as health care, child care, and wage subsidies than cash welfare.[34] As we detail in chapter 6, the research from behavioral economics supports the view that such paternalism not only increases public support for aid to the poor but is also more consistent with much that we now know about human behavior. If people often behave in ways that are not in their own long-run self-interest, and if public policy is able to nudge them in a more constructive direction, it should do so.

Fourth, research on what determines people's sense of well-being and the importance of social context leads us to the conclusion that relative economic status matters. In an affluent society with a great deal of inequality, the rich can afford to share with the poor. The public's concern about the poor has grown in response to evidence of increasing inequality. In the next chapter, we turn to just how much poverty and inequality there is in the United States in the first decade of the twenty-first century.

three
The Changing Fortunes of the Rich, the Poor, and the Middle Class

Facts are stubborn things; and whatever may be our wishes, our inclinations, or the dictates of our passion, they cannot alter the state of facts and evidence.

JOHN ADAMS

In 1980 President Ronald Reagan famously asked, "Are you better off than you were four years ago?"[1] In a similar vein, in this chapter we ask, Who moved ahead and who lagged behind over the past three or four decades? Our answer, in brief, is that real incomes have grown but that income inequality—gaps between the rich and the poor—have also risen.[2]

We give special attention to the poor, for whom progress has been spotty at best. The War on Poverty, launched by President Lyndon Johnson in the mid-1960s, does not seem to have succeeded if the goal was to promote personal responsibility and independence from government welfare benefits. Despite considerable efforts to provide the poor with various kinds of assistance, their ranks have not been reduced except among the elderly and female-headed families. This lack of progress is primarily related to changes in family composition, especially the growth of single-parent families, and stagnant or declining wages for unskilled workers. Moreover, some of this lack of progress is a mirage, due to the way in which the government calculates the poverty rate. Specifically, a shift in emphasis from providing the poor with cash assistance (welfare) to providing them with various noncash benefits and work-based support, although not captured in the government's official data on poverty, has clearly made them better off.

The middle class has not done a great deal better than the poor. The real income of the typical family (the family in the exact middle of the income distribution) has risen by less than 1 percent a year on average since 1979.[3] At the same time, wages for men in their thirties are actually lower than for their fathers' generation.[4] However, because more women work, incomes for the typical middle-class family have increased modestly. Put differently, for most families, it now takes two earners to enter the middle class. The primary reasons for disappointing wage growth in recent years, especially for men, seem to be related to the automation or outsourcing of many midlevel jobs and to the fact that college enrollment rates for men have not been increasing. The limited progress for this group has led to a high degree of anxiety, even pessimism, for many middle-class families. In light of this anxiety and its political implications, including its possible effects on the poor, we address these issues in more detail in chapter 7.

Another striking feature of recent decades is the chasm that has opened up between the middle class and the rich and, even more strikingly, between the rich and the super rich. The sharp increase in incomes at the very top of the distribution has become in recent years the primary driver of income inequality. Income and wealth in the United States have not been this concentrated in the hands of a few since the 1920s. Possible reasons for this development include fierce competition for the "winners" or "top talent" in most fields, a failure of corporate governance to limit excessive pay, the growing size and complexity of most corporations, and a shift in pay practices, especially more emphasis on performance in setting compensation at the top of the distribution.[5]

As this book went to press in 2009, the United States was in the midst of a very serious recession, and there is no way of knowing how long it will last and exactly what effects it may have. However, there is little question that it will lead to much higher rates of joblessness than that of recent decades, will extinguish much of the wealth held by the rich as well as the middle class, and will swell the ranks of the poor. Each percentage point increase in the unemployment rate is likely to raise the poverty rate by about half a percentage point. And we are already seeing rising applications for various safety net programs such as unemployment insurance and food stamps.[6] However, this book is focused not on what to do about the immediate recession but rather on what should be done to create an opportunity society over the longer term.

We have more to say about policy responses to the widening gap between rich and poor later in the book. This chapter is devoted to providing "just the facts." To paraphrase Senator Daniel Moynihan, we are all entitled to our own opinions but we are not entitled to our own facts.

Widening Gaps between Rich and Poor

The American economy grew quite smartly between 1979 and 2007. GDP per person, roughly $27,500 in 1979, was over $45,800 in 2007 (in 2007 dollars).[7]

Figure 3-1. Household Income Growth, by Income Percentile, 1979–2007[a]

Percent growth

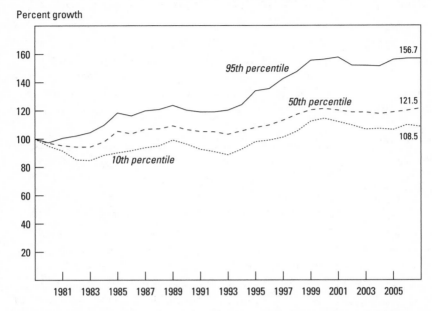

Source: Authors' calculations based on U.S. Census Bureau, *Current Population Survey, Annual Social and Economic Supplement.*
a. Income is adjusted for household size using the square root equivalence scale (household income divided by the square root of the number of people in the household).

This growth would seem to provide the raw material to increase the economic well-being of all Americans, but income has not grown at comparable rates all along the income distribution (figure 3-1).[8] Those in the top of the distribution enjoyed a 57 percent increase in their incomes, while those in the middle gained just 21 percent and those at the bottom a still more paltry 8 percent.[9] This pattern contrasts sharply with the more broadly distributed income gains that prevailed in the 1950s and 1960s (figure 3-2).[10]

What explains this growing gap between rich and poor in recent decades? Some of the rise in income inequality is related to changes in family composition. The growth of single-parent families and smaller households along with the increased tendency for high earners to marry each other can explain roughly half of the increase in inequality between 1979 and 2004.[11] The remainder is the result of rising wage inequality.

Although wage increases have been robust at the top, they have been moderate in the middle and, after a long period of decline followed by a recovery, virtually nonexistent at the bottom. Workers at the tenth percentile actually

Figure 3-2. Family Income Growth, by Income Quintile, 1947–2007

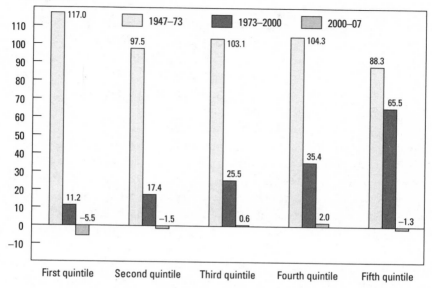

Percent growth

Source: Lawrence Mishel, Jared Bernstein, and Heidi Shierholz, *The State of Working America 2008/2009* (Washington: Economic Policy Institute, 2009), figure 1H.

earned slightly lower hourly wages in 2007 than they earned a quarter of a century earlier.[12]

In their attempts to explain growing wage inequality, most experts emphasize that changes in the economy—such as new technologies, the shift from manufacturing to services, and the introduction and spread of computers— have increased the demand for more educated workers. Because the supply of more educated workers has not kept pace with the demand, wages have increased for the most skilled but remained flat or declined for the less skilled.[13] One result of the failure of the supply of educated workers to keep pace with the demand has been a sharply rising wage premium for those with the most education.[14] Since 1979 the difference between the median income of men with a bachelor's degree and men with a high school degree has increased from around $12,400 to close to $25,500, all measured in 2007 dollars.[15]

When we divide the past quarter century into two subperiods, another interesting pattern emerges. The gap between low-wage and middle-wage workers widened in the 1980s, but all of the rise in inequality since the late 1980s has been concentrated in the top half of the distribution. Put differently, there has been a polarization of the labor force over the past two decades that has favored both low-wage and high-wage workers over those in middle-wage jobs.

This polarization of wages appears to be due to the different ways computer-based technologies have affected jobs. These technologies have enhanced the demand for educated professionals and managers who have the cognitive and interpersonal skills needed in a high-technology world, reduced the demand for the routine tasks done by many midlevel blue- and white-collar workers, and had little effect on the demand for those in lower-paid service jobs, such as health aides, security guards, janitors, and waitresses.[16]

Other possible reasons for rising wage inequality over this period include the declining power of unions, the failure of Congress in the 1980s to adjust the minimum wage for inflation, the rising share of low-skilled immigrants in the labor market, and the effects of global competition on the wages of domestic workers. However, none of these competing explanations can reconcile the fact that trends in inequality in the 1980s and in the 1990s were different.

For example, the decline in the real value of the minimum wage can explain some of the rise in inequality during the 1980s, but since that time all of the increase in inequality has been concentrated at the top end of the wage scale and thus cannot be explained by changes in the minimum wage.[17] The decline in union bargaining power has contributed to male wage inequality since the late 1980s but not necessarily in the way most people expect. Unions have traditionally increased wages for midlevel jobs, not for jobs at the bottom of the wage distribution. Thus the decline of unions has widened the pay gap between high-level and midlevel jobs but has narrowed the gap between midlevel and low-level jobs.[18]

Estimating the degree to which complex and evolving market forces like trade and immigration affect wage inequality is more difficult. Many economists have studied the effect of trade on wages, and most find that trade has had only modest effects.[19] The effects of immigration on wages appear to have been relatively modest as well. The rising share of poorly educated immigrants from less-developed countries could be expected to hold down wages at the bottom, but no empirical study has found that immigration has had a large effect on the overall trend in either inequality or poverty.[20] Nevertheless, because the public perceives trade and immigration to be far more important than the experts, we engage in a broad discussion of these topics and their political ramifications in chapter 7. For now, our conclusion is that each of the above factors may have played a small role in explaining rising wage inequality but that none has been as important as the increasing value of education and skills to employers.

Whatever the ultimate causes, the rise in wage inequality combined with slower productivity growth after 1973 has had devastating effects on entry-level wages for high school educated men. If productivity growth after 1973 had continued along the same path that prevailed from 1960 to 1973, and if this growth had been equally distributed across the population (as it was in the earlier period), the typical man with a high school education would have been earning $71,000 by 2007 (figure 3-3). But because productivity growth slowed down and mainly benefited those at the top of the wage distribution, the typical high school graduate just entering the labor market was earning only $23,600 in 2007. Roughly speaking, half of the gap was due to slower growth and the other half to growing inequality.[21]

The Poor

If most of the gains in income over the past few decades have gone to those at the top of the distribution and very little to those at the bottom, this means that, in relative terms, the poor are falling further and further behind. In chapter 2 we argue that relative poverty is a better measure of individual well-being than absolute poverty, because social context and community norms about what it means to be poor change over time, implying that the poverty line should be adjusted as economic growth makes everyone better off. But the current measure of poverty in the United States is absolute rather than relative. The advantage of an absolute measure—one that defines poverty as income below some level that is adjusted only for inflation and not for the rise in real incomes over time—is that economic growth should make it easier to raise everyone or almost everyone above some minimum threshold representing the amount of money needed to buy the bare necessities. Even this more modest goal, however, has proved difficult to achieve.

Measures of Poverty

In 2007 the official poverty threshold for a four-person family was about $21,000. For an individual it was about $10,500.[22] The official threshold, developed in the 1960s, was based on research showing that typical families spent about three times as much to meet all their needs as they spent on food. Thus the poverty level was defined as three times the amount of a low-cost diet adjusted for family size.[23]

This official measure of poverty has come in for some criticism, with conservatives tending to argue that it overstates the problem and liberals responding that, if anything, it is biased in the opposite direction. Conservative arguments tend to focus on the fact that many people are poor for only

Figure 3-3. Wages and Productivity, Three Scenarios, 1973–2007[a]

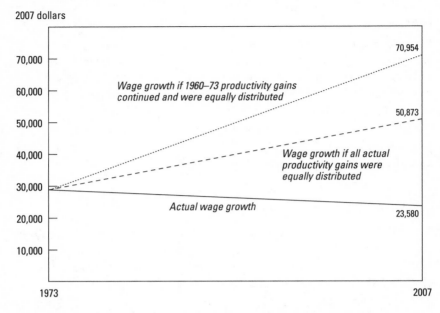

2007 dollars

Source: Authors' calculations based on Lawrence Mishel, Jared Bernstein, and Heidi Shierholz, *The State of Working America 2008/2009* (Washington: Economic Policy Institute, 2009), table 3.19; U.S. Bureau of Labor Statistics, *Productivity and Labor, Major Sector Productivity and Costs Index* (various years).

a. Data are entry-level wages for high school–educated men in 1973 and 2007 (in 2007 dollars). Annual wages assume forty hours a week and fifty weeks a year of work.

short periods of time, that they seem to have access to material goods that were once considered luxuries, and that the official measure doesn't include the value of many of the government benefits received by the poor, such as food stamps and the Earned Income Tax Credit. More liberal arguments emphasize that the official poverty measure has never been updated to reflect rising standards of living for most families in recent decades.

The argument that poverty is often a temporary condition is at least partially borne out by the facts. Census data on poverty do not follow the same individuals or families from one year to the next. So the people who are poor one year may not be poor the next. Researchers using alternative longitudinal data sets confirm that poverty is not a chronic condition for the majority of those who are counted as poor in the annual census.[24] For example, in the three years 2001 through 2003, only a little more than 2 percent of the population was poor for the entire period. However, during that same period,

32 percent of the entire U.S. population was poor for at least two months.[25] So persistent poverty is much less common than is often assumed, while temporary bouts of low income occur much more frequently. Although there is a great deal of movement in and out of poverty, most people don't move very far, and many experience repeat spells. Moreover, there is a small group—but a group that dominates the poverty data because they are always "there" to be counted each year—who are persistently poor and who tend to be poorly educated, black, and living in female-headed families.[26]

Measures of consumption such as access to certain consumer goods (TV sets, microwave ovens, cell phones) show that the poor are not quite so poor after all. Using consumption data, W. Michael Cox and Richard Alm find that the poverty rate fell from 31 percent in 1949 to 13 percent in 1965 to 2 percent at the end of the 1980s.[27] Similarly, Bruce Meyer and James Sullivan find that income is substantially underreported among the most disadvantaged families. Measures of consumption indicate that these poor families are considerably better off than their reported incomes would suggest.[28] For instance, average expenditures for families below the tenth percentile of the income distribution are nearly four times their average income. While consumption-based measures are not without flaw, they nevertheless provide further insight into the living circumstances faced by the poor and suggest that they are not as destitute as their income would indicate.[29]

A continual problem with the official income poverty measure is its failure to include noncash benefits available to poor families, such as food stamps, housing assistance, and subsidized health insurance through Medicaid, as well as its failure to measure income net of taxes (including the Earned Income Tax Credit). If tax credits and noncash transfers are improving the material conditions of the poor, then it makes sense to include these provisions in income measures. The National Academy of Sciences (NAS; now the National Academies) addressed this issue along with several others, such as a broader measure of need (reflecting not just the cost of food as in the current measure but also shelter, clothing, and utilities), variation in the cost of living in different areas of the country, the way in which family size affects needs, and a measure of health care expenses.[30]

In the meantime, many scholars point out that the official poverty measure is flawed primarily because it is not adjusted to keep pace with rising standards of living. While the poverty threshold in 1963 was equal to about 50 percent of the median income, strong income growth since that time has lowered the line to about 28 percent of the median.[31] Thus many argue that the poverty line no longer provides an adequate gauge of whether a family is meeting its basic needs, as those needs are defined in the current context.[32] By contrast, in the European Union poverty is defined as falling below 60 percent of the median income in a given country.[33] With a relative measure of poverty such as this, the poverty line increases in step with increasing standards of living.

The 1995 NAS study recommends updating the poverty line using a quasi-relative approach, which would base the threshold on typical expenditures for food, clothing, shelter, and other essentials, using a moving average of three years of consumption data. Hoping to reap some of the benefits of both an absolute and a relative measure with this approach, the authors observe that "our intent was to recommend a concept and procedure that would update the initial reference family poverty threshold for changes in real consumption but in a conservative manner."[34]

While some of the details are still being worked out, consensus around a NAS-based measure is growing. In 2000 more than forty prominent economists signed an open letter to the director of the Office of Management and Budget urging him to implement an alternative poverty measure based on NAS recommendations.[35] As this volume went to press, several attempts to update the poverty measure were under way, and several bills modeled after the NAS recommendations have been introduced into the U.S. Congress. In addition, in the summer of 2008 New York City unveiled a measure, modeled on the NAS recommendations, that the city is using to track progress in reducing poverty. Thus it seems likely that a new measure of poverty, one based more on the relative incomes of the poor and where they are positioned in overall income distribution may soon be adopted. In the meantime, because most past research and data are based on the current definition of poverty, we use it in what follows unless otherwise noted.

In 2007 the official poverty rate was 12.5 percent, and the number of poor was 37.3 million.[36] However, the poverty population is diverse. Relative to the rest of the population, the poor are more likely to have little education, to live in female-headed families, and to lack a full-time worker.[37]

Trends in Poverty

Poverty declined sharply in the 1960s, due in part to President Johnson's War on Poverty, but little additional progress in reducing the overall poverty rate has occurred since that time (figure 3-4). Among both children and working-age adults there was a remarkable decline ending in the late 1960s or early 1970s. But since the early 1970s, poverty has increased and, in the case of children, has not reached its 1969 low. Among the elderly, poverty fell precipitously until the mid-1970s and has continued to decline (though more

Figure 3-4. Poverty Rate, by Age Group, 1959–2007[a]

Percent

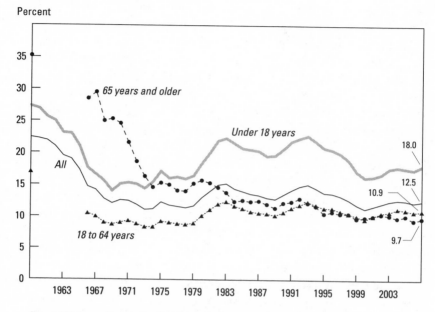

Source: U.S. Census Bureau, Historical Poverty Tables (various years), tables 2 and 3.
a. Poverty rates for adults and the elderly not available for 1960 through 1966.

slowly), reaching a low of about 10 percent in 2007. Given the miserable economy, poverty probably increased in 2008 and will increase again in 2009 and perhaps later years.

Later we address why poverty has dropped so precipitously among the elderly. But why has the nation not made more progress with other groups? One reason may be the generosity of Social Security benefits compared to welfare, since the public fears that higher welfare benefits might discourage work. Two other broad reasons stand out: changes in family composition and changes in the economy that affect wages or employment opportunities for less-skilled workers. We consider each of these in turn.

Family Composition. Poverty among female-headed families with children is typically about five times greater than poverty among married-couple families.[38] Thus any increase in the share of the population living in female-headed families with children will increase the poverty rate. In the past half century the American family has undergone something like a revolution. The changes began with a rise in divorce rates, rates that have now leveled off and even declined a bit. Still the probability of divorce is nearly 50 percent, with low-income couples showing a greater propensity to divorce than middle-class couples.[39]

A rapid rise in nonmarital births has also produced more single-parent families. Almost 40 percent of all babies are now born outside marriage, the majority of them to black or Hispanic mothers.[40] About half of these newborns live with their cohabiting parents, but these relationships are notoriously unstable, and within a few years many have dissolved, leaving the mother and child to live alone or perhaps with another partner.[41] Almost 30 percent of all children (and 57 percent of black children) were living in a single-parent family in 2007, up from just 12 percent in 1968.[42]

These increases in family dissolution make the task of reducing poverty much more difficult. If the United States had the same proportion of children living in single-parent families as in 1970, all else equal, today's poverty rate would be roughly one-quarter lower than it is.[43] The reasons for this earthquake in the composition of the American family have been sharply debated, with some arguing that it results from a lack of jobs and decent wages for less-skilled men and others arguing that it reflects a more fundamental shift in societal norms with especially devastating effects in low-income and minority communities. Our view is that both contribute; but we revisit this debate in chapters 6 and 10.

The Economy. The economy creates the jobs and earnings that constitute the first line of defense against poverty. When jobs are easily available (and unemployment is low), when poor people are willing and able to take such jobs, and when wages are sufficient to support a family, then poverty will decline. When none of these three conditions apply, poverty is likely to rise.

The exceptionally strong economy of the 1960s produced dramatic reductions in poverty, giving rise to President John Kennedy's "A rising tide lifts all boats." Over the decade, the economy grew by 35 percent as measured by per capita GDP, and poverty in families fell by almost half (table 3-1). In each of the next three decades the economy continued to grow, albeit more slowly, yet poverty fell only 5 percent in the 1970s and actually increased by 12 percent in the 1980s. Only during the 1990s, especially the latter half of the 1990s, did economic growth once again lead to a substantial reduction in poverty, in this case by nearly 10 percent. But from 1999 to 2007 the family poverty rate again increased—by 5 percent. One thing that the late 1960s and the late 1990s had in common was low unemployment rates. In both cases, the unemployment rate dropped well below 5 percent, a level that was almost unprecedented over the rest of this period. Recent research by Rebecca Blank shows that the poverty rate remains very sensitive to the level of unemploy-

Table 3-1. Economic Growth and Poverty, by Decade, 1959–2007
Percent unless otherwise indicated

Years	Change in GDP per capita	Family poverty rate		Change in poverty rate	
		Start	End	Percentage points	Percent
1959–69	34.6	18.5	9.7	−8.8	−47.6
1969–79	23.8	9.7	9.2	−0.5	−5.2
1979–89	22.9	9.2	10.3	1.1	12.0
1989–99	22.2	10.3	9.3	−1.0	−9.7
1999–2007	12.9	9.3	9.8	0.5	5.4

Source: Richard Freeman, "A Rising Tide Lifts . . . ?" in *Understanding Poverty*, edited by Sheldon H. Danziger and Robert H. Haveman (Harvard University Press, 2001), table 3.1; authors' update through 2007 using U.S. Census Bureau, *Statistical Abstract of the United States: 2008*.

ment. For each 1 percentage point increase in the unemployment rate, the poverty rate increases by an average of 0.45 percentage point.[44] The sharp increase in unemployment rates experienced in 2008 and 2009 can be expected to produce a big increase in poverty rates as well, although the official poverty rates for these years are not available as of this writing.

But high unemployment rates during recessions are not the only problem. One of the puzzling trends over the past few decades has been declining employment rates among men, especially less-skilled minority males (figure 3-5). Over the past thirty years there has been a 35 percent decline in work among less-skilled black men. By contrast, black female high school dropouts increased their work effort, especially during the mid-1990s. Whatever the exact cause of these trends, the fact that work levels for men decreased while work levels for women rose rapidly—and that these opposite movements occurred during both strong and weak economies—shows that factors other than the state of the economy have an impact on the decision to work. Just what those factors are remains something of a mystery. Declining wages for unskilled men can explain some of the trend, but economic factors cannot account for most of the decline, especially over the last two decades.[45]

The work rates of black female dropouts are especially interesting because they show such a remarkable increase over the 1990s, especially leading up to and after welfare was reformed in 1996. This law required practically all of the nearly 5 million mothers on welfare to work or have their cash welfare benefit reduced or even terminated. The cash welfare program was also changed so that participants could receive federal benefits for no more than five years (including repeat enrollments). In addition to these momentous changes in welfare, the federal government has modified existing programs and created

Figure 3-5. Employment Rates for Black High School Dropouts Ages Eighteen to Thirty, by Gender, 1979–2007

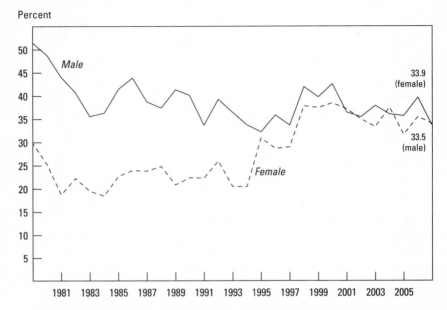

Percent

Source: Authors' calculations based on U.S. Census Bureau, *Current Population Survey, Annual Social and Economic Supplement.*

new ones that are designed to support low-income working families. The Earned Income Tax Credit, for example, was expanded to provide bigger wage subsidies for low-income workers, health insurance coverage of low-income families was expanded, and funds for child care were greatly increased. In short, poor women already on welfare or tempted to go on welfare were both required to work and given financial incentives to do so. In the words of President Clinton, the federal government "made work pay."[46] These policies of both requiring and rewarding work, along with the strong economy and low unemployment rates of the late 1990s, contributed greatly to the rise in employment rates for women.

In the meantime a large number of unskilled men remain disconnected from the labor force, and it is not clear how they are supporting themselves. They may be working sporadically, be involved in crime or the informal economy, or be living with girlfriends or on the streets. The extent to which lack of work among this group is due to their inability to find a job or their unwillingness to accept the low-paid jobs for which they qualify remains

Figure 3-6. Government Spending on Means-Tested Programs, 1968–2004

Billions of 2007 dollars

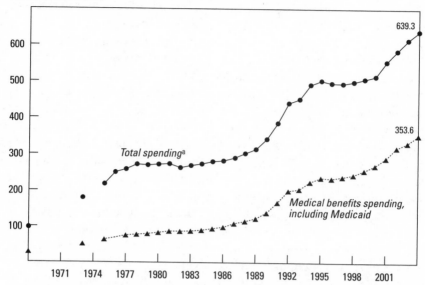

Source: Congressional Research Service, "Cash and Noncash Benefits for Persons with Limited Income: Eligibility Rules, Recipient and Expenditure Data, FY2002–FY2004," RL33340 (Washington: 2006), tables 2, 5.
a. Total spending includes federal, state, and local spending.

unclear. We return to this issue in chapter 6, where we explore the debate on cultural versus structural perspectives on poverty.

In the end, it is the combination of a willingness to work, the availability of jobs, and rising wages at the bottom that can reduce poverty. If any of the three is lacking, the struggle against poverty becomes more difficult. Although jobs appear to have been available through most of this period, wages at the bottom stagnated or declined, and for this and other reasons (including high rates of incarceration and dropping out of high school) less-skilled men, especially minority men, left the labor force in large numbers.

Government Antipoverty Programs

Spending by federal and state governments on programs for the poor has grown in most years, beginning from a low base in the mid-1960s (figure 3-6). Not only has spending grown, but the number and diversity of programs has risen as well. The most recent comprehensive data available on all federal and state spending on means-tested programs (for 2004) show that real spending on health programs grew especially fast. In recent years, health care spending has grown at about twice the rate of inflation, and there is no prospect for it to slow down any time soon.[47] Even so, spending on many other categories of programs is considerable and in most cases continues to grow.

Of course, the spending data tell us simply that spending on means-tested programs has grown faster than inflation. But there are other ways to measure spending growth, one of the most important being to compare it to GDP. This comparison shows that means-tested spending increased from 2 percent of GDP in 1968 to 5 percent of GDP in 2004; and even omitting Medicaid, that spending was a little more than 1 percent of GDP in 1968 and just over 2 percent of GDP in 2004. As noted above, poverty among the elderly fell much more than poverty among other groups over the past thirty years, largely because of Social Security payments. Obviously, one foolproof way to reduce poverty in America is to give people enough money to raise them above the poverty line. As originally conceived, Social Security paid benefits too small to lift most of the elderly out of poverty. But the program grew rapidly in the 1960s and 1970s, covering more people and paying bigger benefits, and the poverty rate among the elderly declined sharply—from 35 percent in 1959 to 10 percent in 2007 (figure 3-4) and to much lower than 10 percent if the values of health insurance, food stamps, and subsidized housing are included.[48] A careful analysis of the impact of Social Security on poverty rates among those born between 1885 and 1930 shows that Social Security can explain the entire decline in the official rate of elderly poverty.[49]

So is the main problem the fact that we are not spending enough money on the poor? In a simple-minded exercise, if we divide annual federal and state spending on means-tested programs by the number of people in poverty, there would be more than enough money to lift everyone in America above the poverty line. Indeed, there is enough money from federal and state spending on means-tested programs to provide each poor person with $15,000 a year, or each three-person family below the poverty line with $45,000 a year.[50]

But there are at least two problems with this approach to solving poverty. First, the American public believes that able-bodied people should work.[51] Giving money to the elderly and the disabled is one thing, but giving money to able-bodied poor people on a more or less permanent basis is not acceptable to the American public. A major reason that a Republican Congress and President Clinton were able to reform welfare in 1996 is that the public was opposed to families—especially single mothers—raising children on welfare and not working.[52] Second, there is no bright line between those just below and those just above the poverty line in terms of need. Thus suddenly cutting off all assistance to those just above the poverty line would severely penalize the near poor and would be widely regarded as unfair. For these reasons, most government programs target the poor and gradually reduce benefits as income rises.

Also for these reasons, policymakers are not likely to cash out all the nation's means-tested programs, including the increasing proportion that provide noncash benefits, and transfer the money to able-bodied adults in poverty. But the trends in poverty among Social Security recipients show that, not surprisingly, giving money to families would in fact reduce poverty.

It is not only Social Security that has been effective in reducing poverty. An analysis done for the *Green Book,* a compendium of U.S. tax and social programs compiled periodically by the Ways and Means Committee of the House of Representatives, shows clear evidence of the impacts of government programs on the poverty rate among children living in families with unmarried heads of household. If the government benefits received by these families are ignored, children in these mostly female-headed families would have experienced a poverty rate of 38 percent (figure 3-7). But including the value of government cash and noncash transfer programs, such as Supplemental Security Income and food stamps, knocked the poverty rate down to 28 percent. Adding income from the Earned Income Tax Credit reduced poverty further, to 24 percent. No doubt most people would want the poverty rate among these families to be less than 24 percent, but policymakers can take satisfaction that public programs reduced the poverty rate by just over 35 percent among these vulnerable children.

Another approach to assessing the effectiveness of government anti-poverty programs is to calculate the poverty gap before and after the receipt of government assistance. The poverty gap is the difference between the amount of income that poor households actually have and the amount they would need to bring them all up to the poverty line. An analysis by John Karl Scholz, Robert Moffitt, and Benjamin Cowan estimates the poverty gap in 2004 before most taxes and transfers at $30 billion a month (in 2007 dollars). Total transfers in that month were over $65 billion.[53] Using a broad measure of income, which includes the value of such things as food stamps, housing assistance, and a variety of other programs, Scholz and others find that the transfer programs cut the household poverty gap by more than a quarter.[54] This result reinforces the conclusion that the current system of cash and non-cash transfers has been effective at reducing poverty. Moreover, they are roughly as effective now as they were twenty-five years ago, although total transfers per person (excluding Medicare and Medicaid) are slightly smaller than they were in the mid-1980s. If the insurance value or actual per person

Figure 3-7. Poverty Rate for Children Living with Unmarried Heads of Household, before and after Government Programs, 2002

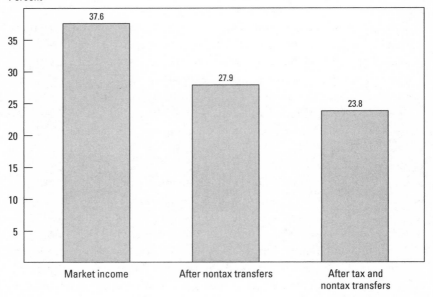

Percent

Source: Staff of House of Representatives Committee on Ways and Means, 2004 *Green Book*, WMCP: 108-6, table H-21.

spending of Medicare and Medicaid are added, government per capita spending on the poor is much greater than it was twenty-five years ago.

Still another approach to assessing the effectiveness of government programs on how different groups are faring is to compare measures of income inequality before and after taxes and transfers. According to Andrea Brandolini and Timothy Smeeding, these government tax and transfer programs reduced a summary measure of inequality (the Gini coefficient; see below) by 23 percent.[55] This compares to 28 percent in Canada, 33 percent in the United Kingdom, 43 percent in Germany, and 47 percent in Denmark. We conclude that government programs do help the poor and reduce disparities in market incomes, but the experience of other countries shows that the United States could do more.

The Middle Class

As with the poor, there is no single definition of the middle class. One approach is to define the middle class as those who are in the exact middle of the income distribution at any point in time. This approach leads to a focus on median household income ($50,233 in 2007) or on those with incomes in the middle fifth of income ($39,100 to $62,000 in 2007) or even those in the middle three-fifths—that is, the 60 percent of all households with incomes between $20,291 and $100,000 in 2007.[56] These definitions are analogous to defining poverty in relative terms, such as those in the bottom 20 percent of the distribution. And like relative poverty, there will always be a middle class, defined in this way.

Another approach is to define the middle class as all those with incomes in a certain specific (inflation-adjusted) dollar range, say, $30,000 to $75,000. Using an absolute measure of this sort, it is possible to show that the middle class is not only shrinking, it is also moving up the income scale.[57]

A final approach is far more subjective. It involves asking people if they consider themselves middle class. The National Opinion Research Center (NORC) at the University of Chicago has been asking people what class they belong to since 1972. Based on the cumulative results from these surveys, the self-reported middle class makes up 46 percent of the population—those with incomes between $45,000 and $200,000 in 2005. Another 46 percent of the population classified themselves as working class, while only 3 percent of the population classified themselves as upper class and only 5 percent classified themselves as lower class.[58] It should not be surprising that, in a society in which even the word *class* makes people uncomfortable, so few want to think of themselves as anything other than middle class or working class. Even those with very high incomes tend to consider themselves middle class.

The middle 20 percent of the income distribution is demographically different from the poverty population in some important ways.[59] Over two-thirds of the middle class is in married-couple families, compared to less than a third of the poor. Adults in the middle class are also much more likely to be well educated and to be full-time, full-year workers.[60] These characteristics of the middle class make them quite different from the poor. (In chapter 4 we focus on how education, work, and a stable family contribute to moving people into the middle class.)

Trends in Middle-Class Income

Median household income in the United States trended upward between 1979 and 2007 (figure 3-8). Although the general direction of income was up, growth fluctuated with the state of the economy, peaking as the economy rose and falling as the economy went into recession, usually with some lag. From the first peak in 1979 to the last in 1999, median income increased from $43,814 to

Figure 3-8. Median Household Income, 1979–2007[a]

2007 dollars

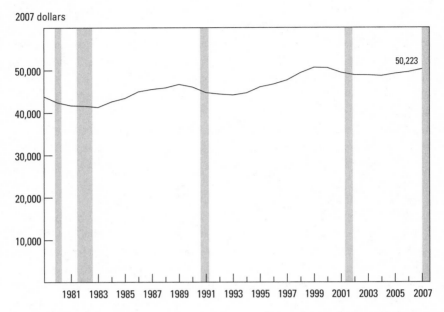

Source: U.S. Census Bureau, Historical Income Tables: People (various years), table H-10; National Bureau of Economic Research, "Business Cycle Expansions and Contractions" (Cambridge, Mass., various years).
a. Grey shading indicates period of recession. Household income above is not size adjusted (unlike figure 3-1).

$50,641, or by a little over 15 percent in dollars adjusted for inflation. However, since 2000, the typical household income has stagnated, with 2007 median income hovering just below the year 2000 high, at $50,233.

By contrast, looked at in absolute terms, the middle class is doing very well. Over the period 1980 to 2007 a growing proportion of the population moved from income categories below $75,000 to categories above this level (figure 3-9). Specifically, 32 percent of households earned $75,000 or more in 2007, compared with just about 20 percent in 1980. Thus a major achievement of the American economy has been enabling a growing share of individuals or couples to earn incomes in excess of $75,000.

Once again, using relative or absolute definitions of income leads to very different conclusions. Based on an absolute income measure, adjusted only for inflation, the middle class is doing well. Based on a relative measure, adjusted for where a family sits in the distribution—in this case, exactly in the middle—the middle class is making much more modest progress.

Figure 3-9. Households, by Income Group, 1980–2007[a]

Percent

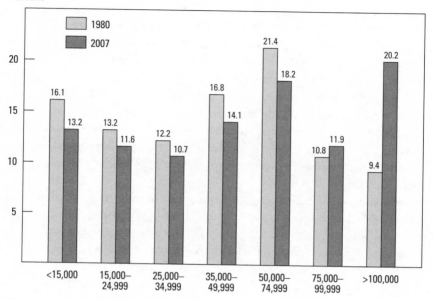

Source: Carmen DeNavas-Walt, Bernadette D. Proctor, and Jessica C. Smith, "Income, Poverty, and Health Insurance Coverage in the United States: 2007," Report P60-235 (U.S. Census Bureau, 2008), table A-1.
a. Household income data measured in 2007 dollars.

Explaining the Trends

Household income depends on the number of earners in the household, the number of hours they work, and hourly wages. Although wage gains have been modest to nonexistent, with increases reserved primarily for those with a college education, families have benefited from the fact that far more of them have two earners. In addition, since a rising share of compensation takes the form of employer-provided health insurance, and most of the data on income omit the value of these and other employee benefits, progress may be underestimated.[61] Finally, because families are smaller, whatever income they have supports fewer people. Working in the opposite direction, families dependent on two earners have much higher work-related expenses, especially for child care.

If middle-class families are doing so well, why is there so much talk about families struggling to make ends meet? This is such an important question that we devote an entire chapter (chapter 7) to it. In that chapter we explore several possible answers to this question. These answers are worth a brief summary here.

First, expectations may have increased even faster than incomes. As noted above, if the middle class is hollowing out, it is not because more of them are falling to the bottom of the distribution but because more of them are moving into a category that most people would call affluent (above $75,000). To be sure, their incomes have not grown as fast as they did during the decades immediately following World War II, and particularly since the 1980s. Moreover, they may be comparing their situations to the lifestyles enjoyed by the rich and famous. Anyone who has lived through the past half century recognizes that the typical family today has a higher standard of living—bigger houses, newer cars, more gadgets, nicer clothes, more expensive vacations—than similarly-aged families in the 1950s.

Second, today's families are caught in a time squeeze because far more of them either have two earners or are headed by a single parent. Third, most of them are working very hard. Earlier predictions that economic growth would enable people to consume more leisure have not come to pass. Compared to adults in other advanced countries, for example, American men and women work a similar number of hours a week but far more weeks a year.[62]

Fourth, many middle-class families feel economically insecure: one paycheck away from not being able to pay their bills. In chapter 7 we review the evidence on whether family incomes are subject to wider year-to-year swings than in the past. In that chapter we also review the extent to which changes in the economy, especially more trade and higher rates of immigration, have contributed to the problem. Our conclusion is that, despite all the political talk about these issues, they have had less impact on the economic well-being of the middle class than is usually assumed.

The Rich

If there is some disagreement about how well the middle class has fared, there is almost universal agreement that recent decades have seen historic increases in both income and wealth at the very top of the income distribution.[63] Yet Americans are not bitter about the rich or even about the rich getting richer, if for no other reason than they hope and believe that they themselves or at least their children may be rich someday. But as we show above, most of the considerable growth in income and productivity is going to the top of the distribution. So great have been the rewards going to the top that serious analysts are now claiming that the age of the robber barons has returned.[64] A brief review of the growth of income and wealth at the top of the distribution shows just how spectacular the American economy has been for those at the top.

Trends in Income at the Top

We have touched on the economic well-being of those at the top of the distribution (see, for example, figures 3-1 and 3-2), but some of the best data on the incomes of the wealthy come from income tax returns. Based on a careful analysis of these data, Thomas Piketty and Emmanuel Saez find that, after about 1980, the income share of the top 1 percent of earners shot up from about 8 percent to almost 18 percent by 2006 (the most recent data available), nearly equaling the previous high for the twentieth century of almost 20 percent in 1928.[65] If the income of the top three executives of the 101 largest publicly traded American companies is any indication, incomes at the very top have grown even more (figure 3-10).[66]

Examining the income of top executives in historical perspective, we find that after a slight decline during World War II, total compensation was flat or rose slightly, until the 1970s. But by the early 1980s compensation began growing rapidly—by more than 7 percent a year between 1982 and 1990 and by close to 14 percent between 1992 and 2000—with only a few short interruptions. After a modest drop between 2001 and 2003, compensation renewed its growth in 2004 and 2005. From its low of about 23 times the pay of average full-time workers in 1971, the median pay of top executives rose to almost 120 times the pay of average workers in the year 2000; in 2005 (the most recent data available) median total executive compensation was still worth a staggering 110 times the pay of average workers.[67]

Explaining the Trends

Rapidly rising incomes at the very top of the income distribution could be the result of greater competition for top talent in an increasingly integrated national and international economy. Although this competition has probably played some role, it does not explain why the U.S. experience has diverged from that of Japan and advanced countries in Europe. Another potential explanation is the ability of top executives to control their own compensation while complicit or weak boards of directors look the other way and shareholders lack the power to limit the excesses. This explanation is hard to square with changes in laws and regulations that in recent years have made boards more independent, pay practices somewhat more transparent, and excessive reliance on stock options less common.[68] Moreover, the phenomenon of seven-figure incomes extends well beyond CEOs to include celebrities in the worlds of entertainment and sports and even to lawyers and financiers. Yet

Figure 3-10. Median Executive Compensation and the Ratio to Average Earnings, 1936–2005[a]

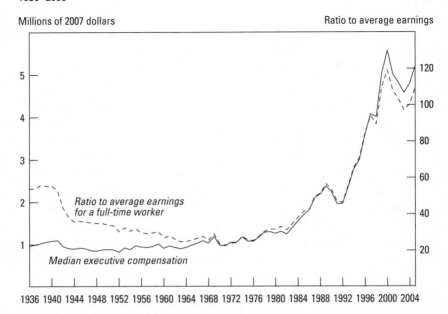

Source: Carola Frydman and Raven Saks, "Executive Compensation: A New View from a Long-Term Perspective, 1936–2005," Working Paper 14145 (Cambridge, Mass.: National Bureau for Economic Research, 2008), figure 1.

a. Total executive compensation is composed of salary, bonuses, long-term bonus payments, and stock option grants for the three highest officers in a firm. Ratio to average earnings is defined as total compensation divided by total wage and salary accruals for full-time-equivalent employees from table 6.6 of the National Income and Product Accounts.

another hypothesis is that larger and more complex companies require higher-paid executives, a thesis with some modest empirical support. Chances are that each of these factors has played some role.[69]

At least part of the explanation for wage increases among those at the top 20 percent of income is greater pay for performance. Thomas Lemieux, W. Bentley MacLeod, and Daniel Parent find that the share of male workers whose pay is linked to their performance increased from 30 percent in the late 1970s to over 40 percent in the late 1990s and that this can explain about 25 percent of the increased inequality in compensation over this period.[70]

Government Benefits and Taxes for the Rich

Most upper-income families receive few government benefits, at least during their working years. They do qualify for Social Security and Medicare and a few other universal programs, but the main way government affects them is

Figure 3-11. Posttax Income, by Income Quintile, 1979 and 2005[a]

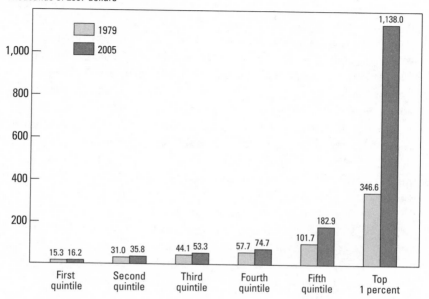

Thousands of 2007 dollars

Source: Congressional Budget Office, "Historical Effective Federal Tax Rates: 1979 to 2005" (December 2007), appendix table 1C.

a. Comprehensive household income equals cash income plus income from other sources, including in-kind benefits. See CBO for details.

through the tax code.[71] Under this country's progressive tax system, the overall effective tax rate in 2008 was an average of 1 percent in the lowest-income quintile and 26 percent in the highest.[72] The wealthy not only pay a larger proportion of their incomes to the government, but because their incomes are high, they pay a large share of all federal taxes: over two-thirds of all federal taxes in 2008 were paid by the richest fifth of the population.[73]

Over the past several decades, however, the progressiveness of the American tax system has declined. While average federal tax rates for the middle class have remained relatively constant, large decreases in tax burdens at the very top (among the top 1 percent) have significantly eroded the progressivity of the system.[74] As the result of this decline in progressivity, together with a very large increase in pretax income inequality, posttax incomes have grown at very unequal rates (figure 3-11). Although recent tax cuts have exacerbated the increasing inequality, they are not the primary culprit; that has been the dramatic increase in pretax income and wage inequality already noted.[75]

Wealth and Inequality

Most of the concern about the growth of inequality in the United States focuses on income inequality. Much less concern has been expressed about wealth inequality. This lack of attention to wealth is unfortunate because wealth is a vital component of family economic well-being. Wealth can provide a stream of income that families can use for current consumption, collateral for loans to boost consumption, security during periods of unemployment or other disruptions of income, and security for retirement. Wealth can also be passed to children or others, at death or before. In a less measurable vein, substantial wealth often contributes to influence in the community, including political influence. Negative wealth or debt is also a major determinant of well-being. In the extreme, persistent debt can lead to bankruptcy, which not only results in loss of most assets but usually constitutes a formidable barrier to obtaining credit in the future.

Wealth is assets minus debt. In most definitions of wealth, assets include financial assets such as checking accounts and stocks and bonds as well as nonfinancial assets such as real estate holdings, businesses, jewelry, art, boats, and vehicles. Debt includes home mortgages, loans against real estate, credit card balances, and installment loans.[76]

Growth of Wealth

The growth of wealth in the United States was strong over the 1989–2004 period. Data from the Federal Reserve Board's Survey of Consumer Finances (SCF), the best source of data on wealth in the United States, show that wealth doubled over this period, growing from $25.9 trillion to $50.3 trillion.[77] Thus as with GDP and income, wealth in the United States has grown substantially over the last quarter century.

However, wealth is unevenly distributed and getting more so (table 3-2). Net worth improved all along the distribution between 1989 and 2004. That is, almost everyone gained in wealth. Even so, net worth at the tenth percentile was exceptionally small. These families have great difficulty accumulating assets that exceed their debts, and their net worth typically hovers around zero. In contrast, people at the top (in the ninetieth percentile) not only have a very large proportion of all wealth but also saw their net worth increase from $540,000 to $830,000, or by over 50 percent, over the period.

The concentration of wealth at the very top of the distribution can be seen in figure 3-12. The bottom half of families controlled less than 3 percent of the wealth in 2004; the top 1 percent, 33 percent. Though its share of wealth

Table 3-2. Net Worth of Households, by Selected Percentiles of Wealth Distribution, 1989–2004

Thousands of 2004 dollars

Wealth percentile	1989	1992	1995	1989	2001	2004
Tenth	0.0	0.0	0.1	0.0	0.1	0.2
Twenty-fifth	8.1	9.6	12.3	11.5	13.6	13.3
Mean	277.9	246.1	260.7	328.5	423.9	448.0
Median	68.8	65.3	70.8	83.2	91.7	93.1
Seventy-fifth	216.2	194.6	197.8	242.2	301.7	328.5
Ninetieth	539.5	470.2	469.0	572.9	782.2	831.6

Source: Arthur B. Kennickell, "Currents and Undercurrents: Changes in the Distribution of Wealth, 1989–2004" (Federal Reserve Board, rev. August 2006), p. 9.

peaked in 1995 and then declined slightly (and may be declining even more sharply as this book goes to press), the top 1 percent still laid claim to an enormous piece of the wealth pie in 2004.

Millionaires and Billionaires

The growth of wealth at the top of the distribution is also apparent in the rising number of households worth at least $1 million. The number of millionaires more than doubled in raw numbers and increased by 77 percent as a share of the population between 1989 and 2004. If the rise in millionaires is impressive, the rise in households worth $10 million or more is more impressive still, with a rise of over 430 percent.[78]

As hard as it might be to believe, the SCF data reviewed so far are likely to underestimate wealth at the top of the distribution. Most rich families refuse to even be interviewed. In addition, even if they agree to an interview, it is difficult to gain a full picture of all their assets because they are so extensive. A well-known attempt to gauge the true wealth of families at the very top of the distribution is the annual list of the 400 richest individuals in America compiled by *Forbes* magazine. *Forbes* invests considerable resources in trying to learn about the wealth of people they target as likely to be among the richest Americans. They search court documents and records of the Securities and Exchange Commission, interview business associates and even ex-spouses, and review articles in newspapers and magazines in their attempt to obtain a complete list of the assets and debts of those they target.

Whether all this effort yields an accurate picture is difficult to know, but the picture nonetheless suggests how spectacular the fortunes of America's richest individuals have become. For openers, since 2006 no one made the *Forbes* 400 list with wealth of less than $1 billion.[79] While we do not yet know if the current financial meltdown will drastically shake up the *Forbes* list in

Figure 3-12. Share of Net Worth, by Percentile, 2004[a]

Percent

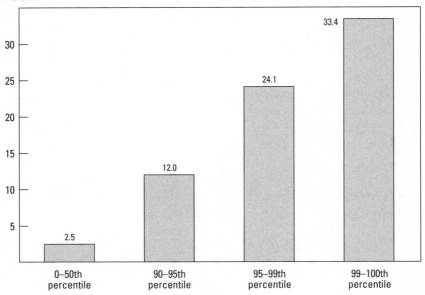

Source: Arthur B. Kennickell, "Currents and Undercurrents: Changes in the Distribution of Wealth, 1989–2004" (Federal Reserve Board, 2006, rev.), p. 11.

a. Shares do not add to 100 because the 50th to 90th percentiles are omitted. This missing group holds 27.9 percent of total wealth.

2009, it is clear that the wealth of those at the top far outstrips what an average or even above average American can ever hope to obtain.

Given the increasing wealth at the very top of the distribution, it is not surprising that wealth is more unevenly distributed than income. According to calculations based on SCF data, the 2004 Gini coefficient (a common measure of the distribution of wealth or income, ranging from 1 when one person or household controls all the income or wealth to 0 when everyone has the same income or wealth) for wealth was 0.80, while that for income was only 0.54.[80]

Conclusion

Based on our review of trends in both income and wealth, we conclude that both are becoming more unequal. In addition, there has been only modest progress in reducing poverty. Changes in family composition, stagnant wages at the bottom, and the failure to count noncash benefits that are an increasingly important part of the safety net have all played a role in explaining why official measures of poverty are no lower now than they were back in the 1970s (except for the elderly and female-headed families). In the meantime, the middle class has seen only modest economic gains in recent decades, and most of those gains have required more effort on the part of the adults in those families, leading to a time squeeze and a greater sense of vulnerability to economic shocks or personal misfortune. By contrast, the rich have done extraordinarily well over this period. Their income taxes have declined as a percent of their income, giving a further boost to their already high earnings.

four
Opportunity in the United States

Understanding what lies behind any particular distribution of incomes very much influences our perceptions of whether that distribution is "good" or "bad" and what, if anything, needs to be done about it. Those who believe that the distribution fairly reflects each person's talents and energies will have one view. Those who believe it is a deck stacked to reward those fortunate enough to have started with the right cards will have another.

DANIEL P. McMURRER AND ISABEL V. SAWHILL

In chapter 3 we show that incomes have become increasingly unequal in recent decades and that poverty has been persistent.[1] These facts are disturbing to most people and would seem to call for greater efforts to distribute government assistance more broadly and provide a more robust safety net for the poor. In later chapters we propose some policies that would do just that. But we also want to argue, along the lines of an earlier volume authored by Daniel McMurrer and Isabel Sawhill, that focusing on income inequality and poverty provides a narrow and to some extent misleading picture. As stated in this earlier volume:

> This single-minded focus on income inequality has led to a preoccupation with what are only the symptoms of a deeper set of forces that badly need to be understood. Where one ends up in the income distribution reflects, after all, where one began, who one's parents were, what kind of education one received, race and gender, and a host of other factors—including just plain luck. . . . Understanding what lies behind any particular distribution of incomes very much influences our perceptions of whether that distribution is "good" or "bad" and what, if anything, needs to be done about it. Those who believe that the distribution fairly reflects each person's talents and energies will have one view. Those who believe it is a deck stacked to reward those fortunate enough to have started with the right cards will have another. One cannot judge any particular distribution of incomes without knowing what produced it.[2]

Put in another way, there are at least three reasons to focus on economic opportunity and not just on poverty or inequality. To begin with, as highlighted in chapter 2, Americans believe they live in a meritocracy. They care more about equal opportunity than they do about equal results. This belief has deep roots in our culture and our history and, as we shall see, distinguishes us sharply from the citizens of other advanced countries. This faith in the American Dream has made the public less willing to redistribute income than their counterparts in other countries.

Second, concerns about income inequality beg the question of how much inequality is too much. Almost no one favors a completely equal distribution of income. That would undermine incentives to work, to save, and to contribute to wealth creation. However, current inequalities may well exceed what is needed to foster behaviors that lead to economic growth. Indeed, some argue that by breeding insecurity current inequalities are actually retarding risk taking and growth.[3] Nonetheless, these arguments about insecurity won't satisfy everyone, especially those who are persuaded that inequality is the price we pay for a dynamic economy.

A third reason to focus on economic opportunity is because it suggests a redirection of public policy from treating symptoms to preventing misfortune in the first place. We should not deny assistance to those who fail to succeed by their own efforts, but it would be far better if we could ensure that they had the tools and capacities to achieve economic security on their own.

So it is not only the distribution of income and the level of impoverishment that should concern us but also the system that produces these outcomes. In chapter 2 we distinguish between substantive and procedural fairness. When people believe that the system producing any particular distribution of income is fair, they are less concerned about the outcome and may tolerate a large amount of inequality and poverty. To use the typology developed in that earlier chapter, it matters whether the United States is a meritocracy, a class-stratified society, or a fortune-cookie society in which where you end up is primarily a matter of luck. Even if the distribution of income were the same in all three cases, most people would prefer to live in a meritocracy. The fairness of the process is what seems to matter, not a specific outcome.

Greatly complicating this picture is the fact that not everyone is dealt the same genetic hand or is exposed to the same home environment, topics to which we return in chapter 5. So even if an economically level playing field was created—by redistributing income so that every child had the same amount—these children would still vary in competence, and their ultimate position in society would still tend to affect the next generation. Any attempt to create an opportunity society needs to deal with these core inequalities and with the need for unequal treatment in favor of the most disadvantaged as a precondition to moving toward the goal of ensuring that everyone has a decent shot at the American Dream.

Economic Opportunity as a Concept

By economic opportunity, we mean the ability of people to move up or down the economic ladder in one or two generations. Most studies of this topic focus on family income or individual earnings, although sociologists often study occupational prestige or some other measure of socioeconomic status. Economic mobility also has a time dimension. One can talk about mobility between generations (comparing children to their parents), over a lifetime (comparing, for example, an individual's income at age fifty-five to his or her income at age twenty-five), or over a short period of time, such as a year or two. Thus one can distinguish between intergenerational mobility, intragenerational mobility, and short-term income volatility.

In addition, one can measure people's relative economic position or their absolute economic position. Strictly speaking, in considering relative economic mobility, for everyone who moves up, someone else must move down. But in a growing economy, it is possible for most real incomes to advance, at the same time that people are re-sorting themselves in relative terms. That is, economic growth can be an uneven process, advancing some people's fortunes more than others'. Imagine the economy as a ladder upon which everyone is perched at some level. This ladder may be getting taller as the result of economic growth—and therefore boosting everyone's opportunities. At the same time, the rungs on the ladder may be getting closer together or further apart as incomes become more equally or less equally distributed. The ability of people to move from one rung to another may be changing as well, depending on their relative mobility.

Much prior research and public discourse has focused on the rate of economic growth and on the fact that income inequality has been increasing in recent decades. Much less has been written about relative economic mobility, since it requires following individuals' incomes over their life course or over several generations. Such studies are important, however, because degree of relative economic mobility is related to societal fairness.

We begin the exploration of economic opportunity with a discussion of relative mobility across generations, briefly addressing trends in intragenerational mobility, based on recent research completed by our colleague Julia Isaacs in collaboration with the two authors of this volume.[4] We then explore what it takes to achieve the American Dream, showing that if you graduate from high school, work full time, and marry before you have children your chances of becoming a member of the middle class are greatly enhanced.

Intergenerational Mobility

As noted, Americans believe that opportunities to succeed are abundant. In a 1999 survey of twenty-seven middle- and high-income countries, some 69 percent of Americans agreed with the statement, "People are rewarded for intelligence and skill," compared to an average of just 39 percent for all the countries surveyed (figure 4-1).[5] What's more, just 19 percent of Americans think that being born to wealth is very important in getting ahead, compared to an average of 28 percent among all respondents. It follows that Americans are more accepting of economic inequality: just one-third believe that the government should take responsibility for reducing income disparities, compared to more than two-thirds in other countries surveyed. Does this faith in the fairness of the process bear scrutiny? Are we the land of opportunity as celebrated in a thousand grade school textbooks, or are we becoming more stratified than many would find acceptable? The answer is less clear than either critics of, or true believers in, American exceptionalism have been willing to acknowledge.

As it turns out, economic success is greatly influenced by the socioeconomic circumstances of the family into which one is born (figure 4-2). For example, 42 percent of the children of families in the bottom fifth of the income distribution end up in the bottom fifth as adults (with annual incomes less than $40,300 in 2006 dollars); this is twice the percentage that would be expected by chance alone.[6] Family incomes in this group were not much higher in the late 1990s than they were in the late 1960s: median income at the bottom grew only 18 percent between the parents' generation and the children's generation, while median income of the top quintile grew 52 percent.

Furthermore, rags-to-riches outcomes are uncommon. Just 6 percent of poor Americans move from the bottom fifth to the top fifth of the income distribution (above $116,700 in 2006 dollars) in one generation. Individuals born to middle-income parents have better prospects: 19 percent climb from the middle fifth to the top fifth. Contrast these low- and middle-income groups to individuals whose parents were in the top fifth. They have a 39 percent chance of staying in the top fifth and only a 14 percent chance of moving down to the middle ($62,000 to $84,000 in 2006 dollars). America, then, is not a rigidly class-stratified society, but neither is it immune to the influences of class.

Figure 4-1. Mobility and Inequality in Twenty-Seven Countries, 1999

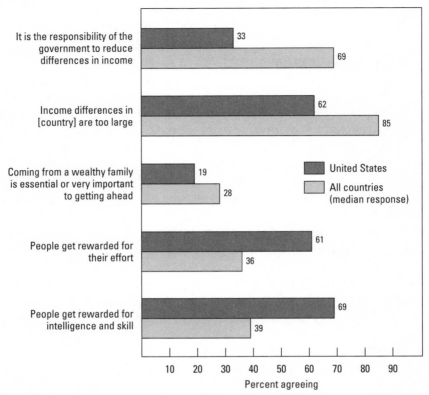

It is the responsibility of the government to reduce differences in income — United States 33, All countries 69

Income differences in [country] are too large — United States 62, All countries 85

Coming from a wealthy family is essential or very important to getting ahead — United States 19, All countries 28

People get rewarded for their effort — United States 61, All countries 36

People get rewarded for intelligence and skill — United States 69, All countries 39

□ United States
□ All countries (median response)

Percent agreeing

Source: Julia B. Isaacs, Isabel V. Sawhill, and Ron Haskins, *Getting Ahead or Losing Ground: Economic Mobility in America* (Brookings and Economic Mobility Project, an Initiative of the Pew Charitable Trusts, 2008), figure 1. (Brookings tabulations of data from the 1999 Social Inequality III module of the International Social Survey Program; data collected 1998–2001.)

While 42 percent of those born into the bottom fifth of the income distribution remain poor as adults, the remaining portion do move to a higher-income quintile. Thus there is significant mobility. The relevant question is whether there should be more.

These statistics do not tell us why mobility is less than perfect—why class or socioeconomic status matters. Parents at the top may buy success for their children through their command of economic resources such as access to good schools, safe neighborhoods, and good health care. Or the underlying personal characteristics shared between successful parents and their children (such as strong verbal or mathematical skills, a winning smile, or a strong work ethic) may be at work. Or higher-income parents may adopt more suc-

Figure 4-2. Family Income of Adult Children, by Parents' Family Income[a]

Percent of adult children in each income quintile

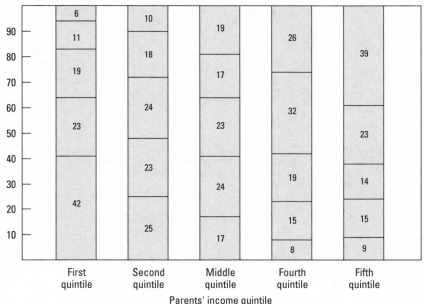

Parents' income quintile

Source: Julia B. Isaacs, Isabel V. Sawhill, and Ron Haskins. *Getting Ahead or Losing Ground: Economic Mobility in America* (Brookings and Economic Mobility Project, an Initiative of the Pew Charitable Trusts, 2008), figure 4.

a. Columns may not add to 100 due to rounding. Family incomes are five-year averages from the Panel Study of Income Dynamics (PSID) for 1967–1971, when parents were forty-one years old on average, and again in 1995–2002 when their adult children were thirty-nine years old on average.

cessful childrearing practices and expose their children to a wider range of educational experiences (museums, books, travel, other successful children and adults). In chapter 5, we delve more deeply into these issues. The point for now is that some relationship between the economic circumstances of parents and their children is inevitable. It is thus difficult to say whether the mobility glass is half full or half empty. But we can ask how the American experience compares to other affluent democracies.

Comparing Intergenerational Mobility across Countries

By the benchmark of intergenerational mobility America comes up short compared to some other advanced countries. Obtaining data that are comparable across countries is a challenge, especially because to make these comparisons requires income data from two generations. Typically, researchers have

Table 4-1. Economic Mobility, Men with Fathers in the Bottom and Top of Earning Distribution, Six Countries[a]

Percent

	Bottom fifth			Top fifth		
Country	Remained in bottom fifth	Climbed 1–3 steps	Climbed to top fifth	Dropped to bottom fifth	Dropped 1–3 steps	Remained in top fifth
Denmark	25	61	14	15	48	36
Finland	28	61	11	15	50	35
Norway	28	60	12	15	50	35
Sweden	26	63	11	16	47	37
United Kingdom	30	57	12	11	60	30
United States	42	50	8	10	55	36

Source: Markus Jäntti and others, "American Exceptionalism in a New Light: A Comparison on Intergenerational Earnings Mobility in the Nordic Countries, the United Kingdom, and the United States," Discussion Paper 1938 (Bonn: IZA, 2006), table 4, p. 18, and table 12, p. 33.

a. Sons were born around 1958, and earnings of both fathers and sons were observed near age forty. Sons' earnings are generally measured between 1992 and 2002.

used data on the earnings of sons compared to their fathers (table 4-1).[7] In the United States, the pattern is very similar to the more comprehensive mobility statistics presented above: 42 percent of American sons whose fathers had earnings in the lowest quintile remained stuck at the bottom. In contrast, the comparable percentages ranged from 25 to 30 percent in Denmark, Finland, Sweden, Norway, and the United Kingdom. What's more, a slightly smaller fraction of American sons rise from the very bottom to the very top.

Other studies, moreover, tell much the same story, finding less mobility in the United States than in Canada, Germany, and France.[8] Poor Americans do have some chance of moving up through hard work (and luck). But the idea that equality of opportunity is a distinctly American strength is a myth.

Mobility patterns of middle- and upper-wage earners, however, were quite similar across the six countries in which the earnings of fathers and sons were compared. Middle-income workers were fairly mobile in each nation, and stickiness at the top of the earnings ladder was the rule. Some 30 to 37 percent of those whose fathers had earnings in the top fifth of the earnings distribution themselves ended up in the top fifth of the earnings distribution in most countries.

Trends in Intergenerational Mobility in the United States

Comparisons of mobility across time face even more daunting data challenges than comparisons among countries. Many surveys do not go back far enough to track earlier generations. Moreover, we can't know whether mobility has gone up or down in the last few decades because children born since the early 1980s are not yet old enough for us to track their adult careers.

But we do know that relatively young workers are facing greater challenges than earlier generations. In the past, a growing economy ensured that each generation was better off than the previous one, creating an effective engine of upward mobility for most families. From 1947 to 1973 the typical family's income roughly doubled. Since 1973, however, growth in family incomes has been limited to a relatively paltry 22 percent.[9] And all of that gain for families comes from the addition of second (almost always female) earners. Men in their thirties actually earned less in real terms in 2004 than their fathers' generation averaged at the same age: $38,430 for the current generation, down from $44,507 for their fathers' generation (data in 2007 dollars).[10]

With the economic tide plainly failing to raise the incomes of all families, the issue of mobility becomes all the more important. Indeed, in the absence of robust and broadly shared growth, movement to a higher rung on a largely stagnant income ladder has become pretty much the only way to live better than one's parents. To be sure, mobility is a double-edged sword: in the absence of economic growth, for every family that moves up in the ranks, another must move down. Still, the chance to improve their lot matters to most people. And in the eyes of some, an increase in relative mobility would help offset the near stagnation and growing inequality of family incomes.

However, hopes that increased social fluidity have worked to counter the effects of slower growth and less equal incomes are not supported by the evidence. Some researchers, among them Gary Solon of Michigan State and Chul-In Lee of SungKyunKwan University, South Korea, conclude that the rate of relative mobility has not changed significantly since the 1970s.[11] Others, including Bhaskar Mazumder and Daniel Aaronson of the Federal Reserve Bank of Chicago, find a decline in mobility.[12] Perhaps most troubling, some research suggests that there is a link between a high degree of inequality in a society and low mobility: if the rungs of the ladder are far apart, it becomes harder to climb from one rung to another.[13] At the same time, with greater inequality, the prizes for success and the penalties for failure are bigger, making it even more important that the process determining where people end up be fair and open. So greater income inequality has two effects: it makes mobility more difficult and the absence of mobility more consequential.

Comparing Groups

While the broad picture is important, what's happening within subgroups defined by gender, race, and country of birth may have an impact on social stability and the perception of social justice.

We find very few differences in relative mobility by gender. For both men and women (but especially for women) there is an additional source of upward mobility beyond earning a good income, namely, marrying well. If women tend to marry men whose economic prospects are similar to those of their own fathers, marriage becomes another vehicle, along with success in the labor market, for transmitting economic status across generations. And the data show that both sons' and daughters' family incomes resemble the incomes of their parents.

In contrast, mobility differences between black and white families are striking. Some 54 percent of blacks, as compared to 31 percent of whites, born to parents in the bottom fifth of the income distribution remained in the bottom fifth as adults. Thus a disproportionate source of the stickiness at the bottom is driven by the experiences of African American families.

In addition, whereas 37 percent of the children of white middle-income families moved up relative to their parents, only 17 percent of black children born to middle-income parents moved up. More disturbing still, 45 percent of black children whose parents were middle income in the late 1960s ended up falling to the bottom fifth, compared to only 16 percent of white children.[14]

Immigrants are still another story. If America has been seen as the land of opportunity, one reason is because so many immigrants have been able to improve their lot by coming here. That's still true. Although workers, particularly those with little education, earn relatively low wages in the United States, they earn far more than they could back home. This reality is largely ignored in the research reported here because we lack data on immigrants' parents. Yet immigrants are an important part of the mobility story, with around 1.5 million immigrants entering the country each year, and with most of them able to improve their economic status in absolute terms.[15] (Even though they are absolutely better off, their families may have had relatively high status in their country of origin.)

And the children of immigrants tend to do even better than their parents. George Borjas of Harvard compared first-generation immigrants in 1970 and second-generation immigrants in 2000 and found that second-generation immigrants made more money than their parents, with a wage gain of 5 to 10 percent, on average.[16] Thus the immigrant experience generally reinforces the idea that America remains a land of opportunity. However, Borjas cautions that changing political, economic, and social forces may diminish the gains made by future generations of immigrants and their children. Because recent immigrants actually report lower wages than their native counterparts, Borjas predicts that their children may also be less advantaged, suffering a wage deficit of 10 to 15 percent relative to native-born workers by 2030 if current trends continue.[17] Thus while economic assimilation continues to provide a step up for immigrants, the children of more recent and typically less-skilled immigrants may have more difficulty reaching economic parity with nonimmigrants.

Intragenerational Mobility

Individuals move up and down the economic ladder not only across generations but also across the life course. Thus a snapshot of a family's income in any particular year is not necessarily a good indicator of how that family will fare over a more extended period of time. A typical pattern is for incomes to be low when people are young, to rise to a peak when they are middle aged, and to decline again in old age. However, there is considerable variation in this pattern. Family income may rise rapidly as the result of greater experience on the job, promotions and raises, the addition of a second earner, or a business success. Income may fall because of the loss of a job, a divorce, a serious illness, a business failure, retirement, or a family member taking time out of the labor force to continue his education or to care for children. Thus there is some re-sorting of families' relative position over the course of their working lives. If everyone were poor at age twenty-five but rich at age fifty-five, we could still say that lifetime incomes were equally distributed. Yet by conventional measures, it would appear to be a highly unequal society because we would be lumping together people at very different stages of their careers. For this reason, we need to understand how much income mobility there is over the life course and whether there is more or less now than in the past.

A series of studies, pioneered by Isabel Sawhill and Mark Condon—and extended in important ways by Gregory Acs and Seth Zimmerman for recent decades—examines mobility over the periods 1967–76, 1977–86, 1984–94, and 1994–2004 using the Panel Study of Income Dynamics. What these and other studies show is that about 60 percent of all families in their prime working years (ages twenty-five to forty-four at the beginning of a given decade) change quintiles over a ten-year period.[18] The proportion of families moving out of the bottom quintile over the same time period is roughly 47 percent, proportions that have not changed significantly since the 1960s.[19]

What determines who moves up or down over a decade's time? Acs and Zimmerman explore this question and find that non-Hispanic whites, men, those with more education, and home owners are the most likely to exit the bottom income quintile.[20] High rates of relative downward mobility are associated with being black or Hispanic, being poorly educated, and having a disability.

The implications of this research are twofold. First, lifetime incomes are more equally distributed than incomes measured over a shorter time period, since any snapshot of the distribution includes people at very different stages of the life cycle and thus exaggerates the inequality in incomes over an entire career. Second, rising income inequality in recent decades has not been offset by an increase in mobility. If intragenerational mobility were increasing, then the picture provided by one-year snapshots would be a misleading and an upwardly biased indicator of the extent to which lifetime income inequality is increasing. But since rates of intragenerational mobility have not changed since the 1960s, it follows that the one-year snapshots are a decent proxy for what has been happening to lifetime incomes. In short, although lifetime income is more equally distributed than annual income, lifetime income inequality appears to be increasing along with the more conventional one-year measures of income inequality.[21]

Achieving the American Dream: What Are the Prerequisites?

In chapter 2 we sketch our philosophical orientation, which is to provide assistance to those who are playing by the rules. We also note that taxpayers are more willing to support those who are making an effort to support themselves and their families than they are to support those whom they perceive to be shirking this obligation. Personal responsibility matters. In particular, we expect people to at least graduate from high school, to work full time (if jobs are available), and to not have children outside of marriage. We believe these social norms are widely if not universally endorsed.

To what extent does compliance with these norms enable people to join the middle class? In table 4-2 we show how it matters whether the head of the family has completed high school and works full time (assuming that person is not elderly or disabled) and whether families with children are married (or widowed) and whether the family head waited until at least her twenty-first birthday to have children. As the table shows, families that adhere to these norms or expectations have a very high probability of entering the middle class. Indeed, adhering to all three norms virtually eliminates the possibility of a family living below the poverty line.[22]

Individuals in families headed by an able-bodied adult between the ages of twenty-five and sixty-four have a 98 percent chance of escaping poverty if the family adheres to all three social norms. By contrast, 76 percent of those living in families that do not adhere to any of these norms are poor. In short, the likelihood of reaching the middle class improves dramatically for those

Table 4-2. Income Class, by Adherence to Social Norms, 2007

Percent

Income class[a]	All persons[b]	Persons in families by number of norms[c]		
		All three	One or two	None
Poor	11.4	2.0	26.9	76.0
Lower middle	32.1	24.2	47.9	17.1
Middle	25.8	31.3	16.2	3.5
Upper middle	14.7	20.0	5.1	2.0
Upper	15.9	22.5	4.0	1.4
N (thousands)	237,994	154,203	80,416	3,375
Total	100	64.8	33.8	1.4

Source: Authors' calculations based on the U.S. Census Bureau, *Current Population Survey, Annual Social and Economic Supplement.*

a. Income classes are family-size adjusted and refer to individuals living below poverty, 100–299 percent of poverty, 300–499 percent of poverty, 500–699 percent of poverty, and more than 700 percent of poverty, respectively. For the average three-person family, these income classes correspond to about $0–$16,530; $16,530–$49,590; $49,590–$82,650; $82,650–$115,710; and more than $115,710.

b. Table excludes individuals living in families with heads under age twenty-five and over age sixty-four as well as individuals living in families with heads that receive disability income. Observations with negative income are included and coded as living below the poverty line.

c. The three norms are complete high school, work full time, wait until age twenty-one and marry before having children. High school graduation is defined as attaining a high school diploma or its equivalent. Full-time work is defined as thirty-five or more hours of employment a week for forty or more weeks in 2007.

who finish high school, work at least forty weeks a year, and delay childbearing. Looking at each norm separately, working full time has the strongest association with ensuring one's position in the middle rungs of the income distribution.[23] In chapter 6, we address the debate about whether lack of work is due to a lack of jobs or a failure to take the jobs that are available. For present purposes, we simply note that these data are for 2007, a year in which the unemployment rate was 4.6 percent. (There have been only three years since 1970 when it was lower than this.) Thus this analysis is primarily relevant to the kinds of opportunities that exist in a full-employment economy, not to the kind of economy we entered in 2008.

Of course, we cannot assume that a family's decision to adhere to certain social norms is made in a vacuum. Presumably, families selecting into the norm-abiding and norm-violating groups differ with regard to other relevant characteristics. For example, in the case of high school graduation, it may be that those who complete high school simply have a higher average level of innate ability than those who drop out and would thus command superior wages in the labor market regardless of their decision to obtain a high school diploma. Or in the case of marriage, those with extensive economic resources might be viewed as more desirable marriage partners and thus have more opportunities to marry in the first place. In short, being middle class might be what leads people to get a high school degree or get married, instead of the other way around.

In the research literature this problem of separating correlation from causation is called adjusting for selection effects. However, rigorous empirical research suggests that in these three domains of education, work, and marriage, selection effects are actually quite modest, and the observed relationship between "playing by the rules" and economic success is predominantly causal.[24]

We do not argue that it is easy to meet these norms. The long debate between those who believe that individuals control their destiny and those who believe that they are the victims of adverse circumstances that make education, work, and marriage difficult will not be resolved any time soon. We have more to say about this debate in chapter 6. For now, our goal is simply to show that if people did finish at least high school, work, and marry before having children, most of them would achieve the American Dream.

Conclusion

The research reviewed in this chapter suggests that the American Dream is alive but somewhat frayed. Economic growth means that most families are better off than in the past and better off than their own parents, but slower growth has made the economy more of a zero-sum game, with high stakes for both winners and losers. The United States does not have as much intergenerational mobility as most people think. Nor is there more mobility than in other advanced countries.

If you were born into the middle class, your chances of moving up or moving down the ladder relative to your parents are roughly equal. But there is stickiness at either end of the income distribution. Rags to riches in a generation is pretty much a myth: it happens very infrequently.

The story for African American families is especially troublesome. Even those born into middle-class circumstances back in the 1960s are having difficulty retaining a middle-class income as adults. For many immigrants, on the other hand, America is still the land of opportunity, at least to a degree. Even though many recent immigrants arrive with little education and earn low wages as a result, they are doing better than they would have in their home countries, and their children are likely to assimilate and move up the ladder.

Finally, achieving the American Dream is closely tied to playing by society's informal rules. Education, work, and marriage are the foundations of the middle class. Without them, it is much harder to succeed.

What are we to make of these findings? What is it about growing up in a less-advantaged family that causes the children in these families to be less successful as adults? In chapter 5 we address this question in some detail, examining the role of genes, parenting styles, material resources, and neighborhoods and schooling. In subsequent chapters, we explore policies that could create greater mobility for those at the bottom, especially by improving educational opportunities from preschool through college, by supporting work, and by strengthening families.

five

Why Family Background Matters

About half of the inequality in the present value of lifetime earnings is due to factors determined by age 18.

JAMES J. HECKMAN, *Nobel Laureate*

Family background plays a significant role in who gets ahead and who falls behind from one generation to the next. In addition, a number of good studies find that childhood poverty, especially persistent poverty during early childhood, is associated with worse outcomes for children.[1] Children who grow up in poor families do less well in school, are more likely to engage in risky behaviors as adolescents, and have lower earnings and incomes when they become adults.[2] In short, although many people escape from the poverty they experienced while growing up, many do not; and even those who do escape face obstacles not experienced by children from more advantaged families. But why is this relationship between family background and a child's future prospects so strong?

There are four possible answers. One is biology: the children of successful parents may have a genetic advantage in traits ranging from intelligence to good health. While genes interact with the environment in ways that defy any complete separation of the two, biology clearly matters.

A second possibility is that parenting is a key factor in determining a child's later success. This inference follows from data showing large differences by socioeconomic status in the extent to which parents talk to their children, read to them, and otherwise encourage their development.

A third possibility is that more successful parents have the material resources to provide their children with advantages ranging from good medical care and high-quality child care to comfortable and stimulating home environments and experiences.

A fourth possibility is that more affluent parents live in better and safer neighborhoods and that their children have access to better schools.

In short, children who grow up in low-income families may suffer from bad genes, bad parenting, insufficient income, and bad neighborhoods and schools. All of this may seem obvious; yet a common reaction to learning that family income is predictive of children's success is to assume that giving families more income would produce more successful children. Indeed, it seems natural to conclude that giving poor families greater access to material resources should equalize disparities in upbringing. The purpose of this chapter is to delve more deeply into this hypothesis. For example, what if parental income reflects the parents' own genetically based abilities or cultural capital? Because these attributes are transmitted, in part, to their children, simply giving the parents more resources will not necessarily produce dramatically different outcomes for their children.

Scholars have had great difficulty separating the impact of income or material resources from that of genes, parenting, and neighborhood or school. Most likely all of these factors play some role in the transmission of economic status. Indeed, the four interact in complex ways, and it may never be possible to sort out fully their separate influences. Parents facing economic adversity are likely to be less responsive or more punitive in interactions with their children. Genetic potential is less likely to be expressed in unfavorable environments. Low income limits neighborhood and schooling choices. Thus policies based on the simplistic assumption that all one needs to do to improve children's life prospects is to give their parents more money are likely to disappoint. In 2007 we could have eliminated childhood poverty for $53.9 billion.[3] But as Greg Duncan notes after considering the likely effects of this option: "There is little doubt that children raised in poverty have less enjoyable childhoods. But to what extent does poverty affect developmental outcomes and thereby reduce opportunities for success and happiness in adulthood? In contrast with the apparent precision with which poor children are counted, the effects of economic deprivation on children are not at all well understood."[4]

We concur with Duncan's conclusion. Nonetheless, we review the research that attempts to delineate the importance of each of these four factors in order to set the stage for some of the policy judgments made later in this book. More specifically, we conclude that parents who are working hard at low wages deserve more support. However, we are in favor of providing them with more income less because we think it will substantially affect their children's life chances than because we believe it supports work and is the right thing to do. A better approach to improving children's future prospects, in our view, is to invest more directly in their care and early education, a topic we return to in chapter 8.

Is It Bad Genes?

Not all men (or women) are created equal. Some people are born with physical or mental limitations of various kinds. Others are healthy and energetic from the start. This conclusion is based on the work of behavioral geneticists, who have studied the extent to which twins or siblings reared apart (and who thus have similar genes but experience different environments) still share many of the same traits. It is also based on the fact that children who are adopted often have more in common with their biological than with their adopting parents.[5]

Biological influences may be latent. For example, medical research is increasingly finding that genetic susceptibility to certain conditions varies greatly from one individual to the next; these susceptibilities include alcoholism, drug abuse, and depression. Even one's basic temperament—from being very outgoing to being extremely shy—appears to be partly grounded in one's genetic makeup, creating personality differences that, although not hardwired, are influenced by one's biological inheritance and only partially malleable later in life.[6] Studies of people who share some or all of the same genes, such as siblings or identical twins, suggest that around half of the differences in various measures of achievement, for example, can be explained by genetic background.[7] The authors of a much-cited text on behavioral genetics note that "genetic factors are often as important as all other factors put together."[8] Moreover, it is well accepted within this field that, contrary to most people's beliefs, genetic influences play a larger role, not a smaller one, as an individual ages.[9]

Any serious study of why some people are more successful than others needs to keep genetics in mind. The power of initial endowments means that a major part of life is a lottery. Some find this fact distressing because of its implication that little can be done to change people's life trajectories. Some, including the authors of this volume, believe that because no one can control the biological cards they are dealt (at least not yet), society has an obligation to help those whose initial endowments handicap them in the race. Moreover, no one argues that the environment is unimportant or that its interactions with one's genetic potential don't matter a great deal.

In a controversial volume on this subject, published in 1994, Richard Herrnstein and Charles Murray examine the extent to which success is predicted by cognitive ability.[10] If genes are inherited and largely immutable, as *The Bell Curve* implies, then there is little room for social policy interventions focused on education or other opportunity-enhancing measures to make much of a difference. Moreover, arguing that success in the labor market is more closely tied than in the past to cognitive ability, the book warns of increasing social stratification based on innate aptitude. Finally, by focusing on black-white differences in IQ, and seeming to imply that these, too, might be immutable, the book touched a very sensitive racial nerve.

The book has been reviewed by many scholars. These scholars generally support the view that many traits, including IQ, are partially inherited. In a statement originally published in the *Wall Street Journal* on December 13, 1994, dozens of social scientists, all experts in the field, co-signed a statement that stated in part that "members of all racial-ethnic groups can be found at every IQ level. The bell curves of different groups overlap considerably, but groups often differ in where their members tend to cluster along the IQ line."[11] The statement continues:

> IQ is strongly related, probably more so than any other single mea-sureable human trait, to many important educational, occupational, economic, and social outcomes. . . . Heritability estimates range from 0.4 to 0.8 (on a scale from 0 to 1), most thereby indicating that genet-ics plays a bigger role than does environment in creating IQ differences among individuals. . . . That IQ may be highly heritable does not mean that it is not affected by the environment. Individuals are not born with fixed, unchangeable levels of intelligence (no one claims they are). IQs do gradually stabilize during childhood, however, and generally change little thereafter.[12]

While the importance of genes is not at issue, the specific analysis under-taken by Hernstein and Murray has been criticized for using a measure of IQ, the Armed Forces Qualifying Test, that is far from a pure measure of ability and instead reflects in part what an individual has learned. The study was also crit-icized for not adequately distinguishing the effects of cognitive ability from those of other possible influences on various outcomes. In addition, although not so-argued in the book, a common but mistaken inference is to assume that if IQ or other traits are inherited at the individual level, that group differences are also difficult or impossible to change. Imagine two groups of children, one of which is never allowed any schooling at all and the other of which is given the very best tutoring imaginable. Within each group there will be *individual* dif-ferences in IQ that are inherited, but the average IQs across the two groups will not be the same because members of the two groups have been exposed to very different environments. Genes create the potential to learn, but actual learning is a product of both one's innate ability and one's experiences.[13]

Some research finds that genes affect IQ more among high-income chil-dren than among low-income children. One interpretation of these findings is that environment matters the most for impoverished children but has reduced salience for middle-income and upper-income children for whom environmental conditions are usually adequate if not ideal. In other words, genetic differences are accentuated in favorable environments.[14]

Whatever one's genetic endowment, it interacts with one's environment in ways that defy a strict separation of the two. Babies who are naturally sociable will elicit warmer responses from their parents, thereby further enhancing their sociability. Children who are musically inclined will likely end up being encouraged to sing or play an instrument, setting them on a path to achieving new musical competencies.[15] One study finds that adopted children whose biological parents were antisocial tend to inherit their parents' behavioral problems.[16] These problems led their adoptive parents to be harsher or less nurturing, leading to further problems for the children. These kinds of interactions between genes and the environment have led many researchers to conclude that any strict separation of the two is impossible.

More important for policy, the architecture of the brain develops very rapidly in the first few years of life and is heavily influenced by a variety of environmental factors, including the home environment and parenting.[17] It is those early experiences to which we next turn our attention.

Is It Bad Parenting?

Common sense and the wisdom of countless generations of grandmothers suggest that children are influenced by their parents. Yet this simple proposition has turned out to be more contentious than one might imagine. Some scholars are skeptical that parenting styles have any significant effects. In their book, *Freakonomics,* Steven Levitt and Steven Dunbar argue that genes account for 50 percent of a child's personality and abilities and that "by the time most people pick up a parenting book, it is far too late. Most of the things that matter [for your child's outcomes] were decided long ago—who you are, whom you married, what kind of life you lead. If you are smart, hard-working, well educated, well paid, and married to someone equally fortunate, then your children are more likely to succeed."[18]

But this conclusion is not inconsistent with the idea that parenting matters, because parenting style is associated with many of these same factors, particularly socioeconomic status. Indeed, countless studies by scholars who study child development suggest that parenting styles have some effect on a wide variety of child outcomes. A common way of describing these styles, based on the seminal work of Diana Baumrind, is to delineate authoritarian, permissive, and authoritative styles.[19] The authoritative style, which combines both warmth and discipline, has been found to be the most effective in promoting both academic and social competencies along with good behavior. With so many children growing up in homes where the parents are absent, neglectful, abusive, or simply overburdened, some groups are calling for the creation of authoritative communities to supplement the home environment.[20]

The literature also suggests that parenting styles vary with socioeconomic status. Five decades of research, reflecting a broad array of theoretical perspectives and research methods, show that poor parents are more likely to use harsh discipline, show less warmth and affection, talk less, and talk less responsively to their children.[21] One study argues that middle-class parents typically employ a parenting style designed to cultivate in their children the competencies needed for success.[22] This includes a focus on organizing leisure-time activities for their children, talking and reading to them, reasoning and negotiating with them, and eliciting feelings and opinions from them. In contrast, working-class and poor families are more likely to believe that the major role of parents is to provide economically for their children. They are much more laissez-faire than their middle-class counterparts when it comes to their children's leisure-time activities and their choice of friends. At the same time, they believe there is a clear boundary between parents and children and are thus more directive and less likely to use reasoning in resolving disputes.

If we compare children from the bottom fifth of income with children from the top fifth, the advantaged children live in homes that are four times more likely to have a computer and that have three times as many books. Advantaged children are read to more, watch far less television, and visit museums and libraries more often.[23] In part as a result of these differences in experience, long before children enter school there are large gaps in vocabulary, test scores, and behavior among children from the different socioeconomic groups.[24]

In one of the most remarkable studies of social class differences in child rearing, Betty Hart and Todd R. Risley observed children from welfare families, working-class families, and professional families once a week for the first two and a half years of life. One of the many differences they found among the three groups was that, in the first year of life, children of professional parents heard more than 10 million words, working-class children heard about 6 million words, and welfare children heard about 3 million words. The children of professional parents actually have larger vocabularies at age four than adults who are on welfare. The authors also found extensive differences in the function and complexity of language used by these three groups of parents. These measures of children's language environment were highly correlated with measures of the children's development at ages nine and ten.[25]

Much attention has been focused on early differences in verbal competencies or test scores, but social competencies are equally, if not more, important. Reliability, trustworthiness, and self-discipline contribute to success in school and in the workplace. Take as an example the ability to delay gratification. In a 1989 experiment done by Walter Mischel and colleagues at Columbia University, a group of four-year-olds was told that if they could refrain from eating a marshmallow (provided by the experimenter) for about ten minutes, they would get an additional marshmallow.[26] As it turned out, all of the children had difficulty waiting this long, but some did much better than others. Remarkably, the children who deferred gratification the longest were discovered in a follow-up study in 2004 to have become the most successful adults.[27] Once again, the ability to delay gratification, like most skills, correlates with socioeconomic status. The reasons remain murky; but children from poorer homes may do worse on delayed gratification tests than children from middle-class homes because they are more likely to have their lives disrupted by marital breakdown, violence, or moving. They think in the short term because the long term is less predictable.

In a more recent study, Nobel Laureate James Heckman, in collaboration with other scholars, has attempted to quantify the influence of children's cognitive and noncognitive skills on labor market and behavioral outcomes later in life.[28] Heckman emphasizes that while cognitive skills are more predictive of adult wages, noncognitive skills are more important in limiting risky behaviors such as teen pregnancy or substance abuse among youth. In all of his work, Heckman emphasizes that gaps in both cognitive and noncognitive skills emerge early and then persist. Most of the gaps observed at age eighteen were already present at age five.[29] He argues that as people age, the ability of any intervention to affect the competencies needed for self-sufficiency diminish sharply. The result is that the cost of achieving improved outcomes rises with age. The optimal strategy, in Heckman's view, is to invest early in less-advantaged children and to sustain the early investment by making additional investments as they grow older.[30]

Indeed, it is not just very young children who are influenced by what goes on within the home. Increasingly, studies are finding that older children are also influenced by their parents. Although most parents believe their teenage children are impervious to their advice and rebellious against their values, the research suggests otherwise.[31] Parents play a key role in teen decisionmaking even during college years, when physical proximity between parent and teen is typically diminished.[32] Moreover, a 2006 survey of high school dropouts found that 38 percent of them reported having "too much freedom and not enough rules in my life" as a major reason for leaving school.[33]

While it may be a mistake for parents to preach to their teens about drugs, alcohol, or sex, it is also a mistake to assume that sixteen-year-olds will make the right choices if we simply provide them with sufficient information.[34] Not only do teens have limited experience, but in addition their development, including that of their brains, is not complete.[35] A 2005 Supreme Court decision banning use of the death penalty on offenders under the age of eighteen exemplifies a growing consensus around this notion. The Court's ruling affirms in law the understanding that teens, while increasingly required to make important life decisions, are not yet always fully capable of doing so.[36] The evidence suggests that the development of this decisionmaking ability may actually come in stages, with the capacity to regulate behavior often developing later than intellectual capacity.[37]

These discoveries suggest that efforts to limit risky behaviors among teens should focus on preventing opportunities for the exercise of poor judgment as well as on educating teens about the risks associated with unsafe behaviors such as binge drinking, unprotected sex, and reckless driving. Parents may play an essential role by remaining engaged and setting reasonable boundaries. Research on the effects of welfare reform on children finds that when mothers go to work there are, in most cases, no adverse effects on their children. The one exception to this is in the case of adolescents.[38]

For low-income parents the challenges of parenting are especially hard. They are more likely to be single parents, to be working, and to live in neighborhoods where crime, drugs, and gangs are prevalent. These and stresses associated with being poor undoubtedly make their job much more difficult.

Home visiting programs to teach people how to be better parents and preschool programs that expose children to positive influences at a very early age, as well as mentoring or after-school programs for older children or teens, aim at supplementing what happens within the home. The ability of such extrafamily interventions to compensate for what less-advantaged children don't get at home is considered in greater detail in later chapters.

Is It Insufficient Income?

A popular theory among some social scientists and advocates contends that if we gave parents more income their children's prospects would improve. After all, if poverty produces bad outcomes for children, then the most direct way to improve those outcomes would seem to be to give parents additional income or other concrete forms of help, such as food stamps, housing assistance, or health care subsidies.

However, researchers continue to debate the extent to which increases in family income alone significantly improve child outcomes. Susan Mayer's 1997 book, *What Money Can't Buy,* is one of the most comprehensive investigations on the subject.[39] Using a variety of statistical methods to distinguish the effects of income per se as opposed to all the parental characteristics associated with income on child outcomes, she finds few effects and concludes that more fundamental parental qualities—the kind that employers are willing to pay for, such as diligence, honesty, good health, and reliability—are stronger predictors of child success than income alone.[40] And as common sense would suggest, income makes more of a difference for child outcomes when we are talking about very poor families who lack the bare necessities such as food or shelter than when we are talking about families who are able to meet their most basic needs through some combination of earnings and government benefits.

These findings have not gone unchallenged. Greg Duncan and his co-authors, using an equally creative methodology, find that family income during early childhood predicts later educational success and that the effects continue into adulthood, leading to greater work effort, higher earnings, and less dependence on government benefits.[41] The authors analyze the extent to which closing the early childhood poverty gap from conception to age five would affect a variety of outcomes later in life. They find that an annual $4,326 boost to income during early childhood would increase years of school completed by about a fifth of a year and young adult earnings by 29 percent.[42] The authors acknowledge that their findings do not prove that income is the cause of these positive outcomes since they are unable to completely control for all of the variables that might affect later outcomes.[43] Still, their study goes a long way toward demonstrating that more income when children are very young could improve children's life chances.

Additional evidence on this question comes from a number of experimental welfare-to-work programs.[44] The preschool-age children of mothers who had higher incomes due to work and income supplements did better in school. Because these programs randomly assigned families to the experimental group that then had higher income than the control group, these findings are free of most of the biases of nonexperimental research. One possible reason for the positive effects found in such programs is the greater use of child care by the mothers in the experimental groups. Some speculate that access to quality child care may have, on average, provided a more structured and disciplined learning environment for the children. Because of the uncertainty about what caused these positive effects for children, we still do not know whether more income by itself would produce similar results.

Is It Bad Neighborhoods and Schools?

Social policy researchers in the 1990s favored the theory that disadvantaged neighborhoods are destructive to the well-being of poor families and children. Following on this theory, they believed that, by improving the neighborhood or moving people to better neighborhoods, children would be able to attend better schools and parents would have more employment opportunities. In addition, access to recreation, social services, and decent housing would expand, crime rates would fall, and the generally deleterious effects of racially segregated ghettos would be ameliorated. However, results from a demonstration program financed by the Department of Housing and Urban Development, called Moving to Opportunity (MTO), which involved establishing a housing voucher lottery to help poor families move to better neighborhoods and comparing them to a control group that didn't move, has produced somewhat disappointing results.

So far, moving to a better neighborhood has had no effect on younger children's behavior or school achievement in reading or math. Nor has it affected graduation rates. There has been some decrease in risky behavior among teenage girls (drug use, drinking, and smoking) relative to the control group but an increase in risky behavior and crime among teenage boys.[45] MTO adults were no more likely to be employed, earned no more, and received no less welfare than the control group. However, they did report feeling safer, and levels of anxiety dropped as a consequence of the move.[46]

Poor children don't just live in bad neighborhoods; they are also likely to attend poor schools, where overcrowding, inexperienced teachers, inadequate facilities, and disciplinary problems and other signs of disorder are common.[47] School finance reforms since the 1970s have helped to even out spending between more and less affluent school districts but do not compensate for the fact that less affluent districts have more special-needs children, older facilities, higher salary costs if they are located in urban areas, and greater challenges educating a less-advantaged group of children.[48] In chapter 8 we return to the question of whether greater access to a high-quality preschool and K–12 experience could promote upward mobility for low-income children.

Conclusion

Children from low-income families face a number of disadvantages. Some of these disadvantages are inherited from their parents, some relate to the quality of their home environments and the parenting they receive, and some are exacerbated by insufficient household income, adverse neighborhood conditions, and poor schools. Improving the prospects of children reared in these environments requires operating on several fronts at once. However, our view is that the opportunity to compensate for inadequate home environments and for genetic tendencies is highest in early childhood.

In subsequent chapters we give more attention to the question of how much income support should go to low-income adults and in what form. There are many reasons that supplementing the incomes of low-income families may be the right thing to do. Improving the life chances of children in these families, however, may not be the strongest justification for that assistance. Put differently, there's a trade-off between spending $4,000 a year per child to bring poor children up to the poverty line during their early years and spending a similar amount to provide them with more or better early education outside of the home. The research reviewed in this chapter suggests that children in less-advantaged families are handicapped not so much because they lack material resources as because other aspects of their home environments prevent them from acquiring the cognitive and noncognitive skills they need for later success in school and in the job market. If we want to improve their life chances, we need to do more than provide their parents with income. We need to provide them with high-quality child care or early education and better education during the public school years.

six
Perspectives on Poverty

The core conservative truth is that culture matters . . . and the core liberal truth is that government can reshape culture.

SENATOR DANIEL PATRICK MOYNIHAN

Debates about what the rest of society owes the less fortunate are often based on underlying assumptions about why people are rich or poor, successful or unsuccessful. This chapter examines that debate. As chapter 2 notes, the public is divided in ranking personal effort or outside circumstances as the bigger cause of poverty.[1]

Expert and political opinion on the issue is also equally divided. To many liberals it seems obvious that a large part of the problem is societal, that the very structure of a market economy, which offers low wages and uncertain job prospects for the least skilled, makes it impossible for many people to achieve economic success without robust government intervention. To many conservatives it seems equally obvious that anyone who is willing to obtain an education, work hard, and take advantage of the opportunities that exist in the United States will achieve a modicum of success—as many immigrants to this country have, in fact, done.

Our view—probably most people's view—is that it isn't either-or. On the one hand, low market wages and uncertain job prospects are a fact of life. In addition, and even more important, as emphasized in chapter 5, children don't get to pick their genes, their parents, or their early home environments. These can greatly affect later success yet are not a matter of personal choice. Still, individual choice matters. Decisions about how hard to study, how much to work, and what kind of family life to lead all ultimately contribute to individual success.

In this chapter we begin with a review of the debate between those who believe that poverty is a cultural phenomenon and those who believe it is structural in nature. In chapter 3 we review some of the key data and research that relates to this debate. However, that kind of factual evidence is far from dispositive, so in this chapter we focus primarily on the debate itself and some of the more qualitative evidence upon which researchers draw. Different people can honestly interpret the same facts quite differently. Nor does one explanation fit all segments of the poverty population, which after all is exceedingly diverse. We need to distinguish between someone who is poor because he can't find work and someone who is poor because she is unwilling to work. Statistical data on employment rates cannot distinguish one from the other. In the end, our view is that it is possible to find policies that recognize the importance of both culture and structure in explaining American poverty today.

Cultural Explanations

The debate about whether there is a culture of poverty began in the 1950s and 1960s, with scholars such as Oscar Lewis and Edward Banfield arguing that poverty stems at least in part from insufficient orientation to the future, little sense of self-efficacy, and a too-ready acceptance of life as it is.[2]

Empirical data on these issues are hard to find and even harder to interpret. In a series of papers in the mid-1980s, researchers associated with the Institute for Social Research at the University of Michigan used a longitudinal survey (the Panel Study of Income Dynamics, or PSID) to study the attitudes of the poor. They found that the heads of poor families, when compared to the heads of more affluent families, had less-positive attitudes, greater fear of failure, less orientation to the future, and less confidence that they could affect their own lives. However, these attitudinal measures were, for the most part, not predictive of future economic mobility. Indeed, if anything, the causation ran in the other direction, from economic circumstances to attitudes. For example, in one paper the researchers conclude: "Poor people differ from others on some motivational and personality measures, but the differences appear to have been caused by the events they have experienced. There is virtually no consistent evidence that the motivational and psychological characteristics measured by the study affect subsequent achievement, either within or across generations."[3]

Similarly, reviewing extensive qualitative research from the Urban Poverty and Family Life Study in the mid-1990s, William Julius Wilson finds that the attitudes and values of the poor were not different from those of the middle class and the wealthy in any basic way. If anything, motivation and action are driven by individual circumstance and location, rather than the reverse. According to Wilson,

Our research reveals that the beliefs of inner-city residents bear little resemblance to the blanket media reports asserting that values have plummeted in impoverished inner-city neighborhoods or that people in the inner city have an entirely different value system. What is so striking is that despite the overwhelming joblessness and poverty, black residents in inner-city ghetto neighborhoods actually verbally endorse, rather than undermine, the basic American values concerning individual initiative.[4]

This conclusion is echoed by Katherine Newman, based on her ethnographic study of inner-city fast-food workers:

Given the divergence of experience, the stability of our respondents' views of opportunity and personal responsibility is notable. While one might expect that those who have done well would see the world through positive lenses and argue that everyone is the master of his or her own destiny, it is testimony to the power of mainstream values that even those who have had less positive trajectories generally subscribe to [those same] views. . . . The durability of these views is impressive for the way in which it displays the power of mainstream, middle-class morals. Conservative thought infuses the lives of the working-poor and their fellow job seekers in the inner city.[5]

Although low-income families may accept mainstream values, what stands out in Newman's work is the difficulty many of them have in integrating these values into their own lives.

In contrast to Newman, the Harvard sociologist Orlando Patterson argues that cultural attributes—including the distinctive attitudes, values, and predispositions of a group and the effects such attitudes have on behavior—are critical to understanding why millions of young black males feel disconnected from the American mainstream. He is critical of social scientists who rely heavily on structural factors like low incomes and joblessness as explanations for self-destructive behavior out of fear of blaming the victim or implying that the behavior of certain subgroups is immutable. Instead, Patterson reasons that culture can be a powerful factor in explaining certain behaviors, such as failing to complete high school:

The "cool-pose culture" of young black men was simply too gratifying to give up. For these young men, it was almost like a drug, hanging out on the street after school, shopping and dressing sharply, sexual conquests, party drugs, hip-hop music and culture, the fact that almost all the superstar athletes and a great many of the nation's best entertainers were black. . . . Hip-hop, professional basketball and homeboy fashions are as American as cherry pie. Young white Americans are very much into these things, but selectively; they know when it is time to turn off Fifty Cent and get out the SAT prep book. For young black men, however, that culture is all there is—or so they think.[6]

Bill Cosby and Alvin Poussaint advance a similar view in their book, *Come on, People: On the Path from Victims to Victors.* They write:

> Too often the word *victim* shows up in our discussions. We have all driven through lower economic neighborhoods where there are three and four families living in a one-family house, and the music is loud enough to wake the dead. It seems as if the folks living there are trying to drown out their own feelings. This culture is sedating. It encourages people to see themselves as victims, as being incapable of helping themselves, of feeling anything but totally defeated.
>
> We know that there are forces that make the effort to escape poverty difficult. . . . [But] many people in these communities, who are trying to make it, find themselves struggling against their fellow African Americans who are so lost in self-destructive behaviors that they bring down other people as well as themselves.[7]

A theme in much of this more observationally oriented literature is hopelessness—a sense of passivity or fatalism in the face of limited opportunity. Jason DeParle, a journalist with a distinguished record of covering social policy issues, picks up on this theme in his 2004 book, *American Dream: Three Women, Ten Kids, and a Nation's Drive to End Welfare.* Following the lives of three young women living in Milwaukee in the wake of the welfare reforms of the mid-1990s, DeParle observes that two of his subjects, Angie and Jewell

> offered no theory about what stood between them and conventional success. But one striking part of the story they told is what they left out. They didn't talk of thwarted aspirations, of things they had sought but couldn't achieve. They certainly didn't talk of subjugation; they had no sense of victimhood. The real theme of their early lives was profound alienation—not of hopes discarded but of hopes that never took shape.[8]

A similar view is expressed by Kathryn Edin and Maria Kefalas in their book, *Promises I Can Keep: Why Poor Women Put Motherhood before Marriage,* which is based on interviews with more than 150 low-income single mothers in Philadelphia and its suburbs.[9] In examining how the women approach pregnancy, especially unintended pregnancy, the authors observe the complex and fatalistic view the women often take regarding their own life prospects. Without any defined plans or even dreams for the future, many of the women come to embrace pregnancy quickly, whether planned or not. Edin and Kefalas note that the women are often fatalistic about the challenges (and gifts) that life presents. Two of the subjects in the study, Jasmine and Susan, underscore this mentality when discussing the conception of their own children: Jasmine explains that "I never used anything [when] I got pregnant. *God* is in control. And [my kids] was *meant* to *be.* . . . I feel like, if it happens, it happens." Susan adds that "it wasn't like I could just *plan* things. Things happen, and so you just go ahead. Some things happen you just can't plan!"[10]

In an in-depth and heroic attempt to sort out the relative influence of economic incentives, individual motivation, and culture on people's behavior, Mary Jo Bane and David Ellwood conclude that all three factors play a role, although the influence of each factor depends on the nature of the behavior in question and the circumstances.[11] Economic incentives (or structure) seem to play a larger role in explaining work, and social norms (or culture) play a larger role in explaining family behavior. For example, economic models do a poor job of explaining the decline in marriage or the rise in nonmarital births.

Larry Mead suggests that another way to think about the intersection of culture and structure is to distinguish attitudes from behavior. He postulates that the chronically poor may have conventional values but be unable to convert those values into orthodox behavior. He contrasts this group to three other groups: members of the middle class, who have both conventional attitudes and conventional behavior; bohemians, who have unorthodox values and unorthodox behavior; and political radicals, who combine unorthodox values with more conventional behavior.[12]

One problem in most of this literature is a tendency to paint with too broad a brush. As suggested in chapter 3, the poor are very diverse. Of the nonelderly poor, 60 percent of all people who begin a spell of poverty are only temporarily poor; the adults in these families may have lost a job, become ill, seen a business fail or a home foreclosed, and they will typically get back on their feet within a year or two. The remaining segment (about 40 percent) consists of chronically poor working-age adults and their children, with only about 12 percent of those entering poverty staying there ten years or more. However, precisely because those who are chronically poor have difficulty escaping poverty, the majority of the poor measured at any given time (for example, in an annual cross-sectional survey like that used for the official poverty measure) tends to be the chronically poor. Measured at a given point in time, over 80 percent of the poor have been poor for three or more years, and a little more than half have been poor for ten or more years.[13] If there is a culture of poverty or an underclass in American society, it is drawn from this second group. Indeed, Ellwood concludes that ghetto poverty is hard to explain without reference to cultural variables.[14] But how large a group is this?

In an attempt to answer this question, Isabel Sawhill, in collaboration with Errol Ricketts, earlier offered one possible definition of the American underclass:

> Behavioral norms are not invariant. But in American society . . . it is expected that children will attend school and delay parenthood until at least age eighteen, that adult males (who are not disabled or retired) will work at a regular job, that adult females will either work or marry, and that everyone will be law abiding. The underclass, in our definition, consists of people whose behavior departs from these norms and in the process creates significant social costs.[15]

To estimate the size of this group, Sawhill and Ricketts used census data to identify "underclass areas," or neighborhoods in which the proportion of the residents who failed to achieve such norms was one standard deviation above the national norm for each of these four behaviors simultaneously.[16] They find that in 1980 the proportion of the poor living in such neighborhoods was only 5 percent.[17] Thus as troubling and costly as these behaviors are, the underclass, according to this definition, is very small.

Subsequent research by Paul Jargowsky and Sawhill, using the same definition, finds that the size of the underclass, after rising rapidly in the 1970s, rose only slightly in the 1980s and declined sharply in the 1990s.[18] Four factors may have played a role in this decline.

First, the reform of welfare addressed some of the underlying behavioral problems associated with poverty, especially nonwork. By imposing work requirements on recipients and emphasizing the importance of marriage, the reforms attempted to link assistance to personal responsibility.

Second, changes in federal housing policy, which slowed the creation of high-rise housing projects in favor of vouchers and mixed-use housing, may have reduced the concentration of poverty in many urban neighborhoods.

Third, easier access to abortion reduced the number of unwanted births following the *Roe* v. *Wade* Supreme Court decision of 1973, leading to fewer disadvantaged teens or young adults and, thus, less crime or other antisocial behavior several decades later.[19]

Fourth, in addition to policy changes, a strong economy in the late 1990s undoubtedly contributed to these positive trends.[20]

Whatever the reasons behind these trends, the history of rising and falling numbers of the ghetto poor suggests that culture is malleable and that both societal expectations (such as a shift in welfare policy toward requiring work) and opportunity (such as a stronger economy and more supports for low-wage workers) matter.

Much of the literature on the culture of poverty focuses on the importance of family structure. Daniel Patrick Moynihan famously called attention to this issue in 1965, arguing that "a community that allows a large number of young men to grow up in broken homes, dominated by women, never acquiring any stable relationship to male authority, never acquiring any set of rational expectations about the future—that community asks for and gets chaos."[21]

His message—that the growth in black single-parent households was damaging to children as well as to the entire black community—struck a harsh chord in the media and among many academics for its unequivocal tone. But the disappearance of marriage has continued apace. It has affected not just the African American community but virtually all Americans. The proportion of white children born out of wedlock is now higher than the proportion of black children in 1965, when Moynihan first raised a firestorm over the issue.[22] Indeed by 2007 (the latest available data), almost two of every five children were born outside of marriage.[23]

Subsequent research by several well-respected scholars has convinced most experts that growing up in a single-parent family leads to poor outcomes for children and that a substantial portion of the increase in poverty since the 1970s is the result of the decline of marriage and an increase in unwed childbearing.[24] Some researchers, such as Harvard's William Julius Wilson, argue that the decline of marriage, especially in the black community, is the result of a lack of employed males; however, the empirical evidence in favor of this hypothesis is weak.[25] A more likely explanation is a change in culture and social norms, perhaps exacerbated by the availability of welfare for single mothers and the lack of well-paid jobs for men. Whatever trends in economic conditions may have occurred over the past half century, they are not sufficient to explain the collapse of the two-parent family.

A similar debate swirls around the question of why more poor adults—especially minority men—don't work. Some researchers, such as Wilson and Harry Holzer, contend that the problem is lack of jobs; others, such as Larry Mead, emphasize the willingness to work. In his 1996 book, *When Work Disappears*, Wilson argues that, since the 1960s, the urban poor have largely fallen victim to fundamental and interrelated shifts in the American economy, including the greater use of technology in manufacturing, the rise of global trade, the weakening of unions, and the influx of poor immigrants. The transition away from manufacturing and toward a service economy has also led to a greater suburbanization of employment and an increase in demand for higher-skilled workers, further reducing the jobs available to the low-skill, minority workers living in urban areas.

Harry Holzer similarly argues that the retreat of young black men from the labor market is largely economic in nature, the product of weak employment opportunities and inadequate wages.[26] In one review, Gordon Berlin notes that a 10 percent increase in wages among low-income workers could lead to a 2-to-10 percent boost in employment.[27] Other evidence along these lines comes from programs that guarantee jobs to disadvantaged men, such as the New Hope Project of the 1990s.

In contrast to Wilson, Berlin, and Holzer, Mead argues that work norms among the poor explain much of the joblessness found among the chronically poor:

> Today's urban poverty arose chiefly because work discipline broke down in the mid-twentieth century among low-income people, especially blacks. Somehow, many parents lost their own discipline and thus their authority over children. Fathers failed to work and often disappeared. Their sons then became rootless, seeking to work but not knowing how. Paradoxically, the collapse came just as opportunities for blacks were expanding. To a cultural interpretation, poverty reflects social disorder more than deficient opportunity.[28]

Observing that opportunities to find decent employment have actually been rising over the past several decades for blacks and other minorities in conjunction with civil rights reforms, Mead remains troubled by the number of individuals who continually fail to take advantage of what he sees as promising opportunities. He argues that, beyond providing a direct source of income, employment can represent an organizing principle in one's life and a way to achieve respect. Without this anchor, self-defeating and destructive behaviors like gang activity and nonmarital births flourish. Like Orlando Patterson, Mead points to an oppositional or rebellious culture among young minority men that undermines both their willingness to work and their ability to interact comfortably with supervisors and customers and thus retain the kinds of low-wage jobs for which they qualify.[29] As we show in chapter 4, work is a powerful antidote to poverty. In fact only 3.5 percent of families with at least one full-time worker were poor in 2007.[30]

Finally, the debate about structure versus culture also plays a role in explaining why so many youth fail to graduate from high school with the skills needed to survive in today's economy. A great deal of the education literature focuses on the failures of public schools. But schools cannot improve without the active cooperation of students and their families.[31] When Hugh

Price became the president of the Urban League in 1994, he focused on the large achievement gaps between black and white students as well as the fact that some black students resisted doing well academically because they believed it was tantamount to "acting white." He launched a campaign aimed at encouraging children, families, and communities to care more about achievement. As he explains, "I felt that families and communities had to step up and take responsibility for boosting student commitment to achievement rather than look to outsiders to do that job for them. If an academic culture is truly to take hold and endure, it must be embedded in the hearts and minds—and the belief systems and behaviors—of youngsters, their families, and the organizations that make up their communities."[32]

Similarly, when he was speaking at the 2004 Democratic convention, Senator Barack Obama said, "Go into any inner-city neighborhood and folks will tell you that government alone can't teach our kids to learn; they know that parents have to teach, that children can't achieve unless we raise their expectations and turn off the television sets and eradicate the slander that says a black youth with a book is acting white."[33] President Obama repeated this message in his February 2009 address to a joint session of Congress.

Although people may disagree about why the poor are less likely to finish school, more likely to be jobless, and more likely to form single-parent families, there is no question that these are the underlying causes of their poverty. In a 2003 analysis of census data, we show that if the poor complete high school, work full time, have no more than two kids, and marry as much as they did in the 1970s, the poverty rate would fall by slightly more than 70 percent (figure 6-1).[34] These results parallel the more recent analysis presented in chapter 4 (see table 4-2).

Both our 2003 analysis and the more recent analysis presented in table 4-2 demonstrate that "playing by the rules" (finishing high school, working full-time, marrying before having children) can lead to large reductions in poverty; full-time work is shown to have a particularly large effect. The bad news is that even full-time work leaves some people in poverty. And not everyone can find full-time work, especially in periods of high unemployment. With these facts in mind, we turn next to more structural explanations and, in particular, to how the labor market may restrict opportunities for the poor.

Structural Explanations

Conservatives often assume that markets deliver the best outcomes. While markets efficiently allocate resources most of the time, there are three important exceptions to this rule, all of which especially affect the poor. One exception

Figure 6-1. Poverty Rates, by Influencing Factors, 2001

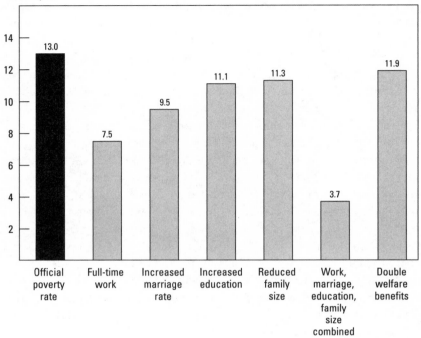

Percent poor

Source: Ron Haskins and Isabel Sawhill, "Work and Marriage: The Way to End Poverty and Welfare," Policy Brief 28 (Brookings, Welfare Reform and Beyond 2003), figure 1.

occurs when the economy goes into a recession and produces too few jobs. A second exception occurs when the market distributes earnings and income inequitably. A third exception occurs when employers discriminate against certain classes of workers on noneconomic grounds, such as race or gender. In these three cases, some government intervention—fiscal and monetary policy to increase the number of jobs, wage supplements or other assistance for low-wage workers, and antidiscrimination laws—are in order. We consider these three cases of market failure and their effects on the poor below.

Lack of Jobs

It is natural to assume that all or most joblessness reflects a lack of jobs rather than a disinclination or inability of workers to fill the jobs that are available. Some joblessness surely does reflect a lack of jobs. We know, for example, that the poverty rate rises during periods of high unemployment. Examining the relationship between the macroeconomy and poverty from the 1960s through 2006, the labor economist Rebecca Blank estimates that a 1.00 percentage point rise in the unemployment rate leads to a 0.45 percentage point rise in the poverty rate.[35] Blank also observes that less-skilled workers experience much higher rates of unemployment and are more affected by changes in the macroeconomy than other workers.[36] We also know that local economic circumstances, such as the closing of a plant, can affect people's job opportunities and cause a sharp drop in their incomes, at least in the short run, and that unemployment rates can vary widely from one area to another. For example, in December 2008 the national unemployment rate stood at 7.2 percent, while state unemployment rates ranged from 3.2 percent in Wyoming to 10.2 percent in Michigan.[37]

Job scarcity, though, is not the major issue among those who are chronically poor (although it is a very important reason for those who are temporarily poor).[38] The U.S. labor market creates between 7 million and 8 million jobs every quarter, even in a year like 2008, when job loss was large and overall employment was declining.[39] There are always some job openings, because people move frequently in and out of the labor market and also in and out of jobs, opening up slots for others. In periods of high unemployment, the ratio of such openings to the pool of those looking for work shrinks, and it becomes harder for those with the fewest skills to compete for the smaller number of available jobs.

Except in times of recession, then, the major problem is not so much a lack of jobs as it is the ability of less-skilled workers to compete for the jobs that are available. Even the poor themselves rarely mention a lack of jobs as their primary problem. When asked why they did not work in the previous year, only 11 percent of poor men and 4 percent of poor women ages eighteen through sixty-four said it was because they "could not find work."[40] Much more important were such factors as being ill or disabled, going to school, retirement, or taking care of home or family (the last-mentioned being especially true for women). Problems with substance abuse, depression, or a prison record also make finding and keeping a job difficult.[41]

These reasons for lack of employment should not blind us to the real difficulties that a period of high unemployment poses for the least-skilled members of the labor force. Because they are likely to be the hardest hit by a recession, countercyclical fiscal policies like those introduced in 2008 and 2009 should be designed to provide extra help to these workers. This help can take the form of greater spending on unemployment insurance, food stamps, Medicaid, cash assistance, and other programs targeting low-income families.

Inadequate Wages

A much more serious problem than a scarcity of jobs during normal economic times is the wages paid in jobs at the bottom of the skills ladder. In 2007, by one definition more than a quarter of the workforce earned poverty-level wages.[42] Moreover, the United States has a higher proportion of workers in low-paying jobs than other rich countries; and differences in the incidence of low pay are correlated strongly with differences in poverty rates across these countries.[43]

To see the effect of low wages on family well-being, consider a single parent with two children who earns $8.00 an hour (just a little above the current minimum wage of $7.25 an hour) and works full time (2,000 hours a year). This worker would earn only $16,000 a year—well below the poverty line of $16,705 for this family. On the other hand, such a family would be eligible for a number of government benefits, which can augment its income significantly (figure 6-2).

However, most poor families do not get all of these benefits. Eligibility requirements can be confusing, and working families may wrongly assume that they are not eligible, or they may be unable to spend the time it takes to secure these benefits. The multiplicity of programs and their different eligibility standards require applicants to visit different offices and complete different application forms for each program—a process that is especially burdensome for working parents.

Even if they do apply, there may be waiting lists for some programs—child care subsidies or housing assistance, for example. Housing assistance, in particular, can provide enormous help to a low-income family. Unfortunately, receiving such assistance is relatively uncommon. Currently, only one in four eligible households receives any housing help at all.[44] Unlike tax credits, food stamps, and free school lunches, housing vouchers are not entitlements, for which the right to participate is based solely on a person's eligibility. Instead, housing vouchers are distributed largely on a first-come, first-served basis, and long and growing waiting lists exist.[45] Many local housing agencies have even stopped accepting new applications because existing waiting periods are so long. Meanwhile, in 2005, 6.5 million low-income renter households that did not receive housing assistance faced "severe housing problems," defined as paying more than half their income for rent or living in severely substandard housing.[46]

Even entitlements like food stamps do not achieve full participation, especially among working families. Evidence suggests that changes to welfare in

Figure 6-2. Estimated Annual Income, Including Taxes and Benefits, for a Low-Wage Household Head, 2007[a]

Thousands of dollars

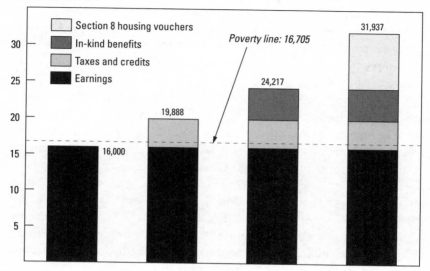

Source: Authors' calculations as follows: Tax liabilities and credits for tax year 2007 estimated using the NBER TAXSIM Model, Version 8.0; food stamp estimate based on data from Dorothy Rosenbaum, "Families' Food Stamp Benefits Purchase Less Food Each Year" (Center on Budget and Policy Priorities, 2007); lunch program estimate based on data from United States Department of Agriculture, Food and Nutrition Service, "National School Lunch Program Fact Sheet" (2007); housing assistance data from John Karl Scholz, Robert Moffitt, and Benjamin Cowan, "Trends in Income Support," paper prepared for conference, "Changing Poverty," Institute for Research on Poverty, May 29–30, 2008.

a. Household is composed of a single parent with two children. Hourly wage is $8.

the mid-1990s designed to move women from welfare to work dissuaded many women from collecting benefits from other government programs. In response, the food stamp program has implemented several important changes in eligibility rules and outreach efforts. Participation has improved substantially since the early 2000s: 67.3 percent of all persons eligible for food stamps received them in 2006 (the most recent data available), up from 53.8 percent in 2002.[47] It is likely that food stamp applications and participation will rise sharply in coming years—as will participation in other benefit programs—as a result of the current economic downturn.[48]

Another valuable form of government assistance not included in these calculations, but vital to low-income families, is Medicaid. Putting a dollar value on medical care for low-income families is difficult.[49] Nevertheless, access to health care does have large benefits for low-income families, even if those benefits are less directly quantifiable than other forms of aid.[50]

Ultimately, those families fortunate enough to qualify for all of this assistance, and that have the knowledge and the fortitude to navigate the system that provides it, will still have a difficult time living in any major American city and supporting several children on less than $31,937 a year. Furthermore, in most programs, working reduces a poor family's benefits, creating a disincentive to work or to earn more.

While current spending on social services in the United States is not insignificant, a global perspective suggests that more could be done. A number of European nations and Canada report much higher spending (as a percent of GDP) on cash and near-cash assistance to the poor, and this spending is strongly correlated with relative poverty rates across countries. As Gary Burtless and Tim Smeeding conclude, "Simply put, the United States does not spend enough to make up for low levels of pay, and so we end up with a relatively higher poverty rate than do other nations."[51] For all of the above reasons, we argue in chapter 9 that it makes sense to provide more assistance to low-income families than at present and to structure that assistance in a way that encourages work or at least does not discourage it.

Discrimination in the Labor Market

White men working full time and year round earned a median wage of roughly $51,000 in 2007, while their female counterparts earned about $38,000, or 74 percent of that amount. Black men earned 73 percent, and Hispanic men 61 percent, of what white men earned. Black women earned 62 percent and Hispanic women 54 percent of the typical earnings for a white man. Somewhat surprisingly, these gaps persist even among those with roughly similar levels of education.[52] Given the extent of pay disparity across groups, it is worth asking what role discrimination may play in constraining labor market opportunity.

The literature on discrimination has been summarized by a number of social scientists, including Devah Pager, Melissa Kearney, and Joseph Altonji and Rebecca Blank.[53] The general consensus is that outright discrimination has declined sharply since the 1950s but that more subtle forms of bias may be playing an increasing role as more explicit forms of prejudice diminish. These more subtle judgments may include the tendency to assess a particular individual on the basis of group averages (statistical discrimination) or unconscious associations made between a subgroup and a given attribute (implicit bias).[54] An example of statistical discrimination would be an employer assuming correctly that women, on average, are not as strong as men but then inferring that a particular woman who happens to be strong cannot be a baggage handler. An example of implicit bias would be an employer who chooses a male over an equally qualified female job applicant because of a deep-seated but unconscious belief that women are less rational or more emotional than men.

Analysts who have used statistical techniques to explain the lower earnings of women find that differences in education and experience cannot explain the gaps noted above.[55] Instead, most of these pay gaps appear to be due to the fact that women work in lower-paid occupations and industries, either out of choice or because of larger cultural forces.[56]

Nearly all of the black-white gap can be explained by racial differences in education, experience, region of residence, measured aptitude, and as in the case of women, the kinds of jobs in which each racial group is found.[57] In a seminal study, Derek Neal and William Johnson look at the black-white gap in test scores on the Armed Forces Qualifying Test (AFQT) and find that adding this proxy for skill explains all of the black-white wage gap for young women and much of the gap for men.[58] Of course, skill or ability as measured by the AFQT may represent the product of earlier discrimination and its effects on opportunities for black children. Nevertheless, this and similar studies tend to indicate relatively low levels of labor market discrimination and high levels of premarket disadvantages associated with childhood experiences for blacks.

Other studies provide a more direct measure of discrimination by testing how employers or others respond to applications that differ by only one particular trait (such as gender, race, and age). These studies, called audit studies, consistently find evidence of bias against women and minorities. For example, in an audit study of high-priced restaurants in Philadelphia, the women in the study are about 40 percent less likely to receive a job offer for a waitstaff position than the men.[59] Similarly, when symphony orchestras started using screens to conceal the identity of job candidates from the hiring team, women's chances of being selected improved sharply.[60]

Harry Cross and colleagues observe similar results in a 1989 audit study of Chicago and San Diego with Hispanic and white job applicants, as do Margery Austin Turner and colleagues in a 1990 audit of black and white applicants in Washington and Chicago.[61] Likewise, in a more recent study in Boston and Chicago, Marianne Bertrand and Sendhil Mullainathan find that resumes bearing white-sounding names received 50 percent more callbacks for interviews than resumes carrying black-sounding names. In light of their results, Bertrand and Mullainathan conclude "that African Americans face differential treatment when searching for jobs, and this may still be a factor in why they do poorly in the labor market. Job applicants with African American names get far fewer callbacks for each resume they send out. Equally importantly, applicants with African American names find it hard to overcome this hurdle in callbacks by improving their observable skills or credentials."[62]

Taken together, this evidence suggests that bias still exists. Indeed, the findings from audit studies are particularly striking. Still, it's hard to conclude that labor market discrimination is currently a major cause of disadvantage. To be sure, earlier discrimination in housing markets, in the education system, and in the criminal justice system may affect labor market participation and must also be taken into account. Still, we maintain that class (family background) is more important than race or gender per se, as are a person's education and training, their "people skills," and their motivation to succeed.

Toward a Synthesis of Conservative and Liberal Views

While one's behavior and one's circumstances are inextricably linked, it is not clear which is the chicken and which is the egg. Conservatives emphasize the fact that those who work hard and play by society's rules will usually get ahead. Liberals emphasize instead the effects of low wages, poor job prospects, and discrimination by race or gender on the ability and motivation to improve one's lot. Surely both are right, and the balance varies depending on each individual's circumstances. Not all poor people are the same.

The two authors of this volume do not always see eye to eye on these matters but we have benefited enormously from working together and have come to a common view that informs the policy proposals we offer in later chapters. Our view might be summarized as follows: We accept the idea that fundamental inequalities are large. As much as we might like to believe otherwise, not all men—or women—are created equal, and children's early environment and schooling as well as their genetic endowment have important effects on later attainments.

Low wages for those dealt a poor hand early in life are almost inevitable. But even low-wage workers can move out of poverty and into at least the lower middle class with the right motivations and the right kind of support. For these reasons, we argue that interventions early in life that compensate for the initial inequalities should be aggressively pursued. As for adults who are working to support their families and for whom such early interventions are too late, we think their struggle to achieve a decent standard of living should be rewarded by help from the public. But in our view, help means linking assistance to people's own efforts to improve their lives, not providing them with unconditional support. We do not argue that it is easy to make the right choices in life. Bad things happen to good people, and many of those from disadvantaged families do not have the cultural capital, the private safety nets, or the supportive peer networks available to their more privileged counterparts. Moreover, as we have noted, their economic opportunities, especially the wages they can earn, may be constrained.

If one accepts the premise that both behavior and circumstances matter, then policy should shore up wages at the bottom but in ways that encourage education, work, and stable families. Good policy should be designed to both encourage and reward behavior that is in people's own long-run self-interest. It should also recognize that there are limits to what good policy can accomplish. Not only will middle-class Americans likely rebel against transferring too much income to the poor, especially if the transfers are not conditional on behavior, but other strategies may actually do more good. For example, even a tripling of welfare benefits would accomplish less in reducing poverty than finding ways to keep most people fully employed.[63] So thinking about how to help people make the right choices is important.

Should Policy Be More Paternalistic?

One reason we believe it's important to encourage people to make the right choices is because new research in economics and psychology suggests that people do not always act rationally. All of us need to be prodded to do things that will improve our long-term well-being, whether it is eating the right foods or setting aside funds for our own retirement. Low-income families are no different. This line of reasoning argues for using public policy as a kind of "soft paternalism" to encourage, or even require, people to do what is arguably in their own long-term self-interest.

If education, work, and family stability are the keys to success, as we believe, then how far should the nation go in encouraging or requiring such behaviors? The nation has compulsory school attendance laws, seat belt laws, airport security checkpoints, abundant restrictions on smoking, and a host of other laws that interfere with individual freedom but imposes such restrictions only when there is a compelling societal interest for doing so. In other areas, the nation may offer incentives for people to work harder, save for their retirement, smoke or drink less, get more education, give to charity, or buy an energy-efficient home or a more fuel-efficient car, but stop short of compelling such behavior. Finally, the nation may simply exhort people to do certain things, through social marketing campaigns, for example, and provide them with more information about the potential consequences of their actions (for example, through food or drug labeling).

Individual freedom and civil liberties are highly valued in the United States and so is tolerance toward those whose behavior fails to conform to mainstream norms. But there are several reasons for accepting some restrictions on people's behavior. The first is because your right to do what you choose may affect me, in which case more than one person's freedom is at issue. If your behavior imposes costs on me, then I may have a right to impose some limits on what you can do. As a taxpayer who pays for welfare or other social programs, for example, I may want to require that you seek work or stay in school as a condition of receiving benefits, and I may want to provide additional benefits through the EITC only if you maintain your commitment to a job.

But quite apart from the rights of taxpayers or other members of society, there is another reason to justify a certain amount of paternalism in social policy; namely, that people often do not behave in ways consistent with their own self-interest. An increasing body of work in psychology, neuroscience, and behavioral economics calls into question the extent to which individuals act in ways that are rational, consistent, future oriented, and self-interested.[64]

In an important article that draws on this literature and spells out its implications in a provocative way, Richard Thaler and Cass Sunstein argue that, because self-defeating behaviors are common, there is a role for government in steering behavior in more positive directions.[65] They call this "libertarian paternalism" or "soft paternalism" because the steering preserves individual choice while making clear to the individual that not all choices are equally constructive, even from the standpoint of the individual's own long-run welfare. An example of such steering can be found in 401k plans. By making automatic participation in such plans the default option, but giving people the option of declining to participate—as opposed to the reverse—more people end up participating, and saving for retirement rises. These kinds of policies are nonetheless paternalistic because they involve the government intervening in people's lives even when there are no benefits or harms to others involved.

Another example of soft paternalism is the effort to reduce smoking through the use of media campaigns and health warnings on packaging. These efforts appear to have contributed to a marked decline in the incidence of smoking. The example of smoking may be particularly salient since it suggests that it is at least possible to change self-destructive behaviors by moving social norms in a new direction.[66] As smoking has become less common and has acquired negative connotations, more people have been encouraged to quit and fewer and fewer people are taking up the habit. Such shifts in norms, once started, often turn into cascades.[67] Other areas where fundamental changes in social norms have occurred—triggered by some combination of public and private action—are the greater acceptance of women in nontraditional roles, the greater use of helmets and seat belts, the growth of recycling, and lower rates of sexual activity among teenagers.

Attempts to use similar approaches to reduce poverty could include efforts to reduce nonmarital childbearing; efforts to reintroduce a marriage-friendly culture into low-income communities, where marriage as an institution has mostly disappeared; conditional cash transfers designed to encourage parents to get their children to school on time or to keep medical appointments; and programs that create a stronger work norm in low-income neighborhoods or housing projects by saturating them with employment-based programs.[68]

Harder forms of paternalism, such as work requirements in welfare, tying college scholarships or tuition assistance to performance in high school, and wage subsides for full-time work, have also been tried with some success. Here we review the evidence from three demonstration programs that have had considerable success in encouraging work: the New Hope Project, operated in Milwaukee from 1994 to 1998; the Minnesota Family Investment Program (MFIP), which started as a pilot program in 1994 and became Minnesota's statewide welfare program in 1998; and the Canadian Self-Sufficiency Project (SSP), which operated from November 1992 to December 1999.[69]

Each of these three programs provided earnings supplements that were contingent on full-time work. The Canadian SSP was a voluntary program available to individuals who had been living on Income Assistance (Canadian welfare) for at least one year. The program offered lucrative earnings supplements to participating workers, but to participate in SSP individuals were required to forgo their welfare benefits. A variant of SSP that yielded even stronger results, known as SSP Plus, offered employment services to its participants in addition to the standard earnings supplements.

The New Hope program offered broader financial supports than SSP, including child care and health care subsidies, along with earnings supplements. For individuals unable to secure employment, the program provided access to temporary community service positions. Participation in the program was voluntary and contingent on the individual working thirty hours a week. New Hope was available to all low-income people, including males and females, those without children, and those currently not receiving welfare benefits.[70]

In contrast to the New Hope program, the MFIP primarily targeted long-term welfare recipients. Participants in MFIP who secured full-time employment saw their basic welfare benefits increased by 20 percent to offset work-related expenses. These participants also benefited from an increased "earned income disregard," which is the amount of income that is excluded in the calculation of a household's welfare benefit. Participation in MFIP was mandatory for long-term welfare recipients. Those who did not find employment totaling thirty or more hours per week were required to participate in employment-focused services aimed at assisting them in their search for a job.[71]

All three experiments were rigorously evaluated by MDRC, a respected policy research organization. MDRC President Gordon Berlin observed that, across all three programs,

> the results were encouraging. The mostly single mothers who were offered earnings supplements in these large-scale, rigorous studies were more likely to work, earned more, had more income, and were less likely to be in poverty than those in control groups who were not offered supplements. . . . The pattern of results also suggests that income gains—and thus the poverty reduction—could be sustained by an ongoing program of supplements.[72]

These programs demonstrate that promoting work through use of incentives or requirements plus incentives can stimulate significant employment and earnings gains among previously unemployed adults. Indeed, long-term welfare recipients, a population typically deemed unemployable, were the most successful at improving their employment rates as compared with similar recipients not offered the work incentives.

Conclusion

This brief review of different perspectives on poverty suggests four conclusions.

First, the debate about whether high rates of dropping out of school, joblessness, and unwed births reflect a failure of individuals to act responsibly or a failure of society to respond to poverty and inequality is hard to resolve. Our view is that it is some of both, with the balance between the two varying across individuals.

Second, the job market for those who don't have sufficient education is not good. It is hard to support oneself, much less a family, in today's economy if one is stuck in a low-skill job. Government benefits for the working poor do make a difference, but they could usefully be expanded in ways we address in chapter 9.

Third, discrimination against women and minorities has not disappeared, even though its role in constraining opportunities has diminished.

Fourth, social norms or culture matter, and a more authoritative or directive set of policies that nudge people in the right direction can make a difference. A little more paternalism in social policy is in order.

These conclusions have clear policy implications. They suggest that higher educational achievement depends not just on fixing schools but also on motivating students. They suggest that policies targeting less-advantaged adults should focus on work, providing greater assistance to those who work full time. They suggest that efforts to bring back the two-parent family would produce good results for adults and children. The principle in each case should be to help those who are "playing by the rules." This principle marries social and personal responsibility, structural and cultural perspectives. It also builds on the idea that we should nudge people to do what is in their own long-term interest. In subsequent chapters, we describe policies that build on this principle.

seven

Middle-Class Complaints

And I think I should note that, when I talk about the middle class, I'm talking about folks who are currently [in] the middle class but also people who aspire to be in the middle class. We're not forgetting the poor. They are going to be front and center, because they, too, share our American Dream. And we're going to make sure that they can get a piece of that American Dream if they're willing to work for it.

BARACK OBAMA

It is no coincidence that President Lyndon B. Johnson declared the War on Poverty during the 1960s, a period when most Americans were doing well and when almost everyone, rich or poor, had benefited from the rapid economic growth following World War II. The relative affluence of the United States compared to other advanced countries, many of which had been devastated by the war, was at a peak. U.S. workers—many of them working in well-paid, union jobs in the manufacturing sector with few rivals in the rest of the world—were achieving the American Dream for themselves and their families.

As we discussed briefly in chapter 3, it is clear that much has changed. America in recent decades has experienced slower growth and a sharply rising inequality of incomes. It has also faced greater competition from other countries, including developing countries such as India and China. In addition, fewer and fewer workers belong to unions or work in high-paid manufacturing jobs, and trade and immigration are producing a more anxious middle class.[1] Not only is the middle class feeling less secure, but in addition its members have become more pessimistic about the future and about the prospects for their children.[2]

In this chapter we review how this new environment is affecting the middle class and the implications for the poor. Such a discussion may seem out of place in a book whose primary focus is the disadvantaged, but we believe it is important for several reasons.

First, the willingness of the broad middle class to provide greater assistance to those who are still struggling to join their ranks may depend on how well they themselves are doing. When the middle class is beset by its own problems and risks, will its members be willing to help the poor? Or are they likely to insist that additional government funds be spent to help solve middle-class problems? Given the size of the middle class relative to the poor, plus the fact that the middle-class votes and donates to campaigns at a much higher level than the poor, politicians know that they ignore the middle class at their peril.[3]

Second, the line between the poor and the middle class is not permanent. People move in and out of poverty over time or generations. In recognition of this blurred line, many government programs, from child care to the State Child Health Insurance Program (SCHIP) and the Earned Income Tax Credit provide assistance to families with incomes above the poverty line. In some cases these programs reach well into the middle class. Not only do many people in the lower middle class need help paying for such services as child care and health care, but also any sharp phaseout of assistance at the poverty line would produce severe disincentives for people to move up the ladder. But the more government extends such assistance to people higher up the ladder, the more expensive that assistance becomes.

Third, most low-income families aspire to join the middle class or at least to see their children do so; but to the extent that middle-class jobs and incomes are under threat, the incentive to climb the ladder and the chances of doing so are threatened as well. There is evidence (reviewed in chapter 3) that midlevel wages have grown only modestly over the past three decades, and evidence reviewed in chapter 4 shows that it is becoming harder than it used to be to move up the ladder.

Fourth, some of the same factors that affect the middle class also affect the poor. Many argue, for example, that technological innovation and globalization, including both trade and immigration, are adversely affecting the wages of both groups. However, it is also possible, as we argue below, that globalization is better for the poor than for the middle class because the poor are more likely to be in service jobs that can't be outsourced and also benefit from the low prices for consumer goods that import competition has produced.

The remainder of this chapter elaborates on these observations. We begin by examining why the middle class may be feeling more anxious. We then explore one solution for eliminating any competition between the middle class and the poor: universal programs. We ultimately dismiss this solution as too expensive, though we support some easing of eligibility standards for today's means-tested programs. Finally, because it has received so much attention in political debates, we address the likely effects of globalization—

both more trade and more immigration—on the middle class and the poor. We conclude that there is more sound and fury than evidence that globalization had major effects on either group. Still, current trends in trade and immigration are disturbing and they may have bigger impacts in the future than they have had to date. We suggest that keeping U.S. borders open to trade may actually benefit those at the bottom and that trade is critically important to the much larger group of poor in the world at large.[4]

The Politics of Aid for the Poor

As noted in chapter 3, median family income in the United States has risen fairly steadily over the past thirty to forty years although not as rapidly as it did in the 1950s and 1960s. More specifically, it increased from about $52,135 in 1979 to a new peak of $61,355 in 2007, or by nearly 20 percent.[5] If our judgment about the well-being of the middle class were based only on longer-term income trends, this rise would allow some room for optimism.

But there are several more subtle issues beyond changes in income that bear on the well-being of the middle class. We refer to a constellation of issues that are often grouped under the term *economic insecurity*. Roughly, economic security means that individuals and families have a steady source of adequate income and protection against what President Franklin Roosevelt called the major vicissitudes of life. The vicissitudes that pose the greatest threats to financial security are job loss, death of a spouse, disability, serious illness, and old age. The Social Security Act, passed in 1935, provides insurance against the results of job loss, death of a spouse, and old age, thereby greatly increasing the economic security of Americans.[6] The federal government enacted legislation in 1956 to cover disability and in 1965 to provide health insurance to the elderly and to the poor and disabled.[7]

These programs have had two important effects. The first has been to dramatically expand the scope of government. Many conservatives were opposed to these social insurance programs when they were created and even today maintain that these programs reduce people's motivation to work and save. Conservatives also argue that such programs reduce people's capacity to take care of themselves and their families.[8] In addition, the cost of these programs is growing at an alarming rate as the result of the aging of the population and rising per capita health care costs. Nonetheless, the programs are immensely popular with the American public. One reason for their popularity is that they are based on insurance principles and are universal. All have dedicated trust funds to which virtually every working American (and every immigrant as well) contributes and to which they can turn in case of need.[9] As a result, these insurance programs should be sharply distinguished from welfare programs. Moreover, as we saw in chapter 3, they have dramatically reduced poverty among the elderly.

Given the broad guarantees against the ravages of unemployment, disability, and old age provided by the nation's popular social insurance system, what is left to trouble the middle class? Possible answers include slower income growth in recent decades, including stagnant earnings for younger men combined with increased pressures on families to have two earners; greater job dislocation and income volatility along with the decline in employer-sponsored health care and guaranteed pensions; rising expectations associated with a culture of affluence; and job security in a time of greater trade and immigration. All of these, along with the rising cost of college (addressed in chapter 8), have arguably fed into the pessimism the middle class expresses about the future and especially about prospects for their children.

Slower Income Growth and Stagnant Earnings for Younger Men

The main reason that family incomes have been growing, albeit slowly, is that more women have gone to work and have been receiving steadily rising wages. If we look at male earnings only, however, it becomes clearer why the middle class is feeling stressed.

Consider four generations of men born between 1925 and 1974, focusing on their individual incomes when they were in their thirties (figure 7-1). During most of our history, each generation of prime-age men has earned more than the previous generation. But for the most recent generation—those in their thirties in 2004—rising wages are no longer the rule. Their median earnings were $38,430 a year in 2004, while men in their father's generation earned $44,507 at the same age. This finding suggests that the up escalator that has historically ensured that each generation would do better than the last is not working very well. Indeed, there has been no progress at all for the youngest generation of males. As a group, men in their thirties are on average 12 percent worse off than their fathers' generation was at the same age.

Although family incomes have risen primarily because of women's work, two-earner families have paid a price. They have less time at home to care for children or attend to other family needs. It is not surprising that they feel stressed. When asked to weigh their priorities in life, middle-class respondents say that having free time is more important to them than having children, a successful career, being married, or being wealthy.[10] Finally, because nearly two-thirds of middle-class families already contain two earners, this source of additional income is slowly being exhausted.[11]

Figure 7-1. Median Earnings and Family Income for Men in Their Thirties, 1964–2004

Thousands of 2007 dollars

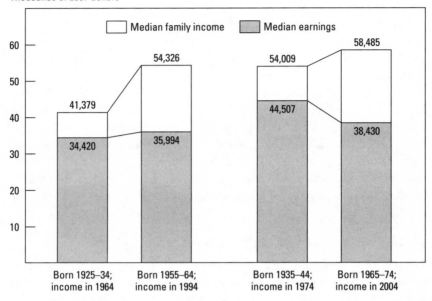

Source: Isabel Sawhill and John E. Morton, "Economic Mobility: Is the American Dream Alive and Well?" (Washington: Economic Mobility Project, an Initiative of the Pew Charitable Trusts, 2007), p. 5.

Economic Insecurity

A second potential cause of middle-class insecurity is what some analysts claim is increasing income volatility. Jacob Hacker is the best-known scholar making this claim. In his widely read 2006 book, *The Great Risk Shift*, Hacker argues that over the past four decades the chance of a family experiencing a sharp drop in income over a short period increased substantially.[12] Since his book first appeared, Hacker and numerous other scholars have completed additional research on this question. In his most recent work, Hacker finds that income volatility essentially doubled from 1969 to 2004.[13] Family income declines of 50 percent or more over a two-year period affected about one in ten nonelderly workers in the early 2000s.[14] Most other studies confirm that family incomes have become less stable over this period.[15] Some of this instability is the result of the business cycle, but there appears to be a long-term trend as well.

It is not yet clear exactly what is producing this instability. The volatility of men's earnings increased up until the 1980s but does not seem to have contributed much to the increasing volatility of family incomes since then. Family income can vary for a host of reasons in addition to earnings instability. Both voluntary and involuntary events—such as divorce, loss of a job, a medical crisis, retirement, or leaving the labor force to start a family or to continue one's education—can lead to income variability.

Peter Gosselin, in his book, *High Wire: The Precarious Financial Lives of American Families,* finds that the risk of divorce, separation, unemployment, disability, illness, or the death of a spouse actually fell slightly from the 1970s to 2005 but that the income drops associated with such events grew larger.[16] Somewhat surprisingly, these income shocks do not appear to be related to the movement of second earners into or out of the workforce. In the end, without knowing more about why this increase in income volatility has occurred, it's hard to know how to assess it. What goes up can also come down, and downward shocks may simply be more frequent and easily tolerated in an increasingly affluent society.

Hacker and like-minded scholars argue that increased income volatility is an integral part of a larger story about risk. This "risk shift," as Hacker terms it, is related not just to greater workplace insecurity or more family instability but also to the inadequacy or erosion of social benefits. These scholars argue, in short, that the safety net is shrinking. In particular, a robust system of guaranteed pensions and affordable health care is rapidly disappearing.[17] And the first line of defense against loss of a job—unemployment insurance—may no longer be as relevant for workers who are permanently dislocated from their jobs. How much truth is there to these assertions?

Unemployment Insurance. Average weekly earnings in the United States were just over $650 in 2007.[18] Unemployment insurance replaces well under half of earnings at that level (the average weekly benefit is about $290, and the typical spell lasts four months).[19] Although more than 90 percent of workers are covered, only about 40 percent of them actually receive payments when they become unemployed.[20] Those who don't receive benefits are primarily those who do not make themselves available for work while unemployed, those who leave their jobs voluntarily, or those involved in a labor dispute. The law disallows unemployment payments under all these circumstances. Less-experienced workers may also be disqualified.

Although some advocates want to liberalize unemployment compensation, our view is that a better solution would be to reform the program to better match the needs of today's workers to retrain for and accept new jobs. In the past, many laid-off workers could count on being reemployed in their old jobs once a downturn in the economy had ended. Today, though, manufacturing companies are being downsized and many white-collar jobs are being outsourced to other countries. These jobs are unlikely to come back. Worse, about a quarter of those who are displaced experience sharp earnings losses once reemployed.[21] For these reasons, proposals to provide wage insurance or retraining assistance are better suited to the times. The basic idea behind wage insurance is not only to encourage workers who have lost their jobs to take new ones but also to partially compensate them for the reduced earnings that many of them may have to accept.[22]

Health Insurance. Health care coverage is a growing concern for both the employed and the unemployed. Only three groups of Americans are guaranteed coverage: the elderly through Medicare, the disabled through either Medicaid or Medicare, and children in low-income families through Medicaid or SCHIP. Most of the people not covered by government programs have private health insurance, usually through their employer. But in 2007 about 46 million Americans had neither government coverage nor private coverage.[23] The uninsured may be treated in emergency rooms, but typically they fail to obtain the kind of routine care afforded those with insurance.[24]

For those who are covered, the value of insurance has risen. This benefit is not included in most measures of wages or family income, but many of today's insured workers are better off than earlier generations for this reason alone.[25] However, even those covered by private insurance face growing problems.

One problem is the threat of losing private insurance: the percentage of employers who offer coverage has been declining in recent years. Just in the seven years between 2000 and 2007 the percentage of companies offering their employees health insurance fell to 59 percent, from 64 percent.[26] A major reason for the decline is that employers are increasingly subject to international competition from companies that do not provide health insurance because their employees are covered by their governments. Another reason employers are trying to reduce their obligation to provide health insurance is that in the years 2001–07 insurance premiums increased by 78 percent; by comparison, wages increased just 19 percent and inflation just 17 percent.[27] A second problem facing those covered by private insurance is the increasing cost of out-of-pocket medical expenses, which grew by 6 percent annually between 1997 and 2002 for middle-class, nondisabled adults with private insurance.[28]

What all these figures add up to is an increasingly valuable benefit for many but both a declining likelihood of coverage and a rising level of personal spending on health care.[29]

Pensions. A few decades ago the typical employee was covered by a defined-benefit plan, that is, a pension that provided a guaranteed annual income during retirement. Of those with retirement benefits, the portion of private sector workers covered solely by defined-benefit plans fell sharply, from 62 percent in 1979 to about 10 percent in 2005.[30] As defined-benefit plans have declined, they have been largely replaced by defined-contribution plans, such as 401k and IRA plans, which permit workers to save for their retirement on a voluntary basis. While giving workers more choice, these plans also contribute to feelings of insecurity, especially during periods when the stock market—and thus the value of such accounts—is subject to wide swings. The sharp decline in the value of these accounts that had occurred at the time this book went to press is a reminder of how vulnerable middle-class workers are to the ups and downs of the market.[31]

Rising Expectations

Although we accept the reality of these new economic challenges, we are also convinced that middle-class expectations have grown with middle-class incomes; indeed, expectations have often exceeded income. Many families have become accustomed to well-furnished homes, fancy cars, designer clothing, high-definition televisions, and frequent trips to Starbucks. A new single-family home is about 50 percent larger now than in the 1980s.[32] Time was when people were overjoyed to have running water; now Americans drink bottled water at $3 a bottle. Savings rates that averaged more than 8 percent of income between 1980 and 1994 had plunged to near zero by 2005 and have continued to hover just above zero in recent years.[33] The subprime mortgage crisis that led to a financial meltdown in late 2008 was fueled not only by those trying to purchase a home but, far more important, by those trying to extract equity from an existing mortgage by refinancing on favorable terms. These home equity loans, in turn, were used to support levels of consumption that often exceeded people's current incomes.

At the same time, the baby boom generation, the wealthiest generation in history by a large margin, is not saving enough for its retirement. According to the McKinsey Global Institute, two-thirds of the early baby boomers (those born between 1945 and 1954) do not have enough assets to retire comfortably.[34] Even though they have earned far more than earlier generations, they have consumed a far higher share of their incomes than their predecessors. This is a serious problem, further exacerbated as this book went to press by a financial crisis that has shrunk everyone's nest egg. Social Security replaces only about 55 percent of the earnings of a low-wage worker, about 40 percent of the earnings of an average-wage worker, and about 35 percent of the earnings of a high-wage worker.[35] Clearly, people planning to retire and live exclusively or primarily on their income from Social Security face a rather bleak future and are likely to demand more help from the government.

Whether such demands are justified, they pose a real dilemma for those advocating on behalf of the poor. When the middle class turns to government for help with health insurance, job dislocation, and retirement, fewer resources will be available to help lower-income families. Above all, members of the middle class are not likely to be in the mood for cuts in either Social Security or Medicare. Yet, as we see in chapter 10, those programs are rapidly squeezing out spending on low-income families and their children, especially programs such as education and job training that are designed to move people up the economic ladder. Given the pending budget crisis, which we explore in greater detail in our final chapter, an already skittish middle class seems unlikely to risk seeing its own security threatened even further for the sake of expanded programs for the poor.

Targeting Assistance

One solution to the political difficulty of reallocating resources from the middle class to the poor is to provide universal, or at least much broader, assistance to the poor and middle class alike. Social Security is an example of such a universal program, and it has done more to reduce overall poverty than any means-tested program in the federal arsenal.[36] Not only do universal programs have broad political appeal, but they also create the right incentive structure, since people do not lose their benefits as they move up the income scale.

The problem, of course, is that universal programs are very expensive. Social Security cost $454.5 billion in 2006, while cash assistance or welfare for the poor (not including the poor disabled or the poor elderly) cost only $4.9 billion in federal spending.[37] In addition, universal programs require that large sums of money flow through the public sector, necessitating higher taxes and a larger government, which can create its own disincentives. Many European countries, for example, have far more generous social programs than the United States, but they also have higher taxes. Research on these countries' economies indicates that, even if their higher tax rates don't create major disincentives to work, save, or invest, their social insurance programs and labor market regulations do.[38]

For these reasons, we favor more targeting of assistance than now exists, even in the United States. But the way we suggest accomplishing this goal is by looser targeting of some traditional antipoverty programs (child care and health care for working-age families) and tighter targeting of some traditional social insurance programs (Social Security and Medicare for the elderly). As currently designed, these latter programs are not really insurance programs. Insurance programs are designed to provide resources to those who face catastrophic losses as the result of such infrequent and unpredictable events as a fire, an automobile accident, or a medical crisis or disability.

Instead these programs have become "entitlements" to coverage of a major portion of even the normal and predictable costs of retirement and health care in old age. These normal costs are almost entirely knowable in advance, and people with good jobs and incomes should be expected or required to save for their eventual costs. Those who work in low-wage jobs all their lives and cannot afford to save very much would continue to be subsidized by other taxpayers. This way of thinking about programs for the elderly suggests that greater income relating of retirement benefits is in order. And greater income relating of these programs would free up resources to put the federal budget on a more sustainable path and also to fund some new assistance for low-income working-age families.

For similar reasons, we also favor tighter targeting of tax expenditures or subsidies designed to support retirement saving, employer-sponsored health insurance, and home ownership among the middle class. Currently, these tax subsidies, such as the mortgage interest deduction, the exclusion of health benefits from income, and the preferential treatment of retirement savings are extremely expensive, and they disproportionately benefit high-income families.[39] As such, they do little to encourage people to save more or acquire more health insurance; instead they function more like welfare for the affluent.

In later chapters we provide more details on how we would use freed-up resources to reward and encourage education and work among low-income families. In the meantime we recognize that there will be strong resistance to reforming tax subsidies for the middle class or cutting Medicare or Social Security benefits for the more affluent elderly. In the former case, what is required is a wholesale reform of the tax system that makes it simpler as well as fairer and more efficient. In the latter case, what is required is not an actual cut in benefits but simply a slower rate of growth. If action is taken now to phase in new rules gradually so that no current or soon-to-retire beneficiary is affected, the politics is less daunting.

Once resources target those who face the greatest need, whether young or old, there is a further question of whether resources should target those most likely to benefit from a program. Peter Schuck and Richard Zeckhauser distinguish, for example, between what they call "bad versus good bets"—that is, between those who are likely to be helped by a program and those who are not. They cite the example of a chronically ill ninety-year-old who receives costly medical care at the end of life with very little benefit to herself or society. They also distinguish between "bad versus good apples." A bad apple is someone who by committing illegal acts or engaging in disruptive behavior makes life difficult for others. An unruly student in a classroom or a person who sells drugs in a public housing project are examples.[40] Public policy should, in our view, target not just those with low incomes but also the "good apples"—those who are motivated to learn, to work, and to support their families and for whom, often as a result, the benefits of government assistance are clear.

In sum, we believe programs should target less tightly those at the bottom of the income scale and more tightly those at the top, regardless of age (a theme we return to in chapter 11, where we argue for a revision of the social contract between less-advantaged working-age families and relatively affluent older Americans). But we also argue for programs that target primarily those who play by the rules and exercise personal responsibility by obtaining an education, working, and supporting their families (themes we return to in chapter 8, on education; chapter 9, on work; and chapter 10, on the family).

Globalization

In chapter 3 we note some of the reasons behind growing wage and income inequality and emphasize the widening gap between the incomes of the rich and the incomes of the middle class. Why has the middle class not done better? Many Americans attribute the problem to both a rising tide of immigrants from low-wage countries and a flood of imports from some of those same countries. Polls show that more than half of Americans want to protect U.S. companies from foreign competition even if that slows growth.[41] According to this view, trade has created, in Ross Perot's famous phrase, "a giant sucking sound," as many high-wage jobs have disappeared and wages for many workers have stagnated or fallen.[42] Most Americans are in no mood to accept these perceived dislocations, and their elected representatives are under severe pressure to adopt protectionist trade policies and tough measures to stem the flow of illegal immigrants into the country. Should advocates for the poor join this chorus? We think not, for the reasons advanced below.

First, most experts on these matters have a somewhat different view from that of the public. The experts argue that increased trade and immigration are beneficial for the economy overall although not necessarily for all groups of workers and areas of the country.[43] They admit that the short-term effects on the availability of jobs and the growth of wages for these groups and geographical regions may be adverse even though the benefits to the entire nation are positive.

Second, attempts to reduce these flows of goods and people across national borders are not only likely to damage the economy but are also likely doomed to failure. The ongoing integration of the world economy made possible by revolutionary advances in communications, information technology, and transportation makes any attempt to stop the process at best futile and at worst counterproductive. A better approach is to recognize that the globalization of the U.S. economy is inevitable and to fashion policies that facilitate or cushion the adjustment process for affected individuals.

Third, protectionist policies or efforts to stop immigration from low-wage countries have adverse effects on global poverty. It would be ironical if advocates for the poor in the United States were to succeed in reducing opportunities for the 2.5 billion people in the world who live on less than $2 a day.[44]

Even though we believe protectionist policies are a mistake, the effects of both trade and immigration on the domestic economy have been hotly debated, so we briefly review some key facts about each.

Effects of Trade

One possible explanation for rising wage and income inequality in the United States is the effects of increased trade on wages. Between 1979 and 2007 the volume of trade (as measured by the share of imports plus exports in the GDP) rose from roughly 20 percent to 29 percent (a 45 percent increase), and the share of imports coming from less-developed, low-wage countries also rose (figure 7-2). Thus U.S. workers, especially those with little education or few skills, are increasingly competing with workers in countries with low standards of living. On average, Chinese workers are paid just 3 percent and Mexican workers 11 percent of what their American counterparts earn.[45] Nonetheless, most experts do not believe these discrepancies in wages have contributed much to rising inequality in the United States.[46]

Whether this conclusion will hold true in the coming decades is less certain. Not only trade in goods (French wine for American movies) but also the outsourcing of production and service jobs have raised alarm. Although Barbie dolls are designed and marketed in the United States, their hair is manufactured in Japan, their dress fabric is manufactured in China, and they are assembled in Indonesia and Malaysia.[47] As far as service jobs are concerned, anyone who has made an airline reservation or who has needed technical support for a personal computer has probably had the experience of talking to a customer representative in India. High-skill services—such as accounting, reading x-rays, and developing software—are also being performed by workers in foreign countries, who receive far lower wages than similar workers in the United States.

It is hard to see an end to this process. Indeed, economic theory and common sense both suggest that in the long run there will be a convergence of wages globally, as cross-border transaction costs decline and businesses seek

Figure 7-2. Exports, Imports, and Balance of Trade as Share of GDP, 1979–2007

Percent

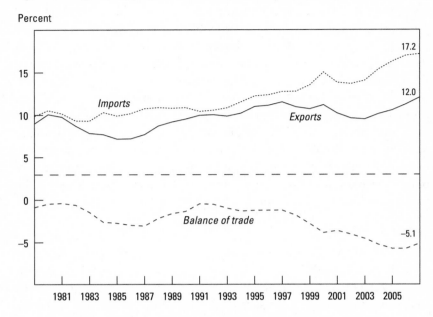

Source: U.S. Bureau of Economic Analysis, *National Income and Product Accounts,* table 1.1.5.

the lowest-cost alternative for producing a particular good or delivering a particular service. We may be going through what the economist Alan Blinder calls the "third industrial revolution," the first having been the movement from an economy based on agriculture to an economy based on manufacturing and the second being the rise of the service sector, which now employs eight in ten American workers.[48]

This third revolution would involve a much greater outsourcing of jobs than we have seen to date. As Blinder and others note, the only tasks that cannot be moved offshore are those that involve face-to-face personal services and nonroutine tasks that require on-site ingenuity and management. In the economy of the future, we may all be cutting hair, delivering pizza, installing carpet, teaching children, taking care of the elderly, or providing management consulting services, psychotherapy, and boring academic papers for other adults. Depending on the ability of the United States to train scientists, engineers, doctors, and other highly skilled professionals, we may retain some comparative advantage in these high-paid jobs. However, technical skill per se may matter less than interpersonal and problem-solving skills, since these will continue to be required of the domestic labor force engaged in personal services, management, and similar tasks that cannot be outsourced.

As noted above, empirical evidence for the proposition that trade has substantially reduced U.S. wages is lacking. However, studies of the effects of trade on wages may not be a reliable guide to the future, for three reasons. First, these studies are based on data that are increasingly out of date. Second, the "Barbie doll effect" makes it difficult to study just exactly how the outsourcing of specific tasks is affecting American workers.[49] Third, although offshoring has so far affected a relatively small number of jobs, some believe it will have much larger effects over the next few decades.[50] If so, protectionist pressures will become even stronger than they are today.

Because protectionist policies, such as trade barriers, would adversely affect standards of living both in the United States and in other countries over the longer run, we believe that giving in to these pressures would be a mistake. However, any new social compact with American workers needs to take into account their growing vulnerability to competition from other countries, especially those, like India and China, with relatively well-educated populations but low wages. Moreover, it is not just trade but technology and many other developments that lead to worker dislocation in a dynamic economy. These economic developments will affect not only the disadvantaged but also the middle class. Indeed, as suggested by the evidence on wage polarization in chapter 3, they appear to be affecting middle-wage workers far more than low-wage workers.

Effects of Immigration

If members of the broad middle class are disturbed about trade, they are even more disturbed—at least of late—about immigration. Their concern may reflect not just economic anxieties but also worries about cultural differences and the impact of immigrants, especially those who are here illegally, on local public services such as schools and hospitals. For these reasons, even though the country is a nation of immigrants, many Americans, including policymakers in Washington and in state capitals, are concerned about the increasing and historically high levels of legal and illegal immigration and the low levels of education of many immigrants now entering the United States.

The number of legal immigrants has risen to almost a million each year since the 1990s (figure 7-3). In addition to these, an estimated 500,000 illegal immigrants come to the United States each year, bringing total annual immigration to around 1.5 million.[51] As a result of this influx, the percentage of U.S. residents who are foreign born increased from a low of 4.7 percent in

Figure 7-3. Annual Number of Legal U.S. Immigrants, by Decade and Region of Origin, 1960–2007

Thousands of immigrants

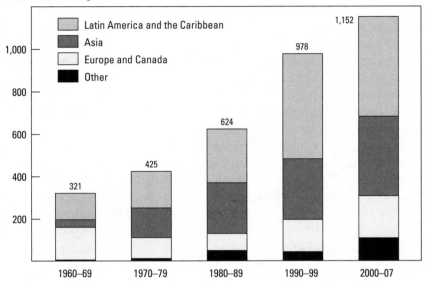

Source: Philip Martin and Elizabeth Midgley, "Immigration: Shaping and Reshaping America," Population Bulletin 61, no. 4 (2006). Updated through 2007 using data from the Department of Homeland Security, *Yearbook of Immigration Statistics: 2007*, table 2.

1970 to 12.5 percent in 2007.[52] Because immigrants tend to be in their child-bearing years, the percentage of U.S. children who are immigrants or who are the children of at least one foreign-born parent is even higher (about 21 percent) according to a 2005 estimate.[53]

More important for our purposes, the characteristics of immigrants have been changing dramatically. Compared with the 1960s, the fraction of immigrants who are from European nations or Canada has declined from about half to under 20 percent, while the fraction from Asia, Latin America, and the Caribbean has increased from about half to nearly three-quarters (figure 7-3). Relative to the average American worker, immigrants are poorly educated, unskilled, and earn low wages when they enter the United States.[54] For example, 32 percent of foreign-born adults, compared with only 11 percent of the U.S. born, lacked a high school degree in 2007.[55]

The inevitable result of admitting immigrants with less education than typical American workers is falling relative wages for immigrants. Work by George Borjas of Harvard shows that the average wage of immigrants, com-

Figure 7-4. Age-Adjusted Wages for First- and Second-Generation Immigrants Relative to Wages for Nonimmigrants, 1940–2000

Percent

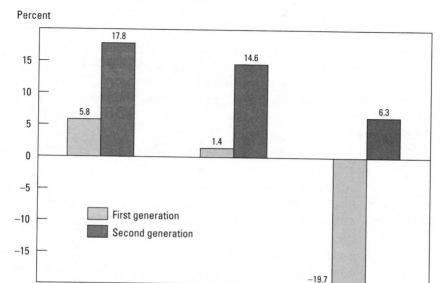

Source: George Borjas, "Making it in America: Social Mobility in the Immigrant Population," *Future of Children* 16 (Fall 2006).

pared with the average wage of the native born, has been falling for several decades and is now about 20 percent below that of nonimmigrant workers (figure 7-4). Despite this fall in relative wages for first-generation immigrants, their children tend to assimilate and climb the economic ladder so rapidly that their wages actually exceed the wages of other workers by the second generation. However, the decline in relative education and skills of first-generation immigrants has been associated with a continuous decline in the average wages of second-generation immigrants as well. Thus in the future, if present trends continue, the wages of immigrant children are likely to fall below the wages of native workers—as the wages of their parents have already done.[56]

It comes as no surprise, given these trends in education and wages, that immigrants also have relatively high poverty rates. In 2007 the immigrant poverty rate was 16.5 percent, compared to a native poverty rate of 11.9 percent.[57] However, because immigrants still make up only about 12.5 percent of the population, their excess poverty rate contributes only modestly to poverty trends and to the overall U.S. poverty rate in any given year.[58] But if immigrants continue to increase as a share of the U.S. population, as they are predicted to do, and if the downward trend in relative wages of both the first and second generations continues in the direction documented above, immigration may come to exert greater upward pressure on the U.S. poverty rate.[59]

What about the effects of immigration on employment opportunities and wages for native-born workers? Foreign-born workers represented 15.7 percent of all employed workers in 2007.[60] If immigrants did nothing but increase the size of the labor force, their effects on the economy would not be much of an issue. Historically, the U.S. economy has proved that it is capable of absorbing new workers, whether the new workers have been GIs returning from war, women entering the labor force, or baby boomers joining the workforce. Indeed, a larger supply of labor, especially if it is complemented by the skills and capital of the native-born population, should actually benefit native-born workers. For example, less-skilled laborers can enhance the productivity of skilled craftsmen. But many analysts fear that the large number of immigrants at the bottom of the skill distribution is putting downward pressure on wages in low-paid jobs.[61]

The evidence on this question is mixed. Some economists, such as George Borjas, believe that immigrants are having an adverse effect on the wages of poor, nonimmigrant workers, especially blacks. Others, such as David Card and Ethan Lewis, believe these estimates exaggerate the impact of immigrants on wages and argue that there has been virtually no impact on native workers' wages or employment. The latter base their research on the fact that even a large influx of immigrants into a local labor market seems to have had no effect on wages relative to wages in other labor markets.[62]

These findings are surprising. How can they be explained? One possibility is that native-born workers simply don't want to do the jobs that immigrants have filled as construction laborers, gardeners, maids, and agricultural workers. Thus the two groups are rarely in direct competition with one another. And the availability of immigrants may have actually increased opportunities for at least some less-skilled Americans to work at jobs a little higher up the skill ladder. Indeed, it is this possibility, among others, that leads us to suggest that the poor may actually gain from globalization.

Why the Poor Might Gain from Globalization

The discussion suggests that trade and immigration have so far had small effects on domestic wages and employment. However, as we also emphasize, the research on these effects is somewhat mixed and far from definitive with respect to what the future holds. In particular, research doesn't speak directly to the likely effects on the American worker if future immigration swells the ranks of the less educated and an increasing number of tasks are outsourced to other countries.

We also emphasize that these effects may vary depending on where in the income distribution a family falls. The outsourcing of jobs, for example, may have affected the middle class more than the poor because low-wage workers tend to be concentrated in service jobs that can only be done here. Janitors and home health aides need not fear for their jobs, but radiologists and airline clerks have already felt the effects of the outsourcing revolution. Further enhancing this differential effect is the fact that the lowest-income families are the most likely to benefit from the lower prices that international competition has made possible. Trade has had its biggest effects on precisely the goods that loom largest in a low-income consumer's budget: food, clothing, and other nondurable goods. Janitors and home health aides may have abysmally low wages, but they pay far lower prices for most of what they buy than they would in the absence of global competition.[63] Much ado has been made about the low wages paid by Wal-Mart, but we should not forget about Wal-Mart's ability to use its purchasing power to pay very low prices for its goods, many of them produced in low-wage countries. The winners in this process, Wal-Mart's consumers, vastly outnumber the alleged losers, their employees.

In sum, middle-class demands for trade barriers could work to the detriment of the poor by raising the prices of what they buy. Immigration, to be sure, could work in just the opposite fashion: producing more competition for jobs at the bottom of the distribution, which reduces the wages of the least skilled. Although we remain skeptical that immigration has significantly depressed wages for the less skilled, we admit that the evidence on this point is equivocal.

Conclusion

The middle class is feeling economically insecure, particularly during the period of serious economic decline facing the country as this book went to press. This fact limits the ability of the political system to respond to the needs of the poor. One way out of this dilemma would be to provide assistance to both groups, to eschew targeted programs in favor of those whose benefits are universal. But this strategy runs into another problem: very large costs and much higher levels of taxation. A compromise could entail providing benefits further up the income scale than in the past but without making them universal.

Much of the anxiety faced by working families is related to their perception that trade and immigration are reducing their economic prospects. We find little evidence that this is the case, although we also emphasize that ongoing trends in both areas may eventually produce more serious consequences. We also remind readers that, whatever the effects of trade on wages, it affects prices as well, with net effects that may help low-income families. Our reading of the evidence is that the nation as a whole is better off because of trade and technological innovation, although some groups and individuals are worse off, at least temporarily. The goal of policy should be to help those negatively effected by these economic forces over which they have no control.

eight
Expanding Educational Opportunity

Once we considered education a public expense; we know now that it is a public investment.

LYNDON B. JOHNSON

Underlying the nation's problem with economic opportunity is the nation's problem with educational opportunity. We believe that the impressive array of programs and research now under way will boost education among the disadvantaged and that more can be done to increase educational opportunity and achievement in America. After providing a brief history of educational attainment and reviewing evidence that establishes the importance of education in promoting opportunity, we develop a set of policy proposals directed at, respectively, preschool, K–12, and postsecondary education. We also hold the view that, despite the reforms we recommend, millions of adolescents will not go to college and additional millions of adults at any given moment will not even have a high school degree. These groups will be joined from time to time by young and middle-aged workers who have lost their jobs, often in declining industries, and who need new skills. Promoting training and employment (or reemployment) for these groups is addressed separately in our chapter on work (chapter 9).

America has long been viewed as the land of opportunity, a country in which everyone has the chance to work hard and get ahead. Hard work may have been enough in the past, but several developments—especially the impact of technology and trade on the economy—have added a new subtext to the story of opportunity in America. Good jobs are now usually based on knowledge and skills. This development, in turn, has made education and training the motor of both economic mobility and the American economy. For most Americans the path to economic success lies through the schoolhouse door.[1]

Despite an economy and a legal system that offer opportunity on a nearly equal basis to all educated people, including immigrants and minorities, and despite the nearly universal understanding that education leads to good jobs and the opportunity for advancement, many young Americans get much less education than they could or should.[2] Nor is the lack of adequate education equally distributed among young people from all ethnic groups or economic backgrounds. Young people from minority and poor families get significantly less education than their more fortunate peers. Below we make several recommendations about public policies that could help disadvantaged youngsters get more education, but once again, as in so many of the policies we recommend, successful interventions depend on changes in the behavior of individuals no less than on good policy.

The issue of individual and group differences in educational attainment begins with the family (chapter 5). There is general agreement among developmental behavioral geneticists that genes exert considerable influence on children's development and their abilities.[3] Even so, all respected theories of genetic influence on behavior leave considerable room for environmental influence. Thus the environment provided by parents is an important factor in accounting for children's development and preparation for schooling. Parents in more advantaged families usually provide a more stimulating environment for their children, especially in the frequency and sophistication of their use of language and in their use of discipline that emphasizes consequences and eschews harshness.[4] By age three, children from poor and minority families are already well behind their more advantaged peers in intellectual development.[5] Without high-quality preschool, by the time poor children reach the public schools they are far behind children from middle-class families.[6]

Nor do the public schools do enough to overcome the substantial impacts of family background that children bring with them to the first day of kindergarten.[7] One of the most famous and widely examined studies in the history of educational research, the Coleman Report of 1966, concludes that family background is a more potent influence on school achievement than any measure of the school environment itself, including per pupil expenditures.[8] That conclusion was mightily resisted by the educational establishment, but the basic finding has been replicated so many times that the immense influence of the family on child development and school achievement is now a settled issue, although more recent studies find factors within the school that have impacts on student achievement.[9] In fact, to a considerable degree our mission in this book is to discover ways to overcome the limitations imposed on disadvantaged children by their family background. Anyone aiming to promote

Figure 8-1. Median Family Income, Ages Thirty through Thirty-Nine, by Education, 1964–2006[a]

2006 dollars

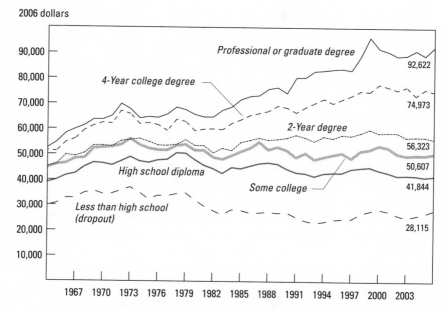

Source: Ron Haskins, Harry Holzer, and Robert Lerman, "Promoting Economic Mobility by Increasing Post-secondary Education" (Washington: Economic Mobility Project, an Initiative of the Pew Charitable Trusts, 2009), figure 1.

a. All men and women ages thirty through thirty-nine, including those with no personal income, are included in these estimates.

educational opportunity and economic mobility must face the fact that success means helping many children overcome the below-average developmental pathway to which their genes and family background contribute so heavily.

The stakes in this enterprise could hardly be higher. In recent decades the returns to educational attainment have been remarkable (figure 8-1). Each higher level of attainment is associated with higher family income. In addition, the pattern of economic progress is different across the various levels of educational attainment. Not only do high school dropouts and students who achieve no more than a high school degree earn less money than those with college degrees and advanced degrees, but also the wages of the former groups have been more or less stagnant or even in decline for three or four decades. Meanwhile, the family income of the two highest-achieving groups has grown, making the gap between those with high educational attainment and those with low attainment even wider. The strong suggestion is that unless something is done to boost the number of young people earning postsecondary credentials, opportunity for millions of Americans will continue to be limited.

Nevertheless, the returns to education shown in figure 8-1 could be misleading. It is well known that people who achieve more education differ in many ways from those with less education. People with more education, on average, have higher IQs, have parents who have more education and more income, have lived in better neighborhoods and attended better schools as children, and so forth.[10] Ignoring all these differences and attributing the entire income effect to education would be a mistake. Orley Ashenfelter and his colleagues, based on twenty-seven empirical studies conducted in the United States and abroad, exhaustively examine these sources of bias and their impact on estimates of returns to schooling.[11] They find that controlling for various sources of bias does reduce the rate of return to education, but their best estimate is that the rate of return after controlling for bias is on the order of 6–9 percent.[12] This is a good rate of return compared to other standard investments such as U.S. Treasury bonds and suggests that in modern economies education produces sizable financial advantages even when other differences between those with more and those with less education are controlled.

Barbara Wolfe and Robert Haveman push the analysis of returns to education far beyond the mere economic returns measured in most studies. Besides economic returns, they identify fifteen nonmarket outcomes that are important to individuals or society for which there is evidence of an educational impact.[13] These outcomes include associations between more education and more productive children, healthier children, healthier adults, less divorce, more charitable giving, more savings, and lower rates of crime. After surveying the studies of all fifteen noneconomic outcomes, Wolfe and Haveman estimate that the total rate of return to schooling is perhaps twice the rate estimated by Ashenfelter and his colleagues based only on economic returns. If true, this rate of around 15 percent makes education one of the best investments individuals can make for themselves and for society.[14] Indeed, this rate of return is so high, and so many of the benefits are social, that government has a direct interest in helping individuals achieve high levels of education. The role of government is especially justified because not even the Wolfe and Haveman analysis includes the importance of an educated populace to the nation's economic future in a globalized economy. The future of the American economy depends in large part on high educational achievement by today's and tomorrow's children.

Given these remarkable financial and nonfinancial payoffs to educational attainment, it might reasonably be predicted that American youth would pursue ever higher levels of education and that parents, the private sector,

Figure 8-2. High School Graduation Rates, by Ethnic Group, 1900–1990[a]

Percent

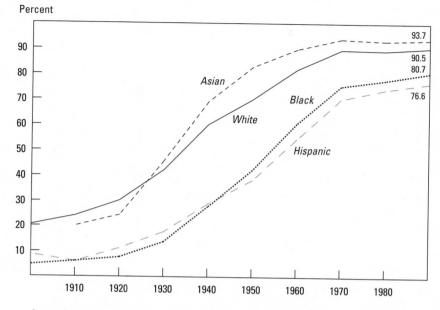

Source: Claude S. Fischer and Michael Hout, figure 2.2 ("High School Graduation Rates for All by Gender, Region, and Racial Ancestry, by Year Person Turned Twenty-One"), in *Century of Difference: How America Changed in the Last One Hundred Years.* © 2006 Russell Sage Foundation. Reprinted with permission.

a. Data are for high school diploma or equivalent (including GED certificate). See note 15 for details on methodology.

and governments at all levels would take strong actions to help them. But this prediction is only partially correct. The twentieth century saw huge increases in the rates of high school completion by all groups (figure 8-2).[15] Although every group advanced rapidly, large gaps in high school completion persisted between whites and Asians on the one hand and blacks and Hispanics on the other.[16] In addition, the trends, especially for blacks and Hispanics, flattened out toward the end of the century and into the first decade of the twenty-first century. Even worse, recent evidence suggests that high schools exaggerate their graduation rates and that the rates have actually been falling in recent years, especially for minorities.[17]

All the ethnic groups and both genders also made great progress in improving their college graduation rates (figure 8-3). Unfortunately, the rate of improvement for blacks and Hispanics in recent decades has been much lower than the rate for whites and Asians, resulting in an enormous gap between the groups, with blacks and Hispanics left far behind. Whites are

Figure 8-3. College Graduation Rates, by Ethnic Group, 1900–1990[a]

Percent

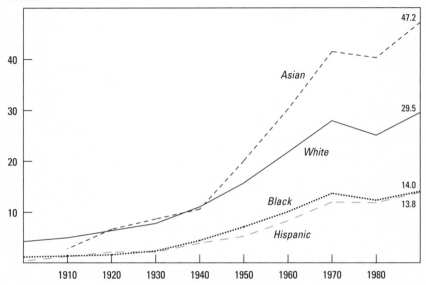

Source: Claude S. Fischer and Michael Hout, figure 2.3 ("College Graduation Rates for All by Gender, Region, and Racial Ancestry, by Year of Twenty-First Birthday"), in *Century of Difference: How America Changed in the Last One Hundred Years*. © 2006 Russell Sage Foundation. Reprinted with permission.

a. Data are for B.A. degree. See note 15 for details on methodology.

now twice as likely to earn a B.A. degree as blacks and Hispanics, while Asians are more than three times as likely.

Changes in the American economy in recent decades have created an economic world in which given demographic groups will not make economic advances unless more of their members complete postsecondary training and education. As long as dropout rates and the gaps in college completion remain as high as they are now—never mind the possibility that they could grow even larger—it will be difficult for blacks, Hispanics, and students from poor and low-income families to achieve greater upward economic mobility. It follows that the task for those who study, enact, and implement policy is to figure out ways to help youngsters from disadvantaged backgrounds increase their rates of achieving postsecondary certificates or degrees.

Our recommendations for achieving this goal are based on three premises. The first is that the promising results produced by high quality preschool programs, combined with improvements in the public schools attended by the graduates of quality preschools, have the potential to produce lasting impacts on student achievement and college readiness.[18] These improvements in preschool and K–12 education should then be exploited by reforms designed to increase the number of poor and minority students enrolling in and graduating from postsecondary institutions. Simultaneous and coordinated reforms at all three levels of education hold greater promise than reforms aimed at a single level.

The second premise is that individual reforms should be supported by good evidence that they affect student outcomes. It would be ideal if we could recommend policies supported by evidence from large-scale, random-assignment evaluations implemented under field conditions that produced benefits exceeding costs, but relatively few policies have superior evidence of this type. When the best evidence does not exist, evidence can nonetheless play a role in policy choice if there have been studies with less than optimum designs that support the policy. In addition, it is reasonable to exploit evidence from small-scale research to gradually expand a program while studying its impacts and gradually improving the program. Most of our recommendations at least meet the test of being supported by evidence, albeit not always ideal evidence.

The third premise is that if we insist that education reforms be based on existing evidence and designed in such a way as to produce new evidence, educational achievement of all groups including the disadvantaged will gradually improve. Accountability in education means that the people crafting and implementing the policy for educating the nation's youngsters acknowledge their responsibility for producing world-class outcomes. In working to fulfill this responsibility, they must ensure that evidence to judge their performance is widely available. High-quality evidence showing the effects of educational programs on student outcomes is the heart of accountability and leads to a system in which the public has information about school success and educators can continuously improve their performance. Thus our recommendations typically include specific proposals for producing additional evidence by which their success or failure can be judged. Given the reality, based on many years of experience, that most new educational interventions fail, best bets supported by reason and evidence must be implemented and subjected to continuous evaluation and improvement.[19]

Our recommendations for new, expanded, or reformed policies for preschool, K–12 education, and postsecondary education are summarized in table 8-1.

Preschool Education

No strategy for reducing poverty and increasing economic mobility in the long run has more support among researchers, advocates, and politicians

Table 8-1. Recommendations and Goals, Preschool, K–12 Education, and Postsecondary Education

Recommendation	Goal
Preschool	
Create competitive grant program for states to expand nurse visitation and preschool programs for children below 150 percent of poverty	To increase the school readiness and long-term success of children from low-income families
K–12 education	
Establish national standards for student achievement	To set one standard nationally and to preempt states from setting low standards
Establish competitive grants for school districts for teacher improvement, to include additional pay for teaching in low-achieving schools	To enhance teacher quality and to provide financial incentives for teachers in schools with predominantly disadvantaged students
Establish and fund more paternalistic schools, on the KIPP model, increasing instructional time, the monitoring of student learning, and hours of instruction	To possibly increase student performance on standardized tests and to increase the number of paternalistic schools for evaluation
Establish and fund a rigorous evaluation of paternalistic schools (by the National Institute of Education Sciences)	To determine whether the effects on student achievement attained by paternalistic schools can be widely replicated and to identify the characteristics of these schools that produce these results
Continue funding research and the What Works Clearinghouse	To ensure that education research uses rigorous methods and that proven programs are widely known and available
Postsecondary education	
Streamline federal support for college preparation programs and convert to competitive grant program based on outcomes after five years	To increase the college preparation of students from low-income and minority families by increasing their academic knowledge and learning skills
Create longitudinal data systems	To help school systems determine whether their programs to increase college enrollment and success are effective

(continued)

than preschool education.[20] This support is based in part on remarkable findings from three well-known studies of model preschool programs, which we refer to as the big three. The big three yield strong evidence that high-quality preschool programs can produce a wide range of long-term impacts on the development of poor children.

Evidence That Preschool Works

Two of these remarkable studies are the Abecedarian preschool program conducted at the University of North Carolina and the Perry Preschool Program

Table 8-1. Recommendations and Goals, Preschool, K–12 Education, and Postsecondary Education (continued)

Recommendation	Goal
Improve counseling for college applications and student aid	To help students select colleges that are matched with their abilities and to help them finance their college careers
Simplify the student aid application process by terminating the Free Application for Federal Student Aid and basing awards on family income and size	To make it easier for students and families to apply for aid and to provide them with early information (at least by ninth grade) about the size of the aid package the student can expect
Simplify federal student aid grant programs by eliminating three grant programs	To make federal grant programs easier to understand and easier to administer at both the federal and university levels
Increase the maximum Pell grant	To provide low-income students with bigger grant awards to increase the probability that they will enroll in and graduate from college
Expand income-based repayment program for student loans by capping maximum repayment at 150 percent of original loan and by cutting maximum repayment period from twenty-five to twenty years	To make it easier for students to repay their loans, thereby making it more likely that they will be willing to incur debt to attend college
Reform state funding of colleges so that part of funding is based on enrollment and graduation of low-income and minority students	To increase the financial incentives for state colleges to recruit and graduate more students from low-income and minority families
Create state programs for helping students from poor and minority families stay in college until they receive a terminal degree	To ensure that students from low-income and minority families get extra help with their studies if they are having academic problems

conducted in Ypsilanti, Michigan.[21] Both studies randomly assigned children to experimental and control groups, collected extensive data on the children and their families, and followed the children until they reached at least their mid-twenties. Both involved a preschool program featuring a carefully designed and administered curriculum implemented by experienced teachers. Both involved parents, but the Abecedarian program did not begin systematic parent involvement until children reached school age; parents were an integral part of Perry from the time children started the program. Abecedarian children began the program by roughly three months of age and attended the program full time, five days per week, for forty-nine weeks a year, until they entered the public schools at age five. By contrast, the Perry program started when children were either three or four years of age (some children attended the preschool for two years).

A major limitation of these studies is that they were both small scale, involving fewer than 125 children, raising the issue of whether a national program for millions of children could produce the same results. Another limitation is that the programs were both of very high quality, raising the question of whether a large-scale program could achieve and then maintain such a high level of quality. Finally, both programs were conducted at only one site, again raising the question of how difficult the programs would be to replicate at many sites.[22]

A third exemplary program, the Chicago Child-Parent Centers, involved more than 1,500 children and operated in twenty schools (with five control schools) in Chicago, thereby reducing concerns inevitably associated with small-scale programs operated at a single site under ideal circumstances (like Abecedarian and Perry).[23] The Chicago program consisted of half-day classes for children ages three and four during the school year, used a formal curriculum that emphasized speaking and listening skills, required parental involvement on a weekly basis, included small classes and individualized assessment as children transitioned to the early elementary grades, and provided comprehensive health and social services. The program affected math and reading as measured by standardized tests, reduced grade retention, reduced placement in special education, improved rates of high school graduation, and reduced arrests. The design was not based on random assignment, causing some critics to argue that the results are subject to doubt.[24]

All three of these model programs produced a range of effects on tests of school achievement in math and reading, grade retention, placement in special education, high school graduation, or college attendance. Although some of the effects on cognitive abilities fade over time, the three programs reduced the likelihood of school dropout by between 24 and 32 percent, and Abecedarian greatly increased the enrollment in four-year colleges.[25] In addition, at least one of the programs, and often more, reduced teen parenting, delinquency or crime, abuse or neglect, abortion, or drug addiction, and all three increased lifetime earnings (table 8-2). These results are exactly what is needed from a national preschool program for children from low-income and minority families, and virtually all the children in these three studies were low-income and black or Hispanic. If results like these could be achieved on a broad scale, a huge investment of tens of billions of dollars, or more, would be justified, as shown by an impressive number of benefit-cost studies of preschool programs.[26]

But there's a problem. Although the Chicago results are notable for being implemented on a fairly large scale, the scale is still modest compared with a national program. The only national preschool program is Head Start. There

Table 8-2. Early Childhood Programs, Later Outcomes

Percent except as indicated

Outcome and program	Control or comparison group	Group in program
Teen parenthood		
Abecedarian	45	26
Perry Preschool	37	26
Chicago Child-Parent Centers	27	20
Well-being		
Health problem (Perry Preschool)	29	20
Drug use (Abecedarian)	39	18
Addiction treatment (Perry Preschool)	34	22
Abortion (Perry Preschool)	38	16
Abuse or neglect by age 17 (Chicago Child-Parent Centers)	9	6
Criminal activity		
Violent assaults per person (Perry Preschool)	0.37	0.17
Juvenile court petitions (Chicago Child-Parent Centers)	25	16
Booked or charged with crime (Head Start)		
Addendum[a]		
Abecedarian	35,531	
Perry Preschool	38,892	
Chicago Child-Parent Centers	30,638	
Head Start	No effect	

Source: W. Steven Barnett and Clive Belfield, "Early Childhood Development and Social Mobility," *Future of Children* 16, no. 2 (2006), table 2.

a. Net earnings gain from participation, in dollars.

are disputes about the strength of evidence from Head Start, but there is some evidence from long-term follow-ups based on national data that Head Start produces lasting influences on children's development.[27] None of the studies of long-term Head Start results, however, are from random-assignment experiments. Further, the results of the first random-assignment national evaluation of Head Start found smaller effects than those produced by the Abecedarian and Perry programs at the end of preschool.[28] The Head Start evaluation will eventually produce information from longer-term follow-up, but it is difficult to expect long-term impacts when those measured at the end of the program are small relative to the big three.[29]

Even so, the Head Start program, which has now been in operation for more than four decades, is popular among policymakers in Washington and most state capitols. Despite the somewhat disappointing findings of the national evaluation, Head Start continues to enjoy a solid reputation among most researchers and immense support from advocates.[30] Based in large part on the mixed success of Head Start and the strong outcomes from the big three, in recent years up to forty states have established their own pre-K programs, and many states are expanding their spending on these programs.[31] Evaluations of several state pre-K programs seem to show that their effects on school readiness are even greater than the effects of Head Start.[32]

The broad effects of the big three, the mixed success of Head Start, and the success of state pre-K programs cause us to be optimistic that preschool can play an important long-term role in boosting school readiness and social development. There is correlational evidence that, if school readiness in math and reading can be boosted, students would also achieve more throughout their school careers.[33] To the extent that preschool can achieve these long-term effects on children's school achievement, quality programs could also contribute to economic mobility.[34]

Expanding Preschool

Preschool programs should be expanded. Our objective is to build on the child care market we now have, which is composed of a range of programs from inexpensive but low quality to high quality but expensive (table 8-3).[35] Further, we would increase the funds available for day care for low-income working parents (see chapter 9) and expand and improve the high-quality sector of the market. The goal is to ensure that every child from a family below some income cutoff, say 150 percent of poverty, receives the kind of care provided by the big three model programs. If we can achieve this goal, poverty would decline and economic mobility would increase. There also could be some decline in poverty contemporaneous with the preschool program, because with full-time, high-quality, inexpensive or free child care, low-income parents might be even more likely to work than they are now—and to work longer hours.

Our proposal, modeled on an earlier proposal by Isabel Sawhill and Jens Ludwig of the University of Chicago, is to spend up to $6 billion a year expanding high-quality programs and carefully evaluating the results.[36] We propose to provide funds on a competitive basis to local consortiums. These consortiums would be composed of Head Start officials, officials from the state pre-K program, representatives of the local school system, and parents who would coordinate Head Start funds, state pre-K funds, and the new money provided by our proposal. We propose that these consortiums would enroll many children from families below 150 percent of poverty while simultaneously maintaining high quality and would also plan an intervention program and coordinate it with children's entry into public school. Our proposal can be summarized in four broad points.

First, the local programs would include a pregnancy and home-visiting program for the most disadvantaged families with infants; an infant and

Table 8-3. State and Federal Spending, Preschoool and Child Care Programs

Millions of dollars

Program	Spending
Department of Education[a]	
Title 1 grants	284
Early Reading First	75
Special education	1,339
(Infants and families)	(437)
(Preschool grants)	(390)
(Grants to states)	(512)
Health and Human Services[b]	
Discretionary Child Care and Development Fund (CCDF)	2,100
Mandatory CCDF	2,717
Transfers from Temporary Assistance for Needy Families (TANF) block grant to CCDF	2,000
TANF direct expenditures on child care	1,580
State CCDF match and maintenance effort payments	2,247
TANF MOE in excess of CCDF MOE	750
Head Start	6,668
Social services block grant (Title XX)	160
Department of Agriculture[c]	
Child and adult care food program	1,940
Tax expenditures[b]	
Child and dependent care tax credit	2,910
Employer-provided child care exclusion	720
Employer-provided child care credit	90
Total	25,580

a. Education spending based on the proportion of children under age five.

b. HHS and tax expenditures are for children of all ages; 53 percent of CCDF children are under age five.

c. Only spending on children included in the estimate.

toddler preschool program for children under age three from very disadvantaged families; a preschool program for all three- and four-year-olds from families under 150 percent of poverty; and a school-age program emphasizing reading and math skills.[37] Second, the local consortiums would be responsible for working with their state and local government and with Head Start programs to make sure that all the funds for high-quality care work in conjunction to pay for the various intervention programs. Third, all home-visiting and preschool programs that meet standards set by the consortium would be eligible to provide services, and parents would have vouchers to pick the program of their choice that meets consortium standards. Fourth, beginning at age four, children would be continuously evaluated; before entry into the public schools they would be expected to meet national outcome standards on intellectual and socioemotional measures of school readiness. Programs that failed to meet standards for student performance would be ineligible to receive federal funds.

The potential of preschool programs to play an important role in reducing poverty and increasing economic mobility is substantial. The long-term impacts of the big three preschool programs show what is possible. State pre–K programs have already proven capable of producing large immediate impacts, and a few studies have reported evidence that, despite its less powerful effects on school readiness and educational outcomes, Head Start does have long-term impacts on social outcomes in adolescence and early adulthood. Our plan, the initial phase of which could be implemented for $6 billion a year, would provide a strong test of whether lasting results can be produced by a national demonstration program. Our proposal includes a comprehensive program—beginning during pregnancy for the most disadvantaged mothers and continuing through the first several years of elementary school—that could serve as a model for every community in the nation. But first we should determine whether a program conducted on a national scale can produce results similar to those achieved by the big three. The data we review show that if big three–type results can be achieved on a national scale, even a $50 billion investment in preschool programs would return benefits that exceed the initial cost.[38] Two final words are in order about our plan.

First, we emphasize the importance of coordinating all preschool programs, including Title I, Head Start, state pre-K, and both federal and state child care programs (table 8-3), that currently make about $26 billion a year available for day care and early education. Coordinating bureaucracies is usually difficult and often fails. But when the nation is spending so much on day care and preschool programs, and most or all of these programs now operate independently of one another in most states, the status quo already represents a failure of coordination. This failure is especially apparent in the $3.7 billion states are spending on their pre-K programs despite the fact that Head Start has been operating for more than four decades to provide high-quality preschool to the same types of disadvantaged children now enrolled in state pre-K classrooms.[39] Our plan would at least increase the chance of coordination between state pre-K funds and Head Start by giving local authorities control over both streams of funding. Similarly, if preschool programs are to be coordinated with the public schools, the consortium of local authorities that must include the public schools again provides at least a chance that such coordination would occur. It is likely that some local consortiums would fail and some would succeed. Those that succeed could then serve as models for other local consortiums and would be eligible for additional federal funding. Growing the programs that succeed is our approach to accountability.

Second, we are also aware that some critics think that low-income parents sometimes make bad choices for their children.[40] However, parent choice is not the only mechanism in our plan aimed at increasing and maintaining quality. Another mechanism is the inclusion of local standards and repeated testing of children to ensure that they are meeting standards. Moreover, to avoid the problem of low standards at the state or local level that has plagued No Child Left Behind, our plan includes minimum national standards of child performance at school entry.[41] Thus parents would be selecting among programs that meet national standards for improving children's readiness for school.

K–12 Education

Since publication of *A Nation at Risk* in 1983, the nation's schools have been the object of continuous criticism.[42] No wonder. Reading achievement by students at almost every grade level has been virtually flat since the early 1990s; the United States does not fare well in international comparisons; school dropout continues to be a major problem; and the achievement gap between whites and Asians as compared with blacks and Hispanics is large and has shown only modest improvement in the past two decades.[43]

Although public schools achieve less than they could or should, several factors may serve as the basis for improvement. These factors include the No Child Left Behind (NCLB) act of 2002; the growth of reform models of middle and high schools in the inner city that seem to be increasing the achievement of disadvantaged students; a growing body of research about educational practices that show promise, including whole-school reform, class size reduction, career academies, good teachers, teacher bonuses, and perhaps parental choice programs; notable progress in student achievement in some big-city school systems; and great improvement in educational research.[44] Against this backdrop of guarded optimism, we offer the following proposals for reform that could strengthen the performance of schools in promoting opportunity and reducing the ethnic achievement gaps that have plagued the nation for decades. These reforms include strengthening NCLB and implementing a plan for promoting teacher effectiveness, especially in schools that disproportionately serve students from poor families. In addition, we endorse recent trends in educational research and urge Congress to continue its generous funding of research.

Strengthening NCLB

The federal No Child Left Behind (NCLB) legislation, despite its flaws, represents an important and radical shift in federal policy.[45] Before NCLB, the federal government's main role in education was to help poor districts and children through a program (Title I of the Elementary and Secondary Education Act) that provides additional funds to districts with high proportions of poor children, a policy that after four decades showed virtually no success.[46] But NCLB moved the federal government, states, and local school districts into the role of promoting accountability.

In the years after *A Nation at Risk*, states and schools had already begun to set standards such as course requirements and competency tests for high school graduation. If minimum requirements and standards represented progress, policymakers and many educators nonetheless came to believe that they were not enough and that states and school districts needed to adopt measures of student progress in achieving the standards. During the 1990s Texas and North Carolina led the way in the accountability movement by setting standards, measuring student progress, and publicizing the results. Both states showed great improvement in student performance, especially among blacks.[47] When George W. Bush, the governor of Texas who played a major role in bringing accountability to Texas public schools, became president in 2000, he worked with Republicans and Democrats in Congress to pass the NCLB act, which in effect expanded the accountability reforms adopted with such success in North Carolina and Texas into a national movement.

We believe that the NCLB represents a step forward because it is difficult to see how schools can be held to high standards unless student performance is measured on a regular basis and the public knows how individual schools and subgroups of students are performing relative to other schools and subgroups. The performance of schools in helping minority groups close the achievement gap is an essential ingredient of accountability and explains the surprising fact that the National Association for the Advancement of Colored People (NAACP) and other civil rights groups support NCLB despite the opposition of teachers unions and many Democrats.[48] Progress in closing the achievement gap is unlikely unless there is continuous public information about the size of the gap and success or failure in narrowing it.

NCLB has not transformed the public schools, but it has created most of the elements of an effective accountability system. Combined with the biennial administration of the National Assessment of Educational Progress (NAEP), a nationally representative achievement test that measures student learning in reading, math, and other subjects at grades four, eight, and twelve, the public and policymakers now have a great deal of information about student performance. NAEP provides national and state scores, while the state tests required by NCLB provide comparable scores all the way down to the school system and school building level. Both assessment systems also yield data on the performance of major subgroups of students. These are vital elements of an accountability system open to public scrutiny and perhaps leading to improved performance. Public information on failing schools could also compel parents to demand better performance and to remove their children from failing schools and place them in more successful schools, as called for in the NCLB law. If the provision of NCLB that allows students to leave failing schools for schools of their choice is aggressively implemented, it is possible that the impacts of NCLB on achievement could increase in the years ahead.[49]

Because progress in improving K–12 education is unlikely unless schools are held accountable for performance, we strongly support NCLB and would strengthen its implementation. The original law requires states to demonstrate that they have "adopted challenging academic content standards and challenging student academic achievement standards."[50] However, the easiest way for states to appear to be achieving high standards—and thereby keep parents and state legislators happy—is to set the bar low in the design of state tests. But not requiring schools to meet world-class standards is a losing strategy in a global economy. If American children are not proficient in math, reading, and other academic skills, they will not be competitive with children from other nations, many of whom already surpass the school achievement of American students.[51] Nor will many of them be prepared to handle the challenges of either college-level academic work or the job market.

We call on Congress to set national standards for student achievement. The standards should consist of both absolute standards in basic subjects by grade level and, to compensate for the fact that the average family background of students varies so greatly from school to school and state to state, standards that provide for year-to-year improvement. Standards are the motor that makes NCLB run, but many states have created a stuttering motor by setting a low bar. The bar should be raised.

Strengthening Teaching

Teachers are the most important ingredient in any plan for promoting excellence in education.[52] Research on effective teachers provides solid information about the effects of good teaching and suggests how good teachers can be identified. One of the first of the new wave of studies of teacher effectiveness was conducted by William Sanders and June Rivers of the University of Tennessee in 1996.[53] The authors followed student test scores in mathematics from grades three through five. Teachers were divided into five groups defined by the improvement in student test scores each year. Teachers whose students scored in the top fifth had student test scores that were substantially better (about 50 percentile points) than students in the bottom fifth. Further analyses show that teachers in the top fifth produced improvements among all students, regardless of the students' original test scores or their ethnic group.

Eric Hanushek of Stanford and his colleagues used similar test score improvement measures to examine teacher effectiveness in a study of Texas students in grades four through eight.[54] Among other findings, Hanushek replicated one of the major Sanders and Rivers findings that good teachers are effective with students at every ability level. Not surprisingly, a review by Rand researchers of the literature on teacher quality based on student change scores concludes that this body of studies stands up well to careful scrutiny and that good teachers do in fact produce major improvements in student learning.[55]

The most striking and innovative feature of these and similar studies is the sophisticated use of students' change scores. The obvious problem in using standardized test scores at the end of a course or grade level is that students start at different levels. Whether the interest is in assessing learning within a school or between schools or demographic groups, outcome scores are deeply flawed because students begin at such different levels. The general idea of change scores, however, is to use complex statistical methods and repeated testing to measure changes in student performance while controlling for non-school influences, such as family background, known to affect test scores. To the extent that this method accurately measures new learning, by in effect subtracting each student's starting score from his ending score while simultaneously controlling for nonschool factors, change scores constitute a greatly improved measure of learning.[56] As such, change scores can be useful in measuring the performance of groups of students, entire schools, and individual teachers.

If teachers contribute directly to student achievement, as these studies strongly suggest, arguably the most direct route to improving student performance is to improve the average quality of teachers. Ron Haskins of Brookings and Susanna Loeb of Stanford have devised a research-based plan for achieving exactly this end.[57] The plan encourages school districts to select the best teachers they can attract, although overreliance on education school graduates and teacher certification is probably a mistake. Schools should also hire people who have had good careers in other fields, graduating college students with high academic performance in college who did not major in education, and teachers from the new array of alternative teacher preparation programs, such as Teach for America.[58] At least as important as trying to select good beginning teachers, however, is a strategy for retaining and promoting successful teachers. School systems that simply grant tenure to teachers after several years of teaching are missing the opportunity to gradually improve the quality of teachers in their system. Here is where the use of the new methods of evaluating teacher performance by using changes in their students' test scores can be useful. Test score improvement should be an important—but not the only—element in a plan for retaining and promoting teachers. Other elements could include principal ratings, feedback from parents, and evaluations by senior teachers. Only teachers who are effective as indicated by these measures, with improvements in test scores playing a central role, should be retained and promoted.

But new teachers should not be left entirely to their own devices in working to develop their skills and effectiveness. School systems should help by creating effective programs for teacher development. As the researcher Heather Hill shows, graduate course work and most other activities now counted as professional development by school systems across the nation are largely ineffective in improving teacher quality.[59] Schools spend about 3 percent of their budget on professional development, apparently without improving teacher quality. Although persuasive evidence on effective approaches to professional development is sparse, school districts should try new approaches, such as extensive training in curriculums being used in their system or direct classroom work with master teachers. Above all, school systems should use evidence of increased teacher effectiveness to evaluate their professional development program.

We recommend that school districts implement clearly defined plans, such as the one outlined above or any of several thoughtful alternatives, for improving average teacher quality.[60] The Teacher Advancement Program—initiated by Lowell Milken of the Milken Family Foundation in 1998 and now operating in 220 schools with more than 6,000 teachers—shows that schools are fully capable of instituting a teacher improvement program of the type we support.[61] Despite merit pay being a central part of the Teacher Advancement Program, the program has been implemented in Chicago and elsewhere with the approval or at least acquiescence of teachers unions. Further, a large-scale study based on longitudinal data finds that the program produced student test score gains in the third and fourth grades, although the study also found negative effects on test scores in the ninth and tenth grades under some specifications of the analysis model.[62]

To encourage the adoption of teacher improvement plans by school districts, and to encourage the placement of highly qualified teachers in schools serving disproportionate numbers of poor and minority children, we support the expansion of an existing federal program for stimulating teacher improvement. The Teacher Incentive Fund, authorized by Congress in 2006, now provides $100 million a year to school districts to pay for teacher improvement plans.[63] The program should be expanded and funded at the level of $1 billion a year, increasing to $2 billion a year over a ten-year period, with $5 million set aside annually to pay for strict evaluations of the effects of the program at the local level.

The goals of the program are to improve student achievement by increasing the quality of teaching in schools that serve disproportionate numbers of students from poor families; reform teacher compensation systems so that teachers are rewarded for increases in student achievement; increase the number of effective teachers serving poor, minority, and disadvantaged students; and create sustainable, performance-based compensation systems. Grants from the Teacher Incentive Fund should be distributed to school systems on a competitive basis. School systems applying for funds would be required to use change scores to evaluate student performance as part of a larger plan for recruiting, training, and retaining effective teachers. They would also be required to provide financial incentives for successful teachers to work in schools serving disproportionate numbers of disadvantaged students.

Promoting High-Achieving Inner-City Schools

Another reason for having some optimism about K–12 education is that a growing number of schools, many located in dangerous urban neighborhoods and only a few blocks away from some of the worst schools in the nation, seem to have produced remarkable results in creating a safe and orderly environment for students and in bringing them, on average, to the performance level of students from more advantaged neighborhoods and schools. A recent book by the former *U.S. News and World Report* writer David Whitman describes six of these schools in great detail and concludes that similar highly successful schools can be created in the midst of the chaos of our inner cities and with students that would fail or perform far below age norms if they went to regular schools.[64]

The schools described by Whitman and others have several common characteristics.[65] Taken together, these characteristics make these schools traditional or even paternalistic in the sense that authorities decide they know best what is good for students and take strong measures to ensure that students actually do what they would decide to do if they made wise decisions. Larry Mead of New York University was one of the first to understand the importance of paternalism and its application to many types of social policies. The authors in a volume edited by Mead in 1997 describe the application of paternalistic policies to social problems as diverse as teen pregnancy, payment of child support by fathers, drug addiction, and mandatory work programs.[66] Since that time, as noted in chapter 6, research by neuroscientists, economists, and psychologists increasingly suggests that paternalistic policies may, in some cases, be more effective than those that rely exclusively on individual self-interest and choice.[67]

Programs based on paternalism attempt to use strong measures, sometimes involving sanctions, to encourage or require people to behave in accord with mainstream values, such as not having babies outside marriage, meeting the paternal responsibility to pay child support, terminating drug use, and getting a job. The education programs described by Whitman set demanding standards that reflect middle-class norms. The schools are especially insistent on order. Students must meet dress codes, walk silently in hallways between classes, sit straight in their seats, attend to the teacher at all times, get permission to talk, and use standard English. Any actions or paraphernalia associated with gangs, such as colored scarves or symbols displayed on notebooks, are dealt with harshly, often by permanent expulsion. Paternalistic schools tend to use both sticks and carrots to persuade students to meet conduct and academic rules. Regarding carrots, students receive points for good behavior and academic achievement, points that can be redeemed for privileges such as field trips and time to engage in leisure pursuits like playing electronic games. But students who do not meet expectations not only lose points but are sometimes compelled to meet in study hall after school, do extra homework, or perform various jobs around the school after regular school hours. Students who repeatedly violate rules are expelled for a period of time or even permanently.

On the academic side, these schools emphasize basic skills. Several of them provide intense remedial instruction when students first arrive because they are often behind in reading and math. Teaching methods tend to be traditional, such as drill and frequent review. Instruction is accompanied by frequent assessments, including standardized tests, to make sure students are mastering the knowledge and skills being taught. One feature of instruction in all the schools is time spent on academic tasks, which is much more than that in regular schools. School hours usually begin by 8:00 a.m. and run until 4:00 or 5:00 p.m. In the KIPP junior high school in the Bronx, for example, Whitman estimates that students receive more than 300 minutes a day of instruction, compared with 185 minutes in other New York City schools. Even this difference is probably an underestimate, however, because like most inner-city schools instruction in regular New York City schools is frequently disrupted by noise, acting out by students, and even violence. As if these huge differences in time on task are not enough, most of the schools studied by Whitman require attendance on Saturdays and at a summer session lasting three or more weeks.

We are reluctant to conclude that any social intervention is successful unless the intervention has been evaluated by the random-assignment design. None of the schools discussed by Whitman has met this standard. Perhaps the most important threat to the conclusion that these schools can boost the achievement of most inner-city and disadvantaged students is that in every case parents played a role in getting their children into the school. Compared with parents who did not make the effort to get their children into an experimental school, parents who make this effort could be different in many ways that could promote their child's achievement. Another potential bias is attrition of the worst students from the schools, which would raise the average level of performance if true.

Despite these caveats, Whitman finds impressive evidence of improved performance of students at each of the six schools on standardized tests and other measures. At the KIPP school in the Bronx, 87 percent of eighth-graders passed the New York State Standards Test, compared with 54 percent of eighth-graders statewide and only about 11 percent of eighth-graders at the three schools nearest to the KIPP school. The results are similar for English proficiency.[68] At the University Park School in Worcester, Massachusetts, 91 percent of students, compared with 69 percent statewide and an average of 45 percent at the two closest inner-city schools, were rated "proficient" or "advanced" in math on the Massachusetts Comprehensive Assessment System, one of the toughest statewide achievement tests in the nation.[69]

Whitman's study suggests that it is possible to have successful inner-city schools. In a rational world, other schools would try to follow the model provided by the schools he studied, especially in their emphasis on order, extra hours of instruction, and emphasis on basics like drill—in a word, paternalism. Indeed, the famed Harlem Children's Zone, initiated by Geoffrey Canada and proposed as a model for expansion to twenty neighborhoods throughout the country by President Obama during the 2008 presidential campaign, features charter schools with characteristics and results similar to those praised by Whitman.[70] But most of the key characteristics of paternalistic programs are anathema to the progressive educators who populate schools of education and the ranks of public school teachers. Another problem is that it seems likely that many teachers could experience burnout from the long hours, and in any case teachers unions will not approve of these long hours without additional compensation.

Still we recommend that local school systems employ the paternalistic model in many of their schools and that they encourage the formation of charter schools based on paternalistic principles. This quiet movement is off to a strong start, but it seems wise to see if the model spreads and continues to have success. Meanwhile, our major recommendation for federal policy would be that the National Institute of Education Sciences fund rigorous ("gold standard") evaluations of several of these programs.

Continuing Federal Support for High-Quality Research

Most of the successful interventions discussed above have been or are now being evaluated using high-quality designs. In part, the increasing quality of educational research is attributable to the Education Science Reform Act of 2002. The act established the Institute of Education Sciences (IES) within the U.S. Department of Education to "apply rigorous, systematic, and objective methodology to obtain reliable and valid knowledge relevant to education activities and programs."[71] One of the more important IES innovations is the creation of a website called the What Works Clearinghouse, which provides information on educational innovations in reading, math, whole school reform, and many other interventions that have been strictly evaluated.[72]

In the years ahead, especially during times in which the American economy is in recession and federal revenues are stable or falling, Congress may be tempted to cut educational research. But this action would be a mistake. Researchers and program evaluators have developed highly effective designs and statistical techniques that allow the field to identify effective programs. High-quality research and program evaluation have moved education out of the period of basing innovation on rumor and fad. New approaches can be effectively evaluated to detect their effects; and failures can be identified and then modified or discarded. As in the case of using achievement test change scores, techniques developed through research can also be used to identify, retain, and promote effective teachers. Congress should at a minimum maintain the budget for educational research and the What Works Clearinghouse.

Postsecondary Education

There is strong evidence that the odds of living in poverty would decline and the odds of moving into the middle class or beyond would increase for every poor child who achieves a college degree (figure 8-4). Adult children with parents in the bottom income quintile, for example, nearly quadrupled their chance of moving all the way to the top quintile by obtaining a college degree (from 5 percent to 19 percent).

College, Opportunity, and Mobility

But how many children from low-income families go to college and how many graduate? Whereas 79 percent of the young people from families in the

Figure 8-4. Family Income of Adult Children, by Education and Parents' Family Income[a]

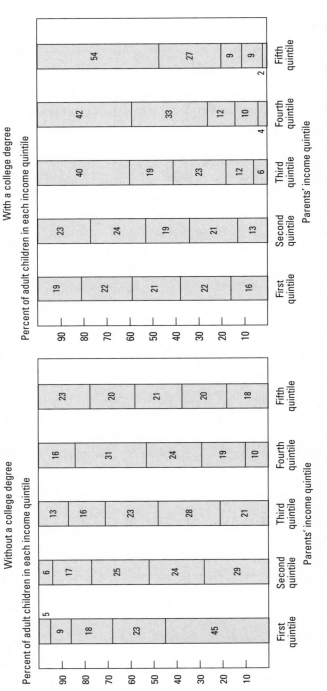

Source: Julia B. Isaacs, Isabel V. Sawhill, and Ron Haskins, *Getting Ahead or Losing Ground: Economic Mobility in America* (Brookings and Economic Mobility Project, an Initiative of the Pew Charitable Trusts, 2008), figure 6.

a. Columns may not add to 100 due to rounding. Family incomes are five-year averages from the Panel Study of Income Dynamics (PSID) for 1967–71, when parents were age forty-one on average, and for 1995–2002, when their adult children were age thirty-nine on average.

Figure 8-5. College Enrollment and Degree Attainment, by Parents' Income Quintile[a]

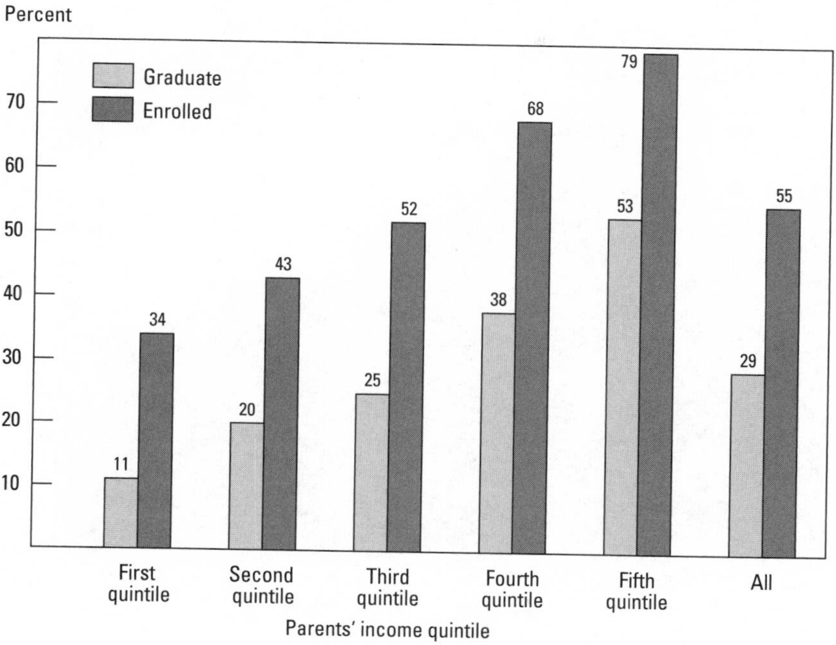

Percent

Source: Julia B. Isaacs, Isabel V. Sawhill, and Ron Haskins, *Getting Ahead or Losing Ground: Economic Mobility in America* (Brookings and Economic Mobility Project, an Initiative of the Pew Charitable Trusts, 2008), figure 5.
a. Family incomes are five-year averages from the Panel Study of Income Dynamics (PSID) for 1967–71, when parents were age forty-one on average, and again in 1995–2002, when their adult children were age thirty-nine on average.

top income quintile enroll in college, only 34 percent of youngsters from the bottom quintile do so (figure 8-5). Similarly, only 11 percent of youngsters from the bottom actually graduate, compared with 53 percent of those from the top.

Family background is a formidable barrier to economic mobility (see chapters 4 and 5). The fact that children from wealthy families have higher achievement test scores and receive higher grades during the K–12 years undoubtedly plays a role in the striking relationship between family income and college degrees. But there are important factors other than family background that affect college going. Consider the relationship between student learning (as measured by math scores in the senior year), parent income, and college enrollment taken from a study by David Ellwood and Tom Kane of Harvard (figure 8-6). The correlation between test scores in the senior year and the probability of enrolling in college for students from all income backgrounds is

Figure 8-6. College Enrollment, by High School Math Score and Parents' Income Quartile

Percent

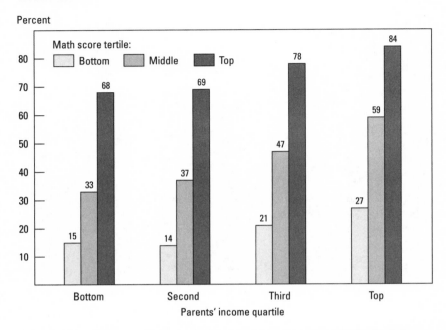

Source: David T. Ellwood and Thomas J. Kane, table 10.2 ("Students in Class of 1992 Enrolling in Postsecondary Schools within Twenty Months, by Parental Income Quartile and Test Scores"), in *Securing the Future: Investing in Children from Birth to College.* © 2000 Russell Sage Foundation. Reprinted with permission.

an indication of whether the nation's universities base enrollment on merit. That high-achieving youngsters from the bottom income quartile have a 68 percent chance of enrolling in college, compared with only a 15 percent chance for their low-achieving peers from poor families, shows that the system is at least partially successful in admitting students from poor families based on merit.

The high rate of college enrollment by high-achieving poor students is good news, probably reflecting hard work on their part, the work of college recruiters and admissions officers, and the availability of student aid. But the findings are not all optimistic. Low-achieving students from families in the bottom income quartile have only a 15 percent chance of attending college, whereas low-achieving students from wealthy families have almost twice as great (27 percent) a chance. Similarly, youngsters from the bottom two income quartiles who achieve math scores in the middle third of achievement have only a 33 percent and a 37 percent chance, respectively, of enrolling in college, compared with a 47 percent and 59 percent chance for young people from families in the top two income quartiles with math scores in the same middle third. Many of the youngsters in the bottom half who don't make it into college could do well there, especially if they were enrolled in two-year schools or nonelite four-year colleges. But far too many either do not enroll or drop out before graduating.

Promoting College Attendance and Graduation

Thus we propose a three-part plan for boosting the college enrollment and graduation rates of low-income and minority students:[73]

—Increased preparation during high school for engaging in academic work at two-year or four-year colleges.

—Reform of the nation's student aid programs and help for disadvantaged students in selecting a college and working out the finances.

—Expansion of college programs that help disadvantaged students stay in college until they receive a certificate or degree.

We develop each of these strategies below. It is notable at the outset that the primary responsibility for implementing our plan is spread across local school systems, parents, state government, colleges and universities, and the federal government. Each of these sectors has a vital role to play and each must become more accountable. (While focusing in this section on postsecondary education, we recognize that many disadvantaged young people will not go to college. In chapter 9 we describe programs that support students not intending to enroll in postsecondary institutions and argue that such programs are also important for reducing poverty and increasing economic mobility.)

Strategy 1: Strengthen Academic Preparation for College. One of the greatest problems in public education is the gap between the achievement of white, Asian, and middle- and upper-income students compared with black, Hispanic, and low-income students.[74] After more than four decades of public policy aimed at reducing the achievement gap, there has been only modest progress. Striking evidence of the difference in college preparation between white and minority students is provided by Jay Greene and Greg Forster.[75] Defining minimum college readiness as receiving a high school diploma, taking courses required by colleges for basic academic preparedness, and demonstrating basic literacy skills, Greene and Forster report that only around 40 percent of white and Asian students are college ready by these criteria. But this figure is twice the rate for black students (20 percent) and more than twice the rate for Hispanic students (16 percent).

An equally compelling picture of the problems faced in college by disadvantaged black and Hispanic students is provided by information on a representative sample of nearly 4,000 white, Asian, black, and Hispanic students attending twenty-eight selective colleges and universities.[76] Conducted by Princeton demographer Douglas Massey and his colleagues, the Source of the River study provides the most complete information on the background and adaptation to college by students of all four ethnic groups. Although the first publication from this massive study includes only information through the first semester of the freshman year in college, two outcomes are already clear.

First, whites, Asians, and middle-class black and Hispanic students come from very different social and economic backgrounds than black and Hispanic students from poor families. Disadvantaged black and Hispanic students have less-educated parents, attended worse schools with poorer teachers, and had been exposed to more violence and disorder in their neighborhoods and schools than students from more advantaged backgrounds.

Second, a significant minority of black and Hispanic students suffer from "stereotype vulnerability," which the authors define as "disengagement from school work that stems from fears of living up to negative stereotypes of minority intellectual inferiority."[77] These students are much more likely than other students from disadvantaged backgrounds to fail at least one course during their first semester.

Clearly, improving the readiness of disadvantaged students to handle college-level academic work is paramount to our vision of increased economic mobility. Improving the education of disadvantaged students traditionally has been the responsibility of state and local government, with modest assistance from the federal government. Our recommendations to strengthen preschool and NCLB and to boost the average quality of K–12 teachers should improve the academic success of disadvantaged students throughout their school careers and enhance their academic readiness for college. But in addition to regular course offerings, many school systems are now implementing programs with the specific purpose of helping disadvantaged students prepare for college.[78] For example, a well-evaluated program in Texas that paid both students and teachers for student success in passing advanced placement courses produced a 30 percent increase in the number of students scoring above 1100 on the SAT or above 24 on the ACT as well as an 8 percent increase in the number of students going to college.[79] The Chicago Public Schools have developed a host of high-quality programs aimed at boosting college enrollment and success among inner-city students. In addition, the Chicago school system formed a research consortium with the University of Chicago, known as the Consortium on Chicago School Research, that has attained a national reputation for evaluating innovative college preparation programs.[80]

But local programs are not the only ones that attempt to address the college readiness of disadvantaged students. For the past four decades the federal government has provided college readiness support for innovative programs designed to help prepare students from poor and minority families for college. The five major federal programs (see table 8-4) begin as early as elementary school; some involve activities in the community, some involve summer and after-school programs, some involve tutoring and mentoring, and some involve promises of financial aid for college.[81] However, most evaluations show that the programs produce modest results.[82] For example, a high-quality evaluation of Project GRAD by MDRC found little or no impact on several measures of student performance. There was some evidence of more students completing a curriculum of academic subjects in the Houston school where the GRAD program started, but when the program was expanded to two additional schools, even this effect faded. There is no evidence in any of the schools of elevated high school graduation rates or increased college enrollment rates.[83] Given these results, it is not surprising that the respected What Works Clearinghouse concludes that Project GRAD had "no discernible effects on progressing in school or on completing school."[84]

Our first recommendation for strategy 1 is to streamline federal college preparation programs and make funding contingent on performance. It is hardly surprising that these programs continue to receive support and funding. Funders, including government, often spend money on programs that are subsequently found to be only partially successful. Those who support the programs often deny or minimize the evidence. But why continue programs that produce small if any effects?

We recommend that, over a period of five years, the federal government terminate four of the five programs shown in table 8-4 and use $0.6 billion of their combined funding of $0.8 billion to create a single new program that encompasses the goals of all four programs.[85] An accountability system for the new program would include standardized test performance during the school years, high school graduation rates, success in getting into postsecondary institutions, and success in graduating from postsecondary institutions. Current programs would have five years to work out the details of data collection and to maximize their performance on these outcomes. But after five years, proposals from current sponsoring organizations and new organizations would be submitted to the Department of Education, and funds

Table 8-4. College Preparation Programs

Program/year established	Sponsoring agencies	2008 budget ($ millions)	Student targets	Type of project	Evaluation
Gear Up and I Have a Dream 1998 197 projects	Agencies for higher education, local education, and state education	303	K–12; postsecondary	Discretionary grant program designed to increase the number of low-income students who are prepared to enter and succeed in postsecondary education; six-year grants to states and partnerships to provide services at high-poverty middle and high schools; college scholarships to low-income students	Gear Up 2007: students had slightly greater changes in overall academic performance grade 8 through 10; slightly more likely to be on track to be college ready in English and reading; slightly more likely to take the core high school curriculum and have plans for college at grade 10. Findings apply to only this cohort; for the other, there was no significant difference in taking the core high school curriculum or having plans for college
Talent Search 1967 471 projects	Agencies for higher education, local education, and state education; nonprofits	143	6–12 grades	Tutorial services, career exploration, aptitude assessments, counseling, mentoring programs, workshops, information on post secondary institutions, and help with college application	Mathematica 2006: more likely than nonparticipants from similar backgrounds to be first-time applicants for financial aid in the 1999–2000 school year; more likely than nonparticipants to enroll in a public college or university in their state
Upward Bound 1964 825 projects	Agencies for higher education, local education, and state education; nonprofits	328	9–12 grades, adults (military veterans only)	Academic instruction in mathematics, laboratory sciences, composition, literature, and foreign languages. Tutoring, counseling,	Mathematica Matched Control Study 2004: no effect on enrollment at postsecondary institutions or postsecondary credits earned by students overall; possible increased enrollment in four-year colleges (6 percentage points) but not statistically

conclusive. Substantial impact on high school and postsecondary outcomes for certain groups of students; consistent positive impact on students who, when applying for the program, did not expect to earn a B.A. degree. Upward Bound has limited overall impact on students' academic preparation for college, although staying in the program longer is associated with better student outcomes.

mentoring, cultural enrichment, and work-study programs also supported. Goal is to prepare students for college

Project Grad
1988
205 projects

Nonprofits (working with public schools)

0[a]

K-16

Nonprofit entity coordinates with entire school system to provide a consistent and quality education in reading and math curriculums in elementary school (feeder schools); encourages community involvement through taxes, mentoring, tutoring, and event sponsorship

MDRC Evaluation through 2002–03: At flagship school, Project Grad had a statistically significant positive effect on the proportion of students completing a core academic curriculum on time (average grade of 75 of 100; four credits in English, three in math, two in science, and two in social studies; graduated from high school within four years).

As Project Grad expanded to two other Houston high schools, these positive effects on students' academic preparation were not evident. Out-comes at the newer Project Grad high schools improved but were matched by progress at the comparison high school. Improvements in graduation rates at the three Project Grad high schools were generally matched by improvements in graduation rates at the comparison schools. Project Grad high schools in Columbus and Atlanta showed improvements in attendance and

(continued)

Table 8-4. College Preparation Programs *(continued)*

Program/year established	Sponsoring agencies	2008 budget ($ millions)	Student targets	Type of project	Evaluation
					promotion to tenth grade that appear to have outpaced improvements at the comparison schools, although the differences are only sometimes statistically significant.
Upward Bound math-science 1990 54 projects	Higher education agencies; public and private agencies	31	9–12	Summer programs with intensive math and science training; counseling; computer training; scientific research under faculty supervision	Mathematica (2007): The program improved high school grades in math and science; increased the likelihood of high school students taking chemistry and physics; increased the probability students would enroll in selective four-year institutions; increased the chances students would major in math and science; and increased the probability of completing a four-year degree in math or science.

Source: U.S. Department of Education, Office of Postsecondary Education Act (www.ed.gov/about/offices/list/ope/trio/index.html#programs; "Using EXPLORE and PLAN Data to Evaluation GEAR UP Programs" (www. act.org/research/policymakers/pdf/gearup_report.pdf). Project Grad available at www.projectgrad.org. "MDRC's Evaluation of Project Grad" (2006; www.mdrc.org/publications/431/summary,html). U.S Department of Education, "A Study of the Effect of the Talent Search Program on Secondary and Postsecondary Outcomes in Florida, Indiana and Texas: Final Report, Phase II, National Evaluation" (2006; www.mathematica-mpr.com/publications/PDFs/ talentseach3state.pdf).

a. Project Grad does not currently receive federal funding but has in the past.

would be awarded on a competitive basis. Programs that fail to improve college graduation rates would be terminated and the money used for more promising programs. Public schools, private schools, colleges (both two year and four year), and other education entities would compete for funds. Around $5 million would be withheld from the $0.6 billion each year for the secretary to conduct evaluations of selected programs, using random assignment designs whenever possible.

An essential part of the new approach would be the construction in every state of longitudinal data systems capable of following students through their K–12 careers and for six years or so after they leave high school. Fortunately, some states have already taken modest steps in this direction. A prime mover in the attempt to build these state data systems is Achieve, Inc., a bipartisan, nonprofit organization formed by governors and business leaders in 1996. Among other goals, Achieve's American Diploma Project (ADP), in which thirty-four states now participate, is working to hold high schools accountable for graduating students who are ready for college or careers and who are capable of completing the requirements for a college degree.[86]

According to Achieve's 2008 annual report, one of the major accomplishments of ADP is helping states create data systems to assess how many students from each high school go on to further education and whether they succeed.[87] Achieve and ADP are now working with the Data Quality Campaign, the National Center for Higher Education Management Systems (NCHEMS), and the federal Statewide Longitudinal Data Systems (SLDS) grant program, which serves as a source of funding, to help states create these state-of-the-art data systems.[88] Given the many obstacles to building these systems, including costs, existing outdated systems, and the difficulty of getting all states to agree on compatible systems, it is to be expected that an arduous process requiring many years lies ahead. We recommend using $0.2 billion of the $0.8 billion now being spent on college preparation programs to increase SLDS funding so the program can help more states develop the new data system.

An important benefit of building a comprehensive data system like the one ADP and its allies are trying to create is that it would permit researchers to conduct studies of the relationship between student characteristics, experiences, and performance during their public school careers and their postsecondary achievements, especially college enrollment and graduation. The field of helping disadvantaged students succeed in college is still not well developed and, as we have seen, has not yet created programs that are notably successful in boosting either college enrollment or graduation. Thus correlational studies can provide useful information to school systems about what school programs and what level of student performance are associated with postsecondary achievement. Even better, the existence of a data system that could follow students into college clears the way for experimental studies that can provide solid evidence of the success of programs in this evolving field.

Our second recommendation for strategy 1 is to provide more and better counselors in inner-city schools. No matter how well prepared poor and minority students are for the academic rigors of college, they need help selecting the right college and obtaining financial aid.[89] Thus every high school should have trained counselors and teachers who will help disadvantaged students select colleges and apply for financial aid. Research shows that schools serving predominantly low-income and minority students have more than 1,000 students per counselor, compared with the national average of about 500 students per counselor.[90] Advising students about college preparation, college selection, and obtaining financial aid is a complex undertaking and requires specialized training and a full-time commitment. States and local school districts should do everything possible to ensure that disadvantaged students have access to competent counselors beginning at least by ninth grade.

Advising poor and low-income students about college selection and financing is an area that has seen impressive innovation. Programs like the Coach program at Harvard and the Strive for College program founded at Washington University in St. Louis mobilize undergraduate students to advise public school students in college selection and receipt of financial aid.[91] The undergraduate "counselors," who have themselves recently endured the rigors of preparing college application and aid forms, work with high school students throughout the senior year to help them select a college and apply for aid. Although these programs have not been evaluated, their use of student counselors saves money, and there is anecdotal evidence that many of the schools served by these student counselors have seen the college attendance rates of disadvantaged students increase. Student counselors can supplement the work of full-time guidance counselors, who should be responsible for figuring out effective and efficient ways to use them.

Another remarkable program aiming to supplement the efforts of public school counselors is the National College Advising Corps, which trains recent college graduates to work full time in schools to advise poor and low-income students in college selection and financing.[92] Advising Corps now has chapters on thirteen college campuses in twelve states and plans to advise 30,000 low-income students in 2009.

These and similar innovative and low-cost programs appear to be growing rapidly and have the potential to expand the reach of regular school counselors at a reasonable price. States and localities should take full advantage of these and similar programs.

Strategy 2: Paying for College. Even if low-income and minority students are academically prepared to succeed in college, nearly all of them need financial aid. Fortunately, a generous system of federal, state, and private student financial aid helps millions of poor, as well as nonpoor, students. Unfortunately, this system is flawed. The report of the Spellings Commission in 2006 summarizes the flaws, concluding that the aid system "is confusing, complex, inefficient, duplicative, and frequently does not direct aid to students who truly need it."[93]

To promote both understanding and effective use, our primary recommendation is that federal aid be simplified. In addition, we recommend that available aid be more narrowly focused on, as the Spellings Commission puts it, "students who truly need" the assistance. Thus our recommendations would serve two purposes: simplifying both the aid programs themselves and the application process; and promoting equity by modestly expanding the amount of aid available and by focusing on students with greatest need. We begin with a brief overview of the major categories of student aid.[94]

Table 8-5 summarizes the major categories of spending by the federal government, state governments, and the private sector to provide students and their parents with grants, loans, and tax breaks to pay the costs of pursuing postsecondary education or training.[95] Of the $162 billion available to students in the 2007–08 school year, 42 percent was for federal, state, and private sector grants; 53 percent was for student loans from all sources; and about 4 percent was for tax breaks. Less than 1 percent was spent on the federal work-study program for low-income students. Total spending and loans have increased slightly more than 100 percent in constant dollars since 1997–98. There are at least thirty-one separate federal programs or provisions across the three categories of grants, loans, and tax breaks, many of them overlapping and redundant.[96]

The effects of student aid must be understood in the context of college prices. Although every category of student aid increased over the decade in dollars adjusted for inflation, college expenses have also been increasing. In the ten years between the 1998–99 and the 2008–09 school years, tuition and fees at the average public four-year college or university increased from $4,380 to $6,590, or by about 50 percent in dollars adjusted for inflation.[97] By contrast, the maximum Pell grant increased by only 23 percent.[98] Clearly, the major source of college funding for low-income students that does not have to be repaid failed to keep up with rising college tuition and fees.

Table 8-5. Cost of Student Aid and Ten-Year Change, by Type of Aid, 2007–08[a]

Type	Cost (2007 $billion)	Ten-year change (percent)
Grant	68.4	82
Loan	85.9	103
Tax breaks	7.0	75[a]
Work-study program	1.2	114
Total	162.5	101

Source: Sandy Baum and Kathleen Payea, "Trends in Student Aid: 2008" (Washington: College Board, 2008), p. 6.
a. For the period 1998–99 to 2007–08, because tax benefits began in 1998–99.

A full picture of the effect of these rising college costs is provided in figure 8-7. Grant aid from all sources and federal tax benefits substantially reduced the net cost of tuition and fees. In the 2008–09 school year, for example, student aid reduced tuition and fees at two-year colleges from $2,400 to $100. This figure represents a decline by nearly four-fifths (from $590 to $100) in the net cost of tuition and fees over the previous decade for two-year colleges.

Trends in net costs at four-year institutions are not nearly as favorable as those for two-year institutions. The cost of tuition and fees at the average public four-year college was reduced by over 55 percent in 2008–09 by student aid. Nonetheless, the net cost of tuition and fees increased by roughly 30 percent over the previous decade. The effect of student aid on costs of private four-year colleges was a reduction in tuition and fees in 2008–09 by about 40 percent. However, as was the case with public four-year colleges, the net cost of tuition and fees increased by more than 20 percent over the previous decade. Student aid, in short, does greatly reduce the net cost of tuition and fees paid by the average student each year, but with the exception of two-year colleges net costs are moving in the wrong direction.[99]

Thus the major sources of college funding that do not have to be repaid (grants from all sources and federal tax benefits) failed to keep up with rising college costs. Now it is even more difficult for disadvantaged students to afford a college education. Simplifying the student aid system, concentrating the dollars on the most needy students, and increasing the amount of grant aid available are more important than ever.

Even though we focus our attention on federal aid, we should not lose sight of the fact that states and the private sector play important roles in helping students pay for postsecondary education. In 2007–08, for example, colleges and universities provided over $29 billion in grant aid to students.[100] Postsecondary institutions get some of their money for student grants from

Figure 8-7. College Tuition and Fees, by College Type, 1998–99 and 2008–09

2008 dollars

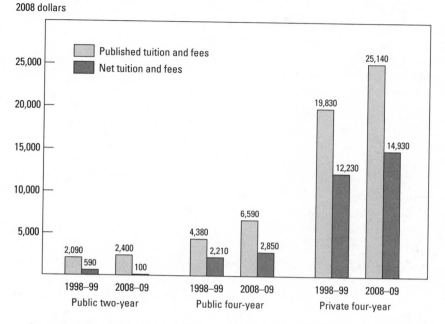

Source: Sandy Baum and Jennifer Ma, "Trends in College Pricing: 2008" (Washington: College Board, 2008), p. 11.

state legislatures, some use endowment money, and some have private contributors and alumni who donate to provide scholarships and other grant aid. Private employers also join in by providing assistance to their employees. And more than $17.5 billion in loans are made to students by private sources.

Our first recommendation for strategy 2 is to simplify the student aid application process.[101] The key step that high school students must take in applying for aid is to complete the Free Application for Federal Student Aid (FAFSA) issued by the U.S. Department of Education. Students must complete the form during their senior year of high school and submit it to the Department of Education. Susan Dynarski of the University of Michigan has calculated that it takes approximately ten hours to complete the FAFSA.[102] The form is five pages long and poses 127 questions, making it, according to Dynarski, more complex that the IRS's form 1040 for filing a tax return.

Dynarski also points out that the student's family does not receive information about the aid package they will receive until the spring of the senior year of high school. Families, especially poor and low-income families, worried about whether they can afford to send their child to college, often don't even know what aid they will receive until a few months before their child must leave for college. A system that operates in this fashion—imposing complexity and time burdens on users and informing parents and students about financial aid so late in the process—misses an important opportunity to increase the college enrollment of students from poor families. The aid package they are eventually offered is likely to be substantial, thereby providing the encouragement we hope for. Simplicity of application and timeliness of information about aid are important criteria and should be central to the process of determining grants and other forms of aid.

To simplify the student aid application process, we would follow the recommendations of both the 2006 Spellings Commission and the Rethinking Student Aid study group.[103] Thus we would completely scrap the FAFSA and base federal grants on only adjusted gross income and family size.[104] The Rethinking Student Aid group laid out detailed recommendations for eliminating the FAFSA and for using information from the IRS to automatically qualify students for federal aid. All families would need to do to initiate the student aid process is to send a simple form to the Department of Education that would include an authorization that the IRS release information from the families' tax documents. In addition, the Rethinking Student Aid group recommends that the Education Department be required to respond to every application by sending, within a few days, an e-mail to the student and the student's parents with a rough, preliminary estimate of the financial aid package they would be likely to receive. Most of the aid packages will be generous, and the family's receipt of information about the size of the aid package will itself serve to encourage them to continue pursuing plans for college.

Our second recommendation for strategy 2 is to simplify and increase grant aid. The aid programs themselves, and not just the application process, need simplification. Consider the blizzard of federal student aid programs in the tables in appendix A. As in so many other areas of policy, once the federal government decides to move into a policy domain, there is no telling where the panorama of programs will stop or how much money will be spent. But even worse, as the number and types of programs grow, there is rarely coordination among them.

The Rethinking Student Aid group makes several pertinent recommendations for reforming the Pell grant program.[105] The Pell grant is the centerpiece of federal grant aid and provided $14.4 billion to students in 2007–08 (table A-1 in appendix A).[106] We support the Rethinking Student Aid group's recommendation that the Pell grant be based on family size and adjusted gross income and that it provide its maximum benefit to families at 150 percent of the poverty level and below and then phase out between 150 percent and 250 percent of poverty. This structure, with a maximum payment of $5,000 in the 2008–09 school year, will ensure that benefits are confined to the neediest students.[107] Basing the Pell grant on only income and family size would allow families to know the amount of grant money for which they would qualify by looking at a simple table for families their size.

We would achieve further simplification of federal aid by terminating the Federal Supplemental Education Opportunity Grant, the Academic Competitiveness Grant, and the National Science and Mathematics Access to Retain Talent (SMART) Grant program (table A-1). This action would not only simplify the federal grant application process but would also save administrative costs and hassle for the federal government and colleges and universities. We would plough the $1.35 billion of savings from ending these grant programs back into the Pell grant to finance the simplification scheme and to pay for the costs incurred by the IRS and the Department of Education in sending Pell grant information to parents. One outcome of this action would be to raise the maximum Pell grant above $5,000, with ripple effects for students receiving less that the maximum grant.

Our third recommendation for strategy 2 is to reduce the loan repayment burden.[108] Given the rising costs of college and the declining ability of grant aid to cover those costs, student loans will continue to be an important part of college financing. A problem with loans is that they must be repaid. From the perspective of a low-income student about to graduate from high school, the idea of taking on $15,000, $20,000, or more in debt to get a college degree is intimidating.[109] A reasonable approach to convincing students in this situation that they are unlikely to be weighed down by debt is to create a repayment system that places only a modest repayment burden on students when they graduate.

In 2007 Congress created an income-based repayment (IBR) system in which payments are applied first to interest, then to loan fees (if applicable), and then to principal. The most attractive feature of the IBR is that the maximum payment is capped at 15 percent of a student's monthly discretionary income.[110] Discretionary income is defined as the difference between adjusted gross income and 150 percent of the poverty level for a family the size of the family maintained by the student. Thus if the student has started or wants to start a family, she can count on her monthly payments being reduced. Because the maximum payment is tied to income, students need to worry less about having to get a high-paying job in order to repay their student loans. Another attractive feature is that former students can stop making payments after a maximum of twenty-five years if they stay current with their repayment obligation. Further, if the student enters a public service occupation, such as teaching, the maximum repayment period falls to ten years.

The Rethinking Student Aid group recommends two changes to the IBR that we support.[111] Total debt, regardless of the buildup of interest if students cannot make their payments due to unemployment, disability, or other causes, should be capped at 150 percent of the original loan. This feature provides yet another reassurance to students from poor families who must borrow to complete their education because even failure to repay their student loan in timely fashion will not throw them into hopeless debt. The second change is to reduce from twenty-five years to twenty years the maximum repayment period. Again, this change provides further limits on the total amount of money students must repay, thereby increasing student confidence in the wisdom of borrowing money to obtain a postsecondary degree.

Our fourth recommendation for strategy 2 is to reform state financing of colleges and universities, such as the radical proposal offered by Robert Haveman and Timothy Smeeding of the University of Wisconsin.[112] In recent years, four-year colleges and universities have admitted more students and provided them with more assistance based on merit, an approach that raises the share of students from wealthy families because these are the students who earn the highest grade point averages in high school and receive the highest scores on standardized tests.

In response, Haveman and Smeeding recommend that state legislatures alter the practice of giving colleges and universities the entire amount of state financial support as lump-sum payments and instead provide part of the support as vouchers for low-income students attending in-state colleges and universities. This approach would force postsecondary institutions to attract low-income students by providing them with additional aid and attractive curriculum opportunities. The federal government could stimulate use of such vouchers by offering matching payments to any state that provides, say, 25 percent of its aid to colleges and universities in the form of vouchers for low-income students. We recommend that the federal government establish a $0.5 billion fund for this purpose. States would be eligible for subsidies in proportion to their share of all low-income students in the nation that they support at their state colleges and universities.

Strategy 3: Helping Disadvantaged Students Stay in College. High school programs designed to improve the academic performance of disadvantaged students are likely to have only gradual results; there will always be students who arrive at the college door with borderline academic skills.[113] This lack of skills is a major reason so many disadvantaged students drop out of college (figure 8-5). Thus an essential component of a plan to increase the share of students from low-income families achieving a college degree is programs to help them stay in college.

There is growing awareness among colleges and universities that the drop-out rate for disadvantaged students is a serious problem, and a number of these institutions are developing programs designed to reduce that rate. One of the most extensive of these programs was established in 2003 by the Lumina Foundation for Education. Called "Achieving the Dream: Community Colleges Count," the initiative focuses on students with the highest dropout rates—those from low-income and minority families. At most recent count, eighty-two institutions in fifteen states had joined the Lumina initiative.[114] Schools receive $50,000 planning grants from Lumina and then $100,000 a year for four years to implement their plan.

Several of these programs have been evaluated by MDRC using high-quality designs. In a program operated at two community colleges in New Orleans, students were offered a $1,000 reward for each of two semesters if they attended school at least half time and earned at least a C grade average. MDRC's evaluation shows that students who received the payments were more likely to enroll full time, pass more courses, earn more credits, and have higher rates of continuing enrollment in the second and third semesters after payments began.[115]

Not all the good news about retention and progress toward degrees comes from community colleges. One of the most impressive programs is at Florida State University (FSU), a large division I institution. The FSU program is aimed at reducing the disparity in graduation rates between blacks and whites. At many four-year colleges, the graduation rate for black students six years after enrollment is 20 percent, or 30 percent lower than the rate for whites.[116] FSU established a program, called the Center for Academic Retention and Enhancement (CARE), with the exclusive responsibility of recruiting and preparing disadvantaged students (both black and white, but disproportionately black) to enter the university and then to perform well when they arrive. The program identifies promising disadvantaged students as early as sixth grade. FSU officials meet with school counselors to encourage them to help these students take college preparatory courses. They also encourage the students to attend summer programs on the FSU campus to provide additional instruction in basic subjects and to acclimate students to the college environment.

In the summer before their freshman year of college, admitted students attend a free seven-week summer session, during which students meet with professors, administrators, and student leaders to learn about life at the university and to take courses. Throughout the academic year, the students become part of what they refer to as a "family" of disadvantaged students, who participate together in social events, award ceremonies, and bimonthly discussions of topics such as adapting to college and keeping up with homework. The CARE program also operates a special resource facility with computers, counselors, and tutors.

The result of this all-encompassing effort is that FSU has a graduation rate for black students that exceeds the state average, including a traditional black college located only a mile from the FSU campus, by 17 percentage points and the national average by 30 percentage points. Although the program has not been carefully evaluated, the graduation rate of its students seems to indicate that the program is successful.[117]

Conclusion

The FSU program and other campus-based programs reviewed here show that it is possible for colleges themselves to help students make up for knowledge and skills they miss in high school. However, research also shows that students who take remedial courses to compensate for deficits they bring with them to the college campus are likely to drop out of college.[118] There is some evidence that campus programs can improve students' grades, rates of course completion, and persistence in school, but in nearly every case these effects are modest. The literature on the impacts of programs once students reach college indicate that truly powerful results are likely to require better preparation for college. We support campus-based programs and urge colleges and universities to adopt them, but we caution that better preparation for college starting as early as pre-K is probably more important than programs aiming to help students once they reach college.

nine
Supporting and Encouraging Work

Work became the cannonball of the Republican welfare reform agenda, blasting
straight ahead through all obstacles. As other issues—time limits, block grants, illegiti-
macy, child care—developed, work remained the central issue of the debate.

RON HASKINS

A major intellectual and political development in social policy over the past
quarter century has been widespread agreement among politicians, scholars,
and the public that the best antipoverty program is a job and that government policy should do everything possible to encourage poor people to work.
Reducing poverty and increasing mobility requires that all who can must
work and earn most of their income.

Before Congress enacted and President Bill Clinton signed the welfare
reform law of 1996, many people in the political and scholarly worlds believed that the first obligation of government was to ensure some basic level
of income and services for the destitute. Many who held this view gave lip
service to self-sufficiency and work, but they also cited numerous reasons the
poor could not work: there were no jobs, the wages of available jobs were too
low, most jobs were in the suburbs, single mothers should be able to stay
home with their children, the unemployed suffered from various afflictions,
and the poor needed more education.[1] But the 1996 legislation was based on
the assumption that policy should nonetheless convey the message that work
and self-sufficiency are expected, regardless of barriers to work that might
exist. Moreover, the legislation was built on the assumption that even if the
poor, given their inferior education and lack of work experience, could only
qualify for low-wage jobs, they would be better off working in these jobs than
staying on welfare because they would serve as a positive role model for their
children and their community and because a host of programs would supplement their income with cash and in-kind benefits and make them finan-
cially better off than if they were on welfare.

Welfare reform clarified what was latent in federal policy for many years: namely, that the able-bodied poor are expected by the public to work.[2] In the more than three decades between President Lyndon Johnson's declaration of the War on Poverty in 1964 and the 1996 welfare reform law, the major thrust of federal and state policy had been to attack poverty through the creation of a bewildering array of means-tested programs that consumed an ever increasing share of both federal spending and the nation's GDP.[3] The innovation of the 1996 legislation was the aggressive use of sanctions and time limits to enforce the expectation of work. There were two parts to the new policy: individuals were required to work, at the risk of losing their cash welfare benefit, and they were promised cash and in-kind support to supplement earnings and lift them out of poverty. Other than simply giving money to the elderly through the Social Security program to reduce poverty, this two-part strategy is the most successful policy the nation has yet devised to reduce poverty among the able bodied.[4]

Our goal in this chapter is to outline policies and programs that will strengthen both parts of this vital national strategy. More specifically, we first make a set of proposals to strengthen work support programs. These programs are designed to help low-income workers supplement their income, improve their standard of living, and possibly even qualify for jobs that pay more and provide employee benefits. We also make a series of proposals to increase the work requirements for welfare programs that provide cash benefits, housing, and food stamps (now the Supplemental Nutrition Assistance Program, or SNAP). Taken together, our proposals would result in more people working and in improved work support benefits for low-wage workers.

Supporting Work

The work support system is composed of programs that provide cash or in-kind benefits to low-income working individuals or families. The goal of the work support system is to boost the income of low-income working families while maintaining work incentive. Eight programs are vital parts of the work support system (table 9-1). Although these programs do not function as a smooth and well-coordinated system, they do provide scores of billions of dollars annually in cash and in-kind benefits and services to low-income working families.[5] We think that the system should provide even more benefits, some of which could be considered investments in human capital. A summary of the recommendations we make for improving the system and for increasing work is presented in table 9-2.

Table 9-1. Work Support Programs

Program	Description
Earned Income Tax Credit	Cash wage supplement paid annually through the tax code.
Child Tax Credit	Reduced tax payment for families with children; payable on limited basis to poor and low-income families who have earnings but not enough to pay income taxes.
Child care	Several programs that pay for or subsidize the cost of care for parents who work or attend school.
Food stamps	Supplemental Nutrition Assistance Program: payments to families through the use of debit cards to pay for food.
Medicaid/SCHIP	Pays for health care for children and, on a limited basis, adults.
Child Support Enforcement	Comprehensive (and usually free) program designed to encourage or force parents who do not live with their children (usually fathers) to pay child support.
Housing	Provides public housing free or at a reduced cost or provides subsidies to pay rent for low-income families.
Education and training	A host of programs that aim to help adolescents not bound for college and poor, low-income, or unemployed adults enhance their literacy or job skills to qualify for better jobs
Other	School lunch; school breakfast; Special Supplemental Food Program for Women, Infants, and Children.

Figure 9-1 provides an idea of both the magnitude of and trends in government spending on selected work support programs, based on work by Sheila Zedlewski and Seth Zimmerman of the Urban Institute. As shown by the last set of bar graphs, between 1996, when the welfare reform law was enacted, and 2005, spending on these four programs increased by $54 billion, or nearly 50 percent. A 50 percent increase in spending seems to indicate a serious commitment on the part of policymakers to creating a well-funded work support system. Closer inspection of the individual programs reveals, however, something quite different.

Consider child care. Child care is one of the most important work supports because low-income working families have much less income left for other necessities when they must pay for child care, especially if they must pay market rates. And yet, after a very substantial increase between 1996 and 2002, government funds available to help low-income families pay for child care actually declined between 2002 and 2005. In a study of child care arrangements of a large sample of low-income families from the nation's largest cities, Nicole Forry finds that only 28 percent of single mothers receive a subsidy for their child care.[6] She also finds that families receiving a subsidy pay nearly $2,400 less a year for child care than families not receiving a subsidy.

Table 9-2. Recommendations, Work Support Programs and Work Requirements

Recommendation	Goal
Work support system reforms	
Change threshold for child tax credit refundability to $8,500 from $12,050.	To increase income of low-income workers; to increase work incentive.
Phase out Dependent Care Tax Credit and Dependent Care Assistance Plan between $100,000 and $150,000 and add savings to Child Care and Development Block Grant.	To reduce work expenses of low-income workers; to increase take-home pay; to increase work incentive.
Modify rules on arrearages so that low-income fathers who pay current support on a regular basis can have their payment on arrearages suspended.	To increase child support payments to mothers; to reduce fathers' problems with overdue child support; to increase work incentive for fathers.
Convert housing to a limited entitlement so that all eligible households receive some benefit; finance by reducing the average size of the housing benefit.	To reduce rental payments of most low-income workers, thereby increasing their disposable income (rents for some workers would increase).
Expand existing apprenticeship program.	To increase employment levels and income for youth who do not attend college.
Expand career academies.	To increase employment levels and income for youth who do not attend college.
Create competitive block grant to fund training in the private sector, sectoral training, career building, and transition jobs.	To increase employment levels and income of youth, unemployed workers, and workers who upgrade skills.
Create mandatory work program for fathers paying child support and fathers leaving prison.	To increase employment and earnings among former prisoners and poor males who owe child support; to increase work incentive.
Create pilot programs that expand EITC for childless workers.	To increase take-home pay of childless workers; increase work incentive.
Reduce mandatory length of sentences for crack cocaine offenses and give judges more discretion in sentencing.	To avoid long sentences in cases in which judges determine that offenders can be handled through probation or relatively short sentences.
Work requirements	
Fund annual inflation adjustment.	To maintain level (inflation-adjusted) funding so states can continue to help families find work and pay benefits to families that cannot work.
Allow more education to count as work.	To allow states to help more low-income workers gain skills needed to get higher-paying jobs.
Create block grant to states to provide job search services and cash to adults who have chronic problems finding and holding jobs.	To reduce number of families that have no income from work or cash welfare; to help multiproblem parents get and hold jobs.
Provide competitive grants to help residents of public housing prepare for and find jobs by increasing work incentives and imposing work obligation.	To increase work rates of public housing residents.
Expand funding for state food stamp work programs that help recipients find jobs.	To increase work rates of food stamp recipients.

Figure 9-1. Federal and State Spending on Work Support Programs, 1996 and 2005

Billions of 2005 dollars

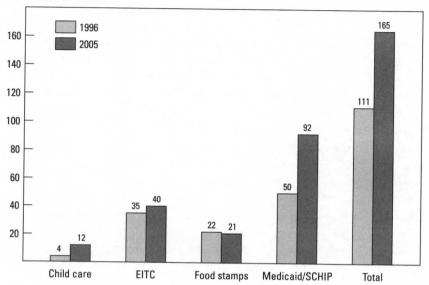

Source: Sheila Zedlewski and Seth Zimmerman, "Trends in Work Supports for Low-Income Families with Children," Brief 4 (Washington: Urban Institute, 2007), figure 1.

These results show that the cost of child care is still a major issue for many low-income working families.

Another issue is that increased spending on the work support system is dominated by health care. Since the State Children's Health Insurance Program (SCHIP) was enacted in 1997, combined spending on Medicaid and SCHIP has been higher than spending on any other type of work support and has increased the most in absolute dollars. Indeed, the increase of $42 billion between 1996 and 2005 represents nearly 80 percent of the total growth of work support spending and in itself is bigger than the total size of any of the other three programs shown in figure 9-1. Americans greatly value health care, and the public believes everyone should be covered.[7] But it is important not to allow these huge increases in spending on health insurance to leave the impression that spending on all or most of the work support programs has greatly increased. It has not.

Strengthening work supports advances most of our policy criteria (see chapter 1). Work supports improve equity because they are primarily financed by the nation's progressive income tax system and go primarily to low-income workers. Similarly, those who work at low incomes are playing by the rules, so our proposals to improve work supports reward an important element of the success sequence. Like most analysts, we favor policies that increase work incentive by increasing the returns to work or by subsidizing work costs, both of which result in a net increase in family income.[8]

Another criterion central to our analysis of work supports was whether there was empirical evidence that the incentives would actually increase work levels or contribute to raising family income. As in chapter 8, we would be prevented from making recommendations if we demanded that every recommendation be supported by stringent evidence. No matter what the state of evidence about a policy might be, we always recommend that funds be set aside to pay for high-quality evaluations of the effects of our recommendations. Continuous improvement based on outcomes established by research and evaluation is a major part of our strategy of developing effective programs.

Cost was another criterion we employed in both selecting policies and in outlining how they would be implemented. Where possible, we discuss benefit-cost evidence, but regardless of the benefit-cost ratios the evidence on benefits is usually modest to weak. Further, benefits occur primarily in the future, while costs are concrete and immediate. Given that we intend to specify how we will pay for all our recommendations, we have few grandiose recommendations for multibillion dollar programs. With these criteria in mind, we turn to recommendations on how to improve the work support system (table 9-2).

Cash from the Tax Code

Both the Earned Income Tax Credit (EITC) and the Child Tax Credit provide cash to working families, although many working families do not earn enough to take full advantage of either program. The EITC has led a charmed life in the nation's capital, enjoying nearly universal support.[9] Even President Ronald Reagan, famous for his skepticism about social programs, praised the bill containing a major increase in the EITC in 1986 by proclaiming that "it's also the best antipoverty bill, the best pro-family measure, and the best job-creation program ever to come out of the Congress of the United States."[10] Signed into law by President Gerald Ford in 1975, the EITC subsequently enjoyed major expansions in 1986, 1990, and 1993. The expansions of 1986 and 1990 were led by Republican presidents while the expansion of 1993 was led by a Democratic president.

As a result of the expansions, the maximum credit for 2008 is slightly less than $3,000 for a family with one child and slightly less than $5,000 for a family with two or more children. The credit phases out beginning at about $16,000 of income and ends completely at about $34,000 for a family with one child and just under $39,000 for a family with two or more children. The EITC also provides a small credit, worth around $450, to poor workers who do not have custody of children.[11] Evidence shows that the EITC is one of the most effective programs for increasing work among single mothers, although it may be associated with some reduction in work among second earners.[12] However, the childless worker credit, probably because of its small size, is much less effective at increasing work. If the childless worker credit is reformed along the lines we suggest below, we think it holds promise for increasing work and income among childless workers, especially men—precisely the group that has been largely ignored by American social policy.

The Child Tax Credit provides a credit of up to $1,000 per child against the federal income taxes of families with children under age seventeen and earnings above and below thresholds stipulated in the tax code. For families that have one child and earn enough to pay $1,000 or more in federal income taxes, the Child Tax Credit is straightforward—these families simply subtract $1,000 from their tax bill.[13]

For families that pay less than $1,000 in income taxes, another provision of the tax code provides a refundable Child Tax Credit, meaning that they get at least some of the money regardless of whether they owe income taxes. The refundable portion of the credit equals 15 percent of earnings above $12,050 in 2008. But because there are many families with earnings above zero but under $12,050, about 6 million children in these families receive nothing from the Child Tax Credit. In addition, in 2008 10 million children were in families that earned above the $12,050 threshold but not enough above to receive the entire $1,000 credit. Thus most part-time workers and those who work sporadically receive less than the maximum credit. A family with one child earning $18,717 would get the full credit of $1,000 (15 percent × [$18,717 − $12,050]).

We propose to increase the number of families and children that receive the full Child Tax Credit as well as to increase the amount of the credit received by millions of additional working families by reducing the earnings at which the refundable credit begins, from $12,050 to $8,500.[14] Thus working families would receive 15 percent of earnings of more than $8,500 rather than $12,050. According to the Center on Budget and Policy Priorities, this reform would extend the tax credit to 2.9 million additional children in working families.[15] Because of the shift in the phase-out range associated with reducing the threshold to $8,500, the credit would increase for families with an additional 10 million children. This proposal, which was actually passed by the House in 2008, would help 480,000 parents who provide health care services for the elderly or disabled; 240,000 who work in child care; 310,000 who work in cleaning and building maintenance; and 470,000 who work as cooks or waiters. The Congressional Budget Office estimates that the cost of our proposal would be about $3.1 billion a year.[16]

The Child Tax Credit and the EITC are the backbone of the nation's work support system because they constitute a work incentive for most families and provide a major boost to the income of low-income workers. Our proposal on the Child Tax Credit would provide an even greater boost to the incomes of families that receive this credit. We have more to say about the EITC below.

Child Care

Arguably the weakest link in the work support system is child care. If government and the public want an effective system for helping parents avoid welfare and for supporting all low-income workers with children, helping parents pay for child care is both necessary and desirable.

Many scholars and advocates argue that child care should be of sufficient quality so that, in addition to supporting work, it supports the goal of enhancing children's development. We support putting children of low-income workers into high-quality nursery, preschool, and afterschool programs (see chapter 8). But these programs are very expensive, and there will still be a need for additional child care to support school-age children, wrap-around care for those in preschool, and care for infants and toddlers who are not in preschool. There is not enough public money available to pay for high-quality care for all low-income children. It follows that, for the foreseeable future, we will need both inexpensive, modest-quality care and high-quality care. Nonetheless, we argue for gradually improving both ordinary day care and preschool education.[17] Grow them both is our motto.

Between 1997, a year after the welfare reform law passed, and 2003 day care spending more than doubled, from $7.2 billion to $15 billion, before falling somewhat in 2004 and 2005 as state budgets came under pressure.[18] The big increase in the years following welfare reform is impressive, but at least two major problems remain.

The first is that too few low-income families receive help. Federal rules allow states to use federal dollars to provide day care subsidies to families with incomes under 85 percent of the state median income, although many states set a limit below this federal maximum.[19] Around 12 percent of families eligible under federal guidelines and 28 percent eligible under state guidelines actually receive child care subsidies.[20] In this respect, government support for child care used by low-income families is like government payments for the housing used by low-income families (see below). Both programs receive a capped amount of money each year from Congress. In the case of child care, the money is then given to states. The states augment the federal funds with their own money—including money from their share of the Temporary Assistance for Needy Families (TANF) block grant—and then ration the money among eligible recipients in such a way that millions of eligible children receive help and millions of equally qualified children do not. This approach, justified exclusively by government budget limitations, is a straightforward violation of the equity principle.

The second major problem is that many of the families that do not receive a day care subsidy wind up paying a significant fraction of their income for child care. In addition to the study by Forry discussed above, nationally representative data from the Census Bureau illustrate the problem: estimates suggest that low-income families (100 to 199 percent of poverty) that paid for care spent an average of 14.5 percent of their income, compared with 5.6 percent of income for higher-income families (200 percent or more of poverty) in 2005.[21] Given that the major goal of the work support system is to increase the net income of low-income working families, helping more families pay for child care would be a big step in the right direction.

To address these problems, the federal government provides support for child care both through the tax code and through grant programs. Here we consider the two major tax code provisions and the two major grant programs.[22]

The two most important tax code provisions are the Dependent Care Tax Credit and the Dependent Care Assistance Program (DCAP). Under the child care credit, parents who work or attend school are entitled to a credit on the cost of their child care (both parents must work or go to school to qualify in the case of two-parent families). The credit equals between 20 percent and 35 percent of child care expenses, with the percentage varying inversely with income, up to a maximum of $3,000 for one child and $6,000 for two or more children. In 2006 the credit provided $2.8 billion in tax benefits to parents.[23] The child care credit is consistent with the principle, reflected by many provisions of the tax code, that tax advantages for both individuals and companies should offset the cost of doing business. Clearly, parents' costs for someone watching their children while they work is a business expense.

However, the tax code should also reflect the principle of equity, under which families with lower income receive a relatively bigger tax break, at least in percentage terms. The Dependent Care Tax Credit in part reflects this principle, because families earning under $15,000 get the full 35 percent credit, which then falls by 1 percentage point for each additional $2,000 of earnings until the credit reaches 20 percent for earnings of $43,000 or more. So far, so good. But because the credit applies only to families with federal income tax liability, single-mother, single-child families with incomes under roughly

$15,000 and two-parent, two-child families with incomes under roughly $25,000 pay no federal income taxes and are therefore ineligible for the credit. Many of these families qualify for child care subsidies under the Child Care and Development Block Grant, but because funding for the block grant is capped, several million eligible families receive no benefits. In short, while millionaires get a federal reimbursement for part of their child care expenses, millions of poor and low-income working families are left out of both the tax and grant programs. Len Burman and his colleagues at the Tax Policy Center show that in 2005, families earning under $20,000 received less than 1 percent of total funds distributed through the child care tax credit, while families earning over $50,000 got 67 percent of the funds.[24] This situation is another clear violation of the equity principle, thereby providing a good argument for reforming the provision. Similarly, the DCAP program, which provides an exclusion of up to $5,000 of spending on child care from pretax income, helps virtually no low-income workers.[25]

In addition to these tax code provisions, the federal government and the states provide child care assistance to families through two major grant programs, the Child Care and Development Block Grant and the TANF Block Grant. The former provides states with $2.9 billion annually in federal dollars that must be partially matched by state dollars to subsidize the child care costs of low-income working families.[26] States have great flexibility in the use of block grant funds as long as they ensure that families are allowed to choose their own provider, the care meets minimum health and safety standards, and spending is confined to low-income families. TANF provides states with $16.5 billion in federal dollars annually, which must also be partially matched, to support poor families with cash or other benefits, to promote the formation and maintenance of two-parent families, and to support work.[27] Every state uses some of its TANF dollars to subsidize child care. In 2006, the last year for which data are available, states used about $3.5 billion of the TANF money to pay for child care.[28]

There are two major problems with the current system of tax benefits and grant programs. The first, already discussed, is the inequity in benefits provided through the tax code. The second is that not enough federal and state money is available through the block grants to subsidize an adequate number of slots of child care.

In view of these two problems, we would increase federal funding of the Child Care and Development Block Grant. We would both promote equity and provide care of modest quality to more families by phasing out payments for married-couple families with incomes of between $100,000 and $150,000 ($75,000–$100,000 for others) from both the tax code's Dependent Care Tax

Credit and the DCAPS exclusion. Phasing out the tax credit would save approximately $1 billion a year, which we would then transfer to the Child Care and Development Block Grant to be used in the same fashion as block grant funds are now used.[29] We would supplement this $1 billion with an additional $1 billion, to bring the total annual increase in the child care block grant to $2 billion, which in turn would increase the number of children receiving full-time, year-round care by 240,000.[30] If states used a sliding fee scale, which many do under current law, they could subsidize more than 240,000 children of low-income working parents.

Health Insurance

Medicaid was a major part of President Johnson's War on Poverty. Enacted in 1965, the program provides health care to the poor and disabled and nursing home care to the poor elderly.[31] As originally enacted, eligibility for Medicaid was tied to welfare.[32] The problem with the link between welfare and Medicaid was that, if parents left welfare for work, they and their children lost their Medicaid coverage. With a policy like this, adults could make a rational decision not to work because most jobs for which they could qualify offered either no or very limited health insurance coverage. During the 1980s, Congress, realizing this antiwork problem with Medicaid, began changing eligibility, making it possible for mothers to leave welfare and retain their coverage and their children's coverage for a limited period of time.[33] On a parallel track, beginning in the mid-1980s Congress enacted a series of reforms that gradually phased in Medicaid coverage for children up to age eighteen in families below the poverty level and provided states with options to cover children up to 185 percent of poverty.[34] The provision is now completely phased in: all poor children under the age of eighteen are covered, and states have options that allow them to expand coverage beyond 100 percent of poverty.

SCHIP began in 1997 when Congress, on a bipartisan basis, again expanded health insurance coverage for children. This program provides states with additional funds to expand Medicaid or to create a Medicaid-like program to provide health insurance to children from families with incomes up to 200 percent of the poverty level (about $34,700 for a family of three in 2008). Today nearly all children in families below 200 percent of poverty are eligible for coverage by Medicaid or SCHIP, and the 2009 expansion of SCHIP, when fully implemented, will provide coverage to more than 5 million additional children.[35] Even before the expansion, the combination of Medicaid and SCHIP had contributed to a remarkable increase in the number of children with health insurance coverage, from 21.3 million in 1995 to 37.7 million in 2008.[36]

Although the nation's health care coverage of poor children can be called a success, the glaring flaw in the system is that their mothers are not covered. The 1996 welfare reform law required states to provide mothers leaving welfare for employment with at least one year of coverage, and some states provide even more than a year. But most mothers who leave welfare lose their coverage after a year, both because their Medicaid guarantee ends and because their jobs tend to have either no health insurance or only a stripped-down form of health insurance. In addition to jeopardizing the health of the mother, the absence of coverage for mothers is an indirect threat to their children's health. Research shows that mothers who do not themselves have insurance are less likely to take their children to the doctor for routine and preventive care.[37]

This spotty coverage for mothers is seen by many analysts and advocates as a serious failure of the work support system, especially since mothers leaving welfare are not the only uncovered group of mothers. Poor mothers who never go on welfare have no comprehensive government health insurance unless they are pregnant or disabled. Thus the lack of coverage for low-income adults is a problem in its own right and constitutes a flaw in the nation's work support system. We have little confidence that coverage by employers will expand to provide this group with better coverage. Indeed, coverage by employers is already shrinking.[38]

But the cost to repair this problem is surprisingly large. Alan Weil, one of the top health policy scholars and practitioners in the nation, has proposed creating a federal earned income health credit, modeled on the EITC, that would enable the working poor to combine their own, their employer's, and public coverage to achieve health insurance for all family members.[39] The cost of his proposal is $45 billion a year. However, we do not support this proposal because we believe it would be better to cover low-income workers as part of an overhaul of the entire U.S. health care insurance system. The large numbers of uninsured, together with the rising cost of health care (which has increased at roughly twice the rate of inflation for several decades), and the fact that health care costs threaten to bankrupt the federal government within two or three decades, mean that fundamental reform is coming, perhaps sooner rather than later.[40] Virtually every serious reform proposal features either universal coverage or something very close to universal coverage.

Food Stamps

The food stamp program gives recipients a debit card, redeemable at most grocery stores, for a fixed amount each month. The maximum annual benefit in 2008 was about $5,000 for a family of three, but the typical working single mother with two children receives a food subsidy worth much less than $5,000 a year because the food stamp benefit begins phasing out at incomes above approximately $5,000 and reaches zero at the program's gross annual income limit of $22,330 for a family of three (or less).[41] Until 2002 the food stamp program was not as helpful to working families as it might have been, largely because states tightly administered the program to avoid errors that could result in federal fines. But a number of changes in the 2002 Farm Bill encouraged states to make it easier for working families to sign up.[42]

Administrative data from the Department of Agriculture show that food stamp participation rates have increased remarkably since the 2002 reforms.[43] Participation increased from just 54 percent of those eligible in 2002 to 67 percent of those eligible in 2006, an increase of nearly 25 percent.[44] There is still plenty of room for improvement, but it seems clear that states are doing a better job of getting benefits to eligible working families. With an average individual benefit of nearly $1,150 a year in 2007, the 25 percent increased participation rate represents an additional $2.1 billion in the pockets of low-income families, many of them working families.[45] These encouraging figures show how important it is to include eligible families in work support programs.

Other than ensuring that eligible working families sign up for food stamps, a topic we address later in this chapter, we have no additional recommendations for food stamp reform (except strengthening work requirements). State performance in getting benefits to eligible families is still improving and thereby already strengthening the work support system.

Child Support Enforcement

Child Support Enforcement is not usually defined as a work support program. But it should be, because child support often results in a stream of money flowing to low-income families headed by working single mothers. Even better, the money is paid by fathers, thereby reducing the burden on taxpayers and perhaps indicating to children living with their mother that their father is concerned about them and makes an effort to support them. But of even greater importance for our purposes, a steady stream of income from child support would allow many mothers to get off and stay off welfare and would simultaneously improve the financial condition of the mothers and children.

Child Support Enforcement is a federal and state program that enjoys immense bipartisan support in Washington and most state capitals. Enacted in 1975, the program has been greatly strengthened by reforms on several occasions, especially in 1996. To locate fathers, establish paternity, establish a child support order, and collect payments, the federal-state system is now highly automated and collects a huge sum of money. Between 1995, the year before the last major set of reforms, and 2007, child support collections increased from $12 billion to $25 billion, almost certainly reflecting the 1996 reforms.[46]

Despite the increased effectiveness of the Child Support Program, though, only about 28 percent of single mothers received any child support in 2006, and low-income mothers are less likely to receive it than wealthier mothers (figure 9-2). For mothers in the bottom income quintile, which includes all single mothers with total incomes under about $17,000 in 2006, only 19 percent received child support payments. Nor are the payments they receive very large. If we ignore the mothers in the bottom two quintiles who received no payment, the average annual payment was $2,500 and $3,250, respectively. Although these amounts improve the economic circumstances of poor mothers, the average amounts are pitiful. After three decades of the program, and after several waves of reform, the typical mother in the bottom income quintile—the mothers we are most concerned about—receives nothing, and the average mother in the bottom two quintiles gets only around $670 a year. It would seem to follow that the prospects are modest for greatly increasing either the percent of mothers who receive payments or the amount they receive.

We strongly endorse the Child Support Enforcement Program, but we think it unwise to count on child support from fathers as a way to increase the income of most poor mothers. Even if we could make the state enforcement programs more efficient, it seems likely that the improvement would be marginal. The biggest barrier to substantially increased collections is low earnings by males, especially the males who owe child support to poor and low-income mothers. Without an increase in both the proportion of young males who have earnings and the amount they earn, it is unlikely that child support collections for low-income mothers and children will increase very much or that child support can become a reliable and steady source of income for most of these mothers.

We recommend one reform that should, in the long run, have a positive effect on the amount of child support paid by fathers. Many young fathers, including those who serve terms in prison, accumulate large child support debt. It is not unusual for a young man to owe $10,000 or more in child support back payments (called arrearages).[47] As a result, he must pay both the current child support amount and then an additional amount to retire his bill for arrearages. The Child Support Enforcement Program is so efficient at locating the employers of fathers who owe child support and automatically

Figure 9-2. Single-Mother Households Receiving Child Support Payments from Fathers, by Income Quintile, 1990–2006

Percent receiving support

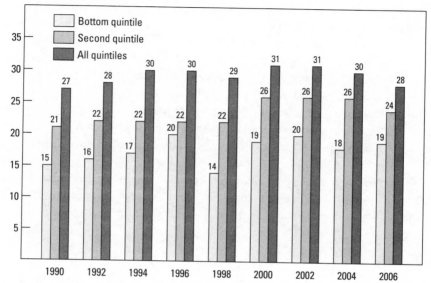

Source: Calculations by Richard Bavier based on data from U.S. Census Bureau, *Current Population Survey, Annual Social and Economic Supplement*, in personal communication, March 20, 2009.

deducting a payment from their paycheck that many of these young men do not have enough money left for themselves. States may deduct up to 65 percent of the father's after-tax earnings.[48] When combined with Social Security and income taxes, the child support payments of these fathers yield an implicit tax rate that could easily reach 70 percent or higher. Under these circumstances, fathers often refuse to accept jobs in the regular economy and work only off the books, sometimes in illegal activities.

The bite from these fathers' regular paycheck could be reduced if federal and state governments and single mothers were willing to suspend arrearage payments on the condition that fathers make regular and timely payments of their current child support amount. If the father pays this reduced amount on a regular basis, mothers would be able to count on a steady stream of tax-free income. Although we would like to impose a requirement on states that they initiate work activities for fathers as part of their child support arrangements between mothers and fathers, too little is known about how and whether this approach would work to propose it as mandatory. Thus our proposal is to spend around $30 million a year for five years to pay for large-scale, voluntary, demonstrations by several states of arrearage suspension. Our proposal involves four components:

—One, establishing procedures and training for negotiators working with mothers and fathers. In effect, the mother is agreeing to suspend her share of the collections on arrearages as long as the father stays current with child support payments. This agreement would be a legal document, which suggests that lawyers or at least paralegal professionals must be involved. States may have to develop specialized units and personnel to conduct these negotiations.

—Two, suspension of the state share of past-due support. We propose that the federal government split this cost with the states.

—Three, suspension of the federal share of past-due support.

—Four, rigorous evaluations of the programs, using random assignment where possible.

The federal government would pay the entire cost of the demonstrations. The secretary of Health and Human Services would select the states, oversee the evaluation, and ensure that the $30 million annual budget was not exceeded.

Housing

The biggest expenditure in the budget of most households is housing. The Department of Housing and Urban Development (HUD) defines housing as affordable if a family spends no more than 30 percent of its income for rent or mortgage payments. Many of the households we are concerned about earn $20,000 or less a year. Ignoring taxes, by HUD standards these households should spend a maximum of $6,000 a year, or $500 a month, for housing. In most markets, $500 a month for housing is a tight squeeze. In some markets, it's all but impossible.[49] Not surprisingly, some low-income households spend 50 percent or more of their income on housing—and even then, the neighborhood is likely to be fraught with problems. Poor neighborhoods have poor schools, and poor schools greatly limit children's chances of achieving economic mobility. Poor neighborhoods are often dangerous, especially for children: in 2005, 1,625 children under the age of eighteen were murdered, mostly in their own neighborhoods.[50] Further, poor neighborhoods may not have easy access to shopping, parks, libraries, and public transportation.

The federal government has been involved in housing since the 1930s, with policies based on the goal of ensuring "a decent home and a suitable living environment for every American family."[51] To achieve this goal, in 2007 the federal government spent $58.7 billion on means-tested programs that supported over 4.7 million households and another $5.1 billion on the Low-

Income Housing Tax Credit (LIHTC).[52] This total of $47.3 billion on low-income housing is more than the federal government spends on any other area of means-tested social policy except health insurance. The appropriated money is spent primarily on four types of housing programs:

—Public housing, which consists of buildings owned and operated by government and rented to low-income families at free or reduced-price rent.

—Project-based rental assistance, in which the federal government pays a subsidy to property owners, sometimes by helping the investor get an FHA mortgage at a favorable rate to build or rehabilitate the property, in return for which the owner agrees to make some of the units available to low-income families for a period of time (twenty to forty years).

—Tenant-based vouchers, in which beneficiaries receive a given amount of money, adjusted for family size and income, to enter the market and rent an apartment of their choosing that meets minimum standards.

—Block grants that provide money to local housing authorities to spend on housing.

When the federal government first entered the housing market before World War II, and then more seriously after the war, an inadequate supply of houses was still a major issue for the nation.[53] But the American housing market, based on technological and organizational innovations, new methods of financing, and the seemingly insatiable desire of Americans for bigger and more expensive housing, exploded in the 1950s and only occasionally slowed down until the housing crisis that began in 2007.[54] Americans are now the best housed people in history, although poor and low-income families struggle mightily to afford a decent place to live. Even among the poor, however, housing has improved greatly over the small and ill-equipped housing that received public support in the 1940s and 1950s.[55]

The origin of federal housing policy in a time of housing shortages is still reflected in support for programs designed to create more housing. According to the housing expert Edgar Olsen of the University of Virginia, "Project-based rental assistance is the dominant form of housing assistance to low-income families in the United States."[56] Nonetheless, over the past two decades or so, there has been a gradual move away from project-based assistance, such as public housing or subsidies for construction, and toward the use of vouchers.[57] In the 1960s and 1970s Congress stopped authorizing construction of high-rise public housing and began ordering its destruction.[58] Since then the number of units of public housing has declined, from a peak of 1.41 million in 1991 to only about 1.16 million in 2007, a decline of more than 20 percent.[59]

But the problem with high-rise public housing is not the only reason the federal government is moving toward vouchers and individual choice. Nearly every study of the relative cost of project-based assistance compared with vouchers shows that project-based housing is between 30 percent and 90 percent more expensive.[60] As Olsen shows, the shift away from government involvement in the construction and management of housing will certainly save money and will do so without reducing the average quality of housing.[61] Choice also allows recipients to pick better neighborhoods and to move closer to work.

The shift toward vouchers, although an improvement over project-based funding, does not solve the single greatest problem with the nation's housing policy, namely, the huge inequity in the distribution of housing benefits. Entitlement programs like food stamps, Medicaid, and school lunch provide guaranteed benefits to all who meet program requirements, and everyone lives under the same set of benefits and rules. Whatever else might be said about these programs, they do a fine job of meeting the equity criterion. By contrast, housing programs are like day care subsidies in that Congress does not authorize enough spending to provide the benefit to everyone who qualifies. As Janet Currie of Columbia University points out, a particularly troubling result of rationing is that 43 percent of the households receiving federal housing subsidies are above the poverty line, while 30 percent of those below the poverty line receive nothing.[62] Similarly, a 1999 HUD study finds that in some cities the wait for housing was six to eight years.[63] When some households receive a monthly housing subsidy of $1,000 or more while other identical, or even lower-income, households receive nothing, policymakers need to take action.

We propose to create an entitlement to housing assistance that would both resolve the problem of inequity and convert housing into an effective element in the nation's work support system. Our vision is to use the resources now devoted to housing to the benefit of all eligible families needing a housing subsidy. To finance our proposal, we would phase out, perhaps over a ten-year period, all programs that support construction, including public housing, project-based assistance, and the Low-Income Housing Tax Credit.[64] We would then put all the savings in the current voucher program, somewhat modified—as outlined below.

Here's the math. We begin with the 2007 appropriation for vouchers and other rental assistance of $25.7 billion. To this we add the $7.3 billion from public housing, the $0.6 billion from "other" housing assistance, and the $7.0 billion from block grants, bringing the total amount available for the housing entitlement to $40.6 billion. We would leave in place the $1.7 billion now spent on programs for homeless households. From this pot of more than

$40 billion, how many households would receive a benefit and how would the size of the benefit be determined?

Our recommendation is based in large part on an intriguing proposal put forth by Edgar Olsen and Jeffrey Tebbs, formerly of Brookings.[65] Their proposal is in turn based on the Housing Assistance Supply Experiment (HASE) conducted in Green Bay, Wisconsin, and South Bend, Indiana, by Rand in the 1970s.[66] A basic concept underlying the reform proposals, current housing programs, and HASE is fair market rent. Fair market rents are generally equal to the 40th percentile of the cost of apartments with a given number of bedrooms in the local housing market.[67] The actual federal subsidy for a given household is the local fair market rent minus 30 percent of adjusted household income or the actual rent, whichever is lower. Thus if the fair market rent for a family of a given size in a particular location were $800 a month and the family had an adjusted income of $1,000 a month, the family would receive a subsidy of $800 minus $300 (30 percent × $1,000), or $500.

Following Olsen and Tebbs, we would guarantee eligible families a subsidy and keep our proposal cost-neutral by adjusting the fair market rent to accommodate the amount of funding available. In other words, we would reduce the average value of housing subsidies in order to provide a smaller subsidy to more families. Recipients could use their voucher to either rent an apartment or pay their mortgage.

Given the pool of a little more than $40 billion created by combining funds in the current housing voucher program with funds from the terminated programs, and our estimate that about 7.2 million households would accept the offer of a voucher, the average voucher would be worth around $5,640 a year.[68] This figure represents about a 20 percent reduction in the average housing subsidy received by households under current law. Our proposal, then, represents a straightforward trade-off: reduce current housing subsidies by about 20 percent in order to provide the subsidy to roughly 3 million additional families. We would, however, phase in the new program over a decade or so in order to minimize the impacts of the subsidy reduction on current recipients, most of whom will drop out of the housing program of their own volition over the ten-year period.[69] To strengthen the likelihood that residents of public housing work, we would also encourage the local housing authority to give subsidies only to families that have jobs, or are exempt from the work requirement because of old age or disability, or meet the local housing authority's work requirements.

In addition to promoting equity in the distribution of federal benefits, our proposal could result in a stronger incentive to work, because millions of additional low-income households would be able to count on a housing sub-sidy. Further, the efficiency of federal housing programs would be enhanced by eliminating construction and government ownership programs. Finally, voucher recipients could choose their own housing and thereby at least have the opportunity to improve the quality of the neighborhood and the schools their children attend.[70] They could also choose to live nearer to employment centers. And all this is purchased for the same number of federal dollars now being spent on the nation's housing programs.

Employment and Training Programs

The lack of mobility of low-wage workers with a high school degree or less convinces us that, although some workers do advance in the low-wage econ-omy, millions are floundering in the bottom of the wage distribution (below, say, $20,000 a year in income).[71] A major cause of the economic mobility prob-lem is that the number of low-skill jobs that pay high wages has diminished greatly in recent decades.[72] Thus promoting economic mobility requires fig-uring out how to boost the skills of low-wage workers. Without doing much to boost the skills of low-wage workers, and concentrating primarily on low-income mothers, the welfare reform strategy of combining work requirements and work supports has done about as much good as it can do. The changes we recommend to the work support system will modestly reduce poverty and boost mobility, but a major impact on either poverty or mobility needs new approaches. These should include a renewed commitment to enroll ever more children from low-income families in high-quality preschool programs, in reading-oriented programs in the early grades, and in postsecondary educa-tion (strategies discussed in chapter 8). But an equally important and more immediate strategy should be to strengthen employment and training pro-grams that provide a boost to the human capital of young people leaving high school and older workers already employed (or unemployed) who are unlikely to ever enroll in four-year colleges.

Again, the equity principle arises. Between the public and private sectors, the nation spends more than $160 billion on grants, loans, and tax credits to students attending undergraduate and graduate institutions.[73] The College Board estimates that in 2007–08 the average aid for each undergraduate stu-dent was around $8,900, or more than $35,000 for a four-year degree; the aver-age aid per graduate student was more than $20,000, or around $80,000 if the graduate degree were completed in four years.[74] The students receiving this college aid are disproportionately from families that are middle class and above.[75] Although it is difficult to get a comparable figure for per capita invest-ments in training programs, federal, state, and local spending on employment and training was slashed from its high of $28.6 billion in 1978 to a little over $7 billion in 2004, a decline of more than 75 percent in constant dollars.[76] Thus it is not surprising that the average investment per participant in Department of Labor job training programs was around $2,900 per person in 2002.[77] These programs disproportionately serve young people from poor and low-income families. As Robert Lerman of the Urban Institute argues, if America's goal of opportunity for all is to be fulfilled, the country will need to spend more money on training programs for those who do not attend college.[78]

Today, after more than four decades of evolving policies, most employment and training programs have been consolidated under the Workforce Investment Act (WIA), which was passed by Congress on a bipartisan basis in 1998. The act requires states to meld several federal employment and training funding streams to create a coordinated system for meeting the needs of those who have lost their jobs, those hoping to find a job, and those trying to upgrade their skills. The evidence suggests that current WIA services probably provide a modest boost to income.[79] A high-quality evaluation of the Job Training Partnership Act, the forerunner to WIA, finds that adults in the group receiving services earn about $1,180 (in 2007 dollars) a year more than controls.[80]

While it is true that employment and training programs are making some difference, too many workers continue to earn low wages even after years of labor market experience.[81] Effective education and training programs could help more workers avoid low and stagnant earnings. These include displaced workers who have lost their jobs, often in declining sectors of the economy; high school dropouts; those who have a tenuous hold on the labor market, earn low wages, and have difficulty finding better jobs; youngsters coming out of high school and not intending to go to college; and poorly educated single mothers. Our proposals are organized around youth, low-wage and unemployed adults, and young males.

Programs for Youth. The evidence on employment and training programs for youth is mixed. The evaluation of the Job Training Partnership Act finds statistically significant though modest effects on adult earnings but no significant impacts on youth employment or earnings.[82] Similarly, a meta-analysis of thirty-one evaluations of training programs for disadvantaged adults and youth finds that the earning effects of the programs were "largest for women, quite modest for men, and negligible for youths."[83] Even scientific evaluations of the Jobs Corps, which reveal significant impacts on youth earnings for up to thirty months after the end of the year-long residential program, find that these impacts fade away by four years after random assignment.[84]

A program called Career Academies has a better track record. Career Academies have three distinguishing characteristics. First, to compensate for the size of large high schools, Career Academies are organized as a school within a school, with 150 to 200 students who attend classes together, have the same teachers, and have the same counselors and administrators. Second, the curriculum is a combination of regular academic courses and technical courses related to employment. Third, the academies form partnerships with local businesses to provide students with direct work experience. There are about 2,500 Career Academies in operation in American schools.

A recent study by MDRC provides strong evidence that Career Academies have a major impact on employment and earnings as well as on marriage rates.[85] The evaluation was based on a gold-standard design that followed more than 2,000 students for eight years after their scheduled date of high school graduation. The design randomly chose the students from among those who attended a career academy and those who attended a regular high school. Males in the academy group had sustained earnings gains that began in the first four years after graduation and held steady during the second four-year follow-up period. Over the entire eight years of follow-up, males in the academy group averaged nearly $2,100 in annual earnings—or a total of almost $17,000—above the earnings of young males who did not attend a career academy. This 11 percent gain in earnings is roughly comparable to the earnings boost received when students achieve a credential from a two-year community college. Nor were these earnings gains achieved at the price of reduced attendance in postsecondary institutions. Critics have long contended that a major problem with vocational education is that it reduces the chances that a high school student would enroll in postsecondary education. But students who attended Career Academies were equally likely to achieve a postsecondary credential as students who did not: about 50 percent in both groups.

Equally remarkable, students who had attended the Career Academies were 33 percent more likely to be married, 46 percent more likely to be a custodial parent, and 36 percent less likely to be a noncustodial parent.[86] Again, these impacts were confined to males. Thus the career academy is one of the few social intervention programs that has been shown to significantly increase marriage rates and decrease the incidence of fathers living apart from their children.[87] This finding suggests that earnings are a key factor in making young males attractive marriage partners.

The success of the Career Academies leads us to place considerable faith in programs that emphasize direct experience in the workforce, combined with classroom study, for young people. The programs that most emphasize work experience in skilled jobs are apprenticeship programs. These programs place youth in jobs for three or four years of learning while also enrolling them in courses that emphasize both theoretical and practical knowledge about their chosen profession. As of 2008 about 450,000 workers were in registered apprenticeship programs.[88] A study by Washington State shows that more than 90 percent of those who complete apprenticeship programs were employed seven to nine months after training; the median hourly wage for those who completed the program and were later employed was over $31, well above the wages of workers who completed any other training program in the state.[89] Jobs that pay at this level are precisely the outcome we want for young people who don't go to college.

The Bureau of Apprenticeship and Training at the U.S. Department of Labor has been in the business of promoting internships and registering qualified programs since 1937. But the bureau operates on an annual budget of only $20 million. We recommend that Congress provide the bureau with another $40 million annually to expand their operations and to hire a third party to conduct a scientific evaluation of representative apprenticeship programs around the country. If over the next decade or so the number of apprenticeships could be quadrupled, as many as 2 million young people could be placed in good jobs with decent long-term prospects. If the Washington State evaluation is any indication, few of these young people would be at risk of falling into poverty, and their economic mobility would rise.

While federal legislation to provide funds for Career Academies and apprenticeships would be useful, we also recommend that state and local governments make major new investments in both Career Academies and apprenticeships. The large-scale evaluation of Career Academies shows that they are one of the most effective interventions yet attempted with young men. The states should now use some of the federal dollars they have through the Workforce Investment Act and other sources to expand Career Academies and apprenticeships. Both of these interventions increase the earnings of youth and could have additional benefits, such as increasing marriage rates.

Low-Wage Adults and Displaced Workers. Two major problems with the employment and training strategy for low-wage adults must be overcome if the strategy is to be effective in reducing poverty and increasing mobility. First, research evidence shows that the programs do not consistently affect employment or earnings.[90] Second, the federal government has drastically cut spending on the programs, so that even if they were successful, there would be too little money to enroll a significant fraction of low-income or unemployed individuals who could benefit from the programs.

Two institutions are the heart of employment and training: the nation's 1,200 community colleges and the 3,400 one-stop centers. Community colleges are vibrant and growing. As we saw in chapter 8, two-year colleges confer a substantial wage boost on those who manage to complete degree requirements.

One of the most attractive features of community colleges, as their name implies, is that they are responsive to local needs. They are also the major delivery system for making more practical, work-oriented training available to both youth and adults. The federal role should be confined to financing evaluation studies, promoting other accountability measures, and providing money for student tuition and expenses. To some extent, the federal government is already fulfilling all three of these roles (chapter 8).

We recommend using both community colleges and one-stop centers to deliver more education and training. More specifically, we support Harry Holzer's recommendation, made in a report for the Brookings Hamilton Project, that the federal government create a new competitive block grant called the Worker Advancement Grants for Employment in States (WAGES).[91] During the initial years of the WAGES program, states would compete for a share of $2 billion a year in funding to implement programs targeted at the working poor, at-risk youth, and hard-to-employ adults. The secretary of the Labor Department would select not more than twenty of the best proposals submitted by states that agreed to put up dollar-for-dollar matching funds. State funds would have to be above the amount the state currently spends on employment and training programs. WAGES programs for low-income workers could include training for employees in the private sector, sectoral training for jobs that can be shown to exist in the local economy, and career-ladder building. Programs for youth could include technical education and Career Academies. Programs for the hard to employ could include transitional jobs and training for jobs that provide opportunities for promotion. All of these types of employment and training programs have been shown to produce meaningful impacts on employment or wages.[92]

States submitting proposals would also be required to provide evidence that local businesses, community colleges, high schools, workforce associations, and other intermediaries have participated in the development of their plan and support the final plan submitted for funding. Proposals would need to show how services would be delivered through existing one-stop centers, community colleges, and other workforce entities. States would be assured of five years of funding as long as they continue to operate the program proposed in their original application. States would be required to agree to third-party evaluations, which the secretary of the Labor Department would arrange, to determine which program models were successful. Holzer presents an interesting analysis, based largely on high-quality evaluation studies, showing that spending on the WAGES program could result in income returns that far exceed the federal and state investment.

Considering the magnitude of the problem, we think an investment of $2 billion a year in this strategy is well worthwhile. If the nation is to develop employment and training programs that allow workers to acquire the skills needed to qualify for jobs with higher wages and benefits, it will be necessary to develop a workforce system operated by experienced managers and case-workers who can design effective programs and guide low-skilled workers into the programs and then into good jobs. The training of program admin-istrators and caseworkers will be critical as will continuous evaluation and continuous program improvement. Careful evaluations show that successful programs are possible; now it is up to states to develop good programs on a larger scale. The Holzer WAGES program could prove an important step toward achieving this goal.

Young Men. It is impossible not to be concerned about young men in America, especially young black men in the inner cities. As we have shown, in recent years young men have had declining work rates and increasing incar-ceration rates, two trends that are in all likelihood related. Yet the nation's social programs largely ignore men. Males, like every poor person, qualify for food stamps, but they are usually not eligible for TANF cash or for Medicaid, and it is nearly impossible for a single young man to obtain a housing bene-fit. The government does have one program in which administrators are anx-ious to have men participate: Child Support Enforcement, a program that has the legal authority to seize over half of a man's income.

We propose above that the Child Support Program modify its procedures so that males owing past-due child support can have their arrearages sus-pended as long as they pay their child support on time in the future. But much more needs to be done than simply helping fathers reduce their bur-densome child support payments. As Larry Mead argues, figuring out how to help young males is especially difficult because many of them participate in what Mead calls an "oppositional culture."[93] As we have seen, Orlando Pat-terson at Harvard has written extensively about the attitudes and behavior of young black men. He argues that the criminal and behavioral problems of black youth are due in part to the "catastrophic state of black family life."[94] As a result, young black men have created what he calls the "cool pose culture," which functions "almost like a drug" in compelling them to hang out on the street, dress sharply, make sexual conquests, use drugs, and listen to hip-hop music with lyrics glorifying violence, misogyny, drugs, and sex.[95] How to break the hold of this culture, which Patterson thinks now has about a fifth of young black males in its grip, is a vital issue for both the black community and the country. We recommend the following three policies.

First, Mead proposes that programs that have some leverage with men, especially Child Support Enforcement and prison release programs, use their authority to require males to conform to societal expectations by working. In the case of Child Support Enforcement, if men refuse to work or to look for work, they could be incarcerated, a policy that is often enforced now. In the case of prison release programs, if males refused to work they would be ineligible for early release from prison.[96]

The second policy, and one that could work in conjunction with Mead's proposal, is to create an EITC-like tax program that would provide a cash wage supplement to workers who do not have custody of children.[97] Several such programs have been proposed by scholars; legislative proposals were introduced in Congress in the 2007–08 session and the Obama administration has expressed its support for a program of this type.[98] The idea of providing such an EITC-like benefit for childless workers (including those who have children but do not have custody) is appealing because it has the potential to increase work incentives among young men who may be reluctant to work for low wages in the only jobs for which their experience and education qualify them. As noted in chapter 6, there is ample evidence from experiments such as New Hope, the Minnesota Family Investment Plan, and the Canadian Self-Sufficiency Project that the combination of work requirements and wage supplements can increase employment and earnings and have several other salutary effects on workers, including men.[99] If fathers leaving prison early on the condition that they work and fathers owing past-due child support could be given help finding jobs and then paid a wage supplement, similar gains might be achieved.

Given the importance of increasing employment among men in poor and minority communities, we recommend that the secretaries of HHS and the Treasury Department be required to plan and conduct a series of experiments working with several states, which would participate on a voluntary basis. These experiments would test the EITC-type wage supplements for childless workers. The experiments would run for a minimum of five years and would be carefully monitored and evaluated. The secretaries would have $2 billion a year to conduct these experiments. In planning with the selected states, the secretaries should consider testing the EITC supplement with fathers who owe child support and fathers leaving prison who agree to work. At least one of the experiments should provide the earnings supplement to all childless adults who work. The experiments would provide Congress and the president with solid knowledge about the expected effects of a national wage supplement for childless workers administered through the tax code on work effort, incarceration, marriage, and other outcomes. This knowledge would provide a basis for deciding whether a national program of wage supplements for childless workers would be a worthwhile investment.

The third policy we recommend is aimed at containing the number of young men who receive mandatory prison sentences for nonviolent crimes. Research shows that for males born between 1965 and 1969, 3 percent of whites and 20 percent of blacks had been in prison by the time they reached their early thirties. More surprising still, 60 percent of black high school dropouts from the 1960s birth cohort spent time in prison.[100]

Proponents of tough sentencing laws argue that incarceration takes criminals off the streets, thereby reducing crime rates.[101] High incarceration rates nonetheless have substantial costs. Recidivism rates are high, the financial costs to society are enormous and rising, families are divided, integration back into family and community life is difficult, and the costs to those imprisoned are almost beyond calculation.[102] In addition to exposing young men to the worst possible selection of new friends and a kind of graduate school of crime, incarceration also confronts them with physical violence, including rape and murder. And as Devah Pager of Princeton shows, their prospects of employment upon returning to society are minimal.[103] Especially in the case of young men who have been convicted of only drug offenses, their "developmental" experiences in prison are almost guaranteed to make them less likely to be productive members of society. Even if we ignore the costs these secondary effects of imprisonment impose on society, direct spending on the police, courts, and jails and prisons has skyrocketed (in dollars adjusted for inflation) from $72 billion in 1982 to over $214.5 billion in 2006.[104]

High-quality prison release programs might reduce recidivism and even pay for themselves.[105] But a policy that could prove even more effective than quality prison release programs would be one that keeps some men out of prison in the first place. Reform of sentencing laws could have the highly desirable effect of reducing the number of young men who receive mandatory sentences for relatively minor drug crimes. In particular, we support the modification of laws that provide for harsh mandatory sentences on those who sell crack cocaine and the modification of penalties for selling crack to the same level as the penalties for selling powdered cocaine. In addition, the discretion of judges in imposing prison sentences should be restored.

The Supreme Court, not exactly a bastion of liberal thought in America, has taken significant steps in support of both of these policies. On December 10, 2007, the Supreme Court issued two 7-2 decisions that provided some relief from the harsh federal sentencing guidelines enacted in 1986.[106] In one case, the Supreme Court reversed an appeals court ruling that had struck down a district judge's decision to give a lighter sentence than recommended by the sentencing guidelines. Writing for the majority, Justice John Paul Stevens said that the "guidelines should be the starting point and the initial benchmark" but that district court judges have a right to depart from the guidelines in making an "individualized assessment." In the second case, the Supreme Court chided the appeals court for overruling a district court judge's "reasoned and reasonable decision" to impose a sentence lower than the one recommended by the guidelines.[107] Both of these cases are consistent with the increasingly urgent recommendations that have been made for several years by the U.S. Sentencing Commission calling for reductions in penalties for sale of crack cocaine. In its May 2007 report the Sentencing Commission emphasized its "strong desire for prompt legislative actions" to reduce the mandatory crack sentences.[108] This recommendation should be followed.

Encouraging More Work

In recent decades work rates have declined among disadvantaged minority men and increased among single mothers. The record for never-married mothers—the group with the least education and work experience—was especially impressive. They took jobs at a modestly increasing rate between the mid-1980s and the mid-1990s, but following welfare reform their work rates increased by nearly 40 percent in just five years. In contrast with this record of increased work effort by disadvantaged mothers—who also assume the primary responsibility for rearing their children—black males with limited education have a dismal record of working. Between the 1970s and 2005, their work rates actually fell by 35 percent. Whatever factors may lie behind this decline, nonwork is a major problem that must be addressed.

Work and the Temporary Assistance for Needy Families Program

Created by the welfare reform law of 1996, TANF is a $16.5 billion block grant that states can use to provide a variety of assistance to poor families with children.[109] The two most common uses of the funds are for cash welfare payments and for activities related to helping families work or prepare for work.[110] The TANF program is generally credited with encouraging states to use strong measures to help, cajole, or require—at pain of losing their cash welfare benefits—able-bodied adults on, or applying for, welfare to enter the workforce. TANF has the strongest work requirements of any federal program. Although we believe the TANF program has been largely successful and that the current work requirements are a model for other programs, TANF could nonetheless be strengthened in three ways.

The first is to amend TANF so that the size of the block grant is adjusted for inflation. The cost of this proposal over five years would be $5 billion.[111] Although many observers argue that the caseload has declined so greatly since TANF was enacted in 1996 that states are actually saving money on the program because the number of families drawing cash welfare has fallen by around 60 percent, inflation has nonetheless cut the value of the TANF block grant by about 40 percent since 1996.[112] States use their block grant funds both to pay for cash welfare and to promote work.[113] States must find the optimum balance between these two policies. If they emphasize work, they must spend more money to help people leave or stay off welfare. If they don't emphasize work, the size of their welfare caseload increases and they must pay more for welfare benefits. Since the 1996 reforms, states have shown that they can help families avoid welfare through their work programs, primarily through job search programs. But the relentless eroding of their block grant by inflation could begin to weaken their programs. Further, as we argue below, the major work-related activity for which states use their block grant is child care. Without child care, many families would come back on welfare. Because the block grant is such a useful and versatile weapon in encouraging work, it seems appropriate for the federal government to at least hold states neutral in block grant funding by providing an annual inflation adjustment.

A second proposed change in the TANF program is that states should be allowed to fulfill up to 50 percent, rather than the current 30 percent, of their work requirement by allowing family heads to participate in educational activities. Experience now shows that many low-income mothers who find jobs make only modest improvements in wages as they gain work experience. There is growing agreement that, without further education or training, many mothers who leave welfare will find it difficult to move beyond jobs that pay low wages and provide modest or no benefits.[114] We do not doubt that work in low-wage jobs is a great improvement over welfare dependency, but if we are to improve economic opportunity, education and training are a must. These programs do not have an impressive track record, but we argue that they can be successful if conducted properly. Certainly there is a wide range of jobs that pay high wages and provide employee benefits—such as welder, electrician, dental hygienist, and machinist—that would increase the economic mobility of low-wage workers. These jobs require training beyond a high school degree but generally do not require even a two-year college degree. The economists Harry Holzer and Robert Lerman estimate that 45 percent of job openings between 2004 and 2014 will fall into this "middle-skill" job category.[115]

The major argument against providing states with more flexibility in the use of education and training programs is the claim that, in the days before the 1996 reforms, states put people into education programs and counted them as working. In other words, states used education and training as a substitute for serious work programs merely to meet their participation requirements. But circumstances have changed greatly since the 1996 reforms. States now know that work-first programs are successful in getting welfare applicants and recipients into low-wage jobs and off welfare. Every state now has more than a decade of experience in helping mothers on welfare or applying for welfare find jobs. Further, states have a fixed amount of money through the TANF block grant to spend on these programs and understand that if their spending on education does not result in people getting off or staying off welfare, they will be wasting their own money. Given these considerations, it is appropriate to allow states more flexibility in counting education as work.

The third TANF change we recommend is that the federal government provide states with financial incentives to mount programs addressed to family heads who have no earnings and have either lost their cash welfare or are at risk of doing so. As Rebecca Blank shows, the number of poor mothers with no cash welfare and no earnings in a given year has risen sharply since 1995.[116] About half of these mothers live with other adults in households that average around $20,000 in income a year. But it is not clear how the other half is living, except that their income puts them and their children in deep poverty.[117] Blank recommends that the federal government provide states with block grant funds of about $2.8 billion annually to help these mothers.

Although we think the Blank proposal is worthy of consideration, we think states should bear the primary burden for designing, conducting, and financing programs for these disconnected mothers. Specifically, we would provide states with additional dollars, at the rate of one federal dollar for every one state dollar spent on a program for these mothers. A total of $0.5 billion would be available to states at this matching rate each year. To qualify for their share of funds, which would be available to states in proportion to each state's share of the number of children in poverty in the entire nation, states would have to present the secretary of the HHS with a plan outlining how the money would be spent to help these mothers address the barriers—such as mental health problems, addictions, transportation, the need to care for disabled members of their household—that are preventing them from working and for providing support to the mothers and their children while the mother prepares for work.

The secretary would be responsible for ensuring that the state plan provides incentives for mothers to gain employment at the earliest possible time. The secretary would also be responsible for requiring states to report basic data about the program and its outcomes, including wage records from the state employment service agency. In addition, using funds from the pot of $0.5 billion for these demonstrations, the secretary would be required to conduct third-party evaluations of a few of the programs and to disseminate information about program effects to other states.

Work and Housing Programs

Each year nearly 5 million low-income households receive some type of federal housing subsidy, at a total cost of about $59 billion (not counting benefits in the tax code).[118] Only able-bodied adults who reside in public housing projects are subject to any work requirement, and the requirement is weak. Worse, most housing programs contain substantial work disincentives, because the rule that beneficiaries must pay 30 percent of their income toward the cost of their unit means that, if they accept a job or increase their hours of work, their rent goes up by as much as thirty cents for each dollar (or additional dollar) of earnings.[119] When this obligation is added to Social Security taxes and state taxes, many workers in low-wage jobs who receive housing subsidies pay 50 percent or more of their earnings in taxes and extra housing payments.[120] It would be challenging to think of a system that would more effectively discourage work.

We think it possible to successfully implement a stronger work requirement in housing programs. Two factors contribute to our optimism. The first is that HUD and local housing authorities have a tradition stretching back to 1984 of creating programs, modest though they may have been, to encourage work. The current version of these programs, implemented in 1991 and now called Family Self-Sufficiency (FSS), is open to residents of public housing and holders of tenant-based vouchers. The participating recipient agrees to a self-sufficiency plan that lays out the steps needed to achieve financial independence over a period of five years. The program features local case managers, who arrange job counseling, education, job training, and support services. FSS includes an innovative provision under which the increased rent that recipients must pay after securing employment is saved in an account and given to them when their plan is completed and they are no longer on cash welfare. Unfortunately, only about 5 percent of working-age, nondisabled voucher recipients and 1 percent of public housing residents participate in the FSS program.[121] In addition, there are no good evaluations of the program so no one knows whether it is producing good results. Nonetheless, it is encouraging that HUD and at least some local housing authorities see work as an important policy goal and have at least started to develop the administrative mechanisms necessary to implement a broad work program.[122]

A second reason for our optimism is that there is strong evidence that a program similar to FSS significantly increased earnings by residents of public housing. Implemented in six sites using a random-assignment design, a demonstration program called Jobs-Plus offered residents of public housing help from specialized staff located on site in preparing for and finding a job. Residents were also offered a financial incentive to work. Specifically, the provision that residents must pay 30 percent of their income in rent was reduced or eliminated. In addition, residents met to discuss work opportunities. The evaluation shows that the program increased earnings over a four-year follow-up period in the three sites where the program was fully implemented. For some subgroups in some sites, annual earnings increased by as much as $3,000 or more.[123]

HUD's experience in conducting employment programs and the success of Jobs-Plus prompt us to recommend that HUD officials launch an initiative to encourage all nonelderly, nondisabled adults with housing benefits to enter the workforce. A large number of adults who do not work or who are underemployed receive housing benefits. The precise number of housing beneficiaries to which our program would apply is difficult to compute, but Jim Riccio of MDRC estimates that about 1.9 million adults receiving benefits are potential workers (not aged, not disabled).[124] Of these, HUD reports that 57 percent had earnings at the time they submitted their annual recertification forms, implying that 43 percent did not work during the previous year (some might have worked for a short period between recertification interviews). About one-third of those who did work earned less than $8,300, suggesting that they did not work full time or year round. These nonworkers and part-time workers are worthy targets for Jobs-Plus-type services.[125]

As we have seen, occupants of public housing are already subject to a weak work requirement. But even this work requirement stipulates that residents capable of work must participate for only eight hours a month in either community service or economic self-sufficiency activities, including training, education, and work. We think that potential workers in both public housing and the rent subsidy programs should be subject to a thirty-hour-a-week requirement and that sanctions, especially reduction of the housing benefit, should be applied to those who do not meet the requirement.[126] We would allow a period of at least sixty days following job loss before a sanctioning period begins. The program should require local housing officials and officials administering the TANF and Workforce Investment Act programs in the local area to coordinate their efforts. In general, the definition of work and the exemptions from the requirement should be the same as those in the TANF program.

Advocates for the poor object to work requirements in housing programs because they fear that sanctions could make some residents homeless. Jobs-Plus, probably because of its voluntary nature, did not create a group of floundering parents who had difficulty staying eligible for welfare or working consistently.[127] The evidence from welfare reform, in which work requirements, sanctions, and time limits created a very big stick, is that sanctions motivate most mothers to work but they also leave some families destitute.[128] Sanctions produce both good outcomes and bad, although the evidence from welfare reform is that the good outcomes outweigh the bad.[129]

But given the possibility that strong mandates could increase homelessness, the approach we recommend to increasing work is to give local housing authorities the power to impose work mandates and sanctions and allow them to decide whether and how to use sanctions, including eviction as a final remedy for able-bodied adults who refuse to meet their work obligation or who turn down jobs. The sanctions could include mandatory civic engagement such as doing work around the public housing site or cleaning up parks as an alternative to financial sanctions. Under our approach, HUD would negotiate with local authorities over such particulars as the percent of the caseload that would be required to participate, the hours of participation, the definition of work, and the types of sanctions. The emphasis would be on private sector jobs, with the work program providing jobs of last resort. Participating local authorities would be allowed to forgive all or part of the 30 percent rent charge on earnings, with resulting lost local revenues compensated by the federal government. If after several years a high percentage of housing beneficiaries still were not working, the approach could be revisited with an eye toward stronger sanctions.

To encourage local areas to experiment with various approaches to promote work, HUD should offer them grants on a competitive basis. Local housing authorities would apply for a fixed sum of money, and the best proposals would be selected by the secretary of HUD. We recommend that Congress appropriate $1 billion a year for five years to conduct these work and housing demonstration programs. This sum would include about $3 million a year for third-party evaluations, using random-assignment designs whenever possible, of the best and most interesting programs as determined by the secretary.[130] The secretary would attempt to solicit at least one demonstration that imposes work requirements backed by financial sanctions as well as at least one that tests the effectiveness of reducing the 30 percent rent payment from earnings or other forms of rent-based work requirements as a work incentive.

Work and Food Stamps

The food stamp program has two work requirements. The first, which applies to all able-bodied adult recipients, stipulates that they must register with the state; accept a suitable job if one is offered; fulfill all state requirements regarding work, job search, or training; and not voluntarily quit a job or reduce their work hours below thirty hours a week without good cause. Numerous recipients are exempt from the requirement, and states have great flexibility in determining what individuals must actually do to fulfill the requirement. However, administrators cannot require recipients to participate in the work program for more hours than their food stamp benefit divided by the minimum wage. Given that the average monthly food stamp benefit (2009) is about $255 and the minimum wage is $7.25 (in 2009), the typical recipient cannot be required to work more than around thirty-five hours a month, or about eight hours a week. Moreover, the statutory language has many loopholes that states can use to minimize the number of recipients required to work. Although states provide some support for child care and transportation, these expenses are reimbursed by the federal government at fifty cents on the dollar (in contrast to the food stamp benefit itself, which is paid entirely by the federal government). The 50 percent reimbursement rate for work expenses creates an incentive for states to run stingy programs so they won't have to spend much of their own money.

The second work requirement applies only to recipients who are between the ages of eighteen and fifty and have no dependents.[131] These recipients must either work or participate in a state-approved work activity (but not including job search) for at least twenty hours a week to receive food stamps for more than three months during any thirty-six-month period. If recipients violate this rule they lose their entire food stamp benefit and can qualify again only when they have worked eighty hours or more during a thirty-day period. The federal government grants waivers of the work requirement to states for recipients who live in areas with high unemployment. In order to receive their share of the federal funds for this work program, a state must pledge to offer education, training, or actual work to adults with no dependents who are about to lose their food stamp benefit because of the work requirement.

The federal government provides some funding to the states to conduct their food stamp work programs, but beyond a base amount these funds have to be matched at a rate of fifty cents on the dollar by the states, making it expensive for them to draw down the full amounts to which they might be entitled.[132] The two food stamp work requirements are reasonable and, compared with those in the housing program, relatively strong. However, they are not aggressively implemented in most states. The solution is to both provide states with more resources to pay for work and training programs for this population, to strengthen state reporting requirements, and to impose administrative fines on states that do not meet the work standards in both sets of work requirements. We recommend that in addition to fines on states that did not meet the work requirements, the secretary of the Agriculture Department be given an additional $200 million a year to help states strengthen the implementation of both work requirements. The secretary would also be given the authority to waive the 50 percent state match on spending directly on the work programs if states spend funds above their 2008 allocation.

Encouraging Work: Summary

These recommendations for strengthening the work requirements and increasing the resources provided to states to implement them have a decent chance of increasing the number of recipients of TANF, housing benefits, and food stamps who are employed. Many people will earn their way off all three programs as their hours of work and income increase. However, other adults will not earn enough money even to lift themselves out of poverty, let alone take a major step toward upward economic mobility. If the 1996 reforms that created TANF are any indication, we can say that most families receiving housing or food stamp benefits will take jobs that pay around $8 an hour, or about $16,000 a year if they work full time, year round—not enough to remove even a family of three from poverty. For precisely this reason, we emphasize the importance of the work support system and have proposed several reforms of the system that will make it even more effective in helping these families.

A Practical Vision

This chapter shows that over the last two or three decades the federal and state governments have developed a partially successful strategy for getting people to work and supplementing their income. The federal government and the states strengthened work requirements in the leading cash welfare program and created or strengthened a host of programs that provide cash and other benefits to low-income workers. The result is that a single parent working for $8 an hour ($16,000 a year) can enjoy a package of earnings and cash and in-kind benefits worth, in theory at least, as much as $37,000.[133]

Thus the combination of work and work supports is a proven strategy for reducing poverty, primarily among women. A fundamental goal of the nation's social policy should be to maintain and strengthen this basic work and work support strategy. Some supports, such as child care, need to be expanded, and all of the work supports need to be better coordinated and made more readily available to the working poor. We already have more than 3,400 one-stop centers around the country that could form the backbone of a system that not only helps all unemployed or underemployed individuals find work but also ensures that once they are working they receive the work supports for which they are eligible. In addition, especially by more aggressive use of the nation's 1,200 community colleges, the system has the potential to help workers gain the education and training needed to qualify for better jobs with higher wages and benefits.

The potential benefits of such a system can be imagined by considering the impacts of one of the more remarkable work programs of recent decades. Implemented in Milwaukee beginning in the mid-1990s, Project New Hope presented poor inner-city residents with a guarantee: If you work full time, we'll provide child care, health insurance, a wage supplement, and if you have trouble finding work, a community service job. This offer embodies the philosophy of linking personal responsibility in the form of a requirement for full-time work with government's responsibility to then deliver additional benefits to workers, especially those with children, in low-wage jobs. As noted in chapter 6, New Hope produced strong results: not only did work and earnings increase, but in addition the program had positive impacts on children.[134] No other project with which we are familiar produced such a broad range of effects on adults and children.

To us the most enticing aspect of New Hope is that the national work support system we describe and propose to strengthen is very close to the New Hope guarantee.[135] If the United States can implement the work–work support strategy even more effectively than it already has, it can increase work, increase family earnings and income, and have positive impacts on children's development in every state in the nation. That is our vision, and it is achievable.

ten
Strengthening Families

Healthy marriages are not always possible. But we must remember, they are incredibly important for children. Our hearts know this and our nation must recognize this.

GEORGE W. BUSH

Of all the rocks upon which we build our lives, we are reminded today that family is the most important.

BARACK OBAMA

The traditional American family of married parents and their children is in decline. Nearly every trend that could work against the traditional family is going in that direction. Marriage rates are down, divorce rates are high, cohabitation rates are exploding, and nonmarital birth rates are rising. Nearly all of these trends started in the 1950s and picked up steam in the 1960s and 1970s. Most of them have slowed down or stabilized, but in every case they are at or near their historic highs or lows. The result is that the majority of American children will spend some time in a household without at least one of their parents. As these living arrangements become more common, they also become more acceptable, leading to an unraveling of traditional norms.

Some claim that anyone who is concerned about these trends is simply out of touch with modern culture; we respond that, if that be the case, then "modern culture is out of touch with the needs of children."[1] In this chapter we argue for reviving what we (along with Barbara Dafoe Whitehead and Marline Pearson) call the "success sequence."[2] The success sequence refers not just to what people need to do to become successful but also to the order in which they need to do it. First comes education, as discussed in chapter 8. Then comes a stable job that pays a decent wage—made decent by the government if necessary—as discussed in chapter 9. Finally comes family formation: meaning marriage followed by children born to two committed parents. We understand that not everyone will be able to achieve this ordering of life events, but we believe it should be the standard that society sets for each new generation.

After nearly half a century of deterioration in the family environments of children, we would be foolish to conclude that the task of turning around recent trends will be easy or that it will happen without the involvement of all sectors of our society—presidents and other elected officials, faith communities, teachers, parents, business leaders, experts, and the media, to name a few. In this chapter, we tackle the question of why families are important and what might be done to promote the success sequence. Government can help, at least on the margins, by providing resources to organizations that share this goal and by funding programs and media campaigns that work.

Importance of the Two-Parent Family

There is a growing consensus that having two married parents is the best environment for children. Marriage brings not only clear economic benefits but social benefits as well, enabling children to grow up to be more successful than they otherwise might be. We recognize this statement is a generalization to which there are numerous exceptions. Many single parents do an excellent job of raising their children under difficult circumstances. But, on average, the decline of the married-couple family has not been good for children.

Marriage and Children's Development

There has been a steady decline since 1968 in the share of American children living with both parents at a given time, from 85 percent to only 68 percent in 2007 (figure 10-1). These figures represent a tripling of the share of American children living apart from one parent. By the time children reach age fifteen, 40 percent have lived through a breakup, a rate higher than that of any European country.[3] To the extent that living in single-parent families detracts from the well-being of children, an increasing fraction of American children are missing out on the optimum rearing environment.

It is worth emphasizing that families in which both parents are committed to raising their children seem to be more effective than the blizzard of government programs in preventing or solving social problems.[4] A compelling example is the impact of marriage on economic well-being. Consider the relationship between marriage and poverty. In a study based on a simulation model, Isabel Sawhill and our colleague Adam Thomas show that, if the marriage rate in 2001 had been the same as it was in 1970, the poverty rate would have been 20 to 30 percent lower than its actual 1998 value.[5] We arrived at this conclusion by "marrying" single mothers to single men with similar demo-

Figure 10-1. Children in Two-Parent Households, 1968–2007

Percent

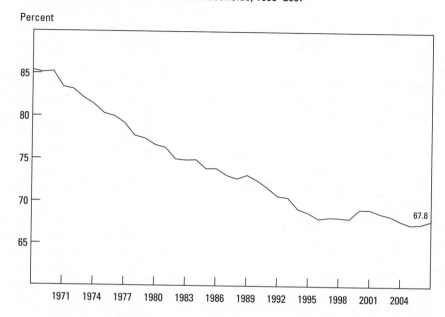

Source: U.S. Census Bureau, *Families and Living Arrangements, Historical Time Series* (various years), table CH-1.

graphic characteristics, based on census data. The single men were less economically successful than men who were already married, but with a few important exceptions, there were plenty of them to go around and they improved the economic status of their new families substantially. The most important exception should be noted: a shortage of young black men. Given the high rates of incarceration among black males, this imbalance between black males and females would be even greater today.[6] For some black women, marriage may be an unrealistic goal. Still, any government program that reduced poverty by 30 percent would be hailed as one of the most successful programs ever.

Beyond its impact on economic well-being, the impact of marriage on children's social development may be even more important to their future. There was a time when social scientists were sanguine about the effects of divorce and single-parenting on children. The general line was that children of divorce might suffer some difficulty at the time of the marital split but that they would soon adapt to their new life.[7]

But social scientists soon began studying the effects of divorce and nonmarital births on the children who actually experienced them. One of the first major studies of this type, somewhat flawed by its method of sample selection and the absence of a comparison group, was conducted by Judith Wallerstein and Joan Kelly on a sample of sixty divorcing families with 131 children.[8] Published in 1980 to widespread attention in the media and the scholarly world, the study describes the serious difficulties experienced by children immediately following and in the first five years after their parents' divorce. Children of divorce were afflicted by school failure, negative social behavior, feelings of bitterness, and high rates of depression.

As the empirical evidence that children are negatively affected by separation from a parent, usually their father, accumulated over the years, reviews of the evidence began to appear. In 1991 Paul Amato and Bruce Keith reviewed the empirical literature and concluded, "The argument that parental divorce presents few problems for children's long-term development is simply inconsistent with the literature on this topic."[9] Even more important to the changing perception of single parenting was the seminal book *Growing up with a Single Parent*, published in 1994 by Sara McLanahan and Gary Sandefur. Although Wallerstein and Kelly's work could be dismissed or minimized by its flawed design, the McLanahan and Sandefur study met high standards of social science research. Based on four nationally representative samples and elegant statistical techniques, which include controlling for a large set of other differences between children from splintered and children from intact families, the authors find abundant evidence that children reared in broken families are worse off. The authors' summary of findings is couched in the cautious language of social science but is arresting nonetheless: "Children who grow up apart from a parent are . . . less likely to graduate from high school and college, they are more likely to become teen mothers, and they are somewhat more likely to be idle [not working, not in school] in young adulthood."[10]

Marriage and Social Science

Evidence like this led more and more people to the conclusion that the decline of marriage is a disturbing development. In 2000 a group of more than a hundred prominent Americans from a cross-section of professions came together to issue a statement on their intention to support "a grass-roots movement to strengthen marriage."[11] The statement makes the case for marriage as a vital economic institution within which both adults and children are nurtured. The statement also argues that marriage is a public issue because it protects children while providing them with a stable and permanent rearing environment and because divorce and nonmarital births impose large economic and social costs on society.

In 2005 *The Future of Children*, a journal that we edit along with our colleagues Sara McLanahan, Cecilia Rouse, and Christina Paxson at Princeton, devoted an entire issue to research and theory about marriage and children. The journal examines economic, demographic, and social developments that have had an impact on marriage; reviews the research on the economic, social, emotional, and intellectual benefits of marriage for adults and children; and focuses special attention on the barriers to marriage faced by poor single mothers. Again, the message is that the trend toward single-parent families is less than optimum for children's development. This consensus view is reflected by the editors in their introduction to the volume: "Although marriage has undergone profound changes in the past forty years, it continues to be the most effective family structure in which to raise children. Low-income children, in particular, stand to reap large gains in terms of family stability if marriage can be restored as the norm for parents."[12]

The growing agreement among social scientists that the decline in marriage is portentous for the well-being of children is further documented by an interesting study undertaken by Norval Glenn of the University of Texas, one of the long-time leaders among marriage researchers. He and his colleagues Thomas Sylvester and Alex Roberts examine 266 articles on the effects of family structure on children published in the *Journal of Marriage and Family* between 1977 and 2002.[13] They rate the articles on a scale of 1 to 5, with a 1 meaning that the author appeared to believe that divorce or unwed births were not an important factor in child well-being and a 5 meaning that the author expressed great concern about family structure and child well-being. They find that the average rating increased from 2.8 in the 1977–82 period to about 3.5 in the 1998–2002 period, with most of the increase occurring in the mid-1980s. They also find that literature reviews (as opposed to empirical articles) on family structure and child well-being published in the *Journal* show the same pattern, with the rating increasing from 2.4 to 3.6 over the same period.

One of the most thorough studies in this literature is an analysis of data from the National Longitudinal Survey of Youth by Carolyn Hill, Harry Holzer, and Henry Chen. Based on differences in household composition at age twelve, and following white, black, and Hispanic children into their early to mid-twenties, the authors find that growing up without both biological parents was correlated with "modest reductions in wages and weeks worked for young adults, and more substantial reductions in educational attainment or achievement as well as greater participation in risky or illegal behaviors." Equally important, they conclude that the higher proportion of black children living in female-headed families is responsible in part for the gap in black-white educational achievement as well as the "cycle of unmarried child-bearing and dramatic increases in crime and incarceration that have affected black youth."[14]

Taken together, these various books, journal articles, and reviews yield persuasive evidence that millions of American children are being raised outside the most effective rearing environment and that, as a result, individuals, families, communities, and the nation are suffering higher levels of poverty and related afflictions than necessary.[15] To be sure, many adults who are trapped in unhappy marriages may benefit from divorce. And few believe that a seriously dysfunctional marriage is the best environment for children or adults. Still, the tripling of the share of American children living in single-parent families over the past half century is making it far more difficult to cope with a host of other problems, from child poverty to juvenile crime. Children raised in single-parent families are more likely to experience such problems as school failure, teen births, teen arrests and time in jail, teen mental health problems, and teen suicide; and in adulthood such problems as welfare use, nonmarital births, joblessness, and incarceration. Some social scientists hold that many of these results are caused not just by being reared without one parent but by other conditions, such as poverty, that are associated with single parenting. True enough. But numerous studies employing statistical controls for these other factors find that the relationship between parent absence and negative outcomes is strong. And even more important, many of the other conditions that lead to negative outcomes (poverty arguably being the most important) are often companions of single parenting. For kids in single-parent families, bad things come in bundles.

Nor are these negative effects on well-being evenly distributed throughout society. As the editorial writer Jonathan Rauch explained in a perceptive 2001 essay: "Marriage is displacing both income and race as the great class divide of the new century."[16] Figures 10-2 and 10-3 tell the story in detail. Nonmarriage is most common among black mothers, followed by Hispanic mothers, and then white mothers, but rates of nonmarriage have been increasing for all groups since the 1960s. Similarly, less-educated mothers are more likely to have nonmarital births than more educated mothers, and the pattern of increasing rates of nonmarital births is directly related to women's education level. Since the early 1970s nonmarital births increased greatly for mothers with less than twelve years of education, somewhat less for moms with just a high school education, a little less for moms with some college, and least of all for moms with sixteen years of education or more. In 2007 the least educated women were six times as likely as the most educated women to have a baby outside marriage.

Figure 10-2. Never-Married Mothers, by Race and Ethnicity, 1968–2008

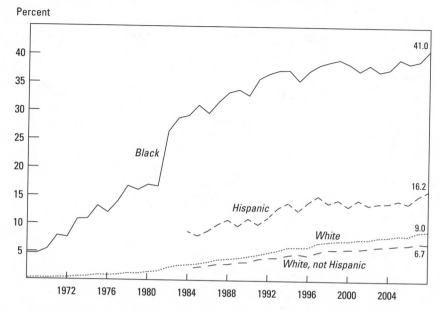

Percent

Source: Authors' calculations based on U.S. Census Bureau, *Current Population Survey, Annual Social and Economic Supplement.*

Many observers of these trends believe that they are a response to the stagnant or falling wages of less-skilled men, to high rates of incarceration among men, and to the desire of low-income women to have children on their own once the option of marriage appears to have faded.[17] Yet the majority of these births to single women are unplanned and end up reducing their chances of ever marrying.[18] And research linking the decline in marriage to the economic prospects of men or any other single factor is weak. David Ellwood and Christopher Jencks sum up the research as follows:

> There is still no consensus about why single parenthood spread, much less about why it spread faster in some populations than others. The most widely cited empirical papers seem to be those that disprove various hypotheses. Indeed, it is only a slight exaggeration to say that quantitative social scientists' main contribution to our understanding of this change has been to show that *nothing* caused single-parent families to become more common. Nonetheless, they did.[19]

A reasonable interpretation of the evidence is that economics and culture interact to produce more single-parent families. Falling wages for low-income

Figure 10-3. Never-Married Mothers, by Years of Education, 1968–2008

Percent

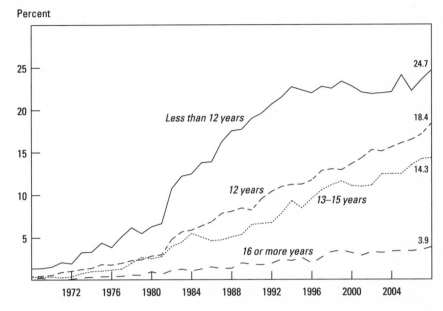

Source: Authors' calculations based on U.S. Census Bureau, *Current Population Survey, Annual Social and Economic Supplement.*

workers, high prison rates for blacks, and changing values all play a role in the decline of the married-couple family, though it is not possible to specify which is the most important or how they interact. But we don't have to understand the exact causes of the decline to know that the major losers have been the poor and their children.

Bringing Back a Marriage Culture

Given the growing evidence of the decline of marriage and its consequences for children, it was only a matter of time before policymakers began to take notice and try to enact policies that might have some impact on the formation of single-parent families. And so it happened that, after taking over both Houses of Congress in the election of 1994, Republicans were intent on reducing nonmarital births, increasing marriage, and increasing work as part of their attempt to revolutionize welfare. Their welfare reform legislation, eventually supported by President Clinton and half the Democrats in the House and Senate, repealed welfare that guaranteed cash benefits and replaced the entitlement to cash with benefits contingent on work. The general strategy of the legislation was to give a block grant to states, called Temporary Assistance for Needy Families (TANF), and to allow states to try any policy "reasonably calculated" to prevent the need for welfare or to help adults on welfare get on their feet and support themselves through work and marriage.[20]

The block grant provides states with $16.5 billion to help people on welfare or at risk for needing welfare and requires that the money be spent on four broad goals. Three of the four goals deal with family composition: states are to use the money to reduce births outside marriage, encourage the formation and maintenance of two-parent families, and reduce welfare dependency by increasing marriage and work (the fourth goal).

The policy of allowing states to decide how best to spend their share of the $16.5 billion TANF grant means that states can use a portion of the money to initiate programs designed to reduce nonmarital births, to stabilize or increase marriage rates, or to strengthen marriages that already exist. Nearly all states initiated programs to reduce nonmarital births, in part because the welfare reform law made states that greatly reduce their nonmarital birth rate eligible for a reward of up to $25 million (this provision has since been repealed). About half the states also have initiated activities—usually modest—to strengthen marriage.[21] Many of these states are building on grassroots movements that existed before the 1996 reforms. Despite these pro-marriage activities in selected states, it would be an exaggeration to say that the 1996 legislation ignited a storm of marriage programs. Every state has mounted programs to help mothers on welfare get jobs, and nearly every state has implemented programs to reduce nonmarital births, but far fewer states have implemented programs to address relationships or marriage among low-income couples, and most of the programs they did mount were limited in scale.

Republicans also wanted to use welfare reform to create a broad set of policies to reduce nonmarital births (table 10-1). The toughest policy on welfare ever supported by either of the political parties in the House is the policy of ending cash welfare payments for nonmarital births. House Republicans did everything they could—though some of their favored provisions ultimately failed—to end cash welfare for mothers under age eighteen who had nonmarital births. This policy was a relatively tame version of a sweeping policy recommended by Charles Murray, in his 1984 book *Losing Ground*, that welfare be completely terminated.[22] Ending welfare in Murray's view was the only way to stop the growing dependency on welfare and the avalanche of nonmarital births that was undermining American society.

Although congressional Republicans judged that ending welfare entirely was neither feasible nor wise, in some versions of their bills unwed mothers

Table 10-1. 1996 Welfare Reform Law, Provisions to Reduce Nonmarital Births

Provision	Explanation
Block grant	States to use funds to pay for any policy designed to reduce teen or nonmarital births
State-set goals	States to set goals and take action to prevent and reduce nonmarital pregnancies, especially teen pregnancies; states to set explicit goals for reducing the ratio of nonmarital to marital births for each year between 1996 and 2005
Bonus for reducing non-marital births	Bonuses of $25 million for up to five states that lead the nation in reducing the number of nonmarital births while decreasing abortion rates
Performance bonuses	Bonuses of $1 billion over five years for overall performance in encouraging work, reducing nonmarital births, and strengthening families
Abstinence education	States provided with $50 billion to establish and conduct abstinence education programs
Family cap	States permitted to end the standard practice of increasing the welfare cash grant when mothers already on welfare have more babies
Welfare termination	States permitted to deny cash welfare to mothers who have babies outside marriage
Teens at home	Unwed teen parents must live at home or in supervised facilities to qualify for cash welfare
Teens in school	Unwed teen parents required to be in school to qualify for cash welfare
Child support	Child Support Enforcement Program strengthened
National strategy to reduce nonmarital births	Secretary of HHS required to publish a national strategy to ensure that 25 percent of the nation's communities have programs designed to prevent teen pregnancy
State rankings	Secretary of the HHS required to rank states on their ratio of nonmarital to total births and annual changes in this ratio

Source: Social Security Act, title IV-A, especially secs. 401, 402(a), 403(a)(4), 408(a)(4), 408(a)(5), 411(b)(1)(B)(ii), and 413(e); title IV-D; title V, sec. 510.

under age eighteen would have lost both their cash welfare and food stamps.[23] These termination policies were exceptionally controversial and widely regarded as draconian, even among many Republicans, especially in the Senate. Bob Herbert of the *New York Times* claimed that Republicans were conducting a "jihad against the poor" and that this "loathsome" policy was "deliberately [designed to] inflict harm" on children and the poor.[24] Even so, the original House bills enacted in 1995 contained a version of the provision that would have ended cash welfare for unwed mothers under age eighteen. This provision, however, was subsequently killed in the Senate, with a majority of Republicans voting against it.[25]

Another controversial policy supported by House Republicans was the family cap.[26] Under this policy, states would be prohibited from using dollars from the TANF block grant to increase the cash welfare benefit of mothers on welfare who had additional babies. Under then-current law, every state increased the cash welfare grant when mothers on welfare had more children. House Republicans saw this policy as an incentive for mothers already on welfare to give birth to children outside marriage that they could not support. Because these mothers were fully aware they could not support new children without public assistance, Republicans argued that taxpayers should not be responsible for supporting the additional children. Like the under-age-eighteen termination policy, the family cap was also defeated on the Senate floor. However, because TANF was a block grant, states could adopt either the termination policy or the family cap under state law if they favored the policy. As it turned out, about half the states did adopt some version of the family cap. However, no state has adopted any version of the policy of terminating welfare for children born outside marriage.[27]

A third highly controversial provision in the 1996 law was abstinence education for teens. Although polls showed that both parents and adolescents believed that abstinence was the best choice for teens, abstinence was often ridiculed by the media and many advocates in Washington as hopelessly out of touch with modern sexual practices.[28] Nonetheless, Republicans elected to swim against the tide of accepting teen sex as inevitable and drafted a legislative provision on abstinence education that provided states with $50 million a year to conduct abstinence education programs. The legislation contained a strict definition of abstinence education, which, along with subsequent rules issued by the Department of Health and Human Services (HHS), prohibited programs from including education about contraception or advocacy for the use of contraception.[29]

Other parts of the Republican effort to reduce nonmarital births were less controversial and most appear to have been implemented willingly by most states. In addition to abstinence education, two of the provisions defined in table 10-1 targeted teenagers. One required teen mothers to live at home or with another adult in order to qualify for welfare payments; the other required teen moms to be in school or job training if they had not completed a high school degree. In addition to these policies, many states used some of their TANF money to fund after-school programs or mentoring for teens. It is difficult to separate out the effects of these many provisions, but there is nonetheless interesting evidence that the rules on living at home and staying in school reduced teen births. Thomas DeLeire and Leonard Lopoo used sophisticated methods and detailed data on births from the National Center for Health Statistics to examine the impact of these two provisions. They find that they were associated with an 11 percent reduction in the birthrate for fifteen-to-seventeen-year-olds.[30] The study does not meet the highest standards of social science research, so caution is required in drawing conclusions, but it nonetheless suggests that policies of this type may be successful in reducing teen births.

Given the rather modest response by states to the 1996 welfare reform law's emphasis on marriage, the administration of George W. Bush created a strong federal role in trying to strengthen marriage from its earliest days in office.[31] The new administration's marriage initiative was strongly supported by powerful conservative interest groups like the Heritage Foundation, the Family Research Council, and Focus on the Family. Equally important, President Bush appointed a clinical psychologist, Wade Horn, to a senior post at HHS to head the marriage initiative. A true believer in marriage, an experienced federal bureaucrat, and an influential inside player in the nation's capital before his appointment, Horn was full of ideas about how to create an aggressive marriage agenda.

When the time to reauthorize welfare reform arrived in 2002, the administration was ready to dramatically expand the marriage activities that it had already undertaken using unobligated funds at HHS. Under Horn's leadership and with full support from the administration, the White House worked with Republican leaders in the House and Senate to include an expensive marriage initiative in its welfare reauthorization bill. After three years of often bitter partisan debate over the administration's bill—especially its strong work requirements and to a somewhat lesser extent its marriage initiative—Republicans passed their reauthorization bill under special rules on a partisan basis in 2005.[32] The final version of the bill contains the marriage grant program, but it had been pared back from $300 million to $100 million a year.

The Bush marriage agenda consists of three initiatives:

—Demonstration grants initiated by HHS starting as early as 2002 using existing funds and administered by a number of offices within the Administration for Children and Families at HHS.

—Research and evaluation programs initiated in 2002 and employing gold-standard evaluation designs, including marriage education programs and communitywide initiatives.[33]

—Competitive grants funded by a $100 million pot of marriage funds that are part of the welfare reform reauthorization of 2006.[34]

Taken together, these three prongs of the Bush marriage agenda constitute an ambitious if controversial set of programs to stimulate and sustain a marriage movement in America (appendix B provides details on Bush's marriage initiative). These programs have been subjected to considerable criticism. However, the initiative addresses what is generally agreed to be one of the most troubling social problems faced by the nation; namely, the decline in the share of children living with both of their parents. And because programs to improve relationships and increase marriage rates are in their infancy, the initiative was designed to stimulate advocates and community groups to start a diverse set of activities and to conduct high-quality evaluations of promising programs.

Public Policy and Family Composition: Where Do We Go from Here?

Although there is now widespread agreement that changes in family composition have adverse impacts on children, there is less agreement about what can or should be done about these changes. To some, any attempt to change patterns of family formation is an unwelcome intrusion into a private domain. Others (including Isabel Sawhill) believe that government should primarily focus on reducing births to young women who are not yet married and worry less about promoting marriage. The argument for giving priority to reducing nonmarital births, especially those to very young women, goes as follows. The problem is not so much a failure to marry as it is a failure to delay childbearing until marriage. In short, the issue is one of timing. Delaying marriage and childbearing, as most well-educated women are doing, is a sensible response to the fact that a modern society requires ever increasing amounts of education and career preparation before one is ready to take on family responsibilities. The challenge is to provide less-well-educated men and women with the motivation, skills, and resources to plan their families the way their better-educated peers are already doing. Marriages by adults who have completed their education are more stable than those undertaken at an early age, and older parents are usually better parents as well.

Still others (including Ron Haskins) believe that the agenda to increase opportunity should include efforts to encourage marriage. If young people in their twenties are not married, they will inevitably have sex, and sex will often produce babies unless couples are vigilant about birth control. But if they marry in their twenties, this problem will be reduced. Moreover, substantial benefits accrue to children raised in low-conflict marriages. This view leads to a more explicit focus on programs that can help people see the value of marriage and learn the skills needed to succeed in a relationship.

Each of us sees some value in the other's perspective, and in what follows we cover both approaches. We also recommend a third approach: direct efforts to change the culture through a social marketing campaign. The campaign would be organized around the theme that young people need to be encouraged to follow a path that until recently was the norm in American society. As we have emphasized several times, this path includes finishing high school (at least), waiting until your twenties to marry, and having children only after you marry. As William Galston and Stephen Goldsmith argue so eloquently:

> The link between preventing teen pregnancy and parenthood and ensuring that more children grow up in stable, two-parent families is powerful, but woefully overlooked. Those in the world of teen pregnancy prevention tend to focus too narrowly on abstinence and contraception while those concerned with marriage and out-of-wedlock childbearing often neglect the value of preventing early pregnancy and childbearing in the first place.... The teen years are a time when young people's "habits of the heart" are first formed and when *half* of first out-of-wedlock births occur.[35]

Reducing Nonmarital Births

More than half of nonmarital births are unplanned.[36] Many of these births are to cohabiting couples who later break up, typically after living together for just a few years. (Recommendations for discouraging such births and encouraging marriage are summarized in table 10-2.) Although 70 percent of nonmarital births are to women over the age of twenty, as Galston and Goldsmith note, almost half of out-of-wedlock childbearing begins in the teenage years (figure 10-4). Once these young women have their first baby, their marriage prospects diminish, and many go on to have additional children outside marriage in their twenties or thirties.[37] So we first focus on teen births, 80 percent of which occur outside marriage, and then turn to the twenty-somethings, for whom the majority of births are now also occurring outside marriage.

Teen Births. Of all the programs we examine for helping stop family dissolution, the greatest success has been in reducing teen births. Since at least the 1980s reducing teen pregnancy and births has been an important item on the agenda of policymakers, advocates, and the American public. While all this attention was focused on teen pregnancy, it did in fact decline, along with teen abortions and the teen birth rate, over a remarkably long period, beginning in 1991 and extending without interruption until 2006 and 2007, when the teen birth rate rose (figure 10-4).[38] Over that period, teen births declined by one-third. Given that four of every five teen births are out of wedlock, the decline in the teen birth rate contributed substantially to the mid-1990s' leveling off of the proportion of children born outside marriage.[39] The subsequent slowing of the decline followed by a recent uptick in the teen birth rate is having the opposite effect.

Table 10-2. Recommendations to Strengthen Families

Recommendation	Goal
Prevent unplanned pregnancy among teens and twenty-somethings	
Create block grant for states to reduce teen pregnancy (with research set-aside)	To fund state programs that emphasize abstinence and family planning to reduce pregnancy and sexually transmitted diseases among teens
Terminate Title V abstinence education programs	To avoid redundant programs and save money, the block grant to reduce teen pregnancy would replace the Title V program
Expand Medicaid family planning coverage	To reduce unplanned pregnancy and sexually transmitted infections among women who are now somewhat above the income cutoff for Medicaid eligibility, regardless of whether they have children
Create competitive block grants for community college pregnancy reduction programs	To provide funds for community colleges to support instruction and information about abstinence education, family planning, and contraceptive use; funds could be used for direct services and to provide training to faculty, staff, or students to work in the programs
Create research fund for secretary to pay for research and demonstration programs on unplanned pregnancy	To provide the secretary with resources to conduct basic research and demonstration programs on the causes and prevention of unplanned pregnancies among couples in their twenties and early thirties
Encourage marriage	
Continue healthy marriage research initiatives	To allow experiments to be completed on the effects of marriage programs, especially on children
Continue healthy marriage and fatherhood grant programs	To ensure the continuation of healthy marriage, healthy relationship, and fatherhood programs at the state and local levels to strengthen marriage and single parenting
Create a ten-year social marketing campaign supporting the success sequence (finish education, get a job, get married, have children)	To encourage responsible behavior among youth regarding education, sexual activity, marriage, and employment

The immediate sources of the decline in teen pregnancy rates until 2006 include both less sex among teens (especially boys) and better use of contraception, although more effective contraception and more frequent use appear to have been more important.[40] The reasons for these changes in behavior are not well understood, but they appear to have been driven by some combination of more conservative attitudes among recent generations of teenagers, greater fear of sexually transmitted diseases (especially AIDS), welfare reform with its emphasis on an unwed mother's responsibility to work and on the father's requirement to pay child support, greater use of more effective long-acting contraceptives (especially among black teens), and an expansion of prevention efforts at the local level.[41] We would rate this achievement as

Figure 10-4. Births to Women Ages Fifteen through Nineteen, 1980–2007[a]

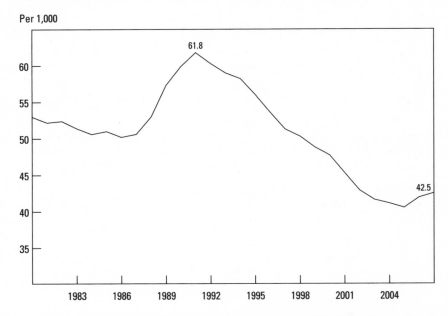

Per 1,000

Source: Joyce A. Martin and others, "Births: Final Data for 2006," National Vital Statistics Reports 57, no. 7 (2009), table 4; Brady E. Hamilton and others, "Births: Preliminary Data for 2007," National Vital Statistics Reports 57, no. 12 (2009), table 2.
a. Birth rate is births per 1,000 women in the specified age group.

somewhat analogous to the decline in smoking and the increased use of seat belts over recent decades.[42] All are examples of change that can occur when there is national consensus on the importance of a social problem, when parents and public figures speak with one voice, when public attention is aroused through word of mouth and media campaigns, and when national and local programs addressing the problem proliferate.

Literally hundreds of programs attempting to reduce teen pregnancy, most at the local level, have been conducted, and a fairly high-quality research literature has built up over the years. This literature has been capably reviewed by Douglas Kirby for the National Campaign to Prevent Teen and Unplanned Pregnancy.[43] Analyzing more than 450 studies, Kirby finds that there are a host of factors that put teens at risk for pregnancy or protect teens from getting pregnant. These factors include knowledge and beliefs about sex and the norms surrounding sexual activity, knowledge about contraception, skills in avoiding sexual advances by partners, mentoring by adults, and participation in community activities, especially during after-school hours.

The typical program in most communities or schools is comprehensive sex education. As the label "comprehensive" implies, these programs emphasize both abstinence and the use of condoms or other contraceptives for youth who are sexually active. Two-thirds of forty-eight well-evaluated programs of this type produced at least one significant effect on sexual behavior, including delayed age of initiation to sex, a reduced number of partners, or increased use of contraceptives. Equally important, none of the evaluations find evidence that the programs induced sex at an earlier age or increased the frequency of sex. Communitywide programs have also been somewhat successful. These programs include components implemented simultaneously, including classroom instruction, mentoring, meeting with students to discuss reproductive health, and community events. Four of six studies of these programs find significant effects on outcomes, such as delayed first sex, increased use of contraceptives, and lower rates of pregnancy.

In an attempt to reform sex education to focus less (or not at all) on contraception than on abstinence, the 1996 welfare reform law provided $50 million a year to states to operate abstinence education programs. Subsequently, Congress and the Bush administration created additional funding streams, bringing the total commitment to abstinence education to $177 million a year.[44] None of this money could be used to promote or teach students about family planning or birth control. Conservatives argue that programs should not tell youth that abstinence is the best choice but then tell them how to use birth control to avoid pregnancy. To conservatives, this mixed message defeats the purpose of convincing adolescents to abstain from sex entirely. As far as we can tell, there is no evidence from good studies that this mixed message actually does contribute to increased rates of sexual activity or higher pregnancy rates among teens.

Congress also appropriated funds to conduct a high-quality evaluation of abstinence education. The evaluation, conducted by Mathematica Policy Research with assistance from officials at the Department of Health and Human Services and in consultation with several of the conservative advocates who had supported the abstinence provision, was based on four of the best abstinence education programs in the country.[45] Several years later, when the evaluation results had been analyzed, the programs were found to have had no impacts on the attitudes or sexual behavior of participating adolescents.[46] These results caused many—but not all—observers to conclude that abstinence education does not work.

Of course, not all of the comprehensive sex education programs that aim to prevent teen pregnancy have worked, and the effects of even the successful programs are usually modest. But on balance, well-designed and implemented programs that emphasize both abstinence and contraception have a track record of success and pass a benefit-cost test.[47]

For this reason, we think the federal government should approve a block grant of $500 million a year, which would allow states to expand sex education and related services for vulnerable teens. States would have considerable flexibility in how to use these funds in order to accommodate local values and norms. The secretary of HHS would be required to use up to $50 million of the $500 million to conduct research and demonstration programs to pinpoint effective strategies for reducing teen sexual activity, preventing pregnancy, and avoiding the spread of sexually transmitted infections. The legislation would encourage the secretary to fund programs at multiple sites using random assignment designs.

We both believe that abstinence is the best choice for adolescents and that every sex education program for teens should feature a guided discussion and factual presentations that emphasize that abstinence is the only certain way to avoid both pregnancy and sexually transmitted infections.[48] The public appears to agree. More than 90 percent of parents and teens believe that society should give a "strong message" that young people "should not have sex until they are at least out of high school."[49] However, even after participating in the most successful abstinence programs—and there seem to be some—many students fail to remain abstinent.[50] Today about 65 percent of students graduating from high school have had sex; and about 20 percent of the girls who have had intercourse become pregnant.[51] These students should not be left without advice on how to avoid pregnancy and achieve at least some protection against sexually transmitted infections if they become sexually active. Yet good evidence indicates that this is precisely what is happening. Using data from two respected national surveys, researchers at the Guttmacher Institute and Columbia University find that, between 1995 and 2002, reports of receiving formal instruction about birth control methods declined among adolescent boys (from 81 percent to 66 percent) and girls (from 87 percent to 70 percent).[52] Around half the states feel so strongly about the need to provide students with information about contraception that they refuse to accept the abstinence-only education funds.[53] When states turn down federal dollars, something is amiss.

Our solution is, in effect, to use the funds now being used for abstinence education to fund (in part) the block grant proposed above that would allow states and local communities more flexibility in the use of federal dollars. Even though a strong abstinence message is consistent with public values, we make this recommendation because the idea that the federal government can, or should, prescribe or monitor what goes on in every classroom through detailed curricular guidelines (like those now found in the abstinence education statute) is not appropriate in a federalist system of government, especially in an area as sensitive and complicated as this one. Instead, family and community values, informed by the best research and not a federal mandate, should prevail. Some conservatives believe that there is more discussion of birth control than of abstinence in many comprehensive sex education curriculums, and there is considerable evidence to support this claim.[54] Liberals, on the other hand, often dismiss abstinence as a sop to the religious right and fault some of the information provided by abstinence education programs as medically inaccurate. Under our block grant, each side has the opportunity to argue at the state and local level for the approach most consistent with their particular values. A one-size-fits-all policy is inconsistent with the pluralistic nature of our democracy.

Twenty-Somethings. Even if the nation continues to make great progress in the battle against teen pregnancy—and the trend now appears to be moving modestly in the wrong direction—the war against nonmarital births would be less than half won. As shown in figure 10-5, as the nonmarital birthrate of teens declined after roughly 1990, the birthrates of young unwed women between ages twenty and twenty-four increased. In fact with the exception of a few years, birthrates for young women over age twenty have been increasing almost every year since 1980.

The trends shown in figure 10-5 are troubling. The increase in births to women in their twenties and early thirties seems to suggest that many unmarried women avoid births through their teen years but not as they grow older. Keeping in mind that in earlier generations a higher fraction of women in their twenties and thirties would have been married and therefore by definition unable to have a nonmarital birth, we can begin to appreciate the fact that preventing nonmarital births among older single women will be difficult. If marriage rates decline further or even stabilize at their current low level, the number of years women are at risk for a nonmarital birth will be very high or even continue to rise. Some view this trend toward more births outside marriage as relatively benign. But births outside marriage not only have adverse consequences for children but are also creating new class divisions in American society and further impeding upward mobility among the less educated and their children.

Thus it is especially unfortunate that we have so little information about how to prevent nonmarital births among twenty-somethings, let alone among women in their thirties. Even so, at least three worthy ideas have emerged among analysts and advocates for preventing unplanned pregnancies among couples in their twenties.

The first is a proposal to expand Medicaid coverage of family planning. Under the regular Medicaid program, states provide family planning services

Figure 10-5. Births to Unmarried Women, by Age of Mother, 1980–2006

Percent per 1,000 women

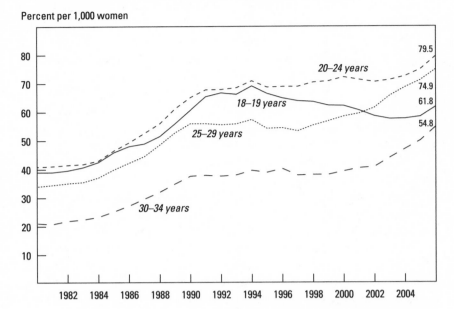

Source: Joyce A. Martin and Others, "Births: Final Data for 2006," *National Vital Statistics Reports* 57, no. 7 (2009), table 19, p. 55.

primarily to women who meet the test for low income (which varies greatly across the states but is usually below 185 percent of poverty) and who are already pregnant or are parents. Since 1993, however, twenty-eight states have been granted a waiver to expand Medicaid eligibility specifically for family planning services. Most states with waivers now offer family planning services to all women, even if they don't yet have children, under an income limit that is higher than the limit for the state's regular Medicaid program. By 2006 Medicaid spending on family planning was $1.3 billion, more than twice the level of 1994 spending, primarily because of the waiver program. Although the waivers vary from state to state, typically women (including those with no children) made eligible are from households with incomes between 185 percent and 200 percent of poverty. An analysis by Melissa Kearney and Phillip Levine finds that the program in states with waivers dramatically increased the number of women receiving family planning services.[55] They also find that birth rates to women in their late teens and early twenties fell by between 5 percent and 7 percent in these states. Women in states with waivers did not reduce their sexual activity, but they were more likely to use contraception than women in states without waivers. At a cost of $188 per additional recipient of family planning services, which equates to a cost of only $6,800 for every birth avoided, the Medicaid waivers appear to have more than paid for themselves.[56]

Evidently the nonpartisan Congressional Budget Office (CBO) agrees with this assessment. CBO concludes that requiring every state to pay for family planning services for women whose family income is under 200 percent of poverty would save as much as $100 million a year when fully implemented.[57] The CBO scoring of this provision makes it easy for us to recommend that Congress require states that have not already done so to raise their eligibility threshold for Medicaid family planning to 200 percent of the poverty level (and offer the service to all women, even if they are not yet mothers).

The second reform we recommend is that the federal government support a competitive grant program to help community colleges and other postsecondary education and training entities to establish programs that help their students avoid pregnancy. The secretary of HHS would be required to withhold $5 million each year for high-quality evaluations of the success of exemplary community college programs and to disseminate results. This reform is based on the fact that around 6.6 million young (and many not-so-young) adults are enrolled in the nation's 1,200 public community colleges.[58] The first step in any intervention is gaining access to the group of people expected to profit from the program. With the possible exception of churches, there is no other institution in American society that attracts so many young adults with modest incomes, exactly the group at highest risk for a nonmarital birth.

About half of the students at community colleges have either been pregnant or gotten someone pregnant. The consequences of a pregnancy while attending community college are especially serious for women: 61 percent of them who have children after enrolling fail to finish their degree, a rate 65 percent higher than the rate for women who don't have children.[59] The grants, which we suggest be funded at $250 million a year, would be awarded to community colleges on a competitive basis and could be used for a wide range of activities designed to reduce unplanned pregnancy and the need for abortion. These activities would include education in marriage and healthy relationships; instruction in pregnancy prevention during orientation or as part of an academic course; innovative programs to reach students through use of technology; access to free or low-cost health services on campus or through referral; and instruction and training for faculty, staff, and student leaders in how to discuss pregnancy prevention with students.

As an example of what might be accomplished by such a program, consider the fact that encouraging young adults to shift from using condoms or the pill to using long-acting contraceptives, such as the IUD, and providing them with the health services and information needed to facilitate this shift, could reduce unplanned pregnancies quite dramatically. Our Brookings colleague Adam Thomas, based on a simulation model, estimates that if 10 percent of pill users, condom users, and noncontraceptors were to switch to long-acting methods, there would be about a 10 percent decrease in nonmarital births, pregnancies to unmarried teen women, abortions by unmarried women, and children born to poor unmarried women.[60]

The third reform we recommend is that Congress provide the secretary of HHS with $25 million a year to fund research and demonstration projects aimed at reducing nonmarital births among women in their twenties and thirties. Expanding Medicaid's family planning services is the only intervention with twenty-somethings for which we have good data indicating that real improvements are likely. Yet the problem of nonmarital births among women in this age range is likely to continue growing and imposing ever rising costs on individuals, especially children, and on government. Where little is known, research and demonstration is the best strategy. If funds are available to support these activities on a competitive basis, highly qualified investigators, research firms, and program operators will respond.

Encouraging Marriage

Government programs to support healthy marriage are controversial. Critics of marriage promotion rest their case on three arguments.[61]

The first is that government should not favor one form of family composition over another. Frank Furstenberg of the University of Pennsylvania, one of the most respected scholars studying adolescent pregnancy, holds that it is "morally indefensible" for government to "privilege legal marriage over other relationships as the target for the intervention."[62] But if marriage is best for children, and particularly if it promotes their development and reduces the odds that they would live in poverty, wouldn't it be better to ask, not whether government should favor marriage, but under what circumstances it would be justified in favoring marriage, especially if it could do so without reducing support for single mothers and their children? Numerous federal and state policies that taken together cost tens of billions of dollars are designed to promote child development. If married-couple families promote child development more than other family forms, it makes sense for government to favor marriage. There is little doubt that increasing marriage rates would reduce the incidence of poverty and reduce economic inequality and thereby reduce the need for some government spending.

Furstenberg's argument would have more traction if government policy tried to compel people to get married. But there is no evidence that government policy, as represented by the many initiatives now taking place around the nation, is using coercion. Rather, government policy seems to be directed at showing people how both they and their children would receive a wide range of benefits if they form stable marriages while simultaneously providing adults with the skills and discipline needed to improve their relationships. There is also abundant evidence, especially from the Fragile Families study, that many cohabiting couples and couples that have had babies together want to get married—and even think that someday they will marry each other.[63] Under these circumstances it would seem justified for government policy to provide benefits, such as income supplements, that are contingent on marriage. Paternalistic policies of this type provide incentives to get people to make the choice they would make for themselves and their children if they considered the longer-term consequences of their actions. As we argue repeatedly in this book, paternalistic policies are justified as long as people have options.[64]

The second argument against government promotion of marriage is that marriage programs have not been shown to work. This argument is mostly true, with some modest exceptions, but is not entirely persuasive. Many progressives who argue against marriage programs on the grounds that they lack evidence of success support a range of other programs for low-income families that have little evidence of success. If evidence of success were a binding requirement for every government program, the federal budget would be spared scores of billions of dollars in current spending on programs for which the evidence is somewhat thin.[65]

Moreover, marriage programs are relatively new and have not had time to demonstrate their possible effectiveness. As detailed in appendix B, there are now a number of experiments being conducted to determine whether marriage programs produce measurable outcomes. Most policy analysts believe that new programs should be tried on a relatively small scale and that high-quality evaluations should be put in place as the programs are implemented.[66] Meeting this ideal model for testing new social policies is one of the most important strengths of the Bush marriage initiative. Although we wish there were more evaluations of the 125 or so marriage grant programs, the large-scale, multisite evaluations of the Building Strong Families, Supporting Healthy Marriage, and Community Healthy Marriage programs (see above and appendix B) promise to yield reliable information about whether marriage education and services can increase couple relationship skills, marriage rates, and child well-being. These results will begin appearing in 2010. Until then, the current scale of programs seems about right.

The third argument against programs designed to change family formation is that they cannot work. The patterns of low marriage rates, high cohabitation rates, and rising nonmarital births are by now deeply ingrained patterns of

American culture and cannot be easily changed, goes the argument. While we admit that the problem is in large part cultural and may require more than a programmatic response as a result, we reject this counsel of despair. Many social and cultural patterns of behavior in America have been slowed or reversed by the deliberate decisions of policymakers and public and private leaders at all levels of society. Smoking, a behavior deeply ingrained in both individual biology and American social norms, was cut in half in a generation.[67] Equally remarkable, the entire culture of smoking has changed. Americans cannot smoke on airplanes, in many public buildings, or even in bars and restaurants in many cities and counties. At a party one of us attended recently a guest commented on her way outside to smoke a cigarette in the dead of winter that she had to "join [her] friends on the deck of shame." Similarly, wearing seat belts, once a preoccupation of the fainthearted, is now almost universal.[68] Regular exercise, previously confined to school gym classes and athletic fields, has now become a consistent part of the routine of millions of Americans.[69] These examples show that deeply ingrained patterns of behavior can change. Why should it be any different with patterns of sexual behavior and family formation?

Marriage Education. We recommend that some parts of the Bush marriage agenda (see appendix B) be continued. However, we make this recommendation while stipulating that the Bush initiative is highly unpopular among some important advocacy groups and among many liberals. Yet as President Obama has made clear both in his books and in his public statements, he thinks marriage is vital to children and to the nation's future. Indeed, in his best-selling *The Audacity of Hope,* he explicitly endorses "marriage education workshops" that can help "married couples stay together" and encourage "unmarried couples who are living together to form a more lasting bond." He goes on to say that access to these programs, especially if they include job training and medical coverage, "should be something everybody can agree on."[70]

If President Obama can so clearly state his support for a policy very similar to the Bush initiative, it is time for conservatives to tone down the rhetoric and look for every possible way to compromise on the marriage initiative. The compromise by conservatives should include an explicit endorsement of services for both young married and unmarried low-income couples as well as an endorsement of birth control for young couples who want it. In addition, the already inclusive marriage projects, which feature mandatory attention to domestic violence, should continue to seek ways to cooperate with both domestic violence and fathers' groups. The wave of the future is to seek accommodation among these groups so that their agendas receive public support and their advocacy groups can work together.

One item on this common ground agenda should be support for the three sets of random assignment experiments initiated during the Bush administration that will soon yield important information on what works in improving couples relationships and on how to organize communitywide initiatives. The general approach to improving couples' relationships is marriage education combined with services. There are fifteen marriage education programs working with unmarried parents or married parents employing this basic approach but with some local variation in curriculum, breadth of services, and other important distinctions that could affect the outcomes. All the sites are also collecting information that will permit tests of whether children whose parents participate in relationship and marriage enhancement programs do better on standard tests of development or on school performance. It will also be possible to determine whether the programs have an impact on marriage rates, either by increasing marriage in the case of young unmarried parents or by reducing divorce in the case of couples who are already married. Given how far along all these programs are, combined with the fact that they are expected to begin publishing results by 2010, it would be a mistake to stop them in midstream. They can be continued for about $20 million a year, an expenditure that we support.

We would also continue the $100 million competitive grant program on marriage and the associated $50 million competitive grant program on fatherhood enacted in 2006. The money to complete the current five-year authorization is already in the budget baseline, so additional appropriations will not be required. Having visited some of the programs, met with program operators and HHS officials, and spoken with scholars evaluating the programs, we have no doubt that a number of the programs are poorly organized and have little or no hope of producing good results or yielding valuable information about how to influence marriage at the local level. Indeed, HHS has already terminated some of the programs for poor performance.

Thus the secretary should take action to determine which of the approximately 120 programs should be continued and then make a new round of grants on a competitive basis, requiring all current and new programs to compete for funding. We would broaden the language of the block grant so that states would have more flexibility than they now have to provide or pay for services, including activities that would help couples avoid second pregnancies and help them find employment. All programs should be required to report a standard set of data on program participants, types of intervention, attendance, and perhaps other basic information. In addition, the secretary should withhold $5 million a year from the $100 million marriage grant and $3 million from the $50 million fatherhood grant to conduct gold-standard evaluations of the most promising programs.

Tax Reform. Given the enormous complexity of the federal tax code, it seems doubtful that most couples can easily understand whether getting married will expose them to higher or lower federal and state taxes.[71] For low-income families, there is the added complexity of the impact of marriage on benefits such as TANF and food stamps. Nor is it easy for policymakers to understand the specific incentives and disincentives imposed on married couples. To address this problem, in 2006 the Department of Health and Human Services published a "marriage calculator" developed by researchers at the Urban Institute.[72] The calculator is Internet accessible and can be used by anyone to determine the financial impact of marriage on low-income couples residing in any state. The calculator applies federal and state benefit and tax policies to the income of unmarried couples with given characteristics and determines whether they will experience penalties or benefits if they marry. This calculator can be used by both federal and state legislators to determine which provisions of benefit and tax law are likely to impose penalties on low-income couples who want to marry.

The effect of marriage on the benefits and taxes of cohabiting couples, a group that has grown exponentially in recent years, has been studied by Gregory Acs and Elaine Maag of the Urban Institute. They selected cohabiting couples with combined incomes of less than 200 percent of poverty from their nationally representative sample of families to determine the impact on both EITC and TANF payments if the couples marry.[73] They divided the sample into two groups: those that received TANF cash benefits and those that did not. Of the 14 percent of all couples that received TANF, more than 70 percent would receive a higher EITC payment if they married; the higher payments would average nearly $3,400 annually. However, these same families would experience a loss of TANF cash benefits averaging around $2,000. Still if their gain from the EITC and loss from TANF are combined, this small share of cohabiting couples has net gains from marriage averaging $1,400. These are average figures and disguise the fact that about 4 percent of couples on TANF would actually have a net loss of income if they decided to marry. In the case of the 86 percent of low-income couples not receiving TANF, a little more than 10 percent would receive net penalties averaging around $1,800, while just over 75 percent of couples would receive a net bonus averaging around $2,300. Generally, the Acs and Maag study shows that the combined federal tax and welfare system imposes penalties on only a small minority of cohabiting couples who marry and, at least in the case of couples with incomes under 200 percent of poverty, that the EITC provides a substantial marriage incentive.

Analyses of this sort could be used by federal and state legislators to locate provisions in their welfare or tax policies that could be reformed to remove marriage disincentives. In the Acs and Maag example, it is clear that a policy that allows couples receiving TANF or food stamps to continue their benefits for a year or two after they marry would reduce a marriage disincentive. Both federal and state policymakers should explore these analyses to determine reforms that would reduce marriage disincentives in their benefit and tax policy.

An important reason that the current federal tax system is often friendly to low-income couples who marry is a set of reforms of the tax system, especially the Child Tax Credit, that were made as part of tax cuts enacted in the early 2000s. The reforms included an increase in the standard deduction and a widening of the 15 percent rate bracket for married couples. The law also extended by $3,000 the income level at which the EITC begins to phase down for married couples.[74] Another marriage-friendly provision of the 2001 reforms expands the refundability of the Child Tax Credit so that more couples would be eligible for the credit and most couples already eligible would receive a bigger check from the IRS. According to the Tax Policy Center, the Child Tax Credit is now the biggest provision in the tax code to help families with children. In 2007 it provided an average of around $1,450 to 31 million families at a total cost of $45 billion.[75]

From the perspective of making the federal tax code friendlier to marriage, these were excellent reforms. Nonetheless, these provisions, like the entire tax code, are bewildering to all but tax experts. They are so complex that even low-income couples, despite the fact that they use relatively simple IRS forms, often find it necessary to spend part of their scarce income to pay a professional tax preparer to complete the forms.[76] Thus we believe that further steps to reduce marriage penalties and simplify the tax code could be an important part of any future overhaul of the tax system.

Marriage penalties will always exist as long as taxes are progressive and government provides means-tested benefits such as TANF, food stamps, and other low-income programs.[77] However, as the refundable Child Tax Credit illustrates, it is possible to provide more income to low-income families while simultaneously encouraging work and marriage. Not only did the refundable Child Tax Credit reduce marriage penalties more than any other reform of the tax code since the vast 1986 overhaul of the entire code, but it also now provides more than $5 billion a year in benefits to around 9 million low-income and moderate-income couples and more than 18 million children.[78]

Changing the Culture. We have recommended several new policies designed to reduce nonmarital births and promote marriage. But none of these policies is likely to be very effective unless there is also a change in the wider culture. It is by now a common observation that we live in a culture that, to put it mildly, glorifies casual sex and is not supportive of marriage. Sex in the media is not only ubiquitous, it rarely has any serious consequences for those involved. Yet research shows that those who are exposed to high levels of sexual content on TV are more likely to have a nonmarital birth than those who are exposed to low levels of sexual content.[79] Nor, with a few exceptions, are there many happily married couples on primetime TV shows.

In light of these obstacles, we think it vital that public figures at all levels of society speak out forcefully in favor of childbearing within marriage and the importance of children living with their married parents. In addition, we recommend that Congress appropriate $500 million a year to plan and implement a social marketing campaign similar to the National Cancer Institute's "5 A Day for Better Health" to improve nutrition and the American Legacy Foundation's "truth" campaign to reduce smoking among youth. Typically, such campaigns use both print and electronic media—and increasingly the Internet-based new media and the social networks they have spawned—to reach a broad group of teens and young adults with new messages that give them positive reasons (such as, it's "cool" to not smoke) for adopting new behaviors.[80] The message of the campaign we recommend should be that great advantages accrue to individuals who follow the success sequence: finish school, get a job, marry, and have children—in that order. This message need not be delivered in a way that sounds preachy. Instead, the younger generation needs to be convinced that it is in its own best interest, as well as its children's, to bring back the informal but culturally powerful norms of the success sequence and that these particular norms are the ones that can work to make their own dreams a reality.

What research we have on the effectiveness of media campaigns on behavior suggests that when they are well designed and implemented they can have substantial effects.[81] A meta-analysis of forty-eight health-related media campaigns, from smoking cessation to AIDS prevention, finds that on average such campaigns increase the preferred health-related behavior in about 9 percent more people than in a comparison group.[82] The "truth" campaign is estimated to have been responsible for roughly 22 percent of the decline in youth smoking between 1999 and 2002.[83] Even when the effects of such campaigns are small, which they typically are, they have a major impact because of the very large numbers of people that can be reached through the media. In contrast, most intervention and service programs, because they are expensive and require well-trained staff and other resources, are unable to saturate a population enough to change social norms.

Conclusion

Our recommendations in this chapter are based on our belief that the nation's task of reducing poverty and promoting economic opportunity will be much more difficult if such a large share of children continue to be reared by single parents, especially if these children continue to be disproportionately from low-income families. There is not a more important divide between the middle class and the poor than the much higher share of middle-class children being raised by both parents.

The good news is that an increasing number of influential voices recognize that marriage is the cultural first choice for rearing children. Examples include recent books by Bill Cosby and Alvin Poussaint and by Juan Williams, along with the public statements of our last two presidents, quoted at the beginning of this chapter.[84] If their statements are any indication, the cultural tide supporting married, two-parent families may be growing. Let us hope it is a tsunami.

eleven
Paying the Bills

We need a new intergenerational contract that invests more in people when they are young, but then expects them to assume somewhat greater responsibility for their own support during their retirement years.

ISABEL SAWHILL

Let's pretend we're a family sitting around the kitchen table discussing the condition of our budget. Recently we wanted to take a well-deserved vacation and make some repairs on our house. The total cost was more than we could afford based on our income, so we did what millions of other Americans do and simply put the costs on our credit card. Now we have a chance to buy into some very promising investments—all but certain to generate a reasonable return at some point in the future—but we don't have the cash to pay for the investments. We could borrow some more, but we already have an alarming level of debt.

This little household tale describes the current state of the federal budget. In one of the greatest abdications of fiscal responsibility in the nation's history, starting in the early 2000s policymakers of both parties abandoned reasonable and time-tested budget principles, ignored the needs of future generations, and spent money in every imaginable way—and several ways no normal person could have dreamed up—while simultaneously cutting taxes.[1]

As the federal government accumulated one of the largest piles of IOUs in the nation's history, the nation's poverty continued at a high level and inequality reached heights not seen since the Roaring Twenties. Wages stagnated, middle-class jobs are under threat, and those at the bottom of the income ladder are having difficulty climbing up, especially if they are African American. Simultaneously, the nation's public schools have slipped into mediocrity, and a number of nations have passed the United States in both the share of their young people graduating from high school and college and student performance on international tests of academic achievement. We show in the previous three chapters that there are solid proposals that reason and evidence suggest hold promise for producing returns that will benefit both individuals and society in the short and long run. They would also encourage behaviors that move individuals and families out of poverty and into the middle class. Most of them are also consistent with our emphasis on encouraging personal responsibility and rewarding it when it occurs. Taken together, our proposals have the potential to help millions of younger families and their children and to move the country and its economy back into a position of international educational and economic leadership.

Even so, the two of us cannot simply recommend that the federal government spend the money necessary to pursue these worthy ends and ignore the deficit implications. Along with our colleagues at Brookings and at other organizations in Washington representing widely differing political perspectives, for the past several years we have devoted considerable time and energy to studying, writing about, and traveling around the nation trying to inform the public about the fiscal crisis.[2]

All of this work led us to recommend raising taxes and cutting spending. These are the necessary ingredients to extricate the nation from its impossible financial promises.[3] We cannot in good conscience now turn around and recommend billions of dollars of new spending without explaining how we would finance the spending. Evidence suggests that most of the spending may produce economic and social returns at some point in the future, but we cannot be certain of that. Rather, in this chapter we intend to do what we call on policymakers to do: lay out a plan that identifies how to pay for any new spending.

We begin with a brief review of the fiscal challenges facing the country. We then summarize the costs of our proposals. Next we outline a general approach to paying for new investments (both those recommended in this book and others) that involves revising the intergenerational contract now defining what younger and older Americans owe each other. We end with specific recommendations for paying for the proposals advanced in this book.

Deficits Unbound

After exemplary budget discipline by the Congress and the first President George Bush during the early 1990s, and even greater budget discipline by the Clinton administration and the Republican-controlled Congress during the mid-1990s, President George W. Bush and Republican and Democratic Congresses not only reversed the discipline achieved in the 1990s but also greatly exacerbated the nation's budget problems. None of the presidents or Congresses dealt seriously with the underlying forces driving the nation's long-term deficit. When the financial crisis hit in 2007 the Bush administration, and the Obama administration later, felt compelled to add several trillion dollars to the nation's debt to rescue the financial system and to get the economy moving.[4] Now it appears that the nation will have annual deficits in the range of $1 trillion far into the future.[5]

But this tale of budget woe over the next decade or so is not the worst of our financial problems. The federal government has promised to provide cash payments and health coverage to the elderly (including long-term care) that it cannot afford. Not only did recent Congresses and the Bush administration fail to address the problem, they actually made it worse by passing the Medicare drug benefit in 2003 and cutting taxes in 2001, 2002, and 2003. Each year that Congress and the president wait to solve the looming crisis of Medicare, Medicaid, and Social Security makes the required budget reforms more and more radical—which is to say that they will hurt more and more Americans, even if taxes are raised as they must be.

Perhaps there would be some excuse for federal policymakers if the budget projections were exaggerated or uncertain. Of course, there is always uncertainty in any projections, but as projections go those for Social Security and Medicare are about as solid as any projections can be. In the case of Social Security, payments will exceed income beginning in 2017, and the fund will run out of money in 2042. The seventy-five-year projection reveals an unfunded obligation of $4.3 trillion.[6]

The Medicare Trust Fund is in even worse shape. The fund is already being depleted because costs now exceed income; between 2008 and 2017 the fund's assets will fall from $326 billion to $96 billion. By 2019 the fund will be completely exhausted.[7] In fact for the past three years the financial condition of the Medicare Trust Fund has been so dire that the trustees have been required by statute to issue a "Medicare funding warning" and the president has been required to submit legislation to the Congress that addresses Medicare's funding problem (which Congress has ignored).

Clearly, the trustees' recent reports have been grim. An equally grim picture of the impact of Medicare, Medicaid, and Social Security on the federal budget is provided by figure 11-1. From about 9 percent of GDP and 40 percent of all federal spending in 2007, the three big entitlements are expected to grow to 18 percent of GDP and 100 percent of federal revenues by around 2040. After 2040 the programs just keep growing, reaching about 28 percent of GDP by 2080. There is nothing in sight to change any of these projections by any appreciable amount. Thus the current strategy of the federal government, which can be succinctly summarized as "What, me worry?" will soon lead us into uncharted waters that could sink the ship of state.[8]

Figure 11-1. Projected Spending for the Major Entitlement Programs, 2007–82

Percent of GDP

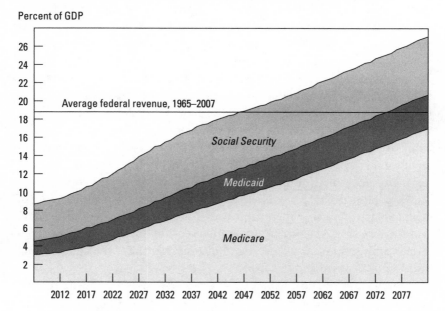

Source: Congressional Budget Office, *Long-Term Budget Outlook, 2007,* figure 1-1; Congressional Budget Office, *Long-Term Outlook for Health Care Spending, November 2007,* figure 1-1; unpublished data from Congressional Budget Office (http://cbo.gov/ ftpdocs/87xx/doc8758/11-13-LT-Health.pdf).

There are many reasons to be alarmed by projections like those in figure 11-1. One is that America is now dependent on foreign investors to maintain its level of spending. The Chinese, Japanese, and Saudis especially are responsible for buying up U.S. debt. Foreign investors have purchased more than 75 percent of the new debt issued by the Treasury Department since 2004.[9] What if foreign investors decide that the opportunity to invest is better in other countries or demand higher interest rates for their money? At worst, this could lead to an unprecedented economic crisis. At best, it could erode standards of living, as an increasing slice of U.S. incomes has to be earmarked to pay creditors. Interest payments were $249 billion in 2008 and are now headed much higher over the next decade, especially if interest rates rise.[10]

The budget problem isn't just an economic issue; it's a moral issue as well. The country has been putting new spending and tax cuts on the national credit card, expecting that its children and grandchildren will pick up the tab. An unfortunate aspect of passing on the debt is that the population is becoming

increasingly composed of minorities, especially Hispanics, who are dispropor-
tionally less educated and low income. As the predominantly white older workers retire, their Social Security and Medicare benefits will be financed in part by
the taxes paid by those who have difficulty supporting their own families, let
alone the families of the more advantaged elderly.

A less direct but more worrisome aspect of the federal government's continuing profligacy is the culture of debt accumulation it has helped to create
in America.[11] Perhaps people get the government they deserve, but given the
sturdiness of American democracy and the track record of its elected leaders
rising to the occasion in a crisis, it could be hoped that the federal government would pay its bills and stand against the rising tide of red ink, thereby
serving as an example of financial rectitude that all Americans could follow.
But instead the federal government led the way in establishing the culture of
debt and lack of regard for consequences. Is it any wonder that, with a government like this, Americans simply followed suit and borrowed so much
money against so little collateral and income that the financial crisis that
began in 2007 was all but inevitable?

Ironically, one certain outcome of the financial crisis is that the federal government has had to borrow still more money to try to prop up the nation's
financial system and to stimulate the economy. As a direct result of the financial crisis, the Committee for a Responsible Federal Budget estimates that the
federal government spent at least $2.4 trillion on bailouts and stimulus pack-
ages in 2008. Although the numbers are sure to change as the financial crisis
progresses, the committee now estimates that total exposure (the amount the
federal government might lose in the long run) of the federal budget on all the
2008 stimulus and bailout actions at several trillion dollars.[12] The human
mind struggles to even understand numbers this huge, let alone the size of the
hole the country is digging for itself and its children.

A Summary of Our Spending Proposals

Taken together, our proposals cost a little more than $20.5 billion a year
(table 11-1). We propose $8.5 billion in spending on preschool and postsec-
ondary education, $10.9 billion on work and work supports, and more than
$1 billion on reducing nonmarital births and promoting two-parent families.
Most of the spending is on grant programs for which spending can be tightly
controlled.

A number of our major proposals reflect our faith in the ability of researchers to design gold-standard evaluations that will guide policy implementation and lead to ideas about how programs can be improved. We pre-

Table 11-1. Federal Costs of Strengthening Education, Work, and Families: A Summary

Billions of dollars

Proposal	Cost
Improve education (chapter 8)	
Preschool	
Institute new competitive grants for early childhood education	6.000
K–12	
Institute a competitive grant to be used for teachers' bonuses	2.000
Carry out research on paternalistic schools	0.010
Postsecondary	
Terminate federal programs that support college preparation	−0.800
Create single competitive grant program to support college preparation	0.600
Increase federal grant program for state longitudinal data systems	0.200
End four federal student aid grant programs	−1.35
Increase Pell grants	1.35
Create incentive grants for state college financing voucher programs	0.500
Subtotal	8.510
Support and encourage work (chapter 9)	
Lower the threshold of the Child Tax Credit	3.100
Phase out Child Care and Dependent Tax Credit between $100,000 and	
$150,000 for married couples ($75,000 and $100,000 for others)	−1.000
Expand Child Care and Development Block Grant	2.000
Continue Child Support Enforcement	0.030
Create employment and training apprenticeships	0.040
Institute employment and training block grant	2.000
Institute an EITC expansion for young males	2.000
Create an inflation adjustment for TANF	1.000
Institute a TANF grant for disconnected mothers	0.500
Link housing grant program with increased work	1.000
Expand food stamps work programs	0.200
Subtotal	10.870
Strengthen families (chapter 10)	
Institute teen pregnancy block grant	0.500
Terminate abstinence education Title V program	−0.050
Expand Medicaid for family planning	−0.100
Institute community college grant program to reduce pregnancy	0.250
Carry out research on reducing pregnancy among twenty-somethings	0.025
Continue Bush multisite demonstration programs	0.020
Institute a social marketing campaign	0.500
Subtotal	1.145
Total	20.525

sent strong evidence that a number of small-scale programs aimed at improving education, supporting work, and reducing teen pregnancy have produced significant benefits. However, scaling up small programs is tricky. The difference in results between evaluations of the Perry Preschool and Abecedarian programs compared with the national evaluation of Head Start is a striking example. The best solution to this long-standing problem is to gradually expand the model programs while continually evaluating and adjusting.

The need to invest more in the education and training of children and adolescents is supported by a large majority of the public.[13] Moreover, unlike many areas of the federal budget, most of the education and training investments we recommend can improve the future productivity of the nation. Greater investments in early childhood education could bring society long-term benefits that exceed their costs. Investments in youth entering the labor force, investments to help teenagers and twenty-somethings avoid nonmarital pregnancies, and investments to provide financial aid to college-bound youth could also pay for themselves in the long run. Other proposals, such as expanded funding for child care and housing, will help those who play by the rules, ensure that prosperity is more broadly shared, and promote self-sufficiency.

Reframing the Budget Debate

But if we are to fund the types of investment we recommend, we first need to reframe the debate about the federal budget. Specifically, we need a new intergenerational contract that invests more in people when they are young but then expects them to assume greater responsibility for their own support during their retirement years. If we make wise investments in the young, their ability to be more self-sufficient during their later years will be enhanced, as will their productivity, so they can contribute to increased national wealth and pay taxes to finance the health care and retirement needs of those who have been less fortunate. But the country must start now. The longer it waits, the more likely that today's children and young adults will be incapable of supporting either themselves or their parents during the latter's golden years.

The need to reframe the intergenerational contract is premised on a number of assumptions.[14] First, linking investments in the young to the reform of entitlements for the elderly could have bipartisan appeal because it emphasizes both personal and social responsibility. Second, the current allocation of resources between the young and the old is premised on outmoded assumptions about the relative needs of each. Generational equity requires a recalibration of the needs of the different age groups. Third, if any changes to the intergenerational contract are phased in slowly and with careful attention to the genuine needs of the older population, no one will be seriously hurt in the process. If change is begun now, commitments to current beneficiaries can be maintained, a robust safety net for vulnerable groups can be provided, and more public resources can be reallocated to the young.

We are convinced that unless the country makes major investments in the education of the young and in workforce programs, future generations will not be better off than previous ones and the economy will not be as competitive as it needs to be. Money alone will not solve all of the problems. However, whether it's addressing the fact that the early home environments of young children put them at risk for school failure, the fact that one-third of young people don't graduate from high school on time, or the fact that almost half of children born into poor families are still poor when they reach adulthood, money is surely needed.[15] So where is this money to come from? According to Eugene Steuerle of the Peterson Foundation, rising costs in entitlement programs for the elderly will absorb most of the currently projected federal revenue growth.[16] Not only will there be no new money for children, there will be a fiscal squeeze on existing programs for children. In other words, if the nation continues along the federal spending path it is on, not only will it fail to make the types of investments we recommend here, but it will be forced to actually cut currently projected spending on children and families.

Dead-End Budget Ideas

Many progressives assume that the solution is simply to raise revenues enough to simultaneously keep deficits at a reasonable level and to pay for the most promising investments in children and their families. Many conservatives assume we can eliminate congressional earmarks along with fraud, waste, and abuse to fund similar efforts. But these assumptions are wrong.

Why can't the necessary revenue be obtained simply by raising taxes? First of all, poll after poll shows that the public is not enamored of new taxes.[17] But even if the taxes (required by our scenario of funding some new programs and simultaneously addressing existing and future deficits) are imposed, these higher taxes would also impose perhaps untenable burdens on typical working-age Americans. The incomes of most members of the middle class have been stagnant, and their jobs and incomes are increasingly insecure. Reducing their take-home pay to fund these investments is neither politically realistic nor a wise idea. Further, higher taxes on productive workers and investors at some point would begin to have a serious impact on the growth of the American economy.

Why can't the needed revenues be achieved by cutting earmarks and waste? Spending on earmarks totals less than $20 billion a year.[18] Even entirely eliminating earmarks would make only a small dent in a federal budget that totals close to $3 trillion a year or in a deficit well in excess of $1 trillion. Similarly, although there is certainly waste, fraud, and abuse in the federal budget, the Government Accountability Office estimates that only a few billion could be saved with tough legislative provisions to prevent waste and fraud. Again, even a few billion is modest compared with the magnitude of the deficits the country faces.[19] Certainly waste, fraud, and abuse should be attacked with vigor, but even eliminating most of it would be at most a baby step compared with the giant steps needed to substantially reduce the deficit.

Another hope is that a major overhaul of America's broken health care system will free up resources that can then be devoted to other national priorities. This, too, is wishful thinking. Most improvements in the health care system—from the adoption of electronic medical records to covering the currently uninsured—will actually cost more than the current system.[20] Over the long haul, learning what works to improve health, and linking reimbursement of providers to evidence that their treatments are effective, could bring down costs, but not any time soon.[21] In the meantime, one of the most effective ways of getting more value for each health dollar spent is to put more emphasis on education rather than on health care per se. Education is associated with major improvements in people's health, independent of their income, their age, or the amount of health care they receive—probably because the more educated are more likely to adopt healthy lifestyles and to be intelligent users of health care.[22]

A final possibility is that elected officials, faced with such daunting federal deficits, will continue to simply say, in effect, "deficits be damned." What harm do they do anyway? In this case, advocates for children would do well to remember that it is the young who will suffer the consequences of this loose and wishful thinking. The national debt, and the amount we owe foreigners, constitutes a stealth tax on future generations. At this writing, net interest payments on the federal debt are scheduled to soon resume their position as the fastest growing item in the federal budget, and the country is financing most of each year's deficit by borrowing from abroad.[23] Eventually creditors will have to be paid back, and with interest.

The preceding statements should not be misinterpreted. The country can and should raise more revenues both to move the budget toward balance and to fund new investments. It can and should rein in earmarks and fraud. It can and should reform the health care system to cover the uninsured, improve quality, and contain health care costs. There may be some savings associated with the drawdown of troops in Iraq, but these savings will need to be reinvested in Afghanistan. None of these steps will be sufficient to fund a robust agenda of investments in working-age families and their children. For this reason, the nation should consider ways in which it can rein in future commitments to the elderly while simultaneously protecting lower-income seniors, the disabled, those in poor health, and the truly aged.

Forging a Bipartisan Compromise

Democrats in Congress are not going to preside over any dismantling of the New Deal or the Great Society that created today's Social Security, Medicare, and Medicaid programs. Not only are these programs extremely popular with the public, but Democrats fear that any savings produced by even modest changes in these programs may be devoted to providing tax cuts to those who need them least. This fear is understandable in the context of recent history. However—especially now that Democrats control both the legislative and executive branches of the federal government—such political concerns should not stand in the way of a robust discussion of the relative needs and responsibilities of people when they are young and when they are old. Still, from a Democratic perspective, any proposal to reform entitlements will need to be combined with assurances that some of the money saved can be reinvested in other areas.

Similarly, Republicans are not going to support more investments in the young if they believe the investments will require bigger government and a substantially higher burden of taxation. From their perspective, any proposals to invest more in education or other areas need to be accompanied by a commitment to reform entitlements for the elderly and to keep spending from exploding. While hardly ideal from either party's perspective, this linking of entitlement reform with greater investments in the younger generation, including lower-income families in particular, has the makings of a political compromise with long-term benefits for the nation. With strong leadership from the White House, this compromise has a decent chance of success.

Still another concern is that reallocating resources between the young and the old seems to entail pitting one group against another. However, this concern rests on a basic misunderstanding of the life-cycle process. Almost everyone who is young will eventually become old. So putting some transition issues aside for the moment, our proposals are not about a competition between the young and the old but rather about making more investments in people when they are young so that they will be in a better position to support themselves and others when they are older. Individuals have the capacity, if not always the foresight, to smooth consumption over the life cycle. They do not have the capacity to eliminate differences in ability, health, and productivity that are the products of their differing genetic and cultural endowments, and especially in the case of children from poor families, of changing investments society did or did not make in them during their childhood and adolescence. By adopting a life-cycle perspective, the country can move beyond stale arguments about generational warfare.

Generational Equity: Reassessing the Relative Well-Being of the Young and the Old

The traditional intergenerational contract has been in force since Social Security was enacted in the 1930s. It was expanded in the 1960s with Medicare and Medicaid and yet again in the first decade of the twenty-first century with the addition of prescription drugs to Medicare. These social insurance programs are built on a number of assumptions: that no one should be expected to work after the age of sixty-five; that most seniors have insufficient resources to pay for their own retirement and health care; and that younger Americans are, on average, better off than older Americans. The system relies almost entirely on contributions from working-age Americans to finance these benefits while simultaneously supporting the other major dependent population, their children. For the most part, the traditional contract has been a huge success, enabling people to retire at a reasonable age and greatly reducing insecurity and poverty in old age.

Nevertheless, the contract hasn't kept up with the times (table 11-2). First, consider the facts about today's elderly. Like other age groups, they are a very diverse population. But whether we look at their income, their assets, their health, their longevity, or their own preferences to stay connected to work and community, the elderly have far more capacity to contribute to their own well-being and to society's than in the past.[24] For example, the inflation-adjusted, median household income of those sixty-five and older increased 89 percent between 1967 and 2007, while the median income of those in their prime earning years, aged thirty-five to forty-four, increased by only 27 percent.[25] Even more striking is the decline in poverty among the elderly, from 35.0 percent in 1959 to 9.7 percent in 2007.[26] Compare this poverty rate to the much higher rate of 13 percent among nonelderly households and the still higher rate of 20 percent among children under age six. Equally striking is the fact that 80 percent of people sixty-five and over own their own homes and that three-quarters of these elderly homeowners own them free and clear of a mortgage.[27]

Tomorrow's elderly—meaning today's baby boom generation—will be the wealthiest generation in history. Projections by the McKinsey Global Institute indicate that by age sixty-five average disposable income for late baby boomer households will be a little over $100,000 a year, or about 50 percent higher than the incomes of those currently that age. Although incomes fall as people retire, even those in their seventies, according to McKinsey, will have average incomes of about $80,000 a year.[28] The problem, as the McKinsey Institute and others note, is that boomers are saving too little during peak earning years,

Table 11-2. Comparative Statistics, the Elderly and the Nonelderly

Unit as indicated

Measure	Under age 65	Age 65 and older
Poverty rate (percent)	12.7	9.4
Average income per household member (dollars)	26,350	24,095
Mean income (dollars)	72,906	41,928
Median income (dollars)	54,726	27,798
Annual change in real income, 1994–2006 (percent)	0.74	1.11
Annual change in real income, 2000–06 (percent)	−0.71	0.47
Median net worth (thousands of 2004 dollars)	69.40	190.10
Home ownership (percent)	64.3	80.0
Home owners with no mortgage (percent)	24.0	75.0
People covered by health insurance (percent)	82.2	98.5

Source: Isabel V. Sawhill, "Paying for Investments in Children," in *Big Ideas for Children: Investing in Our Nation's Future* (Washington: First Focus, 2008), table 1.

with the result that there may be pressures not just to maintain but to increase the government benefits they receive when they retire. However, the solution to inadequate saving is not additional government benefits. It is policies that encourage, or even mandate, greater savings when people are young. This approach must be part of the new intergenerational contract: public policy must nurture or mandate the kind of personal responsibility that goes hand in hand with greater public investments in earning capacity at a young age.

Of course the country must maintain a robust safety net for the elderly. But all the evidence suggests that many older Americans—with or without government assistance—will be comfortably well off in the future, assuming they have access to good jobs and save enough during their working years. Even now, there are more than 1 million people over the age of sixty-five with incomes exceeding $100,000 a year.[29]

Not only are the elderly economically better off than they used to be, they are living longer and healthier lives as well. Many of the elderly are experiencing what experts, such as the Stanford researcher James Fries, call "compressed morbidity"—meaning a decline in disability rates.[30] Because this decline in disability has exceeded the decline in mortality, it has extended not just life but also healthy life and the ability to work. We should celebrate this progress, some of it made possible by the fact that the elderly, unlike the nonelderly, have universal health care.

Although the elderly have improved their situation greatly since the intergenerational contract was formed in the 1930s, working America has also gone through immense changes. In the economy of the 1950s and 1960s, the United States dominated world markets, jobs could last a lifetime, a high school education was sufficient for achieving a middle-class lifestyle, and firms could readily afford to provide generous benefits in the form of health care and defined-benefit pension plans. At the same time, educational opportunities expanded and the proportions graduating from high school and going on to college rose steadily. Today the United States has seen high school graduation rates decline over the last few decades, and it no longer leads the world in the proportion of high school graduates who enroll in or graduate from college.[31]

There are many other signs that working-age Americans and their children are struggling. Over the past three decades young men have seen their wages stagnate. They are earning less, in inflation-adjusted terms, than their fathers' generation did at the same age.[32] Family incomes have crept up but only because more wives have gone to work. Poverty rates are now stuck at 1970s levels (except for female-headed families and the elderly), income inequality is as high as it was in the Roaring Twenties, and access to affordable health insurance has been sharply eroded. The cost of a college degree has increased much more than the rate of inflation, causing millions of young people to either forgo a college education or to go into debt.[33] According to UNICEF, on a range of indicators from education to health care to rates of poverty, children in the United States rank twentieth in well-being compared to children in twenty other advanced countries.[34]

The role of government in boosting the economic mobility of workers and in providing better education and job training for their children is therefore more important than ever. And yet the historic commitment made to the elderly by the traditional intergenerational contract is placing a real burden on the working-age population. Although many people believe that Social Security and Medicare benefits are fully funded by the payroll taxes they paid into the system during their working years, the reality is that these programs are not prefunded; instead tax dollars paid into the Social Security and Medicare accounts each year are used by the federal government to pay current expenses. Every dollar of benefits that goes to the elderly must, sooner or later, come out of the income of younger, tax-paying Americans. So the importance of balancing the needs of one group against the other must become part of our thinking. Those who argue that the way to handle the needs of both groups is to raise taxes to a much higher level seem to forget that the people who will pay those taxes are already struggling economically.

The Miracle of Compound Interest

One of the strongest arguments in favor of gradually reallocating resources from the old to the young is the growth dividend these investments can produce. Spending to make the young more productive is qualitatively different from spending that enables the old to consume. It is the reason people take out loans to go to college but not (one hopes) to go on a cruise or buy a new set of golf clubs.

When the nation invests in the young, assuming those investments are wisely chosen, the power of compound interest ensures that future earnings and GDP will be greatly enhanced. Most economists believe that the rate of return on investments in education, for example, is at least 8 percent and could be as high as 15 percent (see chapter 8).[35] Moreover, the value of such investments can compound over time, since learning begets more learning, both in school and in the workforce.[36] Assume conservatively, and with some discounting of future benefits, that the nation could earn a rate of return of 5 percent on investments in the young (figure 11-2). At the end of twenty years (when today's infants will be in college and today's ten-year-olds will be well into their work lives), the value of $1 would be $2.65. At the end of fifty years, it would be $11.47. If the rate of return were 10 percent, the value of a $1 investment after fifty years would be a spectacular $117.39. While we would not argue that all government programs targeted on children and younger families can achieve these kinds of returns, the point is that investing early in high-quality programs should still pay big dividends.

High-Priority Investments and How to Pay for Them

We recommend funding our proposed increases in spending on working-age families and their children with modest changes in programs for the elderly (table 11-3). Two funding options would impose minimal sacrifices on the elderly, while providing more than sufficient funds to pay for our agenda and still achieve nearly $26 billion in deficit reduction. One option would entail leveling the playing field between elderly and nonelderly citizens with the same incomes by taxing Social Security benefits more fully. Currently, only half of Social Security benefits are taxed for those with incomes above $25,000 ($32,000 for a couple), and up to 85 percent are taxed for those with incomes above $34,000 ($44,000 for a couple).[37] Fully taxing these benefits, after an exemption for the individual contributions made into the system, would raise $36.6 billion in 2012.

A second option would be to change the way Social Security benefits are indexed for inflation. Many experts believe that the current consumer price index for urban wage earners and clerical workers (CPI-W), which is used to adjust benefits, now overstates the rate of inflation because it fails to account for the fact that people's spending patterns shift in response to a change in prices. For example, when gas prices increase, people drive less or purchase

Figure 11-2. Compound Interest on Investment for Three Rates of Return, Ten through Fifty Years

Dollars

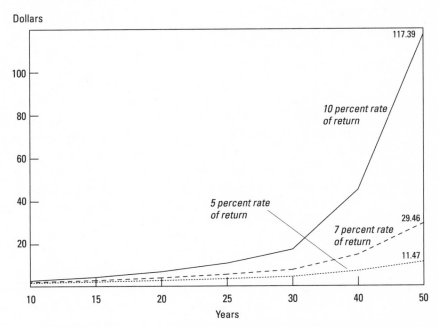

Source: Isabel V. Sawhill, "Paying for Investments in Children," in *Big Ideas for Children: Investing in Our Nation's Future* (Washington: First Focus, 2008), chart 3.

more fuel-efficient cars. An index that more accurately accounts for these changes in purchasing patterns would, if introduced now, save $9.3 billion in 2012. If this reform were introduced for Social Security, it should also be introduced as a better way to index all benefit and tax changes. The extra resources produced by applying the improved inflation adjustment to all benefit and tax programs that are adjusted for inflation could be used to protect low-income beneficiaries.

These short-term steps need to be combined with longer-term efforts to slow the growth of entitlement spending in a way that will bring projected deficits under control, reassure financial markets, and restore confidence in government. Policy changes to accomplish these objectives need to be enacted now and phased in gradually so that they enable people to plan for the future. Our plan also provides for investments in the younger generation that would enhance their productivity and thus their ability to afford their own and their parents' retirements. In other words, the gradual phase-in of the reforms we propose, combined with upfront investments in children, is exactly what is needed to ensure that those receiving the extra help when they are young are

Table 11-3. High-Priority Investments and How to Pay for Them, 2012

Billions of dollars

Investment	Amount
Cost-effective investments	
Strengthen education	8.510
Strengthen work	10.870
Strengthen families	1.145
Total	20.525
Possible ways to pay for them	
Tax Social Security and Railroad Retirement Benefits like defined-benefit pensions (by 2012)	36.600
Base Social Security cost-of-living adjustments on an alternative measure of inflation	9.300
Total	45.900
Deficit reduction after paying for investments	25.375

Source: Isabel V. Sawhill, "Paying for Investments in Children," in *Big Ideas for Children: Investing in Our Nation's Future* (Washington: First Focus, 2008), table 2.

the same people who are asked to contribute more as they age. To jump-start the process, it may be necessary to ask for some new taxes, some belt tightening among the currently retired population, and some forbearance of continuing deficits in the short run. But over time, each generation would be expected to invest in the next while in their prime earning years, in return for which members of the younger generation would be expected to take more responsibility for themselves as they aged.

The major Social Security options that should be debated include a gradual increase in the full retirement age (now about sixty-six) so that increased longevity does not lead to ever-higher lifetime benefits; progressive indexing of Social Security benefits that maintains future benefits for the less advantaged but entails a slower rate of growth in benefits for the most affluent; and changes in a variety of policies that might encourage later retirement. Currently, most people retire at age sixty-two or sixty-three. Some of this early retirement appears to be induced by the fact that the eligibility age for Social Security is sixty-two. Even though people get actuarially reduced benefits as a result of retiring before age sixty-six, the eligibility age sends a strong signal that may have led to a change in social norms about the appropriate time to retire. In the meantime, people are living longer and healthier lives, and far fewer jobs require the kind of physical strength or stamina that may have necessitated such early retirement in the past.[38]

The challenge of slowing the growth of Medicare will be much greater than the problem of restoring solvency to the Social Security system.[39] Like Social Security, Medicare is affected by the aging of the population. However, in addition, its explosive growth is fueled by rapidly rising health care costs per person. Many experts now believe that the most promising long-term approach to this problem is to learn what works and to base reimbursement policies for providers on this knowledge. Because Medicare is the single largest payer in the system, it can lead the way in collecting this evidence and redesigning reimbursement policies accordingly. But it will be many years before any cost savings are actually realized.

By revising the intergenerational contract, we can create a better future for all Americans, young and old. The investments we recommend would both increase the productivity of our economy and enhance the odds that every child, regardless of family background, would have a chance to do well in school, go to a two-year or four-year college, and get a good job. But programs alone will not be enough. Young Americans will need to adopt the success sequence of education-employment-marriage-parenthood that we so strongly recommend. This, along with the policies recommended in this book, would greatly improve the chances that our investments would pay off for them and for their country.

Grants, Loans, and Tax Provisions for Postsecondary Students

This appendix provides an overview of the three main types of student aid—grants, loans, and tax breaks—and traces changes in spending on aid over the past decade. We also present a brief comparison of changes in grant aid with the rapidly rising costs of tuition and fees at private and public four-year and two-year colleges.

Grants

Within the federal grant program category, the major program, which distributes about 70 percent of federal grant funds, is the Pell grant (table A-1). The grant is based on need and operates through more than 5,000 postsecondary institutions that honor the federal payment. The amount of the grant depends on the student's expected family contribution, the cost of the college in which the student is enrolled (or has been accepted), and whether the student is full time or part time.[1] Pell grants have increased by 75 percent in real terms over the last decade. About 5.4 million students received a Pell grant in 2007–08, an increase of 3.4 million over the last three decades.[2] Although the maximum Pell grant of about $4,700 in 2008–09 seems generous, the maximum grant would have to be about $10,000 to cover the same proportion of the cost of attending a public four-year college as it did three decades ago.[3] Low-income students hoping to attend college must figure out how to make up the difference.

Another major type of federal grant aid to students pursuing postsecondary education is aid to veterans and active duty military personnel. After congressional expansions in 2008, veterans programs provided about $5.1 billion, up nearly 100 percent over the past decade.[4] The G.I. Bill may not

Table A-1. Student Grant Programs, 1997–98 and 2007–08

	Billions of 2007 dollars		Percent
Grant	1997–98	2007–08	change
Federal			
Pell	8.22	14.40	75
Federal Supplemental Educational Opportunity			
Grant	0.76	0.77	2
Leveraging Educational Assistance Partnership	0.07	0.07	1
Academic Competitiveness Grant	. . .	0.35	. . .
SMART Grants	. . .	0.23	. . .
Veterans	1.75	3.52	101
Military and other	0.95	1.63	72
Total	11.73	20.95	79
State and private			
State grant programs	4.42	7.96	80
Institutional grants	16.33	29.07	78
Private employer	5.05	10.44	107
Total	25.80	47.47	84
Total	37.53	68.42	82

Source: Sandy Baum and Kathleen Payea, "Trends in Student Aid: 2008" (Washington: College Board, 2008), p. 6.

play as substantial a role in postsecondary education as it once did, but the $5.1 billion in aid for veterans and active-duty military supports around 520,000 students and offers exactly the path to better jobs and economic security for students from poor and low-income families that we hope to widen.[5] The military, arguably the institution in our society with the least discrimination based on race, ethnic group, or economic background, is a viable pathway to the middle class for youth from low-income families.[6]

Nonfederal sources of grant aid, at over $47 billion, are also substantial. The biggest single source is institutional grants, at a little over $29 billion. This category includes contributions to postsecondary institutions from a variety of sources, including state legislatures, alumni, and other individuals and groups interested in helping students based on need or merit or both. The approximately $8 billion from state legislatures is for both merit-based and need-based grants and scholarships. Typically, these funds are designated for specific schools within the states, usually public colleges and universities, and then the college distributes the funds under state guidelines.[7]

In addition to all of these sources of financial aid, state and local governments spend vast sums of revenue on general support for their colleges and universities. According to the State Higher Education Executive Officers, in 2008 state and local governments spent more than $85 billion supporting their colleges and universities.[8] Most economists find that these expenditures are regressive in the sense that the large subsidies go to flagship schools that mostly serve middle-to-upper income students.[9] If these subsidies are included in calculations of public support for higher education, the entire package would probably look less progressive than it does when we focus on student aid alone.

Private employers contribute over $10.4 billion for grants and scholarships at postsecondary institutions. There are at least two major categories of funding sources within this $10.4 billion. First, many employers pay for their employees to take courses or complete degree requirements at postsecondary institutions. Second, a host of individuals and organizations, including foundations, service and fraternal organizations, corporations, research centers and institutes, and individuals, create scholarship programs. Like nearly every other source of student aid, private sector spending is increasing annually.[10]

If spending is any measure, the last decade has seen a growing commitment on the part of the federal government, state government, state and private colleges themselves, and the private sector to helping Americans attend college. Each sector has increased its support for postsecondary grants by nearly 80 percent or more in dollars adjusted for inflation. This constantly increasing level of investment in postsecondary education by so many sectors of American society indicates the great value our society places on postsecondary education and the faith these sectors have that their investments will produce returns to individuals and society. That such a large fraction of this spending is directed to students from disadvantaged families demonstrates the confidence this wide swath of American society has in the ability of postsecondary institutions to help students improve their prospects. In both of these senses, the public and private sectors are in alignment, and their investments are working together to produce exactly the outcome we are pursuing; namely, reducing poverty and increasing economic mobility through postsecondary education. The money could—and we argue should—be used to help even more disadvantaged students.

Loans

Since President Johnson's Higher Education Act of 1965, the federal government has been heavily involved in helping students and families get loans for postsecondary education.[11] It is easy enough to see why. The costs of a college education are substantial and growing: the cost of a four-year education for in-state students at a public university at 2007–08 prices averaged about $54,000; for out-of-state students about $96,000; and for private colleges about $129,000.[12] Nor are these formidable prices stable. The National Center for Educational Statistics estimates that the average increase in the annual cost of attending a four-year college over the decade ending in the 2005–06 school year was about 30 percent in dollars adjusted for inflation.[13] Many families cannot afford to pay these costs without help.

A possible solution to this problem is for students themselves to borrow money. However, the typical seventeen-year-old who wants to go to college is short on all three qualifications—collateral, earnings from secure employment, and a solid credit history—that loan institutions look for. Moreover, from the student's perspective, it takes a certain amount of faith in future income to go many thousands of dollars in debt. If the policy goal is to give young people good reason to continue their education, throwing them into the regular loan market where, given their collateral, earnings record, and credit history, they would undoubtedly pay high interest rates, is not an ideal approach. But with the federal government guaranteeing the loans or providing the loans directly, students can get the money they need to attend postsecondary institutions at reasonable interest rates. Government or private sources can subsidize all or part of the loan and arrange generous repayment terms.

Like all the other categories of assistance for students, the commitment to loans from both government and the private sector has been growing rapidly (table A-2). Over the decade ending with the 2007–08 school year, federal loans increased by 70 percent, adjusted for inflation. Loans sponsored by states more than tripled, while loans from the private sector grew by nearly 600 percent.[14] That the private sector is growing so rapidly suggests that there may be some difficulty with the federal loan system, causing students to borrow from private institutions at rates that are probably much higher than the rates offered by the federal programs.

There are two major types of federal student loan programs. The Stafford Federal Family Education Loan Program (FFELP) provides money from the private sector, usually banks and other lending institutions. The federal government stipulates a maximum interest rate and guarantees the loans. In addition, some of the loans based on need are offered interest free with the federal government picking up the tab for the interest.[15] The second type of loan is the Ford Direct Student Loan (FDSL). In this program, the federal government uses its own resources to provide the loans, thereby cutting out the private sector. Both of these major types of loans can be further subdivided into subsidized and unsubsidized loans. In the subsidized loan programs, which are available only to needy students, the federal government pays the interest while the students are in school and for six months thereafter. By contrast, in the case of unsubsidized loans, which are available to stu-

Table A-2. Student Loan Programs, 1997–98 and 2007–08

Loan	Billions of 2007 dollars		Percent change
	1997–98	2007–08	
Federal			
Subsidized Stafford			
Federal Direct Loan Program	7.23	5.81	−20
Federal Family Education Loan Program	13.69	22.63	65
Unsubsidized Stafford			
Federal Direct Loan Program	4.28	4.86	14
Federal Family Education Loan Program	8.92	21.65	143
PLUS			
Federal Direct Loan Program	1.17	2.29	96
Federal Family Education Loan Program	2.30	8.30	261
Perkins	1.38	1.10	−20
Other	0.28	0.17	−40
Total	1.66	66.82	70
Nonfederal			
State sponsored	0.45	1.46	224
Private sector	2.54	17.60	592
Total	2.99	19.06	537
Total	42.25	85.88	104

Source: Sandy Baum and Kathleen Payea, "Trends in Student Aid: 2008" (Washington: College Board, 2008), p. 6.

dents regardless of financial need, interest accumulates from the date the loan is issued. The interest rate in the unsubsidized program is now fixed at 6.8 percent; Congress has dropped the rate in the subsidized program to 3.4 percent, which is gradually being phased in. Counting both subsidized and unsubsidized loans in the two major programs, the federal government was responsible for $54.95 billion in loans in 2007–08, up by over 60 percent from $34.12 billion in 1997–1998 in dollars adjusted for inflation.

In addition to the two major programs for students, the federal government operates the PLUS loan program for parents. Parents can get either direct loans or FFELP loans but the total amount borrowed by parents cannot exceed the cost of attending school minus all other financial aid. PLUS loans have also been increasing rapidly, growing from $3.47 billion in 1997–98 to $10.59 billion, or by over 200 percent in 2007–08.

The smallest federal loan program is Perkins loans. Congress has not appropriated any new money for Perkins loans since 2005, so the only new federal money comes from loan cancellations. The structure of the Perkins program is unique. Each of the approximately 1,800 participating postsecondary institutions has a revolving loan fund to supply the cash for student loans. Funds from the federal government are distributed to participating postsecondary institutions based on a formula. The actual loan is taken from the institution's revolving fund, to which the school must add a matching contribution equal to at least one-third of the federal allocation for that year. Money that is repaid by students is returned to the revolving fund and used to finance new student loans.[16]

Tax Breaks

The fundamental purpose of the tax code is to raise money to pay for government. In doing so, there is nearly unanimous agreement among scholars, policymakers, and the public that the income tax should be progressive. The widely praised tax reforms of 1986 greatly increased the progressivity of the federal income tax by removing nearly all poor and many low-income families from the tax rolls.[17] It is estimated that about one-third of all households, and about half of families with children, pay no federal income taxes.[18] In addition to the fundamental goal of creating an income tax system that reflects the principle of equity, the tax system has increasingly been used to give tax breaks for socially valued activities. The Congressional Joint Committee on Taxation has analyzed thirty-seven tax provisions designed to provide tax advantages (including exclusions, exemptions, deductions, preferential rates, deferrals, and credits) related to socially valued outcomes such as saving for retirement, purchasing health insurance, reducing poverty, promoting education, promoting employment, and overcoming disability.

Several of the provisions are tax breaks for college expenses.[19] According to Pamela Jackson, an analyst at the nonpartisan Congressional Research Service, before 1997 the collective cost of the modest tax provisions designed to promote education was less than $2 billion a year.[20] But under the urging of the Clinton administration, in 1997 Congress enacted four new provisions that doubled the number of tax provisions for education and greatly expanded their cost. There were two major tax credits (the Hope Credit and the Lifetime Learning Credit), a deduction of interest on student loans, and an exclusion of earnings from the previously established federal Coverdell savings accounts. The two tax credits alone now cost about $7 billion a year. In 2001 yet another tax provision—an above-the-line deduction for higher education expenses—was added to the tax code.[21]

Here is an overview of the federal tax provisions for postsecondary education:[22]

Hope Credit: Enrolled half-time; first two years of college only; 100 percent of first $1,000; 50 percent of second $1,000; maximum credit of $1,800; applies to qualified tuition and related expenses; phases out between $96,000 and $116,000 for married taxpayers filing jointly (for 2008); adjusted for inflation; cannot have a felony drug conviction.

Lifetime learning tax credit: 20 percent of first $10,000 of tuition and related expenses; phaseout same as Hope Credit; can be used for graduate school; can be enrolled for any number of courses

Parental exemption for students: Parents who pay for college expenses of their children can continue to claim them as an exemption through age twenty-three.

Business expense deduction: Taxpayers can deduct the costs of qualifying work-related education expenses (tuition, fees, books, certain travel costs). However, expenditures on work-related education that would qualify the taxpayer for a new trade or business cannot be deducted.

Business deduction of student loan interest: Businesses can deduct from their income expenses associated with education provided to their employees.

Family deduction for student loan interest: Qualified education expenses (tuition, books, room and board, fees) up to a maximum of $2,500 can be deducted; the deduction is phased out ratably over the range from $115,000 to $145,000 for couples, indexed for inflation.

Section 529 plans: Under prepaid 529 plans, investors can purchase tuition credits from state colleges and universities at current rates to be used in the future. Under 529 savings plans, growth comes from an underlying investment, usually in mutual funds. The rules for both types of education investments are established by states, within federal guidelines. Distributions from these plans are exempt from federal income tax.

Coverdell education savings accounts: Similar to 529 plans, Coverdell accounts allow money to accumulate and be withdrawn tax free for qualified education expenses at a qualified institution. A maximum of $2,000 a year per child can be contributed. Unlike any other tax provision, qualified spending includes spending on elementary and secondary education.

Above-the-line deduction for higher education expenses: Qualified educational expenditures (defined in the same manner as for the Hope Credit) can be deducted before adjusted gross income is computed; maximum deduction of $4,000 a year for up to $130,000 income for couples; maximum deduction is $2,000 for couples with income between $130,000 and $160,000.

Exclusion for employer-provided education assistance: Employers may pay and deduct a maximum of $5,250 for college (including graduate school) expenses under an educational assistance plan for their employees (but not dependents). The education does not have to be job related.

Exclusion for interest on U.S. Savings Bonds: Redeeming tax bonds is interest free for bonds purchased after 1989 by someone age twenty-four or older if the money is used for education; tax exclusion is phased out ratably between income of $100,650 and $130,650 (indexed to inflation).

Exclusion of scholarships: Most scholarships and grants are tax free if the recipient does not work for the payment.

None of these provisions fits well with the long-standing emphasis of federal education policy on helping poor and low-income families because they have little or no income tax liability against which to claim the credit. The credits, as well as the other recent tax provisions, are designed to help the middle class. But here's the problem: neither of the education credits is refundable. If they were, families without federal income tax liability would receive a check from the federal government equal to the amount of the credit for which they qualify.

Given this structural issue with tax credits, it is hardly surprising that Leonard Burman and his colleagues at the Tax Policy Center find that, in sharp contrast with the Pell grant, education credits give most of their benefits to families that are neither poor nor low income.[23] Their analysis shows that less than 5 percent of either credit goes to families with incomes under $20,000. Instead, more than half the benefits go to families with incomes of more than $50,000.

These tax credits appear to be motivated by the desire of Congress to do favors for the broad middle class. Middle-class parents are highly motivated to send their children to college, and many parents help their children with college costs. Thus with costs rising at a remarkable pace, more and more middle-class parents complain to their elected officials.[24] President Clinton and Congress saw an opportunity to help the middle class and did so. But as the analysis by Burman and his colleagues shows, in doing so they provided virtually no help to students from poor and low-income families.

The Bush Marriage Initiative

In the early years of the Bush administration, Wade Horn, the assistant secretary for children and families at the Department of Health and Human Services, used his authority to require several offices and programs within his agency to test ways that couple relationship building and marriage could be encouraged within existing programs. Before Horn left the administration in 2007, one or more of these marriage projects were initiated by the Office of Child Support Enforcement, the Office of Refugee Resettlement, the Children's Bureau, the Office of Head Start, and others.

Healthy Marriage Demonstration Grants

Across the agencies, more than 100 grants were awarded to conduct a wide range of activities to strengthen couple relationships and provide specialized services. These activities include strengthening the relationship of poor unwed parents to encourage fathers to provide support for their children; providing training to local leaders with heavy refugee populations so they could create programs to help refugee couples solve problems associated with adapting to a new culture; and offering relationship and marriage education and support services to parents adopting children and to low-income couples at risk of committing child abuse or neglect. These grants aimed both to convince the diverse administrative units within the Department of Health and Human Services (HHS) to consider how they could use their discretionary funds to help couples and parents improve their relationship and work more effectively together to solve their problems.

More broadly, Horn hoped to create a network of grassroots programs that could stimulate the already existing but tiny marriage movement. The underlying theory was that the traditional problems addressed by HHS— getting fathers to pay child support, helping refugees adapt to America, helping parents avoid abuse and neglect, getting parents involved in their child's education—could all be addressed by strengthening the bond between parents and by helping them work together to address the problems at hand. If programs of this type could be created all over the country, the traditional problems addressed by HHS might diminish, because married-couple families could learn to support themselves and their children.

As these grant programs were getting under way, Horn began to emphasize the importance of marriage education. Marriage education programs had a solid track record of helping middle-class couples strengthen their marriages. HHS funded a comprehensive review of the literature on these programs by the respected Urban Institute in Washington. The review was conducted under the leadership of Matthew Stagner, a former senior official at HHS in the Clinton administration and a widely respected researcher of poverty issues and issues regarding abused and neglected children. Stagner and his team of researchers examined abstracts of nearly 13,000 studies and articles and selected thirty-nine studies that met their criteria for quality. They concluded that "marriage and relationship programs provide benefits for the couples they serve." Specifically, the programs greatly increased relationship satisfaction and moderately improved communication.[1]

Although the conclusion is good news for supporters of marriage education programs, two caveats are important. First, almost all the programs were conducted with white, middle-class couples. Because the focus of the Bush marriage initiative was on low-income, minority couples, it is not clear that the types of marriage education programs found to work well by Stagner and his team will produce the same hopeful results when used with low-income couples. Second, few of the studies reviewed by Stagner followed their couples for more than a few months after they participated in the program. Even if marriage education does produce good results with low-income couples, there are no data from the Stagner review to suggest that these effects would last. For both of these reasons, we cannot be more than cautiously optimistic, based on the social science literature, that the Bush marriage education programs will produce meaningful impacts over the long run.

Healthy Marriage Competitive Grants

Using the $100 million allocated for competitive grants by the welfare reauthorization bill, in October 2006 HHS awarded 125 grants ranging in size from $132,000 to $2,342,000, with an average of about $610,000.[2] The grantees are nonprofit, community-based organizations, colleges and universities, county and state governments, for-profit organizations, and faith-based organizations. Most of the grant funds are being used to conduct programs on healthy relationships and marriage education, but other marriage-related activities are being supported as well. These include public advertising campaigns, marriage education in high schools, divorce reduction programs, marriage mentoring using married couples as mentors, and programs to reduce the marriage penalty inherent in many means-tested programs. Well over half the awards went to nonprofit, community-based organization, most of which had previously received federal grants. All the programs are required by federal rules to include consultation with domestic violence providers as the programs are developed and implemented.

In addition to consulting with domestic violence experts, many of the programs use a formal protocol that provides guidance in how to handle situations in which domestic violence has occurred or is suspected.[3] The National Healthy Marriage Resource Center, funded by HHS to provide technical assistance and training to the competitive grant programs, published a packet of resource materials on domestic violence. As often happens with competitive grant programs like the Bush marriage initiative, few if any of these 125 projects are being evaluated by high-quality designs. Thus the possibility of learning whether any of the programs are improving marriage quality or the well-being of adults or children is minimal. On the other hand, it seems likely that the Bush administration did not propose this program primarily to learn whether certain approaches to promoting marriage and relationship skills would produce impacts. As shown in chapter 10, the administration had a clear plan and numerous high-quality research studies in place to produce knowledge of this type. Rather, it seems likely that the administration had two purposes for proposing the national competitive grant program.

First, the program funds many ongoing but cash-starved community marriage programs sponsored by faith-based organizations and other nonprofit organizations in communities throughout the nation. For at least a decade before the Bush presidency there had been a nascent promarriage movement consisting of scholars, faith-based organizations, ad hoc community-based groups, and a few state and local governments.[4] The Bush strategy was to insert dollars into the programs that made up this modest movement and into their sponsoring organizations so the programs could grow and perhaps reach a critical mass, at which point they could become lasting fixtures of the cities, counties, and states they served. The grant funds also supported entirely new programs, many in communities that had not previously had marriage programs. It will be several years before enough evidence has accumulated to evaluate the success of this strategy, the outcome of which could be a growing and vibrant marriage movement with impacts on marriage rates and children's well-being at local and state levels.

The second purpose of these grants was to create a national network of influential individuals and organizations that are strong supporters of the marriage initiative. When the time arrives, probably in 2010, to reauthorize the welfare reform law and the $100 million of support for the marriage movement, these individuals and organizations could constitute a formidable force arguing on behalf of continuing the competitive grant program. Again, it will not be obvious until the moment of reauthorization arrives whether the Bush administration's plan to create a permanent marriage lobby has produced the intended effect.

Multisite Evaluations

Ironically, although often accused of ignoring science and even withholding data that did not support its positions, the Bush administration in 2002 launched sophisticated and far-reaching experiments on marriage programs.[5] These experiments can be divided into three groups.

The first experiment, known as Building Strong Families (BSF), has been testing the effects of marriage education and associated services in seven states.[6] Across all the sites, around 5,000 couples have been randomly assigned to a program group or a control group. All couples had or were about to have a baby outside of marriage at the time of assignment. Couples attend a dozen or more one- or two-hour sessions spread over six months, usually with three or four other couples, on how to effectively communicate with each other, how to control their emotions and avoid conflicts that could lead to arguments or worse, how to develop trust in each other, how to manage and work with their children, and other topics important to marriage. A typical format for the sessions is that two trained professionals introduce the marriage issue to be discussed in that session, provide basic information, and raise questions. Couples then join in, and a lively discussion usually ensues. Some of the sessions involve watching videos or role playing. Booster sessions, mentoring, marriage coaching, and social events often follow the curriculum session.[7] The program includes other group sessions with facilitators trained to connect couples with community services like help in getting jobs, child care, mental health care, and domestic violence intervention.

Attendance is a serious problem. Only around 60 percent of the couples assigned to the program show up for at least one session (although in some projects 80 percent have shown up for one or more sessions).[8] The typical couple attends between half and one-third of the sessions, their attendance declining steadily between the first and last scheduled sessions, despite the fact that most of the programs have a family coordinator who works directly with the families and encourages attendance.[9]

The second experiment, called Supporting Healthy Marriage (SHM), is similar to Building Strong Families except that the couples are already married and the goal is help them create or maintain a healthy, low-conflict marriage. The outcome of the experiment will be knowledge about whether marriage education can improve the relationship between married parents and thereby promote the well-being of both the parents and their children. Nearly 6,500 couples are participating or have participated in the SHM projects at eight sites operating in seven states.[10] Like the BSF experiment, this one also features a marriage curriculum, community services, domestic violence prevention, and a family coordinator.[11]

Although it will be 2010 or later before results from the BSF and SHM experiments are ready for publication, our direct observations and discussions with program operators at several sites lead us to conclude that two problems are already apparent. The first is that attendance is low in most programs. Averaged across all sites, about 70 percent of couples attended less than 40 percent of the twenty or so curriculum sessions.[12] Some of the projects report that attendance by males is especially challenging. The second issue is that the programs are quite expensive. Mathematica estimates that the per couple cost of the BSF program is around $10,000, not counting research costs. At $10,000 per couple, the costs of a national program would be substantial, although it seems likely that refinements of the original programs could somewhat reduce costs.

The third experiment is known collectively as the Community Healthy Marriage initiative and is radically different from BSF and SHM.[13] The underlying idea is that many organizations in local communities that have an interest in marriage can work together to reestablish the norm of marriage as the most important and fulfilling relationship between couples and the best environment for raising children. Churches, antipoverty groups, business clubs, fraternal organizations, businesses, and local governments all have a stake in promoting healthy marriages and thriving children. The goal of community initiatives is to knit together as many of these organizations as possible to create a bottom-up movement to nurture marriage as the community norm.[14] As early as 2002 Horn's Administration for Children and Families (ACF) used child support demonstration funds and local child support offices to stimulate community marriage initiatives. When new marriage grant funds were authorized by the 2006 welfare reauthorization, ACF funded fourteen community initiatives as well as an elaborate evaluation to compare three communities with initiatives with three communities without.[15] The marriage initiative communities were coalitions of secular and religious organizations that cooperated with local governments to plan and implement such marriage-supportive activities as relationship and marriage education, train-the-trainer programs, high school courses, and messages on billboards, radio, and television about the importance and value of marriage.

The initiative in Grand Rapids, Michigan—one of the early initiatives funded by HHS through the Child Support Enforcement program—is coordinated by a nonprofit organization that has signed participation agreements with a number of community partners. Among the most important partners are ten neighborhood organizations in low-income, primarily black, communities. In these communities, service providers that offer employment, child care, and mental health services added marriage and relationship skill training to their programs. More than 2,000 individuals and couples have attended these programs, although participation by women was higher than participation by men. A survey of participants shows that, although they initially had low expectations, they believed they had made progress in partner problem solving, listening, and making decisions together. They also say they learned about independence, responsibility, compromise, and better ways of working with their children.[16]

Summary

The Bush marriage initiative is one of the few strikingly new directions in American social policy (along with Child Support Enforcement, the Earned Income Tax Credit, and mandatory work programs) since the outpouring of innovation at the beginning of the War on Poverty.[17] The initiative addresses one of the most important social problems in the nation, namely, the decline in both marriage and the share of children living with both their parents. Further, there is growing agreement that if a greater share of children lived with both parents, poverty would decline, and a number of important measures of child well-being—including high school graduation rates, mental health, teen pregnancy, delinquency and crime, inactivity in early adulthood—would improve. But because programs to improve relationships and increase marriage rates are in their infancy, the Bush marriage initiative is based on the assumption that the best approach is to conduct high-quality evaluations of program models and to encourage advocates and community groups to initiate activities that could lead to new program models. The hope would then be that second- and third-generation programs could improve on the original models and produce even better results.

Notes

Chapter One

1. U.S. Bureau of Economic Analysis, *National Income and Product Accounts* (2009), table 2.1.

2. Lyndon B. Johnson, Commencement Address at Howard University, "To Fulfill These Rights," *Public Papers of the Presidents of the United States: Lyndon B. Johnson, 1965* (Government Printing Office, 1966), vol. 2, p. 636.

3. Robert Haveman and Timothy Smeeding, "The Role of Higher Education in Social Mobility," *Future of Children* 16, no. 2 (2006).

Chapter Two

1. James Q. Wilson, *The Moral Sense* (New York: Free Press, 1993).

2. Adam Smith, *The Theory of Moral Sentiments* (1759), as cited in ibid., p. 31.

3. Edward O. Wilson, "The Biological Basis of Morality," *Atlantic Monthly*, April 1998, p. 59.

4. J. Wilson, *The Moral Sense*, p. 60.

5. Ibid., p. 64.

6. Alan Sanfey and others, "The Neural Basis of Economic Decision-Making in the Ultimatum Game," *Science*, June 13, 2003; J. Wilson, *The Moral Sense*, pp. 62–63.

7. J. Wilson, *The Moral Sense*, pp. 29–39.

8. E. Wilson, "The Biological Basis of Morality," p. 59.

9. World Bank, "Public Attitudes Matter: Political Economy in the Design of Safety Nets Policies," Social Safety Nets, Primer 12, 2003. Data suggest that the more similar a country's middle class is to the poor, the stronger the political support for the poor. Similarly, less racially diverse countries, including many Latin American countries (Chile, Uruguay, Costa Rica), are more likely to have advanced social insurance and safety net programs relative to racially diverse countries (Mexico, Brazil), in which poverty is concentrated among indigenous populations.

10. J. Wilson, *The Moral Sense,* p. 36.

11. This typology was developed by Daniel P. McMurrer and Isabel V. Sawhill, *Getting Ahead: Economic and Social Mobility in America* (Washington: Urban Institute, 1998). Also see Isabel Sawhill and John Morton, "Economic Mobility: Is the American Dream Alive and Well?" (Washington: Economic Mobility Project, an Initiative of the Pew Charitable Trusts, 2007); for more information on the Economic Mobility Project, see www. economicmobility.org/.

12. This emphasis on procedural fairness in a U.S. context is often conflated with a strong orientation toward believing that markets are not only efficient but also fair. Professional economists have long argued that markets do produce efficient outcomes—at least under some highly simplified assumptions—but they have never maintained that these outcomes are inherently equitable. The ultimate fairness of a society can only be determined through the democratic process.

13. Robert Plomin and J. C. DeFries, "Genetics and Intelligence: Recent Data," *Intelligence* 4, no. 1 (1980).

14. John Rawls, *A Theory of Justice* (Harvard University Press, 1971).

15. Robert Nozick, *Anarchy, State, and Utopia* (New York: Basic Books, 1974).

16. Christopher Jencks, "What Happened to Welfare?" *New York Review of Books,* December 15, 2005.

17. Amartya Sen, *Development as Freedom* (New York: Knopf, 1999). Inspired by Amartya Sen's discussion of capabilities, economists Robert Haveman and Andrew Bershadker reevaluated U.S. poverty using a measure they call self-reliant poverty. An individual is among the self-reliant poor if he would still be poor working full time, year around, at the expected wage given his education, age, race, marital status, geographic location, and other factors. According to Haveman and Bershadker, self-reliant poverty almost doubled between 1975 and 1997, while the official poverty measure grew by roughly a quarter. See Robert Haveman and Andrew Bershadker, "The 'Inability to Be Self-Reliant' as an Indicator of Poverty: Trends for the U.S., 1975–97," *Review of Income and Wealth* 47, no. 3 (2001).

18. European Commission, *Portfolio of Overarching Indicators and Streamlined Social Inclusion, Pensions, and Health Portfolios: April 2008 Update* (http://ec.europa.eu/ employment_social/spsi/docs/social_inclusion/2008/indicators_update2008_en.pdf).

19. United Nations Development Program, *Human Development Report 2007/2008* (New York: 2007).

20. Rafael Di Tella and Robert MacCulloch, "Some Uses of Happiness Data in Economics," *Journal of Economic Perspectives* 20, no. 1 (2006), p. 27.

21. Richard A. Easterlin, "'Does Economic Growth Improve the Human Lot? Some Empirical Evidence," in *Nations and Households in Economic Growth: Essays in Honor of Moses Abramovitz,* edited by Paul A. David and Melvin W. Reder (New York: Academic Press, 1974). Also see Carol Graham, "Happiness, Economics of," *The New Palgrave Dictionary of Economics,* 2nd ed., edited by Steven Durlauf and Larry Blume (New York: Palgrave Macmillan, 2008). Note, however, that recent research has called

into question the veracity of the Easterlin paradox, particularly with regard to cross-country comparisons. Using higher quality and more recent worldwide polling data, some researchers have discovered a direct linear relationship between happiness and income across poor and rich countries, which suggests that absolute income does play a fundamental role in determining well-being. However, the matter is still up for debate, with some arguing that a host of measurement issues—including the sample of countries included, the framing of the happiness survey question, and the specification of the income variable—may influence the true functional form of the relationship. For more on this debate, see Justin Wolfers and Betsey Stevenson, ""Economic Growth and Subjective Well-Being: Re-assessing the Easterlin Paradox," *Brookings Papers on Economic Activity*, no. 1 (2008); and Carol Graham, Soumya Chattopadhyay, and Mario Picon, "The Easterlin and Other Paradoxes: Why Both Sides of the Debate May Be Correct," in *International Differences in Well-Being*, edited by Ed Diener, John Helliwell, and Daniel Kahneman (Oxford University Press, forthcoming).

22. Another explanation emphasizes adaptability. As an entire society prospers, people adjust their aspirations or expectations upward. Goods and services that may have once seemed like luxuries come to be seen as necessities (examples are washing machines, indoor plumbing, electrical refrigerators, automobiles, central heating). Similarly, at an individual level, those who receive a big raise at work or win the lottery may experience a temporary burst of psychic pleasure, but such feelings tend to be transitory. Psychologists studying how people react to good or bad events note that levels of psychological well-being are related more to individual differences in psychological temperament (what psychologists call one's internal set point) than to external events, at least in the long run. See Daniel Kahneman and Alan B. Krueger, "Developments in the Measurement of Subjective Well-Being," *Journal of Economic Perspectives* 20, no. 1 (2006), p. 14. Also see Daniel Gilbert, *Stumbling on Happiness* (New York: Knopf, 2006).

23. Alberto Alesina, Rafael Di Tella, and Robert MacCulloch, "Inequality and Happiness: Are Europeans and Americans Different?" *Journal of Public Economics* 88, no. 9-10 (2004). The authors suggest two hypotheses about why the relationship might be stronger in Europe than in the United States. The first is that Europeans may prefer more equal societies. The second is that social mobility is perceived to be higher in the United States, so that being poor is not seen as affecting future income or societal failures. The empirical evidence supports the second hypothesis.

24. U.S. Census Bureau, *Income, Poverty, and Health Insurance Coverage in the United States: 2007* (2008), pp. 12, 45. As we note in chapter 3, the exact poverty line varies according to family size to account for resource sharing among groups of individuals living together.

25. Shaohua Chen and Martin Ravallion, "Absolute Poverty Measures for the Developing World, 1981–2004," Policy Research Working Paper 4211 (Washington: World Bank, 2007). Annual figures measured at 1993 international purchasing power parity.

26. U.S. Census Bureau, *Historical Income Tables: Families* (2008), table F-8.

27. See, for example, Daniel Kahneman and Amos Tversky, eds., *Choices, Values, and Frames* (Cambridge University Press, 2000), p. xii.

28. Rafael Di Tella and Robert MacCulloch, "Some Uses of Happiness Data in Economics," *Journal of Economic Perspectives* 20 (2006); Carol Graham and Stefano Pettinato, *Happiness and Hardship: Opportunity and Insecurity in New Market Economies* (Brookings, 2001).

29. Compare to Benjamin Friedman, *The Moral Consequences of Economic Growth* (New York: Knopf, 2005).

30. For more on this seemingly incongruent belief system, see Benjamin I. Page and Lawrence R. Jacobs, *Class War? What Americans Really Think about Economic Inequality* (University of Chicago Press, 2009). Page and Jacobs, p. 3, describe what they call conservative egalitarianism.

31. Pew Research Center for the People and the Press, "Trends in Political Values and Core Attitudes: 1987–2007" (Washington: 2007).

32. National Public Radio, Kaiser Family Foundation, and Harvard University Kennedy School, "Poverty in America," 2001 (www.npr.org/programs/specials/poll/poverty/summary.html).

33. Ibid.

34. Since money is fungible, this view is itself quite naïve but still politically salient.

Chapter Three

1. "Debating Our Destiny," Second Presidential Debate, October 28, 1980, Cleveland, Ohio (www.debates.org/pages/debtrans80b.html).

2. In chapter 4, we address the question of whether increased inequality has been offset by greater mobility. In other words, have bigger gaps between rich and poor been accompanied by more opportunity for people to move up and down the income ladder? To anticipate chapter 4, our answer is no. Neither mobility over the life cycle nor mobility between generations appears to have increased over the past three or four decades. That means that lifetime inequality is also increasing.

3. U.S. Census Bureau, *Historical Income Tables: Families* (various years), table F-6.

4. Isabel Sawhill and John E. Morton, "Economic Mobility: Is the American Dream Alive and Well?" (Washington: Economic Mobility Project, an Initiative of the Pew Charitable Trusts, 2007), figure 4.

5. Although there has been an increased emphasis on performance in setting compensation for high-paid professionals and managers, there have nonetheless been several widely cited examples in recent years of highly compensated executives who were given big bonuses or golden parachutes while their company's bottom line plummeted. These dramatic though exceptional examples do not negate the general principle of high pay for high performance in the corporate world.

6. Between November 2007 and November 2008 food stamp program participation rose 14.4 percent. U.S. Department of Agriculture, Supplemental Nutrition Assis-

tance Program, "Program Data" (2009). The four-week moving average for the week of January 31, 2009, for unemployment insurance initial claims increased by 72 percent from the same week the previous year. U.S. Department of Labor, "Unemployment Insurance Weekly Claims Report," news release, February 5, 2009.

7. U.S. Census Bureau, *Statistical Abstract of the United States: 2009,* table 657; U.S. Bureau of Economic Analysis, table 1.1.9. (www.bea.gov/national/nipaweb/Index.asp).

8. Income figures presented in this chapter are based on household income unless otherwise noted. The Census Bureau defines a household as all the people who occupy a housing unit. Though using household income may overstate the degree to which individuals living together share economic resources, as in the case of young single workers living with platonic roommates, we feel that this measure best captures overall trends in how resources are distributed across the population. This measure differs from a measure of family income. The Census Bureau defines a family as a group of two people or more related by birth, marriage, or adoption and residing together. As such, measures of family income, particularly those published by the Census Bureau, tend to omit incomes of single individuals living alone or with other unrelated individuals.

9. We also looked at a posttax, posttransfer household income measure that includes adjustments for changes in household size. From 1979 through 2006 (the most recent data available), the top ninety-fifth percentile grew 61 percent, the fiftieth percentile grew 23 percent, and the bottom tenth percentile grew 10 percent. While these data show that current tax and transfer policies do have a small, but positive, effect on overall well-being, the trend remains similar to that observed in figure 3-1, mainly that growth is disproportionately concentrated at the top. The money income and the posttax, posttransfer figures both calculate family-size adjustments using the square root of the number of household members. Family-size adjustments attempt to give us a better idea about actual material well-being: for example, a family-size adjustment would take into account the fact that a married couple with an income of $40,000 may actually have more resources at their disposal than a family of six with the same income. An equivalence scale that uses the square root of household size (instead of just dividing by the number of household members) also attempts to capture the fact that some resource sharing is inevitable among people living together.

10. Figures 3-1 and 3-2 use slightly different measures of income. While figure 3-1 is based on household income for all individuals, figure 3-2 is based on family income, which excludes from the counts primary individuals living alone. Despite these differences, however, overall trends remain stark. Moreover, Mishel, Bernstein, and Shierholz observe that the inclusion of realized capital gains would reveal much more significant growth for the top quintile over the most recent period shown in figure 3-2. Lawrence Mishel, Jared Bernstein, and Heidi Shierholz, *The State of Working America, 2008/2009* (Washington: Economic Policy Institute, 2009), p. 61.

11. Gary Burtless, "Globalization and Income Polarization in Rich Countries," Issues in Economic Policy 5 (Brookings, 2007), p. 19.

12. Workers at the tenth percentile earned $7.87 an hour in 1979 and $7.79 an hour in 2007, all in 2007 dollars. This amounts to about a 1 percent decline in wages over the period. Workers at the fiftieth percentile (median) experienced an 8 percent increase in wages over the same period, while workers at the ninety-fifth percentile experienced a 36 percent increase. Mishel, Bernstein, and Shierholz, *The State of Working America, 2008/2009*, table 3.5.

13. For a more detailed discussion, see David H. Autor, Frank Levy, and Richard J. Murnane, "The Skill Content of Recent Technological Change: An Empirical Exploration," *Quarterly Journal of Economics* 118, no. 4 (2003); David H. Autor, Lawrence F. Katz, and Melissa S. Kearney, "Trends in U.S. Wage Inequality: Revising the Revisionists," *Review of Economics and Statistics* 90, no. 2 (2008). These works emphasize how shifts in the demand for workers have altered the wage structure. Alternatively, Claudia Goldin and Lawrence Katz focus on how changes in the supply of educated workers have affected trends in wages; see their "Long-Run Changes in the Wage Structure: Narrowing, Widening, Polarizing," *BPEA*, no. 2 (2007). Goldin and Katz argue that skill-biased technological change (SBTC) has existed for much of the past century, growing monotonically for much of that time. As such, although recent technological advances may have polarized wages (as described by Autor, Katz, and Kearney), recent supply changes reinforce and perhaps even overshadow such shifts in demand. In their 2006 review, David Card and John DiNardo present an even stronger challenge to the SBTC hypothesis, arguing that no one explanation can fully account for the trends observed over the past several decades because the trends of the 1980s and 1990s varied so significantly from one another. Card and DiNardo caution that "although factors beyond simple supply and demand are an important feature of the labor economics literature, they seem to have been pushed into the background by a focus on the technological change hypothesis." They emphasize that even if technological change is behind changes in wages over the past several decades this observation alone does not have clear policy implications. See David Card and John DiNardo, "The Impact of Technological Change on Low-Wage Workers: A Review," in *Working and Poor: How Economic and Policy Changes Are Affecting Low-Wage Workers*, edited by Rebecca M. Blank, Sheldon H. Danziger, and Robert F Schoeni (New York: Russell Sage, 2006), p. 114.

14. Golden and Katz, "Long-Run Changes in the Wage Structure."

15. U.S. Census Bureau, *Historical Income Tables: People* (various years), tables P-16 and P-17. Note that education definitions change slightly in 1991, from years of schooling to educational attainment. The earlier measure may erroneously count some workers with four years of high school or four years of college as having a diploma.

16. Autor, Levy, and Murnane, "The Skill Content of Recent Technological Change"; Autor, Katz, and Kearney, "Trends in U.S. Wage Inequality," p. 318.

17. Thomas Lemieux, "The Changing Nature of Wage Inequality," *Journal of Population Economics* 21, no. 1 (2008).

18. Ibid.

19. See William R. Cline, *Trade and Income Distribution* (Washington: Institute for International Economics, 1997); Robert C. Feenstra, ed., *The Impact of Interna-*

tional Trade on Wages (University of Chicago Press, 2000); Gary Burtless, "International Trade and the Rise in Earnings Inequality," *Journal of Economic Literature* 33, no. 2 (1995); Paul R. Krugman, "Trade and Wages, Reconsidered," *BPEA,* no. 1 (2008); Robert Z. Lawrence, *Blue Collar Blues: Is Trade to Blame for Rising US Income Inequality?* (Washington: Peterson Institute for International Economics, 2008).

20. Although the poverty rate for immigrants remains higher than for the native born (16.5 percent and 11.9 percent, respectively, in 2007), the two rates have followed similar trends over the last decade and a half, with the foreign-born poverty rate actually falling faster than the native rate. Though the share of immigrants has also grown over this period (from 8.7 percent in 1993—the earliest year for which we have consistent data from the U.S. Census Bureau, *Current Population Survey, Annual Social and Economic Supplement*—to 12.5 percent in 2007), an analysis by the Economic Policy Institute demonstrates that the decline in the immigrant poverty rate has largely offset the effect of increases in the foreign-born population on the total U.S. poverty rate. See Mishel, Bernstein, and Shierholz, *The State of Working America, 2008/2009,* p. 309.

21. Some of the failure of wages to keep pace with productivity is related to two measurement issues. One is the fact that nonwage compensation, especially health insurance benefits, has increased faster than wages but is excluded from these figures. See Gary Burtless, "Income Progress across the American Income Distribution, 2000–2005," testimony before U.S. Senate Committee on Finance, May 2007. The other is that the deflators used to measure productivity and wages are different, exaggerating the gap between the two series. See Lawrence, *Blue Collar Blues,* p. 18

22. U.S. Census Bureau, *Poverty Thresholds by Size of Family and Number of Related Children under 18 Years* (2007), table POV 35.

23. This amount was computed for families of various sizes in the mid-1960s. These poverty thresholds have been adjusted for inflation every year since the 1960s, but otherwise they are the same as when they were established. See Mollie Orshansky, "Counting the Poor: Another Look at the Poverty Profile," *Social Security Bulletin* 28, no. 1 (1965, reprinted in *Social Security Bulletin* 51, no. 10 [1988]). For details of Orshansky's original work, see Gordon Fisher, "The Development of the Orshansky Poverty Thresholds and Their Subsequent History as the Official U.S. Poverty Measure," Working Paper (U.S. Census Bureau, 1997, rev.).

24. To fully understand the dynamics of poverty, it is necessary to know about and count everyone who has ever been in poverty as well as how long they were in poverty, including repeat spells if they fell back into poverty after leaving. The longitudinal data sources most commonly used in the United States to measure the duration of poverty spells are the Survey of Income and Program Participation (SIPP) and the Panel Study of Income Dynamics (PSID).

25. Sharon M. Stern, "Poverty Dynamics: 2001–2003" (U.S. Census Bureau, 2008), figure 1.

26. See Ann Huff Stevens, "Climbing Out of Poverty, Falling Back In: Measuring the Persistence of Poverty over Multiple Spells," *Journal of Human Resources* 34, no. 3

(1999). A seminal work on the dynamics of poverty spells is Mary Jo Bane and David T. Ellwood, "Slipping into and out of Poverty: The Dynamics of Spells," *Journal of Human Resources* 21, no. 1 (1986).

27. W. Michael Cox and Richard Alm, *Myths of Rich and Poor: Why We're Better Off than We Think* (New York: Basic Books, 1999), p. 16.

28. Bruce D. Meyer and James X. Sullivan, "The Well-Being of Single-Mother Families after Welfare Reform," Policy Brief 33, Welfare Reform and Beyond (Brookings, 2005); Bruce D. Meyer and James X. Sullivan, "Three Decades of Consumption and Income Poverty," Working Paper 0416 (Chicago: Harris School of Public Policy Studies, 2006, rev. 2008), p. 3; Bruce D. Meyer and James X. Sullivan, "Further Results on Measuring the Well-Being of the Poor Using Income and Consumption," Working Paper 13413 (Cambridge, Mass: National Bureau of Economic Research, 2007).

29. New research by Richard Bavier suggests that consumption poverty can be better reconciled with income poverty when a more comprehensive definition of income is used. Constructing a posttax, posttransfer income measure of poverty following National Academy of Sciences panel recommendations, Bavier finds that poverty rates under his comprehensive measure are much more comparable to consumption poverty rates than the official poverty rate for 1984 to 2004. However, the debate is far from settled, with consumption poverty researchers continuing to advocate that measuring income is an inferior tool for understanding hardship and deprivation. For a flavor of the ongoing debate, see Richard Bavier, "Reconciliation of Income and Consumption Data in Poverty Measurement," *Journal of Policy Analysis and Management* 27, no. 1 (2008); Meyer and Sullivan, "Further Results on Measuring the Well-Being of the Poor Using Income and Consumption."

30. Constance F. Citro and Robert T. Michael, eds., *Measuring Poverty: A New Approach* (Washington: National Academy Press, 1995); Rebecca Blank, "Presidential Address: How to Improve Poverty Measurement in the United States," *Journal of Policy Analysis and Management* 27, no. 2 (2008).

31. Blank, "Presidential Address," p. 235.

32. Ibid. Also see Robert Haveman, "What Does It Mean to Be Poor in a Rich Society?" paper prepared for conference, "Changing Poverty," Institute for Research on Poverty, May 29–30, 2008.

33. If the United States were to use a similar standard, the poverty rate would be far higher. Daniel Meyer and Geoffrey Wallace find that 16 percent of Americans lived with posttax, posttransfer incomes below 50 percent of the median in 2006, considerably higher than the 12.6 percent of individuals living below the official poverty line. Daniel R. Meyer and Geoffrey L. Wallace, "Poverty Levels and Trends in the US and the US in Comparative Perspective," paper prepared for conference, "Changing Poverty," Institute for Research on Poverty, May 29–30, 2008.

34. Citro and Michael, *Measuring Poverty*, p. 154.

35. Conveners of the Working Group on Revising the Poverty Measure, "An Open Letter on Revising the Official Measure of Poverty," August 2, 2000.

36. Carmen DeNavas-Walt, Bernadette D. Proctor, and Jessica C. Smith, "Income, Poverty, and Health Insurance Coverage in the United States: 2007," Report P60-235 (U.S. Census Bureau, 2008).

37. Over 70 percent of poor adults have only a high school degree or less, almost 50 percent of poor, nondisabled adults are nonworkers, and close to 38 percent of the poor live in single-family households. Authors' calculations based on the U.S. Census Bureau, *Current Population Survey, Annual Social and Economic Supplement.*

38. For example, in 2007 the poverty rate for female-headed families with children was 37 percent, compared to 7 percent for married-couple families with children. The poverty rate for single-mother families fell dramatically over the 1990s, from a high of 47 percent in 1991 to a low of 33 percent in 2000. Since 2000 the poverty rate crept back up to a new high in 2007. U.S. Census Bureau, *Historical Poverty Tables: Families* (various years), table 4.

39. Andrew J. Cherlin, "American Marriage in the Early Twenty-First Century," *Future of Children* 15, no. 2 (2005).

40. Brady E. Hamilton and others, "Births: Preliminary Data for 2007," Report 57 (National Center for Health Statistics, 2009), table 1.

41. Data suggest that the parents in these fragile families rarely marry: according to one study, one year after the birth of the child only 15 percent had married and 26 percent had separated. See Cherlin, "American Marriage in the Early Twenty-First Century," p. 36.

42. U.S. Census Bureau, *Families and Living Arrangements, Historical Time Series* (various years), tables CH-1, CH-3.

43. Adam Thomas and Isabel Sawhill, "For Richer or for Poorer: Marriage as an Antipoverty Strategy," *Journal of Policy Analysis and Management* 21, no. 4 (2002).

44. Rebecca Blank, "Economic Change and the Structure of Opportunity for Less-Skilled Workers," paper prepared for the conference, "Changing Poverty," Institute for Research on Poverty, May 29–30, 2008.

45. Earlier work by Chinhui Juhn ("Decline of Male Labor Market Participation: The Role of Declining Market Opportunities," *Quarterly Journal of Economics* 107, no. 1 [1992]) does find that declining wages partially explain employment declines for men, particularly white men. However, more recent studies observe that this relationship weakened in the 1990s and 2000s. Indeed, while wages at the bottom have stagnated or even risen and employment rates among young white men and Hispanics have stabilized, employment among black men continues to fall. Harry Holzer and Paul Offner examine trends in employment, specifically among black men in the 1990s in "Trends in the Employment Outcomes of Young Black Men, 1979–2000," in *Black Males Left Behind,* edited by Ronald Mincy (Washington: Urban Institute, 2006). The authors generate regressions for employment and labor force participation, using data from the U.S. Census Bureau, *Current Population Survey, Annual Social and Economic Supplement,* to control for several "culprits": the relative availability of blue-collar occupations and jobs in the manufacturing industry, school

enrollment rates among black youth, and the share of employed females and employed black females. The authors find that the declining share of blue-collar jobs and the rising rate of school enrollment were most strongly associated with declining employment among young black men. Ultimately, though, the authors admit that the factors examined (even those with significant correlations) account for less than a third of the decline in employment among young black men and even less of the decline in labor force participation. Using the same data, Harry Holzer, Paul Offner, and Elaine Sorensen ("Declining Employment among Young Black Less-Educated Men: The Role of Incarceration and Child Support," *Journal of Policy Analysis and Management* 24, no. 2 [2005]) examine two additional factors that may have influenced labor force participation and employment among young black men. They again construct regressions for employment and labor force participation for young black males ages sixteen through thirty-four, this time controlling for incarceration rates among black males in each state and increased state activities designed to establish paternity and extract child support payments from noncustodial parents. They find that the two changes together account for a 1 percentage point decline in labor force participation among those ages sixteen through twenty-four and a 7 percentage point decline among those ages twenty-five through thirty-four; this amounts to about half of the decline in labor force participation among the older age group, a little less among the younger. Nevertheless, the authors conclude: "Some of the employment declines we've observed here, especially among those aged 16–24, do not appear attributable to incarceration or child support policy. As indicated elsewhere . . . a range of other policies would likely be needed as well to raise their employment rates. These might include efforts to improve education and training in this population as well as their incentives to accept low-wage jobs," p. 347.

46. See Ron Haskins, *Work over Welfare: The Inside Story of the 1996 Welfare Reform Law* (Brookings, 2006); Jason DeParle, *American Dream: Three Women, Ten Kids, and a Nation's Drive to End Welfare* (New York: Viking, 2004).

47. Peter R. Orszag, "Growth in Health Care Costs," Testimony before the U.S. Senate Committee on the Budget, January 31, 2008.

48. U.S. Census Bureau, *Detailed Poverty Tables* (2008), R&D table 2, definition 15.

49. Gary V. Engelhardt and Jonathan Gruber, "Social Security and the Evolution of Elderly Poverty," in *Public Policy and the Income Distribution,* edited by Alan J. Auerbach, David Card, and John M. Quigley (New York: Russell Sage, 2006).

50. The Congressional Research Service occasionally publishes a volume that provides details on all federal and state means-tested spending. The last volume estimates that spending at a little over $583 billion. In 2004 there were about 37 million poor people. See Congressional Research Service, "Cash and Noncash Benefits for Persons with Limited Income." Charles Murray has endorsed and provided details for a proposal similar to this one, although he would eliminate most government programs that provide money to individuals (not just money for the poor and low income) and provide a grant of $10,000 to every person (not just poor people) beginning at age

twenty-one. Charles Murray, *In Our Hands: A Plan to Replace the Welfare State* (Washington: American Enterprise Institute, 2006).

51. In 2001, 87 percent of those who agreed that welfare reform was effective cited the work requirement as a major reason for its effectiveness. Additionally, 78 percent of people asserted that there are jobs available for most welfare recipients who really want to work. National Public Radio, Kaiser Family Foundation, and Harvard University Kennedy School, "Poverty in America" (www.npr.org/programs/specials/poll/poverty/summary.html).

52. Isabel V. Sawhill. "Distinguished Lecture on Economics in Government: The Economist vs. Madmen in Authority," *Journal of Economic Perspectives* 9, no. 3 (1995).

53. This $65 billion closed 66.2 percent of the poverty gap. John Karl Scholz, Robert Moffitt, and Benjamin Cowan, "Trends in Income Support," paper prepared for conference, "Changing Poverty," Institute for Research on Poverty, May 29–30, 2008.

54. The other benefits included in this analysis were the EITC, Social Security, unemployment and workers' compensation, Supplemental Security Income, Aid to Families with Dependent Children, Temporary Assistance for Needy Families, and child welfare payments.

55. Andrea Brandolini and Timothy Smeeding, "Inequality Patterns in Western-Type Democracies: Cross-Country Differences and Time Changes," Working Paper 08/2007 (Turin, Italy: Centre for Household, Income, Labour, and Demographic Economies, 2008).

56. U.S. Census Bureau, *Historical Income Tables: Households* (2008), tables H-1, H-10.

57. The economist Stephen Rose observes that, while the middle class under this definition is doing well and is relatively heterogeneous (composed of blue-collar workers, professionals, minorities, and retirees), individual experiences differ tremendously. Statistically, very few blue-collar families and minorities earn more than $90,000, while this amount is just below the median for many professionals. Thus "for many members of the 'middle class,' $90,000 represents the most they can aspire to; for others, it is a stepping-stone on the way to a higher standard of living." Stephen J. Rose, *Social Stratification in the United States: The American Profile Poster* (New York: New Press, 2007), p. 27.

58. Brian W. Cashell, "Who Are the 'Middle Class'?" Report RS22627 (Washington: Congressional Research Service, 2007), pp. 3–4.

59. Authors' calculations based on the U.S. Census Bureau, *Current Population Survey, Annual Social and Economic Supplement* (various years). The middle quintile includes all family members and single individuals. All are assigned a family-size-adjusted income using the equivalence scale underlying the poverty measure. This is done by creating an income-to-poverty ratio based on the adjusted poverty line for each family size. Individuals are then broken into quintiles based on this income-to-poverty ratio. The income-to-poverty ratio for the middle quintile is 2.55 to 3.89.

This equates to 255–390 percent of the poverty line, or between $27,500 and $42,000 for a nonelderly single individual, for example, or between $53,600 and $81,800 for a family of four with two children. The income cutoffs for this quintile are slightly different from the reported household income cutoff figures cited in the text, because those figures do not make any adjustment for family size. While the equivalence scale underlying the poverty measure has come under some criticism, and alternative family-size adjustments abound (such as dividing family income by the square root of the number of family members, as shown in figure 3-1), this system provides the most straightforward way of comparing the middle quintile to the poverty population. There are 60 million people in the middle quintile, compared to about 37 million people in poverty.

60. More than half of adults in the middle class have at least some college education, and almost two-thirds work full time, full year. Only 14 percent of nondisabled middle-class adults are nonworkers. Authors' calculations based on the U.S. Census Bureau, *Current Population Survey, Annual Social and Economic Supplement.*

61. Burtless, "Income Progress across the American Income Distribution," figure 3. Burtless estimates that real average compensation paid to a full-time U.S. worker increased by almost $3,000 (5.6 percent) between 2000 and 2005. However, only a fraction of this growth is the result of increases in money wages: 35 percent is related to rising employer-provided health insurance expenditures, 24 percent to pension contributions, and 12 percent to social insurance expenditures and other miscellaneous costs; only 29 percent (or less than a third) is attributable to an increase in money wages.

62. Alberto Alesina, Edward Glaeser, and Bruce Sacerdote, "Work and Leisure in the U.S. and Europe: Why So Different?" *NBER Macroeconomic Annual 2005,* table 1.

63. For a taste of the debate over the status of the middle class, see a series of web-only articles by Lawrence Mishel and and Stephen Rose, *American Prospect,* October 2006 (www. prospect.org/cs/articles?article=debating_the_middle). For more information, see Steven Pearlstein, "Fair to Middling in the Middle Class," *Washington Post,* May 30, 2007, p. D1.

64. Louis Uchitelle, "The Richest of the Rich, Proud of a New Gilded Age," *New York Times,* July 15, 2007, p. A1.

65. Thomas Piketty and Emmanuel Saez, "Income Inequality in the United States, 1913–1998," *Quarterly Journal of Economics* 118, no. 1 (2003). See the authors' updated supplemental data through 2006 (http://elsa.berkeley.edu/~saez/), table A1. These estimates exclude capital gains.

66. Since the 1930s the Securities and Exchange Commission has required public companies to report the pay of top executives and directors, including salaries, bonuses, stock options, and incentive payments. Figure 3-11 is based on a formulation of this record.

67. Carola Frydman and Raven E. Saks, "Executive Compensation: A New View from a Long-Term Perspective, 1936–2005," Working Paper 14145 (Cambridge, Mass.: National Bureau of Economic Research, 2008), figure 1.

68. The Sarbanes-Oxley Act, also known as the Public Company Accounting Reform and Investor Protection Act, was enacted in 2002 and requires stronger oversight and regulation of corporate governance practices among publicly held companies.

69. For reviews of the literature, see Thomas Piketty and Emmanuel Saez, "The Evolution of Top Incomes: A Historical and International Perspective," *American Economic Review* 96, no. 2 (2006); Robert J. Gordon and Ian Dew-Becker, "Selected Issues in the Rise of Income Inequality," *BPEA,* no. 2 (2007); Thomas Lemieux, "The Changing Nature of Wage Inequality," *Journal of Population Economics* 21, no. 1 (2008); "In the Money," Special Report on Executive Pay, *The Economist,* January 20, 2007. For specific evidence on hypothesis three, see Xavier Gabaix and Augustin Landier, "Why Has CEO Pay Increased So Much?" *Quarterly Journal of Economics* 123, no. 1 (2008). For evidence that tilts more toward hypothesis two, see Lucian Bebchuk and Jessie Fried, *Pay without Performance: The Unfulfilled Promise of Executive Compensation* (Harvard University Press, 2004). On hypothesis one, see Ira T. Kay and Steven Van Putten, "Executive Pay: Regulation vs. Market Competition," Policy Analysis 619 (Washington: Cato Institute, 2008); Ira T. Kay and Steven Van Putten, *Myths and Realities of Executive Pay* (Cambridge University Press, 2007), pp. 243–46.

70. Thomas Lemieux, W. Bentley MacLeod, and Daniel Parent, "Performance Pay and Wage Inequality," Discussion Paper 2850 (Bonn: IZA, 2007).

71. This section focuses on the progressiveness of the federal tax system, currently and historically. Thomas Piketty and Emmanuel Saez note that federal taxes represent about two-thirds of the total tax burden on Americans, though they observe that "overall, state and local taxes are believed to be somewhat regressive, but this depends on the assumed incidence of the property tax. If the property tax is assumed to fall on owners of capital, then overall . . . state and local taxes are very close to being proportional to income across income groups. In that case, ignoring state and local taxes would be of no consequence when assessing overall tax progressivity." Thomas Piketty and Emmanuel Saez, "How Progressive Is the U.S. Federal Tax System? A Historical and International Perspective," *Journal of Economic Perspectives* 21, no. 1 (2007), p. 10.

72. Jeffrey Rohaly, "The Distribution of Federal Taxes, 2008–11" (Washington: Urban Institute, 2008), table 3.

73. Ibid.

74. Piketty and Saez, "How Progressive Is the U.S. Federal Tax System?" However, the share of taxes paid by the wealthy (compared to the tax rate) has continued to rise, at least over the past thirty years, in large part because the pretax incomes of those at the top have been growing so rapidly even as their effective tax rates decrease. Between 1979 and 2005 the share of total federal taxes paid by the top quintile increased from 56.4 percent to 68.7 percent. The share of total federal taxes paid by the top 1 percent almost doubled, from 15.4 percent to 27.6 percent. Tax Policy Center, "Historical Shares of Federal Tax Liabilities for All Households" (www.taxpolicy center.org/taxfacts/displaya fact.cfm?Docid=558).

75. An analysis by the Tax Policy Center finds that, while the wealthy benefit disproportionately from the 2001–06 tax cuts, the overall effect on income is small. In 2007 the top 20 percent received two-thirds of the benefits from the tax cuts, though their posttax incomes increased by only 3.2 percent. Tax Policy Center, "Combined Effect of the 2001–2006 Tax Cuts Distribution of Federal Tax Change by Cash Income Percentile, 2007" (www.taxpolicycenter.org/numbers/displayatab.cfm?DocID=1362).

76. Retirement assets are ignored in most definitions of wealth because they are not liquid. Individual retirement accounts and Keogh accounts, however, are usually included in assets because they permit withdrawals. However, the value of future payments from Social Security and most pension plans are not included because claims against Social Security and most pensions cannot be made until retirement.

77. Arthur B. Kennickell, "Currents and Undercurrents: Changes in the Distribution of Wealth, 1989–2004" (Federal Reserve Board, 2006, rev.), pp. 29–30.

78. Edward N. Wolff, "Recent Trends in Household Wealth in the United States: Rising Debt and the Middle-Class Squeeze," Working Paper 502 (Levy Economics Institute of Bard College, 2007), table 3.

79. The lowest reported wealth on the 400 list rose to $1.3 billion in 2007 and 2008. Matthew Miller and Duncan Greenberg, "The Forbes 400" (www.forbes.com/2008/09/16/forbes-400-billionaires-lists-400list08_cx_mn_0917richamericans_land.html).

80. Kennickell, "Currents and Undercurrents," table 4.

Chapter Four

1. Some of the material in this chapter is included in one or more of the following: Daniel P. McMurrer and Isabel V. Sawhill, *Getting Ahead: Economic and Social Mobility in America* (Washington: Urban Institute, 1998); Julia B. Isaacs, Isabel V. Sawhill, and Ron Haskins, *Getting Ahead or Losing Ground: Economic Mobility in America* (Brookings and Economic Mobility Project, an Initiative of the Pew Charitiable Trusts, 2008); Isabel Sawhill and Sara McLanahan, eds., "Opportunity in America," special issue, *Future of Children* 16, no. 2 (2006); Julia Isaacs and Isabel Sawhill, "Reaching for the Prize: the Limits on Economic Mobility," *Milken Institute Review*, 4th quarter (2008).

2. McMurrer and Sawhill, *Getting Ahead*, p. 1.

3. See Gene Sperling, "Rising-Tide Economics," *Democracy: A Journal of Ideas*, issue 6 (2007); see also Roger C. Altman and others, "An Economic Strategy to Advance Opportunity, Prosperity, and Growth" (Brookings, Hamilton Project, 2006).

4. This discussion is based on Isaacs, Sawhill, and Haskins, *Getting Ahead or Losing Ground*. See also Sawhill and McLanahan, "Opportunity in America." In chapter 7 we consider how an increase in income volatility can contribute to a sense of greater economic insecurity among the middle class and how these trends have affected the typical middle-class family.

5. An earlier version of this section was published in Isaacs and Sawhill, "Reaching for the Prize," and in Isaacs, Sawhill, and Haskins, *Getting Ahead*. We are indebted to

Peter Passell, editor of the *Milken Review,* and to John Morton and Ianna Kachoris, of the Pew Charitable Trusts, for comments and editorial suggestions.

6. Isaacs, Sawhill, and Haskins, *Getting Ahead or Losing Ground,* pp. 16, 19. Family income data for this study come from the Panel Study of Income Dynamics (PSID). As noted in Isaacs, Sawhill, and Haskins, *Getting Ahead or Losing Ground,* p. 22, n. 3, income estimates in the PSID tend to be higher than those measured in the U.S. Census Bureau's *Current Population Survey, Annual Demographic Supplement,* published each March. The CPS is the official source for national estimates on poverty and household income. Isaacs, Sawhill, and Haskins restrict their sample to families with children in 1968, thus excluding those without children at that time, the elderly and very young adults, and immigrants who migrated after that time. These restrictions have the effect of further skewing income estimates upward by excluding those groups with typically low incomes. The dollar-amount quintile cutoffs presented in this chapter should be viewed in light of these methodological choices. However, the authors note that when CPS data are restricted to a similar subsample, median growth across the period is comparable to that observed in the PSID. See chapters 3 and 7 for a fuller picture of national income distributions.

7. See Markus Jäntti and others, "American Exceptionalism in a New Light: A Comparison of Intergenerational Earnings Mobility in the Nordic Countries, the United Kingdom and the United States," Discussion Paper 1938 (Bonn: IZA, 2006). Jäntti and colleagues start their inquiry with the United Kingdom's National Children Development Study (NCDS), sampling those born in 1958. The most recent sweeps occurred in 1991 and 1999, providing researchers with data for this cohort's earnings at ages thirty-three and forty-one. A previous sweep of the same cohort in 1974 provided researchers with family data, including information on the family income of the cohort's parents. The authors then matched data from the other countries examined as closely to the U.K. survey as possible. For the United States, the authors used the National Longitudinal Survey of Youth (NLSY), sampling a cohort born between 1957 and 1964. The earnings of this sample are taken from the 1996 and 2002 surveys, which report income for the previous calendar year (1995 and 2001, respectively). Parental income data are from 1978.

8. Miles Corak, "Do Poor Children Become Poor Adults? Lessons from a Cross-Country Comparison of Generational Earnings Mobility," Discussion Paper 1993 (Bonn: IZA, 2006).

9. Authors' calculation based on data from Lawrence Mishel, Jared Bernstein, and Heidi Shierholz, *The State of Working America 2008/2009* (Washington: Economic Policy Institute, 2009), table 1.1.

10. Isabel V. Sawhill and John E. Morton, "Economic Mobility: Is the American Dream Alive and Well?" (Washington: Economic Mobility Project, an Initiative of the Pew Chartiable Trusts, 2007), figure 4. See chapter 7 for an illustration of this change in income over time among men in their thirties.

11. Chul-In Lee and Gary Solon, "Trends in Intergenerational Income Mobility," *Review of Economics and Statistics,* forthcoming.

12. See Daniel Aaronson and Bhashkar Mazumder, "Intergenerational Economic Mobility in the US, 1940 to 2000," *Journal of Human Resources* 43, no. 1 (2008).

13. See Markus Jäntti, "Mobility in the United States and in Comparative Perspective," paper prepared for conference, "Changing Poverty," Institute for Research on Poverty, May 29–30, 2008.

14. Isaacs, Sawhill, and Haskins, *Getting Ahead or Losing Ground,* chapters 5, 6. New research by Bhashkar Mazumder, "Upward Intergenerational Economic Mobility in the United States" (Washington: Economic Mobility Project, an Initiative of the Pew Charitable Trusts, 2008) also finds that whites experience more intergenerational mobility than blacks, using a different data set, the National Longitudinal Survey of Youth (NLSY). Mazumder finds that while many factors, including years of schooling, self-esteem, and health are associated with mobility differences within racial groups, cognitive ability, as measured by the Armed Forces Qualifying Test (AFQT), plays a dominant role in determining black-white differences in mobility. He concludes that "it is likely that whatever factors explain the large gap in academic skills between blacks and whites will also account for the sources of differences in upward economic mobility between the groups," p. 35.

15. We discuss immigrant population growth and its implications in greater detail in chapter 7. We estimate that the legal immigrant population grows by about 1 million every year and that the illegal immigrant population grows by about 500,000 every year, bringing total immigrant growth to 1.5 million annually. See Department of Homeland Security, *Yearbook of Immigration Statistics: 2007;* Jeffrey S. Passel, "The Size and Characteristics of the Unauthorized Migrant Population in the U.S.: Estimates Based on the March 2005 Current Population Survey" (Washington: Pew Hispanic Center, 2006), for more detail on our population estimates. For information regarding the economic status of immigrants in America versus their home countries, see for example Robert Lerman, "U.S. Wage-Inequality Trends and Recent Immigration," *American Economic Review* 89, no. 2 (1999); Robert Lerman "U.S. Income Inequality Trends and Recent Immigration," in *Inequality, Welfare, and Poverty: Theory and Measurement,* edited by Yoram Amiel and John A. Bishop (Amsterdam: JAI, 2003). Data indicate that the wage premium for immigrants from developing countries to the United States is high and, in many cases, offsets accompanying increases in price for goods and services. See Michael Clemens, Claudio E. Montenegro, and Lant Pritchett, "The Place Premium: Wage Differences for Identical Workers across the U.S. Border," Working Paper 148 (Washington: Center for Global Development, 2008).

16. George J. Borjas, "Making It in America: Social Mobility in the Immigrant Population," *Future of Children* 16, no. 2 (2006).

17. Ibid., p. 61.

18. See Isabel V. Sawhill and Mark Condon, "Is U.S. Income Inequality Really Growing? Sorting out the Fairness Question," Policy Bites 13 (Washington: Urban Institute, 1992); Gerald E. Auten and Geoffrey Gee, "Income Mobility in the U.S.: Evidence from Income Tax Returns for 1987 and 1996," Paper 99 (U.S. Department of the

Treasury, Office of Technical Assistance, 2007); "Income Mobility in the United States from 1996 to 2005" (Department of the Treasury, 2007; typographic revisions 2008). The studies by Auten and Gee use a concept similar to that employed by Sawhill and Condon, and their findings are similar. However, Auten and Gee place greater emphasis on measures of absolute mobility, which show larger increases in real incomes over time as the result of the aging of the population together with the greater labor market experience that this implies. They also look at an alternative measure of relative mobility that allows younger families to enter the sample over the ten-year period, rather than limiting the sample to the working-age population at the beginning of the period.

19. Gregory Acs and Seth Zimmerman, "Like Watching Grass Grow? Assessing Changes in U.S. Intragenerational Economic Mobility over the Past Two Decades," draft (Washington: Urban Institute and Economic Mobility Project, an Initiative of the Pew Charitable Trusts, January 15, 2008). Acs and Zimmerman also provide a summary of other literature on this topic, almost all of which is consistent with the findings of Sawhill and Condon, "Is U.S. Income Inequality Really Growing?"

20. Acs and Zimmerman, "Like Watching Grass Grow?" p. 20. However, while Wojciech Kopczuk, Emmanuel Saez, and Jae Song, "Uncovering the American Dream: Inequality and Mobility in Social Security Earnings Data since 1937," Working Paper 13345 (Cambridge, Mass.: National Bureau of Economic Research, 2007), concur that overall mobility has remained stable since the 1950s, they argue that such stability masks major shifts in mobility by gender. Although women have made major workforce advances over the past five decades, leading to an increase in long-term mobility, men's mobility has suffered a slight reduction or remained stable.

21. Up until now, we have assumed that income mobility is a good thing, at least if it moves people up the ladder rather than down. But too much mobility over a short period can be bad, especially if the mobility takes the form of a sharp drop in family income. Such declines, or the fear of them, may make even middle-class families anxious and insecure, a theme we explore in more detail in chapter 7.

22. A discussion of our methodology for this analysis is available upon request from the authors.

23. The association between work and income is not explicitly shown here. Data available upon request from the authors.

24. A brief review of this literature is available upon request from the authors.

Chapter Five

1. Greg J. Duncan and Jeanne Brooks-Gunn, *Consequences of Growing up Poor* (New York: Russell Sage, 1997); Robert Haveman and Barbara Wolfe, "The Determinants of Children's Attainments: A Review of Methods and Findings," *Journal of Economic Literature* 33, no. 4 (1995); W. Jean Yeung, Miriam R. Linver, and Jeanne Brooks-Gunn, "How Money Matters for Young Children's Development: Parental Investment and Family Processes," *Child Development* 73, no. 6 (2002).

2. Relative to children in families over double the poverty line, poor children "complete nearly two fewer years of schooling, work 25 percent fewer hours," earn roughly 50 percent less, "and are more than twice as likely to report poor overall health or high levels of psychological distress." Adult males who were poor as children are more than twice as likely to be arrested and three times as likely to be incarcerated. Females are five times as likely to have a child out of wedlock before age twenty-one. See Greg J. Duncan, Ariel Kalil, and Kathleen Ziol-Guest, "Economic Costs of Early Childhood Poverty," Issue Paper 4 (Washington: Partnership for America's Economic Success, 2008), p. 4. For an older but detailed review, see Jeanne Brooks-Gunn and Greg J. Duncan, "The Effects of Poverty on Children," *Future of Children* 7 no. 2 (1997).

3. U.S. Census Bureau, *Current Population Survey, Annual Demographic Supplement* (2008), table Pov 28. In 2007, 5,830,000 families with one or more children lived below poverty; the mean deficit below the poverty line for poor families with one or more children was $9,249.

4. Greg Duncan, Jeanne Brooks-Gunn, and Pamela Kato Klebanov, "Economic Deprivation and Early Child Development," *Child Development* 65, no. 2 (1994), p. 297.

5. Robert Plomin and others, eds., *Behavioral Genetics*, 4th ed. (New York: Worth, 2001).

6. See, for example, "Children's Emotional Development Is Built into the Architecture of Their Brains," Working Paper 2 (National Scientific Council on the Developing Child, Harvard University, 2004), p. 3.

7. Linda S. Gottfredson, "Mainstream Science on Intelligence: An Editorial with 52 Signatories, History, Bibliography," *Intelligence* 24, no. 1 (1997), p. 14. See also William T. Dickens, "Genetic Differences and School Readiness," *Future of Children* 15 no. 1 (2005), p. 56; Plomin and others, *Behavioral Genetics*.

8. Plomin and others, *Behavioral Genetics*, p. 2.

9. Ibid., p. 3.

10. Richard J. Herrnstein and Charles Murray, *The Bell Curve: Intelligence and Class Structure in American Life* (New York: Free Press, 1994).

11. Gottfredson, "Mainstream Science on Intelligence," p. 14.

12. Ibid., pp. 14–15.

13. Harold M. Skeels. "Adult Status of Children with Contrasting Early Life Experiences: A Follow-Up Study," *Monographs of the Society for Research in Child Development* 31, no. 3 (1966).

14. Eric Turkheimer and others, "Socioeconomic Status Modifies Heritability of IQ in Young Children," *Psychological Science* 14, no. 6 (2003).

15. William T. Dickens, "Genetic Differences and School Readiness," *Future of Children* 15, no. 1 (2005), p. 62.

16. Committee on Integrating the Science of Early Childhood Development, *From Neurons to Neighborhoods: The Science of Early Childhood Development*, edited by Jack P. Shonkoff and Deborah A. Phillips (Washington: National Academy Press, 2000), chap. 2.

17. Eric Knudsen and others, "Economic, Neurobiological, and Behavioral Perspectives on Building America's Workforce," *World Economics* 7, no. 3 (2006); J. Fraser Mustard, "Experience-Based Brain Development: Scientific Underpinnings of the Importance of Early Child Development in a Global World," in *Early Child Development: From Measurement to Action—A Priority for Growth and Equity*, edited by Mary Eming Young with Linda M. Richardson (Washington: World Bank, 2007).

18. Steven D. Levitt and Stephen J. Dubner, *Freakonomics: A Rogue Economist Explores the Hidden Side of Everything* (New York: HarperCollins, 2005, rev.), p. 161.

19. Diana Baumrind, "Child Care Practices Anteceding Three Patterns of Preschool Behavior," *Genetic Psychology Monographs* 75, no. 1 (1967).

20. *Hardwired to Connect: The New Scientific Case for Authoritative Communities* (YMCA of the USA, Dartmouth Medical School, and Institute for American Values, 2003).

21. Betty Hart and Todd R. Risley, *Meaningful Differences in the Everyday Experience of Young American Children* (Baltimore: P. H. Brookes, 1995), esp. chap. 7; *Parent Education and Public Policy*, edited by Ron Haskins and Diane Adams (Norwood, N.J.: Ablex, 1983); Annette Lareau, *Unequal Childhoods: Class, Race, and Family Life* (University of California Press, 2003).

22. Lareau, *Unequal Childhoods*, pp. 2–3.

23. Valerie E. Lee and David T. Burkam, *Inequality at the Starting Gate: Social Background Differences in Achievement as Children Begin School* (Washington: Economic Policy Institute, 2002), as cited in Jens Ludwig and Isabel Sawhill, "Success by Ten: Intervening Early, Often, and Effectively in the Education of Young Children," Discussion Paper 2007-02 (Brookings, Hamilton Project, 2007), p. 5.

24. Lee and Burkam, *Inequality at the Starting Gate*; Ludwig and Sawhill, "Success by Ten."

25. Hart and Risley, *Meaningful Differences in the Everyday Experience of Young American Children*.

26. Walter Mischel, Yuichi Shoda, and Monica L. Rodriguez, "Delay of Gratification in Children," *Science* 244, no. 4907 (1989).

27. Walter Mischel and Ozlem Ayduk, "Willpower in a Cognitive-Affective Processing System: The Dynamics of Delay of Gratification," in *Handbook of Self-Regulation: Research, Theory, and Applications*, edited by Roy F. Baumeister and Kathleen D. Vohs (New York: Guilford, 2004). The experiment is discussed in David Brooks, "Marshmallows and Public Policy," *New York Times*, May 7, 2006, op-ed.

28. James J. Heckman, Jora Stixrud, and Sergio Urzua, "The Effects of Cognitive and Noncognitive Abilities on Labor Market Outcomes and Social Behavior," *Journal of Labor Economics* 24, no. 3 (2006).

29. James J. Heckman, "Schools, Skills, and Synapses," Working Paper 14064 (Cambridge Mass.: National Bureau of Economic Research, 2008), p. 12.

30. Ibid., pp. 21, 24.

31. See for example Clea McNeely and others, "Mothers' Influence on the Timing of First Sex among 14- and 15-Year-Olds," *Journal of Adolescent Health* 31, no. 3

(2002); Renee E. Sieving, Clea S. McNeely, and Robert Wm. Blum, "Maternal Expectations, Mother-Child Connectedness, and Adolescent Sexual Debut," *Archives of Pediatrics & Adolescent Medicine* 154, no. 8 (2000); B. V. Nelson, T. H. Patience, and D.C. MacDonald, "Adolescent Risk Behavior and the Influence of Parents and Education," *Journal of the American Board of Family Practice* 12, no. 6 (1999).

32. Laura M. Padilla-Walker and others, "Looking on the Bright Side: The Role of Identity Status and Gender on Positive Orientations during Emerging Adulthood," *Journal of Adolescence* 31, no. 4 (2008).

33. John M. Bridgeland, John J. DiIulio Jr., and Karen Burke Morison, "The Silent Epidemic: Perspectives of High School Dropouts," report for the Bill and Melinda Gates Foundation (Washington: Civic Enterprises, with Peter D. Hart Research Associates, 2006), p. 3.

34. Ted O'Donoghue and Matthew Rabin, "Risky Behavior among Youths: Some Issues from Behavioral Economics," in *Risky Behavior among Youths: An Economic Analysis*, edited by Jonathan Gruber (University of Chicago Press, 2001), p. 31.

35. Claudia Wallis, "What Makes Teens Tick?" *Time*, May 10, 2004, p. 65; Laurence Steinberg, "Risk Taking in Adolescence: New Perspectives from Brain and Behavioral Science," *Current Directions in Psychological Science* 16, no. 2 (2007); U.S. Department of Health and Human Services, *The Surgeon General's Call to Action to Prevent and Reduce Underage Drinking* (2007), sec. 2: "Alcohol Use and Adolescent Development."

36. "Less Guilty by Reason of Adolescence," IssueLab Brief 3 (Chicago: MacArthur Foundation Research Network on Adolescent Development and Juvenile Justice, 2006); Laurence Steinberg and Elizabeth S. Scott, "Less Guilty by Reason of Adolescence: Developmental Immaturity, Diminished Responsibility, and the Juvenile Death Penalty," *American Psychologist* 58, no. 12 (2003).

37. Steinberg, "Risk Taking in Adolescence."

38. A synthesis of sixteen welfare-to-work programs finds that such programs have, on average, a negative effect on adolescent school performance; while there is variation in outcomes across programs, the overall magnitude of the negative impacts is small. In particular, adolescent children in participating families experienced a reduction in school performance (as reported by mothers), an increase in grade repetition, and an increase in the use of special educational services. However, school dropout and suspension rates and rates of teen pregnancy among participating families were not significantly different from rates among control groups. The authors speculate that negative effects may be related to increased maternal employment and not program design. They suggest that decreased supervision of adolescents or increased responsibility for adolescents who need to care for younger siblings may negatively impact school performance. Lisa A. Gennetian and others, "How Welfare and Work Policies for Parents Affect Adolescents: A Synthesis of Research" (New York: MDRC, 2002).

39. Susan E. Mayer, *What Money Can't Buy: Family Income and Children's Life Chances* (Harvard University Press, 1997).

40. Ibid., pp. 2–3. Daniel Blau reached a similar conclusion several years later in "The Effect of Income on Child Development," *Review of Economics and Statistics* 81

no. 2 (1999). Though Blau uncovers some correlation between family income over a life course and child outcomes, he concludes that the effects of a direct income transfer would be relatively small, speculating that "it would take an unprecedentedly large income transfer to relatively poor households in order to have a substantial impact on child development," p. 271. Thus both Mayer and Blau contend that, while parental income exhibits a positive correlation with child success, the correlation obscures an underlying and more substantive correlation between parental "ability" (broadly defined) and income.

41. Greg J. Duncan, Ariel Kalil, and Kathleen M. Ziol-Guest, "Economic Costs of Early Childhood Poverty," Issue Paper 4 (Washington: Partnership for America's Economic Success, 2008).

42. Ibid., pp. 4–5.

43. They control for parents' education and test score and also for income during middle childhood and adolescence, which helps to eliminate the effects of other parental attributes that might be driving these results.

44. A 2003 study of the Minnesota Family Investment Program, which provides cash assistance to long-term welfare recipients conditional on employment, finds some evidence of positive school achievement and behavior changes among the children of participants. See Pamela A. Morris and Lisa A. Gennetian, "Identifying the Effects of Income on Children's Development Using Experimental Data," *Journal of Marriage and Family* 65, no. 3 (2003). Though the results are only marginally significant in statistical terms, the authors note that the magnitude of the effects is fairly large with only moderate increases in income. A 2004 study finds similarly positive results for school achievement using pooled data from four studies of eight statewide experimental programs; however, the authors find that the only significant effects occur among preschool-age children. See Pamela Morris, Greg J. Duncan, and Christopher Rodrigues, "Does Money Really Matter? Estimating Impacts of Family Income on Children's Achievement with Data from Random-Assignment Experiments," Working Paper (New York: MDRC, 2004).

45. Jeffrey R. Kling, Jeffrey B. Liebman, and Lawrence F. Katz, "Experimental Analysis of Neighborhood Effects," *Econometrica* 75 (January 2007). According to these authors, underlying survey issues relating to the control group of teenage boys may overstate the magnitude of adverse consequences among boys in the participant group; however, such differences still do not explain the male-female differences in outcomes.

46. Ibid.; "A Summary Overview of Moving to Opportunity: A Random Assignment Housing Mobility Study in Five U.S. Cities" (www.nber.org/mtopublic/MTO %20Overview%20Summary.pdf); Stefanie Deluca and James E. Rosenbaum, "Escaping Poverty: Can Housing Vouchers Help?" *Pathways* (Winter 2008), p. 31.

47. Richard Rothstein, *Class and Schools: Using Social, Economic and Educational Reform to Close the Black-White Achievement Gap* (Washington: Economic Policy Institute; and Teachers College, Columbia University, 2004); Abigail Thernstrom and Stephan Thernstrom, *No Excuses: Closing the Racial Gap in Learning* (New York: Simon and Schuster, 2003).

48. Cecilia Elena Rouse and Lisa Barrow, "U.S. Elementary and Secondary Schools: Equalizing Opportunity or Replicating the Status Quo?" *Future of Children* 16, no. 2 (2006).

Chapter Six

1. National Public Radio, Kaiser Family Foundation, and Harvard University Kennedy School, "Summary of Findings," *Poverty in America*, 2001 (www.kff.org/kaiserpolls/3118-index.cfm).

2. Oscar Lewis, "The Culture of Poverty," in *On Understanding Poverty: Perspectives from the Social Sciences*, edited by Daniel P. Moynihan (New York: Basic Books, 1968); Edward Banfield, *The Unheavenly City: The Nature and Future of Our Urban Crisis* (New York: Little, Brown, 1970).

3. Mary Corcoran and others, "Myth and Reality: The Causes and Persistence of Poverty," *Journal of Policy Analysis and Management* 4, no. 4 (1985), pp. 531–32. See also Martha S. Hill and others, *Motivation and Economic Mobility* (Ann Arbor, Mich.: Survey Research Center, Institute for Social Research, 1985).

4. William Julius Wilson, *When Work Disappears: The World of the New Urban Poor* (New York: Knopf, 1996), p. 179.

5. Katherine Newman, "In the Long Run: Career Patterns and Cultural Values in the Low-Wage Labor Force," *Harvard Journal of African American Public Policy* 6, no. 1 (2000), p. 58.

6. Orlando Patterson, "A Poverty of the Mind," *New York Times*, March 26, 2006, op-ed.

7. Bill Cosby and Alvin F. Poussaint, *Come on, People: On the Path from Victims to Victors* (Nashville, Tenn.: Thomas Nelson, 2007), p. 46.

8. Jason DeParle, *American Dream: Three Women, Ten Kids, and a Nation's Drive to End Welfare* (New York: Viking, 2004), p. 74.

9. Kathryn Edin and Maria Kefalas, *Promises I Can Keep: Why Poor Women Put Motherhood before Marriage* (University of California Press, 2005).

10. Ibid., p. 42.

11. Mary Jo Bane and David T. Ellwood, *Welfare Realities: From Rhetoric to Reform* (Harvard University Press, 1994), chap. 3.

12. Laurence M. Mead, comments, review conference, "Creating an Opportunity Society," Brookings, December 11, 2008. See also Lawrence M. Mead, *The New Politics of Poverty: The Nonworking Poor in America* (New York: Basic Books, 1992), chap. 7.

13. Mary Jo Bane and David T. Ellwood, "Slipping into and out of poverty: The Dynamics of Spells," *Journal of Human Resources* 21, no. 1 (1986), table 2. We define the temporary poor as those who leave poverty one or two years after entering a poverty spell. We define the chronically poor as those who leave poverty three or more years after entering a poverty spell. Because Bane and Ellwood exclude those who are age sixty-five and older, we have little to say about the duration of poverty spells

among the elderly. However, in a similar analysis of poverty dynamics, the economist Rebecca Blank notes that, although overall rates of poverty among the elderly are relatively low, an elderly person who becomes poor is very likely to remain poor for the rest of his or her life. Rebecca M. Blank, *It Takes a Nation: A New Agenda for Fighting Poverty* (Princeton University Press, 1997), p. 23.

14. Bane and Ellwood, *Welfare Realities*.

15. Errol R. Ricketts and Isabel V. Sawhill, "Defining and Measuring the Underclass," *Journal of Policy Analysis and Management* 7, no. 2 (1988), pp. 319–20.

16. Sawhill and Ricketts were not able to obtain data on all of their theoretical constructs, so they identify underclass census tracts as those with a "high proportion of (1) *high school dropouts* (16- to 19-year-olds who are not enrolled in school and are not high school graduates); (2) *prime-age males not regularly attached to the labor force* (males 16 years old and over who are not working regularly, where 'working regularly' was defined as having a full or part-time job for more than 26 weeks in 1979); (3) *welfare recipients* (households receiving public assistance income); and (4) *female heads* (households headed by women, with children). A 'high proportion' for each indicator is defined as a proportion which is one standard deviation above the mean for the country as a whole." A qualifying underclass area must score one standard deviation above the mean on all four indicators. Ibid., p. 321.

17. Ibid., table 2.

18. Paul A. Jargowsky and Isabel Sawhill, "The Decline of the Underclass," Brief 36 (Brookings, Center on Children and Families, 2006), p. 3.

19. For more on this argument, see Steven D. Levitt and Stephen J. Dubner, *Freakonomics: A Rogue Economist Explores the Hidden Side of Everything* (New York: William Morrow, 2005). This research remains controversial among some scholars.

20. Jargowsky and Sawhill, "The Decline of the Underclass."

21. Daniel P. Moynihan, "A Family Policy for the Nation," *America,* September 18, 1965, as quoted in Lawrence M. Mead, "Toward a Mandatory Work Policy for Men," *Future of Children* 17, no. 2 (2007), p. 50.

22. See George Ackerlof and Janet Yellen, "An Analysis of Out-of-Wedlock Births in the United States," Policy Brief 5 (Brookings, 1996), table 1; Joyce A. Martin and others, "Births: Final Data for 2006," *National Vital Statistics Report* 57, no. 7 (2009), table 18.

23. The proportion of births to unmarried women reached a record high of 39.7 percent in 2007. Hamilton and others, "Births: Preliminary Data for 2007," table 1.

24. For more information, consult *Future of Children* 15, no. 2 (2002), which focuses on the complex relationship between marriage and poverty. See in particular Sara McLanahan, Elisabeth Donahue, and Ron Haskins, "Introducing the Issue"; Adam Thomas and Isabel Sawhill, "For Love and Money? The Impact of Family Structure on Family Income"; Paul R. Amato, "The Impact of Family Formation Change on the Cognitive, Social, and Emotional Well-Being of the Next Generation."

25. William Julius Wilson, *When Work Disappears: The World of the New Urban Poor* (New York: Knopf, 1996). Also see David T. Ellwood and Christopher Jencks, "The Uneven Spread of Single-Parent Families: What Do We Know? Where Do We Look for Answers?" in *Social Inequality*, edited by Kathryn M. Neckerman (New York: Russell Sage, 2004); Bane and Ellwood, *Welfare Realities*, p. 113.

26. Harry J. Holzer, "The Labor Market and Young Black Men: Updating Moynihan's Perspective" (Washington: Urban Institute, 2007).

27. Gordon L. Berlin, "Rewarding the Work of Individuals: A Counterintuitive Approach to Reducing Poverty and Strengthening Families," *Future of Children* 17, no. 2 (2007), p. 30.

28. Mead, "Toward a Mandatory Work Policy for Men," p. 50.

29. Ibid., pp. 43–72.

30. U.S. Census Bureau, *Current Population Survey, Annual Demographic Supplement* (2008), table Pov 06.

31. Tom Loveless and Kathleen Mills, "The Parent Trap," *Wilson Quarterly* 23, no. 4 (1999).

32. Hugh P. Price, *Mobilizing the Community to Help Students Succeed* (Alexandria, Va.: Association for Supervision and Curriculum Development, 2008), p. 45.

33. Barack Obama, Keynote Address, Democratic National Convention, July 27, 2004.

34. Ron Haskins and Isabel Sawhill, "Work and Marriage: The Way to End Poverty and Welfare," Policy Brief 28 (Brookings, Welfare Reform and Beyond, 2003), figure 1.

35. Rebecca Blank. "Economic Change and the Structure of Opportunity for Less-Skilled Workers," paper prepared for conference, "Changing Poverty," Institute for Research on Poverty, May 29–30, 2008, p. 27.

36. Ibid., p. 10.

37. Figures are seasonally adjusted. U.S. Bureau of Labor Statistics, *National Unemployment Rate* and *State and Local Unemployment Rates* (www.bls.gov/bls/unemployment.htm).

38. The economist Rebecca Blank observes that, "even with some decline in male labor force participation among less-educated workers . . . the U.S. economy has been the envy of many other countries that have faced much higher unemployment and lower labor force participation over the past two decades. This reflects strong overall U.S. economic growth during these decades, which created a growing number of jobs." Blank, "Economic Change and the Structure of Opportunity for Less-Skilled Workers," p. 11.

39. From December 2007 to March 2008 (the most recent data available), the "number of job gains from opening and expanding private sector establishments was 7.1 million, and the number of job losses from closing and contracting establishments was 7.4 million." Bureau of Labor Statistics, news release, "Business Employment Dynamics: First Quarter, 2008."

40. U.S. Census Bureau, *Current Population Survey, Annual Demographic Supplement* (2008), table Pov 24.

41. See for example M. Robin Dion and others, "Reaching All Job-Seekers: Employment Programs for Hard-to-Employ Populations" (Princeton, N.J.: Mathematica Policy Research, 1999).

42. Lawrence Mishel, Jared Bernstein, and Heidi Shierholz, *The State of Working America 2008/2009* (Washington: Economic Policy Institute, forthcoming), table 3.8. Poverty-level wages are defined as earning, on a full-time basis, less than the wage needed to keep a four-person family above the poverty line in that year (or $10.20 an hour in 2007 dollars).

43. Gary Burtless and Timothy Smeeding, "Poverty, Work, and Policy: The United States in Comparative Perspective," paper prepared for House Ways and Means Committee, Subcommittee on Income Security and Family Support, February 13, 2007, p. 9. Low pay is defined as 65 percent of median earnings. Burtless and Smeeding use OECD and LIS data for the United States, Ireland, Canada, Spain, the United Kingdom, Italy, Netherlands, Germany, Austria, Belgium, Finland, and Sweden to explore the relationship between poverty and low pay.

44. Center on Budget and Policy Priorities, "Introduction to the Housing Voucher Program" (Washington: rev. May 2009), p. 1.

45. However, many local housing agencies do have a policy of targeting those with incomes below 30 percent of the median income for that area as a way of reaching the neediest. On the other hand, the targeting requirement is applied only when families are first admitted to the program. Ibid., pp. 2–3.

46. Ibid., p. 2.

47. Kari Wolkwitz, "Trends in Food Stamp Participation Rates: 2000 to 2006" (Washington: Mathematica Policy Research for U.S. Department of Agriculture, 2008), table 2.

48. Kenneth Finegold, "SNAP and the Recession," Recession and Recovery Brief 4 (Washington: Urban Institute, 2008).

49. John Karl Scholz, Robert Moffitt, and Benjamin Cowan discuss these issues in their 2008 paper, "Trends in Income Support," prepared for the conference "Changing Poverty," Institute for Research on Poverty, May 29–30, 2008, p. 20.

50. Ibid., p. 24.

51. Burtless and Smeeding, "Poverty, Work, and Policy," p. 11.

52. For example, see U.S. Census Bureau, *Current Population Survey, Annual Demographic Supplement* (2008), table Pinc-3.

53. Devah Pager, "The Dynamics of Discrimination," in *The Colors of Poverty: Why Racial and Ethnic Disparities Persist*, edited by Ann Chih Lin and David R. Harris (New York: Russell Sage, 2008); Melissa Kearney, "Intergenerational Mobility for Women and Minorities in the United States," *Future of Children* 16, no. 2 (2006); Joseph G. Altonji and Rebecca M. Blank, "Race and Gender in the Labor Market," in *Handbook of Labor Economics*, edited by Orley Ashenfelter and David Card, vol. 3 (Amsterdam: North-Holland, 1999).

54. For an overview of the varying types of discrimination and a brief review of the literature, see Melissa Favreault, "Discrimination and Economic Mobility"

(Washington: Economic Mobility Project, an Initiative of the Pew Charitable Trusts, 2008).

55. Altonji and Blank, "Race and Gender in the Labor Market." Choice of academic major, particularly whether it is highly quantitative, drives some salary differences, and such choice is often related to gender.

56. The economists Stephen Rose and Heidi Hartmann find that there is distinct occupational segregation by gender in the workforce. They also find, however, that women are much more likely to work in typically "male" jobs than the reverse, and that those women working in typically male jobs earn a wage premium, even when they control for job level (elite, good, less skilled). See Stephen J. Rose and Heidi Hartmann, "Still a Man's Labor Market: The Long-Term Earnings Gap" (Washington: Institute for Women's Policy Research, 2004), pp. 21–22.

57. See Kearney, "Intergenerational Mobility for Women and Minorities," p. 45.

58. Derek A. Neal and William R. Johnson, "The Role of Premarket Factors in Black-White Wage Differences," *Journal of Political Economy* 104, no. 5 (1996). The National Academy of Sciences concludes that the AFQT is a racially unbiased measure of skill, at least in the realm of military duties.

59. David Neumark, Roy J. Bank, and Kyle D. Van Nort, "Sex Discrimination in Restaurant Hiring: An Audit Study," *Quarterly Journal of Economics* 111, no. 3 (1996).

60. Claudia Goldin and Cecilia Rouse, "Orchestrating Impartiality: The Impact of 'Blind' Auditions on Female Musicians," *American Economic Review* 90, no. 4 (2000).

61. Harry Cross and others, *Employer Hiring Practices: Differential Treatment of Hispanic and Anglo Job Seekers* (Washington: Urban Institute, 1990); Margery Austin Turner, Michael Fix, and Raymond Struyk, *Opportunities Denied, Opportunities Diminished: Racial Discrimination in Hiring* (Washington: Urban Institute, 1991). See also Franklin James and Steve W. Del Castillo, *We May Be Making Progress toward Equal Access to Jobs: Evidence from Recent Audits* (University of Colorado at Denver, 1992).

62. Marianne Bertrand and Sendhil Mullainathan, "Are Emily and Greg More Employable than Lakisha and Jamal? A Field Experiment on Labor Market Discrimination," *American Economic Review* 94, no. 4 (2004), p. 1011.

63. Haskins and Sawhill, "Work and Marriage," p. 5.

64. See for example Daniel Kahneman and Amos Tversky, eds., *Choices, Values, and Frames* (Cambridge University Press, 2000). For a brief discussion, see Steven Pearlstein, "The Compromise Effect," *Washington Post*, January 27, 2002, p. H1.

65. Richard H. Thaler and Cass R. Sunstein, "Libertarian Paternalism," *American Economic Review* 93, no. 2 (2003); Cass R. Sunstein and Richard H. Thaler, "Libertarian Paternalism Is Not an Oxymoron," *University of Chicago Law Review* 70, no. 4 (2003).

66. Amartya Sen, "The practical reach of social choice theory, in its traditional form, is considerably reduced by its tendency to ignore value formation through social interactions." Amartya Sen, "Rationality and Social Choice," *American Economic Review* 85, no. 1 (1995), p. 18.

67. Macolm Gladwell, *The Tipping Point: How Little Things Can Make a Big Difference* (Boston: Little, Brown, 2000); Cass R. Sunstein, "Social Norms and Social Roles," *Columbia Law Review* 96, no. 4 (1996).

68. New York City, for example, is implementing several conditional programs under the direction of Mayor Michael Bloomberg. The Opportunity NYC demonstration project currently includes three separate projects to help families, workers, and students link behavior with rewards. The project is being evaluated by the Manpower Demonstration Research Corporation (MDRC). For details, see "Opportunity NYC Demonstrations" (www.mdrc.org/project_16_88.html).

69. Charles Michalopoulos, "Does Making Work Pay *Still* Pay? An Update on the Effects of Four Earnings Supplement Programs on Employment, Earnings, and Income" (New York: MDRC, 2005).

70. Greg J. Duncan, Aletha C. Huston, and Thomas S. Weisner, *Higher Ground: New Hope for the Working Poor and Their Children* (New York: Russell Sage, 2007).

71. These rules applied to MFIP, which ran from 1994 to 1998. In 1998 a modified version of MFIP became state welfare policy. The statewide program maintained much of the same structure but included stricter time limits and also a reduced welfare earnings cap (120 percent of the poverty line, down from 140 percent). L. A. Gennetian, C. Miller, and J. Smith, *Turning Welfare into a Work Support: Six-Year Impacts on Parents and Children from the Minnesota Investment Program* (New York: MDRC, 2005), pp. 5–6.

72. Gordon L. Berlin, "Rewarding the Work of Individuals: A Counterintuitive Approach to Reducing Poverty and Strengthening Families," *Future of Children* 17, no. 2 (2007), pp. 24–25. In a 2005 MDRC review, which examines comprehensively the effects of the three programs along with a fourth program, Connecticut's Jobs First, Charles Michalopoulos finds that "the effects of the programs diminished over time, in part because the programs ended and in part because the early employment effects did not lead to lasting wage gains." Michalopoulos, "Does Making Work Pay *Still* Pay?" p. ES-2. Across programs, the strongest and most persistent effects were observed for the most disadvantaged families, particularly single parents at risk for long spells of welfare receipt. MFIP and SSP both yielded double-digit increases in employment rates of long-term welfare recipients. In turn, these two programs reduced the share of program group members living in poverty by 12–13 percentage points. The weakest effects were observed for new recipients of welfare (or recent applicants to welfare). In general, participants receiving employment services in conjunction with their earnings supplements demonstrated the most substantial employment and income gains.

Chapter Seven

1. See for example "Inside the Middle Class: Bad Times Hit the Good Life" (Washington: Pew Research Center, 2008), p. 44, which documents that 79 percent of people reported in 2008 that it was more difficult to maintain their standard of living

than it had been five years earlier. This compares to 65 percent giving this response in 1986.

2. For example, in 2008 only about half of people (49 percent) predicted that their children's lives would be better than their own, while 21 percent believed that their children's lives would be worse. In contrast, only six years earlier, in 2002, 61 percent believed that their children would be better off, and only 10 percent believed that their children would fare worse. Ibid., p. 43.

3. The November voting and registration supplements to the *Current Population Survey* show large differences in voter turnout by income. In the 2006 congressional elections, adult citizens in families with incomes of less than $20,000 were less than half as likely to vote as those in families with incomes of more than $100,000 (31.3 percent versus 64.2 percent). Turnout by education (often a proxy for income) also increased dramatically by level of attainment (27.4 percent for those with less than a high school degree versus 61.1 percent for those with a bachelor's degree and 69.6 percent for those with an advanced degree). While the CPS figures tend to significantly overestimate official district vote counts (by as much as 25 percent), the general trends displayed across income and educational groups are striking. Trends in campaign donations by income are equally distinct. The political scientists Henry E. Brady, Sidney Verba, and Kay Lehman Schlozman, in "Beyond SES: A Resource Model of Political Participation," *American Political Science Review* 89, no. 2 (1995), use data from the Citizen Participation Study to examine the relationship between socioeconomic status and political participation. They find that political contributions are largely determined by an individual's monetary resources. "It is easy to explain the amount given [to political causes, including elections]: a contributor needs money—and little else in the way of civic skills or political interest—to give money," p. 283.

4. The same is true of the remittances that foreign-born workers provide to their families at home. See for example *Annual Report of the Council of Economic Advisers* (Government Printing Office, 2007), p. 191.

5. U.S. Census Bureau, *Historical Income Tables: Households* (various years), table H-10.

6. Amity Shlaes, *The Forgotten Man: A New History of the Great Depression* (New York: HarperCollins, 2007).

7. Congress and President Nixon enacted the Supplemental Security Income program in 1972 to further augment the income and security of the elderly and the disabled who are poor.

8. See for example David C. John, "How to Fix Social Security," Backgrounder 1811 (Washington: Heritage Foundation, 2004). Modern conservative opposition to Social Security often emphasizes shifting the system to personal retirement accounts. This system would be based upon voluntary individual saving through market investment, not government transfers.

9. Sylvester J. Schieber and John B. Shoven, *The Real Deal: The History and Future of Social Security* (Yale University Press, 1999); Shlaes, *The Forgotten Man*; Gary V. Engelhardt and Jonathan Gruber, "Social Security and the Evolution of Elderly

Poverty," in *Public Policy and the Income Distribution*, edited by Alan J. Auerbach, David Card, and John M. Quigley (New York: Russell Sage, 2006).

10. "Inside the Middle Class: Bad Times Hit the Good Life," p. 16.

11. In 2007, 62.8 percent of families in the middle quintile contained two or more earners. U.S. Census Bureau, *Detailed Income Tabulations from the CPS: Families,* table Finc-06.

12. Jacob S. Hacker, *The Great Risk Shift: The Assault on American Jobs, Families, Health Care, and Retirement and How You Can Fight Back* (Oxford University Press, 2006).

13. Jacob S. Hacker and Elisabeth Jacobs, "The Rising Instability of American Family Incomes, 1969–2004: Evidence from the Panel Study of Income Dynamics," Briefing Paper 213 (Washington: Economic Policy Institute, 2008), p. 2. This overall trend is characterized by several distinct periods: steady growth in the early 1980s, a flattening in the late 1980s, a strong surge in the early and mid-1990s, a dip in the late 1990s, and a moderate increase in the early 2000s. However, the authors—in line with a number of researchers—observe that the strong period of volatility growth in the early and mid-1990s must be viewed with suspicion due to some methodological errors inherent in the Panel Study of Income Dynamics, the data set used for the analysis.

14. Ibid., p. 3.

15. See Karen E. Dynan, Douglas W. Elmendorf, and Daniel E. Sichel, "The Evolution of Household Income Volatility" (Brookings, 2008); Peter Gosselin and Seth Zimmerman, "Trends in Income Volatility and Risk, 1970–2004," Working Paper (Washington: Urban Institute, 2008); Austin Nichols and Seth Zimmerman, *Measuring Trends in Income Variability* (Washington: Urban Institute, 2008). One exception is a Congressional Budget Office study that finds little evidence that individual earnings volatility and household income volatility have increased at all over the last two decades. The CBO findings are based on administrative data, so they avoid the problems of self-reported income used in the Panel Study of Income Dynamics. On the other hand, these administrative data go back only to the mid-1980s, and data for individual earnings exclude the self-employed, who may be prone to larger swings in income. See "Recent Trends in the Variability of Individual Earnings and Household Income" (Congressional Budget Office, 2008).

16. Peter Gosselin, *High Wire: The Precarious Financial Lives of American Families* (New York: Basic Books, 2008). Similarly, Dynan, Elmendorf, and Sichel, "The Evolution of Household Income Volatility," find that the rise in volatility over the past thirty years is related more to the magnitude of income changes among those affected at the extremes (those with drops or jumps of more than 50 percent over a two-year period) than to the frequency at which changes in income occur throughout the distribution.

17. Hacker, *The Great Risk Shift: The Assault on American Jobs, Families, Health Care, and Retirement and How You Can Fight Back*; William Galston, "Reviving the Social Contract: Economic Strategies to Promote Health Insurance and Long-Term Care" (Brookings, Opportunity '08, 2007).

18. U.S. Bureau of Labor Statistics, *Median Usual Weekly Earnings,* in 1982 constant dollars, annual average for 2007. Inflated using CPI-U-RS.

19. While state regulations vary, the average 2007 national potential duration for unemployment insurance was 24.0 weeks. However, actual reimbursement duration was 15.2 weeks. Data available at U.S. Department of Labor, *Unemployment Insurance Financial Data Handbook, 2007* (http://workforcesecurity.doleta.gov/unemploy/hb 394.asp#top).

20. This proportion tends to vary somewhat with the health of the economy and is likely to rise as the current recession continues. In 2007 only 36.3 percent of the unemployed received benefits. See Margaret C. Simms and Daniel Kuehn, "Unemployment Insurance during a Recession," Recession and Recovery Brief 2 (Washington: Urban Institute, 2008); Chad Stone, Robert Greenstein, and Martha Coven, "Addressing Long-Standing Gaps in Unemployment Insurance Coverage" (Washington: Center on Budget and Policy Priorities, 2007).

21. Jeffrey Kling, "Fundamental Restructuring of Unemployment Insurance: Wage-Loss Insurance and Temporary Earnings Replacement Accounts," in *The Path to Prosperity: Hamilton Project Ideas on Income Security, Education, and Taxes,* edited by Jason Furman and Jason E. Bordoff (Brookings, 2008).

22. As an example, a wage insurance program that replaces 50 percent of earnings losses up to a maximum of $10,000 a year for up to two years for long-tenure, full-time displaced workers would cost roughly $3.5 billion a year. See Lael Brainard, "The Case for Wage Insurance," testimony before the Joint Economic Committee, February 28, 2007. It would be possible to make such a proposal budget neutral by some combination of reduced unemployment insurance benefits, an increase in the unemployment insurance payroll tax cap, and a system of earnings replacement accounts, in which workers would be required to self-insure against the short-run costs of unemployment. See Kling, "Fundamental Restructuring of Unemployment Insurance."

23. Carmen DeNavas-Walt, Bernadette D. Proctor, and Jessica C. Smith, "Income, Poverty, and Health Insurance Coverage in the United States: 2007," in *Current Population Reports,* P60-235 (U.S. Census Bureau, 2008), p. 19.

24. In 2007, 52 percent of the uninsured reported having no usual source of care, while only 10 percent of those with Medicaid or other public insurance and 10 percent of those with employer-based or other private insurance reported the same. Kaiser Commission on Medicaid and the Uninsured, "The Uninsured and the Difference Health Insurance Makes" (Menlo Park, Calif.: Kaiser Family Foundation, 2008).

25. For example, Gary Burtless shows that real compensation for the average full-time worker grew 5.6 percent ($2,975 in 2005 dollars) between 2000 and 2005, using National Income and Product Account data from the Bureau of Economic Analysis. However, only 29 percent of that increase was received in the form of higher wages; one quarter of the increase was received as part of pension or profit-sharing plans; and slightly more than one-third was in the form of higher employer contributions to health insurance plans. Gary Burtless, "Income Progress across the American Income

Distribution, 2000–2005," testimony before the U.S. Senate Committee on Finance, May 10, 2007.

26. See U.S. Census Bureau, *Historical Health Insurance Tables* (various years), table HIA-1.

27. Gary Claxton and others, "Health Benefits in 2007: Premium Increases Fall to an Eight-Year Low, while Offer Rates and Enrollment Remain Stable," *Health Affairs* 26, no. 5 (2007), p. 1409.

28. Leighton Ku and Matthew Broaddus, "Out-of-Pocket Medical Expenses for Medicaid Beneficiaries Are Substantial and Growing" (Washington: Center on Budget and Policy Priorities, 2005), p. 5.

29. Diane Rowland, testimony before the House Committee on Ways and Means, "Hearing on Economic Challenges Facing Middle-Class Families," January 31, 2007.

30. Note that the universe for these figures is all participants in retirement plans for active workers in the private sector. Workers not receiving any retirement benefits are not included in these counts. Retirement plan participation (the percent of the workforce that participates in a plan regardless of eligibility) has held somewhat steady over the past two decades. In 2005, 40.9 percent of all workers and 54.8 percent of full-time, full-year wage and salary workers participated in some form of retirement plan. Participation rates for all workers and for full-time, full-year workers peaked in 2000 and 1999, respectively. Employee Benefit Research Institute, "FAQs about Benefits—Retirement Issues" (www.ebri.org/publications/benfaq/index.cfm?fa=retfaq).

31. Possible policy responses to the greater insecurity of health and pension benefits are beyond the scope of this book, but some worthy ideas on this topic have been advanced by our colleague William Galston, "Reviving the Social Contract." Our purpose in raising these issues is to emphasize that attempts to help the disadvantaged, especially if that group is defined narrowly to mean just the poverty population, must compete with a policy agenda catalyzed by some new economic challenges facing the broader middle class.

32. "Inside the Middle Class: Bad Times Hit the Good Life," p. 6.

33. U.S. Department of Commerce, Bureau of Economic Analysis, *National Income and Product Accounts Tables* (various years), table 2.1. Personal saving increased from 0.6 percent of disposable personal income in 2007 to 1.7 percent in 2008, the most recent year for which annual data are available. It is likely that the slowing economy will have some positive effect on the savings rate, at least in the immediate future.

34. Diana Farrell and others, "Talkin' 'Bout My Generation: The Economic Impact of Aging U.S. Baby Boomers" (Washington: McKinsey Global Institute, 2008), exhibit 6.

35. Social Security Administration, *The 2007 Annual Report of the Board of Trustees of the Federal Old-Age and Survivors Insurance and Federal Disability Insurance Trust Funds* (Government Printing Office, 2007), table VI.F10.

36. Engelhardt and Gruber, "Social Security and the Evolution of Elderly Poverty."

37. Social Security Administration, *Annual Statistical Supplement to the Social Security Bulletin, 2007*, Publication 13-11706 (2008), p. 1. Note that the data are for Old-Age and Survivor's Insurance only and do not include disability. See also U.S.

Department of Health and Human Services, Administration for Children and Families, *TANF Financial Data,* table A, "Summary of Expenditures on Assistance FY 2006." Note that, for the TANF figure, cash assistance data reflect expenditures on "basic assistance" only; spending on child care, transportation, training, and other benefits is not included.

38. See for example Alberto Alesina, Edward Glaeser, and Bruce Sacerdote, "Work and Leisure in the U.S. and Europe: Why So Different?" in *NBER Macroeconomics Annual 2005,* edited by Mark Gertler and Kenneth Rogoff (MIT Press, 2006).

39. An analysis using the NBER TAXSIM model finds that half of the benefits from the top thirteen tax expenditures listed in TAXSIM go to the top 10 percent of taxpayers. When the two most important credits for the poor—the Earned Income Tax Credit and the Child Tax Credit—are removed, the top 10 percent receives 70 percent of the total benefits. In this second case, the total benefit received by the bottom half of the income distribution falls from 20.5 percent to 4.5 percent. See Rosanne Altshuler and Robert D. Dietz, "Tax Expenditure Estimation and Reporting: A Critical Review," Working Paper 14263 (Cambridge, Mass.: National Bureau of Economic Research, 2008).

40. Peter H. Schuck and Richard J. Zeckhauser, *Targeting in Social Programs: Avoiding Bad Bets, Removing Bad Apples* (Brookings, 2006).

41. Economic Policy Program, "Perspectives on Trade and Poverty Reduction: A Survey of Public Opinion," key findings report (Washington: German Marshall Fund, 2006), chart 3.

42. Ross Perot, as quoted in "The 1992 Campaign; Transcript of 2nd TV Debate between Bush, Clinton and Perot," *New York Times,* October 16, 1992.

43. Estimates suggest that U.S. incomes are about 10 percent higher than they would be in the absence of trade. Scott C. Bradford, Paul L. E. Grieco, and Gary Clyde Hufbauer, "The Payoff to America from Global Integrating," in *The United States and the World Economy: Foreign Economic Policy for the Next Decade,* edited by C. Fred Bergsten (Washington: Institute for International Economics, 2005).

44. Poverty population estimates are for 2005 at 2005 prices. World Bank, poverty issue brief, September 2008 (http://go.worldbank.org/MVECZVCHX0).

45. Paul Krugman, "Trade and Wages, Reconsidered," *Brookings Papers on Economic Activity,* no. 1 (2008).

46. See, for example, Lawrence, *Blue Collar Blues,* p. 7. In contrast, Nobel Laureate Paul Krugman (see note 45, p. 135) remains somewhat agnostic. Although he argues that growing trade with Mexico and China may likely have had an increased effect on wage inequality in the United States in recent years, he observes that "putting numbers on these effects, however, will require a much better understanding of the increasingly fine-grained nature of international specialization and trade."

47. Gene M. Grossman and Esteban Rossi-Hansberg, "The Rise of Offshoring: It's Not Wine for Cloth Anymore," in *The New Economic Geography: Effects and Policy Implications* (Federal Reserve Bank of Kansas City, 2006), p. 60.

48. Alan S. Blinder, "Offshoring: The Next Industrial Revolution?" *Foreign Affairs* 85, no. 2 (2006).

49. Krugman, "Trade and Wages, Reconsidered."

50. Lawrence, *Blue Collar Blues,* pp. 69–70; Thomas L. Friedman, *The World Is Flat: A Brief History of the Twenty-First Century* (New York: Farrar, Straus & Giroux, 2005).

51. Most researchers who try to estimate the number of illegal entrants or the total number of illegal residents in the United States at any given moment would admit that it is impossible to get an exact count. Even so, some estimates are more reasonable than others. Most observers seem to agree that the most reliable numbers have been produced by Jeffrey Passel of the Pew Hispanic Center. We use Passel's estimate of half a million a year. See Jeffrey S. Passel, "The Size and Characteristics of the Unauthorized Migrant Population in the U.S.: Estimates Based on the March 2005 Current Population Survey" (Washington: Pew Hispanic Center, 2006).

52. Note that the percent of foreign born in 2007 includes anyone who is not a U.S. citizen at birth. This includes naturalized citizens, legal permanent residents (immigrants), temporary residents (such as students), humanitarian migrants (such as refugees), and persons illegally present in the United States. Historical data are largely comparable, though the definition of *foreign born* has been refined over time. Campbell J. Gibson and Emily Lennon, "Historical Census Statistics on the Foreign-Born Population of the United States: 1850–1990," Working Paper 29 (U.S. Census Bureau, Population Division, 1999), table 1; U.S. Census Bureau, *Historical Poverty Tables: People* (various years), table 23.

53. If current trends continue, children of immigrants will make up 30 percent of all U.S. children by 2015. "One out of Five U.S. Children Is Living in an Immigrant Family," Kids Count Data Snapshot 4 (Baltimore: Annie E. Casey Foundation, 2007).

54. Philip Martin and Elizabeth Midgley, "Immigration: Shaping and Reshaping America," *Population Bulletin* 61, no. 4 (2006), p. 18.

55. Though disproportionately less educated, the foreign-born population remains bimodal. The foreign born (17.5 percent) are also almost equally likely as natives (19.1 percent) to be college educated and more likely (10.5 percent versus 9.8 percent) to hold an advanced degree. See U.S. Census Bureau, *Statistical Abstract of the United States: 2008,* table 41.

56. George Borjas, "Making It in America: Social Mobility in the Immigrant Population," *Future of Children* 16, no. 2 (2006).

57. DeNavas-Walt, Proctor, and Smith, "Income, Poverty, and Health Insurance Coverage," table 3.

58. See chapter 3 for more detail on estimates regarding the rise in poverty due to immigration. For a similar analysis, see Hilary Hoynes, Marianne Page, and Ann Stevens, "Poverty in America: Trends and Explanations" Working Paper 11681 (Cambridge, Mass.: National Bureau of Economic Research, 2005).

59. The Pew Research Center on Social and Demographic Trends predicts that 82 percent of the increase in the population between 2005 and 2050 will be due to

immigrants and the children of immigrants. The center estimates that 19 percent of Americans will be immigrants by 2050, a record high proportion. See Jeffrey S. Passel and D'Vera Cohn, "Immigration to Play Lead Role in Future U.S. Growth: U.S. Population Projections, 2005–2050" (Washington: Pew Research Center, 2008).

60. U.S. Census Bureau, *Statistical Abstract of the United States: 2009,* table 572.

61. *Annual Report of the Council of Economic Advisers* (Government Printing Office, 2007), p. 201.

62. Borjas, "Making It in America"; David Card and Ethan G. Lewis, "The Diffusion of Mexican Immigrants during the 1990s: Explanations and Impacts," in *Mexican Immigration to the United States,* edited by George Borjas (University of Chicago Press, 2007). See also a review of the literature by Steven Raphael and Lucas Ronconi, "The Effects of Labor Market Competition with Immigrants on the Wages and Employment and Natives: What Does Existing Research Tell Us?" *Du Bois Review: Social Science Research on Race* (September 2007). Raphael and Ronconi side with Card and Lewis in concluding that "the central tendency of the research evidence suggests that recent immigration has had only a modest effect on the labor market prospects of native-born Americans," p. 414.

63. Christian Broda and John Romalis of the University of Chicago examine gains from trade for low-wage workers using household consumption data on nondurable goods (including cosmetics, toys and sporting goods, and wrapping materials and bags). Because the poor buy a disproportionate share of low-quality, nondurable goods, such as those produced and exported by China to the United States, they benefit more from the lower prices on those goods. Broda and Romalis find that inflation for households in the lowest tenth percentile was 6 percentage points smaller than inflation for the upper tenth percentile between 1994 and 2005 and that one-third of the relative price drop for the poor is associated with the rise of Chinese exports over the last decade. Thus they conclude that traditional measures of inequality may be overstating the relative well-being of the rich compared to the poor. See Christian Broda and John Romalis, "Inequality and Prices: Does China Benefit the Poor in America?" (University of Chicago, 2008); see also Richard Vedder and Wendell Cox, *The Wal-Mart Revolution* (Washington: American Enterprise Institute, 2006).

Chapter Eight

1. Claudia Goldin and Lawrence F. Katz, *The Race between Education and Technology* (Cambridge, Mass.: Belknap, 2008).

2. Charles Murray argues that too many American youngsters go to college. He thinks most of them lack the ability to profit from the rigors of a proper college education and that they should instead acquire skills that would allow them to earn a decent living through apprenticeships and other experiences in the labor market and in short-term training. Murray would then have the nation focus more attention and resources on the roughly 20 percent of youngsters who are gifted and would reform the educational system so that it demands more from them. We agree that appren-

ticeships and other training and work experiences that lead to skilled employment are important, and we make specific recommendations in chapter 9 about how employment efforts of this type should be promoted. But we also believe that a much higher share than 20 percent of youngsters can profit from college and can graduate and qualify for jobs with high pay. Further, we want to ensure that the vast majority of young Americans are pushed toward college and given the experiences and resources necessary to obtain a college education if they want one and are willing to work hard. We are willing to sacrifice some efficiency in the name of opportunity for all and in the name of second chances. Charles Murray, *Real Education: Four Simple Truths for Bringing America's Schools Back to Reality* (New York: Crown Forum, 2008).

3. Robert Plomin and others, *Behavioral Genetics*, 5th ed. (New York: Worth, 2008).

4. Betty Hart and Todd R. Risley, *Meaningful Differences in the Everyday Experience of Young American Children* (Baltimore: Paul H. Brookes, 1995); Annette Lareau, *Unequal Childhoods: Class, Race, and Family Life* (University of California Press, 2003).

5. Christopher Jencks and Meredith Phillips, eds., *The Black-White Test Score Gap* (Brookings, 1998).

6. Valerie E. Lee and David T. Burkam, *Inequality at the Starting Gate: Social Background Differences in Achievement as Children Begin School* (Washington: Economic Policy Institute, 2002).

7. Cecilia Elena Rouse and Lisa Barrow, "U.S. Elementary and Secondary Schools: Equalizing Opportunity or Replicating the Status Quo?" *Future of Children* 16, no. 2 (2006).

8. James S. Coleman, *Equality of Educational Opportunity* (U.S. Department of Health, Education, and Welfare, 1966).

9. Frederick Mosteller and Daniel P. Moynihan, eds., *On Equality of Educational Opportunity* (New York: Random House, 1972). For an analysis of the impact of nonschool factors on student performance, see Richard Rothstein, *Class and Schools: Using Social, Economic, and Educational Reform to Close the Black-White Achievement Gap* (Washington: Economic Policy Institute and Teachers College, Columbia University, 2004). But for a contrary view, see the discussion below of David Whitman's analysis of paternalistic schools: David Whitman, *Sweating the Small Stuff: Inner-City Schools and the New Paternalism* (Washington: Thomas B. Fordham Institute, 2008); Ron Haskins and Susanna Loeb, "A Plan to Improve the Quality of Teaching in American Schools," policy brief (Brookings and Woodrow Wilson School of Public and International Affairs, Future of Children, 2007).

10. Greg Duncan and others, "The Apple Does Not Fall Far from the Tree," in *Unequal Chances: Family Background and Economic Success*, edited by Samuel Bowles, Herbert Gintis, and Melissa Osborne Groves (New York: Russell Sage, 2005); Rothstein, *Class and Schools: Using Social, Economic, and Educational Reform to Close the Black-White Achievement Gap*.

11. Orley Ashenfelter, Colm Harmon, and Hessel Oosterbeek, "A Review of Estimates of the Schooling/Earnings Relationship, with Tests for Publication Bias,"

Working Paper 7457 (Cambridge, Mass.: National Bureau of Economic Research, 2000).

12. The rate of return is the ratio of money gained or lost on any investment relative to the amount of the investment. Rates of return are often expressed as annual rates.

13. Barbara L. Wolfe and Robert H. Haveman, "Social and Nonmarket Benefits from Education in an Advanced Economy," *Proceedings, Forty-Seventh Economic Conference* (Federal Reserve Bank of Boston, 2002).

14. Not everyone agrees that investments in education produce the big returns shown in these scholarly analyses and claimed in numerous stories in the popular media. In 2007 Charles Miller, who headed the Spellings Commission on the Future of Higher Education, wrote a tough letter to the College Board claiming that their estimates of the returns to a college degree are inaccurate. He claims that the College Board and others exaggerate the returns to education by ignoring inflation in their calculations of lifetime earnings, by including people with advanced degrees in their calculations, and by assuming that students finish college in four years (which many do not). Miller also emphasizes the dramatic increase in college tuition and fees in recent years. See Doug Lederman, "College Isn't Worth a Million Dollars" (www.insidehighered.com/layout/set/print/news/2008/04/07/miller).

15. Regardless of when surveyed, individuals are arrayed in the chart by the year of their twenty-first birthday and their highest years of schooling recorded. The advantage of this approach is that if people complete schooling after age twenty-one, their subsequent years of schooling are captured in the data.

16. According to the National Center for Education Statistics, between 1990 and 2000 blacks increased their high school graduation rate by about 9 percentage points; whites increased their rate, from a base nearly 15 percentage points higher than blacks, by nearly 6 percentage points. See National Center for Education Statistics, *Digest of Education Statistics: 2007* (U.S. Department of Education, 2008), table 12 (http://nces.ed.gov/programs/digest/d07/tables/dt07_012.asp?referrer=list).

17. Paul E. Barton, "One-Third of a Nation: Rising Dropout Rates and Declining Opportunities" (Princeton, N.J.: Educational Testing Service, 2005).

18. There is a large literature on the definition of *high quality* in preschool programs, how quality should be measured, and how much high-quality care exists in the United States. There seems to be some agreement that the most important measures of quality focus on the organization of the preschool classroom and the nature of the teacher's interactions with the children, especially the teacher's use of language. For reviews, see Deborah Lowe Vandell and Barbara Wolfe, "Child Care Quality: Does It Matter and Does It Need to Be Improved?" (U.S. Department of Health and Human Services, 2000; http://aspe.hhs.gov/hsp/ccquality00/ccqual.htm); Ron Haskins, "Is Anything More Important than Day-Care Quality?" in *Child Care in the 1990s: Trends and Consequences*, edited by Alan Booth (Hillsdale, N.J.: Lawrence Erlbaum, 1992).

19. Peter H. Rossi, "The Iron Law of Evaluation and Other Metallic Rules," *Research in Social Problems and Public Policy* 4 (1987).

20. Lynn A. Karoly, M. Rebecca Kilburn, and Jill S. Cannon, *Early Childhood Interventions: Proven Results, Future Promise* (Santa Monica, Calif.: Rand, 2005).

21. Craig T. Ramey and Frances A. Campbell. "Preventative Education for High-Risk Children: Cognitive Consequences of the Carolina Abecedarian Project," *American Journal of Mental Deficiency* 88, no. 5 (1984); Lawrence J. Schweinhart, Helen V. Barnes, and David P. Weikart, *Significant Benefits: The High/Scope Perry Preschool Study through Age 27* (Ypsilanti, Mich.: High/Scope, 1993).

22. A careful reanalysis of Perry and Abecedarian data by Michael Anderson of Berkeley finds that more stringent rules for interpreting statistical significance when multiple tests are performed eliminates most of the significant preschool effects for males. However, James Heckman and his students have also reanalyzed the Perry data while correcting for problems in the initial random assignment and using a stepdown multiple testing procedure to correct for problems with significance testing when many tests are performed. After making these adjustments, Heckman and his students find even stronger effects for males, thereby directly contradicting Anderson's results. See Michael L. Anderson, "Multiple Inference and Gender Differences in the Effects of Early Intervention: A Reevaluation of the Abecedarian, Perry Preschool, and Early Training Projects," *Journal of the American Statistical Association* 103, no. 484 (2008), and James Heckman and others, "A Reanalysis of the High/Scope Perry Preschool Program," unpublished manuscript (University of Chicago, April 2009).

23. Arthur J. Reynolds, *Success in Early Intervention: The Chicago Child-Parent Centers* (University of Nebraska Press, 2000); Arthur J. Reynolds and others, "Long-Term Effects of an Early Childhood Intervention on Educational Achievement and Juvenile Arrests: A 15-Year Follow-up of Low-Income Children in Public Schools," *Journal of the American Medical Association* 285, no. 18 (2001).

24. Douglas J. Besharov, Peter Germanis, and Caeli Higney, *Summaries of Twenty Early Childhood Evaluations* (College Park, Md.: Welfare Reform Academy, Maryland School of Public Affairs, 2006).

25. W. Steven Barnett and Clive R. Belfield, "Early Childhood Development and Social Mobility," *Future of Children* 16, no. 2 (2006), table 1 and p. 84.

26. Karoly, Kilburn, and Cannon, *Early Childhood Interventions,* esp. chap. 4; Robert G. Lynch, *Exceptional Returns: Economic, Fiscal, and Social Benefits of Investment in Early Childhood Development* (Washington: Economic Policy Institute, 2004); Clive R. Belfield, "The Promise of Early Childhood Education Interventions," in *The Price We Pay: Economic and Social Consequences of Inadequate Education*, edited by Clive R. Belfield and Henry M. Levin (Brookings, 2007); Julia B. Isaacs, "Supporting Young Children and Families: An Investment Strategy That Pays," in *Big Ideas for Children: Investing in Our Nation's Future*, edited by Bruce Lesley (Washington: First Focus, 2008).

27. Richard P. Nathan, "How Should We Read the Evidence about Head Start? Three Views," *Journal of Policy Analysis and Management* 26, no. 3 (2007); Jens Ludwig and Douglas L. Miller, "Does Head Start Improve Children's Life Chances? Evidence from a Regression Discontinuity Design," *Quarterly Journal of Economics* 122,

no. 1 (2007); Janet Currie, "Early Childhood Education Programs," *Journal of Economic Perspectives* 15, no. 2 (2001); David Deming, "Early Childhood Intervention and Life-Cycle Skill Development," paper prepared for the fall research conference of the Association for Public Policy Analysis and Management, Los Angeles, November 6–8, 2008.

28. U.S. Department of Health and Human Services, Administration for Children and Families, *Head Start Impact Study: First-Year Findings* (2005).

29. The 2003 version of the Head Start Faces survey shows that Head Start children slightly improve their test scores and learn about six additional letters of the alphabet during the Head Start year. See Nicholas Zill and others, *Faces 2003 Research Brief: Children's Outcomes and Program Quality in Head Start* (U.S. Department of Health and Human Services, 2006).

30. Jens Ludwig and Deborah A. Phillips, "The Benefits and Costs of Head Start," *Social Policy Report* 21, no. 3 (2007); Deming, "Early Childhood Intervention and Life-Cycle Skill Development."

31. W. Steven Barnett and others, *The State of Preschool 2006* (Rutgers University, National Institute for Early Education Research, 2006).

32. W. Steven Barnett, Cynthia Lamy, and Kwanghee Jung, "The Effects of State Prekindergarten Programs on Young Children's School Readiness in Five States" (Rutgers University, National Institute for Early Education Research, 2005); William T. Gormley Jr. and Ted Gayer, "Promoting School Readiness in Oklahoma: An Evaluation of Tulsa's Pre-K Program," *Journal of Human Resources* 40, no. 3 (2005).

33. Greg J. Duncan and others, "School Readiness and Later Achievement," *Developmental Psychology* 43, no. 6 (2007).

34. In a 2006 review of the literature on preschool programs and mobility, Steven Barnett and Clive Belfield conclude that "increased investment in preschool could raise social mobility." See Barnett and Belfield, "Early Childhood Development and Social Mobility," p. 91.

35. Ron Haskins, "Child Development and Child-Care Policy: Modest Impacts," in *Developmental Psychology and Social Change: Research, History, and Policy*, edited by David Pillemer and Sheldon Harold White (Cambridge University Press, 2005).

36. Jens Ludwig and Isabel Sawhill, "Success by Ten: Intervening Early, Often, and Effectively in the Education of Young Children," Discussion Paper 2007-02 (Brookings, Hamilton Project, 2007). Our plan has also benefited from the comprehensive infancy and preschool proposal of Arthur Rolnick and Rob Grunewald of the Federal Reserve Bank of Minneapolis, where they are now attempting to implement a program that includes nearly all the characteristics of our plan. Arthur J. Rolnick and Rob Grunewald, "Early Intervention on a Large Scale," *Education Week* 26, no. 17 (January 4, 2007), pp. 34–36.

37. There is evidence that home visiting programs can have substantial impacts on both mothers and children; see David Olds and others, "Long-Term Effects of Nurse Home Visitation on Children's Criminal and Antisocial Behavior: 15-Year Follow-up of a Randomized Controlled Trial," *Journal of the American Medical Association* 280,

no. 14 (1998); for a review of evidence that the Olds program is cost effective, see Julia B. Isaacs, "Cost-Effective Investments in Children" (Brookings, Budgeting for National Priorities, 2007). We would require that states spend at least part of their Title I money from the No Child Left Behind Act on reading and math curriculums. Only high-quality curriculums with tested results as indicated by the What Works Clearinghouse could be used by school districts (http://ies.ed.gov/ncee/wwc/ reports/).

38. Karoly, Kilburn, and Cannon, *Early Childhood Interventions,* esp. chap. 4; Lynch, *Exceptional Returns;* Belfield, "The Promise of Early Childhood Education Interventions"; Isaacs, "Supporting Young Children and Families."

39. Barnett and others, *The State of Preschool 2007,* p. 4.

40. Paul Teske, Jody Fitzpatrick, and Gabriel Kaplan, *Opening Doors: How Low-Income Parents Search for the Right School* (University of Washington, School of Public Affairs, Center on Reinventing Public Education, 2007).

41. Frederick M. Hess and Michael J. Petrilli, *No Child Left Behind: Primer* (New York: Peter Lang, 2006).

42. National Commission on Excellence in Education, *A Nation at Risk: The Imperative for Educational Reform* (Government Printing Office, 1983).

43. See tab "Tables & Figures" on the website of the National Assessment of Educational Progress, U.S. Department of Education, National Center for Education Statistics (http://nces.ed.gov/quicktables/index.asp); Rothstein, *Class and Schools: Using Social, Economic, and Educational Reform to Close the Black-White Achievement Gap*; Daniel Koretz, "How Do American Students Measure Up? Making Sense of International Comparisons," *Future of Children* 19, no. 1 (2009); Paul E. Barton, *One-Third of a Nation: Rising Dropout Rates and Declining Opportunities* (Princeton: Policy Information Center, Educational Testing Center, 2005); Jennifer Laird and others, *Dropout and Completion Rates in the United States: 2006,* Compendium Report NCES 2008-053 (U.S. Department of Education, National Center for Education Statistics, Institute of Education Sciences, 2008).

44. For more, see Abigail Thernstrom and Stephan Thernstrom, *No Excuses: Closing the Racial Gap in Learning* (New York: Simon and Schuster, 2003); Whitman, *Sweating the Small Stuff*; Robert E. Slavin and Nancy A. Madden, *Success for All: Summary of Research on Achievement Outcomes,* Report 41, rev. (Johns Hopkins University, Center for Data-Driven Reform in Education, 2006); Jeremy D. Finn and Charles M. Achilles, "Answers and Questions about Class Size: A Statewide Experiment," *American Educational Research Journal* 27, no. 30 (1990); James J. Kemple, *Career Academies: Long-Term Impacts on Labor Market Outcomes, Educational Attainment, and Transitions to Adulthood* (New York: MDRC, 2008); Haskins and Loeb, "A Plan to Improve the Quality of Teaching in American Schools"; Brian A. Jacob and Jens Ludwig, "Improving Educational Outcomes for Poor Children," Discussion Paper 1352-08 (Madison, Wis.: Institute for Research on Poverty, September 2008); Justine S. Hastings, Richard Van Weelden, and Jeffrey Weinstein, "Preferences, Information, and Parental Choice Behavior in Public School Choice," Working Paper 12995 (Cambridge, Mass.: National Bureau of Economic Research, 2007); U.S. General Accounting Office,

"School Vouchers: Publicly Funded Programs in Cleveland and Milwaukee," Report to Honorable Judd Gregg, U.S. Senate, GAO-01-914 (Government Printing Office, 2001); Charles M. Payne, *So Much Reform, So Little Change: The Persistence of Failure in Urban Schools* (Harvard University Press, 2008).

45. No Child Left Behind (NCLB) aims to improve school performance by increasing accountability for student achievement and improving teacher quality. States are required to reach universal proficiency in reading and math by 2014, but the measure of proficiency is defined by states and can be measured by state-created tests. In moving toward universal proficiency, states must define annual goals, called adequate yearly progress (AYP), that specify how much annual progress individual schools need to make in working their way toward the 2014 goal of universal proficiency. If a school fails to make AYP, it is subject to a series of sanctions, which increase in toughness each year the school fails. If a school fails AYP two years in a row, the school administrators must explain to parents that their school has not met standards. The school must also devise a school improvement plan and explain the plan to parents. The school district must provide failing schools with technical assistance to implement their improvement plan. Finally, the school must inform parents that their child has the right to transfer to any other school within the district that has not failed AYP. If the school fails for a third consecutive year, it must offer its needy students "supplemental education services," such as tutoring, to help them in math and reading. If a school fails for a fourth consecutive year, the school enters "corrective action," in which it must change staff, reform the curriculum, extend the school day or year, or implement other major changes to improve student learning. If the school fails for a fifth consecutive year, the district must turn the school into a charter school, replace most of its teachers and administrators, hire a management company to operate the school, turn the school over to the state, or take other strong action stipulated by the state. NCLB also contains strong provisions requiring schools to have "highly qualified teachers" in every classroom by the end of the 2005–06 school year. For more details, see Hess and Petrilli, *No Child Left Behind*.

46. Marvin H. Kosters and Brent D. Mast, *Closing the Achievement Gap: Is Title I Working?* (Washington: American Enterprise Institute, 2003).

47. For a detailed analysis of the Texas accountability system, see Laurence A. Toenjes and others, "The Lonestar Gamble: High-Stakes Testing, Accountability, and Student Achievement in Texas and Houston," in *Bridging the Achievement Gap*, edited by John E. Chubb and Tom Loveless (Brookings, 2002).

48. Mark Walsh, "The School Law Blog," *Education Week* (Blogs.edweek.org/edweek/school_law/); Jaekyung Lee, "Tracking Achievement Gaps and Assessing the Impact of NCLB on the Gaps: An In-Depth Look into National and State Reading and Math Outcome Trends" (Harvard University, Civil Rights Project, 2006).

49. There is a serious flaw in two NCLB provisions: the provison allowing students to transfer from failing schools and that calling for the restructuring of a school that misses AYP for five years in a row. For these provisions to work, there must be high-quality schools to which students can transfer and effective teachers and admin-

istrators to serve in the restructured school. Whether such schools, teachers, and administrators can be found in the inner city is very much in question.

50. No Child Left Behind Act, Title I, part A, subpart 1 A(b)(1)(A).

51. Koretz, "How Do American Students Measure Up?"; Goldin and Katz, *The Race between Education and Technology,* pp. 325–29.

52. Large parts of this section are based on Haskins and Loeb, "A Plan to Improve the Quality of Teaching in American Schools"; Robert Gordon, Thomas J. Kane, and Douglas O. Staiger, "Identifying Effective Teachers Using Performance on the Job," Discussion Paper 2006-01 (Brookings, Hamilton Project, 2006). See also Susanna Loeb, Cecilia Rouse, and Anthony Shorris, eds., "Introducing the Issue," *Future of Children* 17, no. 1 (2007).

53. William L. Sanders and June C. Rivers, "Cumulative and Residual Effects of Teachers on Future Student Academic Achievement," research progress report (University of Tennessee, Value-Added Research and Assessment Center, 1996).

54. Eric A. Hanushek and others, "The Market for Teacher Quality," Working Paper 11154 (Cambridge, Mass.: National Bureau of Economic Research, 2005).

55. Daniel F. McCaffrey and others, *Evaluating Value-Added Models for Teacher Accountability* (Santa Monica, Calif.: Rand, 2003).

56. For reasonable criticism of the change score methodology, see Jesse Rothstein, "Teacher Quality in Educational Production: Tracking, Decay, and Student Achievement," Working Paper 14442 (Cambridge, Mass.: National Bureau of Economic Research, 2008); Jesse Rothstein, "Student Sorting and Bias in Value-Added Estimation: Selection on Observables and Unobservables," Working Paper 14666 (Cambridge, Mass.: National Bureau of Economic Research, 2009).

57. Haskins and Loeb, "A Plan to Improve the Quality of Teaching in American Schools."

58. A random-assignment evaluation by Mathematica finds that Teach for America teachers produced slightly better student outcomes in math than other teachers. Paul T. Decker, Daniel P. Mayer, and Steven Glazerman, *The Effects of Teach for America on Students: Findings from a National Evaluation* (Princeton: Mathematica, 2004). Teach for America students working with pre-K students in Washington, D.C., also produced learning outcomes that appeared to be better than the outcomes produced by average Head Start teachers (in a national evaluation of Head Start) and by teachers in state pre-K programs. Nicholas Zill, *Promising Results from Teach for America's Early Childhood Initiative: Report to the CityBridge Foundation* (Rockville, Md.: Westat, 2008).

59. Heather C. Hill, "Learning in the Teaching Workforce," *Future of Children* 17, no. 1 (2007).

60. Robert Gordon, Thomas J. Kane, and Douglas O. Staiger, "Identifying Effective Teachers Using Performance on the Job," Discussion Paper 2006-01 (Brookings, Hamilton Project, 2006); Dan Goldhaber, "Teacher Pay Reforms: The Political Implications of Recent Research" (Washington: Center for American Progress, 2006).

61. See www.talentedteachers.org/what/what.taf?page=response.

62. Matthew G. Springer, Dale Ballou, and Art Xiao Peng, "Impact of the Teacher Advancement Program on Student Test Score Gains: Findings from an Independent Appraisal," paper prepared for CESifo/PEPG Conference, Munich, May 16–17, 2008.

63. Funding for the Teacher Incentive Fund was authorized by Congress in Public Law 109-149; see Elementary and Secondary Education Act of 1965, as amended, Title V, part D, subpart 1. The Obama administration has proposed a $420 million increase in the Teacher Incentive Fund budget for 2010.

64. Whitman, *Sweating the Small Stuff*.

65. See also Thernstrom and Thernstrom, *No Excuses*.

66. Lawrence M. Mead, ed., *The New Paternalism: Supervisory Approaches to Poverty* (Brookings, 1997).

67. Richard H. Thaler and Cass R. Sunstein, *Nudge: Improving Decisions about Health, Wealth, and Happiness* (Yale University Press, 2008).

68. Whitman, *Sweating the Small Stuff*, p. 176.

69. Ibid., p. 246.

70. Paul Tough, *Whatever It Takes: Geoffrey Canada's Quest to Change Harlem and America* (New York: Houghton Mifflin Harcourt, 2008). For evidence on the effectiveness of the Harlem Children's Zone's schools, see Will Dobbie and Roland G. Fryer Jr., "Are High-Quality Schools Enough to Close the Achievement Gap?" (Harvard University, 2009; www.economics.harvard.edu/faculty/fryer/files/hcz%204.15. 2009.pdf).

71. Title I, section 102(18)(i) of the Education Science Reform Act of 2002.

72. What Works Clearinghouse, http://ies.ed.gov/ncee/wwc/pdf/wwc.

73. Ron Haskins and James Kemple, "A New Goal for America's High School: College Preparation for All," policy brief (Brookings and Woodrow Wilson School of Public and International Affairs, Future of Children, 2009); Ron Haskins, Harry Holzer, and Robert Lerman, "Promoting Economic Mobility by Increasing Postsecondary Education" (Washington: Economic Mobility Project, an Initiative of the Pew Charitable Trusts, 2009).

74. Thernstrom and Thernstrom, *No Excuses*; John E. Chubb and Tom Loveless, eds., *Bridging the Achievement Gap* (Brookings, 2002).

75. Jay P. Greene and Greg Forster, "Public High School Graduation and College Readiness Rates in the United States," Education Working Paper 3 (New York: Manhattan Institute for Policy Research, 2003).

76. Douglas S. Massey and others, *The Source of the River: The Social Origins of Freshmen at American's Selective Colleges and Universities* (Princeton University Press, 2003).

77. Ibid., pp. 10–12, 206.

78. Kevin Carey, *Graduation Rate Watch: Making Minority Student Success a Priority,* report (Washington: Education Sector, 2008); Melissa Roderick, Jenny Nagaoka, and Vanessa Coca, "College Readiness for All: The Challenge for Urban High Schools," *Future of Children* 19, no. 1 (2009).

79. Clement (Kirabo) Jackson, "A Little Now for a Lot Later: A Look at a Texas Advanced Placement Incentive Program," working paper (Cornell University, School

of Industrial and Labor Relations, 2007; http://digitalcommons.ilr.cornell.edu/work ingpapers/69/).

80. Melissa Roderick and others, *From High School to the Future: Potholes on the Road to College* (University of Chicago, Consortium on Chicago School Research, 2008).

81. In addition to the five programs outlined in table 8-4, the federal government sponsors several other programs: Student Support Services, which provides grants to higher education institutions to help disadvantaged students stay in college; Educational Opportunity Centers, which try to attract qualified adults and prepare them for, and enroll them in, college; the Ronald E. McNair Postbaccalaureate Achievement Program, which helps highly qualified low-income college students prepare for doctoral work; the TRIO Dissemination Partnership Program, which funds public schools and postsecondary institutions that have grants from any of the federal college preparation programs (table 8-4) to help other educational institutions develop college preparation programs; and the Training Program for Federal TRIO Program Staff, which funds conferences, seminars, workshops, and other activities to train staff helping students enroll in postsecondary education.

82. A problem with many evaluations of the college preparatory programs is that the programs tend to enroll students who are motivated to try to do well in high school and to go to college even before joining the program. Random assignment studies might show that students in these programs have no higher rates of high school graduation and college entry than students in the control group. When students in the control and treatment groups are similar at both the beginning and the end of treatment, the program has had no impact and therefore has not proven to be effective. In the MDRC evaluation of Project GRAD, for example, although participants improved their scores on the state achievement tests, students in the comparison schools also improved their performance. Jason C. Snipes, Glee Ivory Holton, and Fred Doolittle, *Charting a Path to Graduation: The Effect of Project GRAD on Elementary School Outcomes in Four Urban School Districts* (New York: MDRC, 2006).

83. Jason C. Snipes and others, *Striving for Student Success: The Effect of Project GRAD on High School Student Outcomes in Three Urban School Districts* (New York: MDRC, 2006).

84. Project GRAD (http://ies.ed.gov/ncee/wwc/reports/dropout/project_grad).

85. We recommend retaining the Upward Bound Math-Science program because a random-assignment evaluation shows that the program increased high grades in math and science, increased enrollment in selective four-year institutions, increased the likelihood of majoring in math and science, and increased the likelihood of completing a four-year degree in math and science. See Robert Olsen and others, "Upward Bound Math-Science: Program Description and Interim Impact Estimates" (U.S. Department of Education, 2007).

86. Efforts to increase the rigor of public school curriculums, one of American Diploma Project's (ADP's) major goals, show promise, but there is concern among some analysts about whether the approach taken by ADP is too narrow and inappropriately mandatory. Some of the requirements for high school graduation are not

used widely in the workforce, while other skills that are necessary for success in the workplace are rarely measured, taught, or evaluated by high schools. Among them are problem solving, teaching, teaming and collaborating, allocating resources, working with others, taking responsibility, communicating well, producing high-quality products, and self-direction. Achieving high-level occupational skills should also be an aim of the high school curriculums.

87. Achieve, Inc., "Closing the Expectations Gap: 2008" (Washington: American Diploma Project Network, 2008).

88. For more detail, see "Data Quality Campaign Announces 3-Year Progress" (www.DataQualityCampaign.org); www.nchems.org/; http://nces.ed.gov/programs/slds/).

89. Roderick and others, *From High School to the Future.*

90. Jennifer Ramsey, "Creating a High School Culture of College-Going: The Case of Washington State Achievers," issue brief (Washington: Institute for Higher Education Policy, 2008).

91. For more on these programs, see www.hks.harvard.edu/service/programs.htm; and www.striveforcollege.org.

92. See www.advisingcorps.org.

93. Spellings Commission on Higher Education, "A Test of Leadership: Charting the Future of U.S. Higher Education" (U.S. Department of Education, 2006), p. 3.

94. See appendix A for details.

95. The American Recovery and Reinvestment Act made major reforms in tax provisions related to the costs of postsecondary education. The Hope Scholarship Credit was temporarily replaced with a new American Opportunity Tax Credit equal to 100 percent of qualified tuition, fees, and course materials of up to $2,000 plus 25 percent of the next $2,000 in qualified tuition, fees, and course materials. The total credit cannot exceed $2,500. In addition, the act for the first time makes the credit refundable (payable in cash to applicants who have no or low federal income tax liability) for up to 40 percent of its maximum amount. In his 2010 budget proposal, President Obama proposes to make the American Opportunity Tax Credit permanent.

96. This count is based on six grant programs plus five grant programs for veterans, eight loan programs, and twelve tax programs. See Sandy Baum and Kathleen Payea, "Trends in Student Aid: 2008" (Washington: College Board), p. 6; David P. Smole and Shannon S. Loane, "A Brief History of Veterans' Education Benefits and Their Value," RL34549 (Washington: Congressional Research Service, 2008), esp. figure 1; Shannon S. Loane, "A Brief Overview of the Post-9/11 Veterans Educational Assistance Act of 2008," RS22929 (Washington: Congressional Research Service, 2008); Pamela Jackson, "Higher Education Tax Credits: An Economic Analysis," RL32507 (Washington: Congressional Research Service, 2007).

97. Sandy Baum and Jennifer Ma, "Trends in College Pricing: 2008" (Washington: College Board, 2008), p. 11.

98. Baum and Payea, "Trends in Student Aid: 2008," p. 6.

99. None of these figures includes the cost of room and board. Surprisingly, the cost of room and board is very similar for students at public two-year colleges and public four-year colleges, $7,340 for the former and $7,750 for the latter in 2008–09. Adjusted for inflation, the cost of room and board had increased by 13 percent over the previous decade for two-year colleges and 27 percent for four-year colleges. The cost of room and board at the average private four-year college was $8,990 in 2008–09, an increase of 16 percent over the previous decade. See Baum and Ma, "Trends in College Pricing: 2008," p. 11.

100. Baum and Payea, "Trends in Student Aid: 2008," p. 6. In addition to the money for student aid, state and local governments spent $85 billion providing general support to their colleges and universities (not counting research support). See State Higher Education Executive Officers, "State Higher Education Finance Early Release FY2008" (www.sheeo.org/finance/shef/shef%20fy08%20early%20release%202.pdf).

101. The Obama administration's budget for 2010 contains language on simplifying the student aid application process. In addition, confidential reports indicate that the administration has been working with the Internal Revenue Service to develop procedures for providing low-income families with information on eligibility for student aid when they submit their tax returns.

102. Susan M. Dynarski and Judith E. Scott-Clayton, "College Grants on a Postcard: A Proposal for Simple and Predictable Federal Student Aid," Discussion Paper 2007-01 (Brookings, Hamilton Project, 2007).

103. Rethinking Student Aid, "Fulfilling the Commitment: Recommendations for Reforming Federal Student Aid" (Washington: College Board, 2008); Spellings Commission, "A Test of Leadership: Charting the Future of U.S. Higher Education" (U.S. Department of Education, 2006).

104. Adjusted gross income is gross income (wages, interest income, dividend income, retirement account income, capital gains, alimony received, royalty income, and a few other sources of income) minus certain deductions. These are difficult to characterize but include certain business expenses, health savings account deductions, certain moving expenses, alimony paid, and student loan interest. The Rethinking Student Aid study group recommends that the IRS compute a moving three-year average of income to help smooth year-to-year variation in income. We emphasize the importance of poor families hearing long before high school that they should be thinking about college for their children and that generous financial aid is available. To help parents understand the aid available to their child, we endorse the proposal of the study group that the IRS notify tax filers with children between ages five and nineteen of the estimated size of the federal student aid grant for which their children would be eligible. Getting this information early and often would increase the chances of convincing low-income families that they can afford to send their children to college.

105. Rethinking Student Aid, "Fulfilling the Commitment."

106. Both in the American Recovery and Reinvestment Act (ARRA) and in its 2010 budget, the Obama administration has either actually made or proposed major changes

in the Pell grant program. The ARRA increased Pell funding by over $17 billion. The Obama budget proposed increasing the maximum Pell grant to $5,500, making the funding mandatory (which would allow the funding to avoid the congressional appropriations gauntlet), and indexing the Pell grant to the consumer price index plus 1 percent.

107. The American Recovery and Reinvestment Act of 2009, otherwise known as the stimulus package, provides $15.6 billion to increase the maximum Pell grant to $5,350 in 2009–10 and to $5,550 in 2010–11. See Center for Law and Social Policy, "Preliminary Summary of Key Provisions of the American Recovery and Reinvestment Act Aimed at Improving the Lives of Low-Income Americans" (Washington: 2009), p. 1.

108. In its 2010 budget the Obama administration proposed several major changes in college loan programs. The most important change would be to move all new federal loans into the direct student loan program (Federal Family Education Loan program). Another important reform would be to revive the Perkins loan program with $6 billion a year to help up to 2.7 million students. The Perkins loans, which allow more discretion in loan allocation to campus financial aid administrators, would also be federal direct loans.

109. The average student who graduates from college is more than $20,000 in debt; see U.S. Secretary of Education Margaret Spellings, "Remarks to the Federal Student Aid Conference," Las Vegas, December 2, 2008.

110. See "Income-Based Repayment" (www.finaid.org/loans/ibr.phtml).

111. Rethinking Student Aid Study Group, "Fulfilling the Commitment."

112. Robert Haveman and Timothy Smeeding, "The Role of Higher Education in Social Mobility," *Future of Children* 16, no. 2 (2006).

113. In its 2010 budget the Obama administration proposed to create a $2.5 billion fund to establish a federal-state-local partnership to improve college success and completion for students from disadvantaged backgrounds. Research on programs that can improve college readiness and completion as well as dissemination of promising practices would be major characteristics of the new fund.

114. Thomas Brock and others, *Building a Culture of Evidence for Community College Student Success: Early Progress in the Achieving the Dream Initiative* (New York: MDRC, 2007).

115. Thomas Brock and Lashawn Richburg-Hayes, "Paying for Persistence: Early Results of a Louisiana Scholarship Program for Low-Income Parents Attending Community College" (New York: MDRC, 2006).

116. Kevin Carey, "Graduation Rate Watch: Making Minority Student Success a Priority" (Washington: Education Sector, 2008), table 4.

117. Ibid.; Shannon Colavecchio-Van Sickler, "More Blacks Succeed at FSU," *St. Petersburg Times*, November 19, 2007, p. 1A; Bill Maxwell, "FSU's Tough Love Gets Results," *St. Petersburg Times*, November 25, 2007, p. 3P.

118. Massachusetts Board of Higher Education and Massachusetts Department of Education, *Massachusetts School-to-College Report: High School Class of 2005* (Malden, Mass.: 2008), p. 9.

Chapter Nine

1. Lawrence M. Mead, *The New Politics of Poverty: The Nonworking Poor in America* (New York: Basic Books, 1992).

2. Ibid.

3. By 2004, the last year for which complete data are available, federal means-tested spending was 18.6 percent of all federal spending and 3.7 percent of GDP. For federal spending figures, see Congressional Research Service, "Cash and Noncash Benefits for Persons with Limited Income: Eligibility Rules, Recipient and Expenditure Data, FY2002-FY2004," RL33340 (2006), table 3.

4. Gary V. Engelhardt and Jonathan Gruber, "Social Security and the Evolution of Elderly Poverty," Working Paper 10466 (Cambridge, Mass.: National Bureau of Economic Research, 2004).

5. Robert P. Stoker and Laura A. Wilson, *When Work Is Not Enough: State and Federal Policies to Support Needy Workers* (Brookings, 2006).

6. Nicole D. Forry, "The Impact of Child Care Subsidies on Low-Income Single Parents: An Examination of Child Care Expenditures and Family Finances," *Journal of Family and Economic Issues* 30, no. 1 (2009), table 2. Forry presents estimates of the child care expenditures of families based on both administrative data and survey data; the figure presented here is the average of her two estimates.

7. Robin Toner and Janet Elder, "Poll Shows Majority Back Health Care for All," *New York Times*, March 2, 2007, p. A1; also see the Polling Report website, which contains results from multiple polls (www.pollingreport.com/health3.htm).

8. What goes up must come down. Work support policies that provide benefits to low-income workers must be phased out at higher incomes or they become too expensive. These benefits provide incentives to work at lower incomes because they boost income beyond wages. However, as benefits phase out, their work incentive declines. At some income levels, depending on what benefits a worker is receiving, an additional dollar of income could actually reduce total income by more than a dollar as the benefit package shrinks.

9. Robert Greenstein, "The Earned Income Tax Credit: Boosting Employment, Aiding the Working Poor" (Washington: Center on Budget and Policy Priorities, 2005; www.cbpp.org/7-19-05eic.htm). Although estimates vary, as much as 30 percent of EITC payments are overpayments or fraudulent. Such huge overpayments undermine support for the program, but the IRS has not figured out how to prevent the fraud without spending billions of dollars. See Robert Greenstein, *What Is the Magnitude of EITC Overpayments?* (Washington: Center on Budget and Policy Priorities, 2003); Internal Revenue Service, *Earned Income Tax Credit (EITC) Program Effectiveness and Program Management FY2002–2003* (2003; www.irs.gov/pub/irs-utl/eitc_effectiveness.pdf).

10. For Reagan's remarks on signing H.R. 3838 (Tax Reform Act of 1986) into law, see *Public Papers of the Presidents of the United States: Ronald Reagan, 1986* (Government Printing Office, 1987), vol. 2, pp. 1414–16.

11. Tax Policy Center, "Historical EITC Parameters" (Brookings and Urban Institute, 2008; www.taxpolicycenter.org/taxfacts/Content/PDF/historical_eitc_parameters.pdf).

12. John Karl Scholz, "Employment-Based Tax Credits for Low-Skilled Workers," Discussion Paper 2007-14 (Brookings, Hamilton Project, 2007).

13. A two-parent, two-child family could claim the maximum credit of $2,000 ($1,000 for each child) with income of $12,050 plus $13,334, or $25,384. The single mother with one child could claim the entire $1,000 child credit with income of $18,717.

14. In the American Recovery and Reinvestment Act, Congress and the Obama administration expanded the Child Tax Credit by temporarily lowering the threshold for the refundable credit from $12,500 to $3,000. President Obama's proposed 2010 budget would make the new $3,000 threshold permanent. If the Obama proposal is accepted by Congress, our recommendation to reduce the threshold to $8,500 becomes superfluous.

15. Aviva Aron-Dine, "Improving the Refundable Child Tax Credit: An Important Step toward Reducing Child Poverty" (Washington: Center on Budget and Policy Priorities, 2008, rev.), pp. 4–5.

16. Congressional Budget Office, *H.R. 6049: Energy and Tax Extenders Act of 2008* (Government Printing Office, 2008). The provision passed by the House would also expand the refundable credit attached to the Alternative Minimum Tax. That provision, which would cost nearly $0.9 billion a year, is not included in our proposal.

17. Ron Haskins, "Putting Education into Preschools," in *Generational Change: Closing the Test Score Gap*, edited by Paul E. Peterson (Lanham, Md.: Rowman and Littlefield, 2006).

18. Douglas J. Besharov, Caeli A. Higney, and Justus A. Myers, "Federal and State Child Care and Early Education Expenditures: 1995–2005" (University of Maryland, Welfare Reform Academy, 2007), table 1.

19. In 2007 median income for a family of three in Mississippi was $44,752, yielding an 85 percent limit for child care subsidies of about $38,000; median income for a family of three in California was $68,070, yielding an 85 percent limit of about $57,850. Data are from the American Community Survey (www.census.gov/hhes/www/income/medincsizeandstate.xls).

20. Assistant Secretary for Planning and Evaluation, Department of Health and Human Services, "Child Care Eligibility and Enrollment Estimates for Fiscal Year 2003," ASPE issue brief (Department of Health and Human Services, 2005).

21. U.S. Census Bureau, *Who's Minding the Kids? Child Care Arrangements: Spring 2005, Detailed Tables*, table 6 (www.census.gov/population/socdemo/child/ppl-2005/tab06.xls). The data from the SIPP survey on which this report is based have serious problems; see Douglas J. Besharov, Jeffrey S. Morrow, and Anne Gengyan Shi, "Child Care Data in the Survey of Income and Program Participation (SIPP): Inaccuracies and Corrections" (University of Maryland, Welfare Reform Academy, 2006).

22. There are many more child care and early education programs than the ones discussed here. The Government Accountability Office (formerly the General

Accounting Office), in a report recommending that Congress streamline the array of child care programs, finds that sixty-nine programs provide care or education to children under age five. See U. S. Government Accountability Office, "Early Education and Care: Overlap Indicates Need to Assess Crosscutting Programs," GAO/HEHS-00-78 (2000).

23. Leonard E. Burman, Elaine Maag, and Jeffrey Rohaly, "Tax Subsidies to Help Low-Income Families Pay for Child Care," Discussion Paper 23, Tax Policy Center (Brookings and Urban Institute, 2005), table 1.

24. Ibid., table 2.

25. For information on the Dependent Care Assistance Program (DCAP), see the summary on the University of Washington website (www.washington.edu/admin/hr/benefits/worklife/dcap.html).

26. The American Recovery and Reinvestment Act of 2009 expanded the DCTC by $2 billion as a one-time infusion of funds. If the provision becomes permanent it would supplement our proposal on expanding the DCTC.

27. U.S. Department of Health and Human Services, Administration for Children and Families, "Fiscal Year 2008 Federal Child Care and Related Appropriations" (www.acf.hhs.gov/programs/ccb/ccdf/approp_2008.htm).

28. House Committee on Ways and Means, *2008 Green Book,* chart 7-2.

29. We thank Jeff Rohaly of the Tax Policy Center for computing this estimate. Our phaseout policy includes a credit against the Alternative Minimum Tax (AMT), because under current law taxpayers who lose the child care credit could have the amount they must pay under the AMT fall, thereby offsetting the effect of the tax credit phaseout and reducing the amount of revenue it produces. The estimated savings achieved by our version of the phaseout grows from about $1.0 billion to $1.4 billion between 2010 and 2019. We have not found a way to estimate the savings from applying the phase-out to DCAPS, but it would be considerable. Whatever it is, we ignore it here.

30. We arrive at this number by subtracting the 4 percent quality set-aside and based on the approximate cost of $8,000 per child for full-time, year-round care. Douglas J. Besharov, Justus A. Myers, and Jeffrey S. Morrow, "Cost per Child for Early Childhood Education and Care: Comparing Head Start, CCDF Child Care, and Prekindergarten/Preschool Programs" (University of Maryland, Welfare Reform Academy, 2007).

31. For a succinct overview of the Medicaid program, see House Committee on Ways and Means, *2004 Green Book,* sec. 15.

32. Either the old Aid to Families with Dependent Children (AFDC) program or the Supplemental Security Income (SSI) program after it was implemented in 1974.

33. Under section 1925 of the Social Security Act, as amended by the 1996 welfare reform law, parents leaving welfare because of increased earnings continue to receive Medicaid for the first six months after leaving welfare. The family continues to receive Medicaid for an additional six months if the family's earnings do not exceed 185 percent of the poverty level.

34. David G. Smith and Judith D. Moore, *Medicaid Politics and Policy, 1965–2007* (New Brunswick, N.J.: Transaction, 2008), pp. 170–83. Although 15 percent of children under 200 percent of poverty remain uninsured, nearly two-thirds of these uninsured children are eligible for public coverage. Kaiser Commission on Medicaid Facts, "Enrolling Uninsured Low-Income Children in Medicaid and SCHIP" (2009; www.kff.org/medicaid/upload/2177_06.pdf).

35. Marilyn Werber Serafini, "SCHIP Leaves Critics Fuming," *National Journal*, February 7, 2009, p. 46; the estimate of 5 million additional children comes from the Congressional Budget Office; see "CBO's Estimate of Changes in SCHIP and Medicaid Enrollment in Fiscal Year 2013 under H.R. 2 (Public Law 111-3), the Children's Health Insurance Program Reauthorization Act of 2009," a table sent to Ron Haskins by Chris Peterson of the Congressional Research Service on March 6, 2009.

36. "Medicaid Enrollment and Beneficiaries, Selected Fiscal Years" (www.cms.hhs.gov/DataCompendium/16_2008_Data_Compendium.asp#TopOfPage), table 4.8. Although there are a few flaws in the data found at this source, the magnitude of the problems should be roughly constant over the period reported in the text.

37. Cindy Mann, "Family Coverage: Covering Parents along with Their Children" (Georgetown University, Health Policy Institute, 2008).

38. Between 2000 and 2007 the percent of people covered by employer-provided insurance fell from 64.2 percent to 59.3 percent. See U.S. Census Bureau, *Historical Health Insurance Tables* (various years), table HIA-1.

39. Alan Weil, "A Health Plan to Reduce Poverty," *Future of Children* 17, no. 2 (2007).

40. Alice M. Rivlin and Joseph R. Antos, eds., *Restoring Fiscal Sanity 2007: The Health Spending Challenge* (Brookings, 2007). As this book goes to press, Congress and the Obama administration are promising some form of expanded or even universal coverage before Congress adjourns in 2009.

41. The maximum benefit was raised 13.6 percent as part of the American Recovery and Reinvestment Act of 2009 for the period April 2009 to September 2009. This action raised the maximum monthly benefit to $526 for a family of three (roughly $6,300 annualized; www.fns.usda.gov/FSP/rules/Memo/09/021809.pdf).

42. The authors thank Dottie Rosenbaum of the Center on Budget and Policy Priorities for her help with this section. The 2002 Farm Bill (P.L. 107-171) contained several provisions to make it easier for working families to receive food stamps, such as reducing barriers (including no longer considering diversion payments as income), increasing the limits on the value of a recipient's car, and increasing the limits on savings and retirement accounts. Elaine M. Ryan, "The Unfinished Agenda: Two Years after TANF," *Policy and Practice of Public Human Services* 56 (1998); American Public Human Services Association, "Why the Food Stamp Program No Longer Meets the Needs of the Working Poor," APHSA issue brief (Washington: 1999); House Committee on Ways and Means, *2004 Green Book,* sec. 15. These reforms cost the federal government about $2.4 billion over five years, again demonstrating the commitment

by Congress to assist low-income families that work. For the CBO estimate of costs, see www.cbo.gov/doc.cfm?index=3385.

43. One study, based on the Survey of Income and Program Participation, shows that between 1996 and 2003 several food stamp and welfare policies had a significant impact on the probability that poor families would receive food stamps. Among the factors related to increased participation were a vehicle exemption policy, longer recertification periods, and expanded categorical eligibility, all of which were reformed in the 2002 Farm Bill. Caroline Ratcliffe, Signe-Mary McKernan, and Kenneth Finegold, "The Effect of State Food Stamp and TANF Policies on Food Stamp Program Participation" (Washington: Urban Institute, 2007).

44. U.S. Department of Agriculture, "Trends in Food Stamp Program Participation Rates: 2000–2006" (2008).

45. See table at www.fns.usda.gov/pd/snapsummary.htm for enrollment increases. The estimate of $2.1 billion is based on the assumption that if the food stamp penetration rate increases 25 percent, the share of increased enrollment is also 25 percent. Thus of the increase of 7.37 million enrollment between 2002 and 2007, about 1.84 million is due to the increased penetration rate. Multiplying 1.84 million additional people by the average annual benefit in 2007 of $1,147 yields our estimate of $2.1 billion.

46. U.S. Department of Health and Human Services, Administration for Children and Families, "Child Support Enforcement, FY 2007, Preliminary Report" (2008), table 3; U.S. Department of Health and Human Services, Administration for Children and Families, "Annual Statistical Report for Fiscal Years 1999 and 2000," table 4.

47. Vicki Turetsky, "Staying in Jobs and out of the Underground: Child Support Policies That Encourage Legitimate Work," Brief 2 (Washington: Center for Law and Social Policy, 2007).

48. According to the Federal Office of Child Support Enforcement, in 2007 non-custodial parents owed $107 billion in past-due child support. Around $7 billion was paid. U.S. Department of Health and Human Services, Administration for Children and Families, "Child Support Enforcement, FY 2007, Preliminary Report" (2008), table 5 (www.acf.hhs.gov/programs/cse/pubs/2008/preliminary_report_fy2007/table_5.html).

49. Consider HUD's 2009 assessment of fair market monthly rents for one-bedroom apartments in various American cities: San Francisco, $1,325; New York, $1,180; Miami, $953; Atlanta, $789; Austin, $749; Charlotte, $682; St. Louis, $593; Pittsburgh, $549; Green Bay, $549.

50. Bureau of Justice Statistics, "Homicide Victims in the U.S.: Homicide Victims by Age" (www.ojp.usdoj.gov/bjs/homicide/tables/vagetab.htm).

51. Housing Act of 1949, P.L. 81-171, chap. 338, sec. 2, stat. 413, title 42 (USCA sec. 1441).

52. See House Committee on Ways and Means, *2008 Green Book*, pp. 15-21, 15-22, tables 15-2 and 15-3; Joint Committee on Taxation, *Estimates of Federal Tax Expenditures for Fiscal Years 2007–2011*, JCS-3-07 (Government Printing Office, 2007), p. 28.

The generous expenditures on means-tested housing programs are dwarfed by the nearly $125 billion in tax benefits for mortgage interest, property taxes, and exclusion of capital gains on home sales that disproportionately benefit middle- and upper-income families.

53. Ron Haskins, along with several hundred other modest-income families, lived in former army barracks that had been converted to low-rent housing in Ypsilanti, Michigan, while his father attended college after World War II.

54. For a colorful review of the explosion of the American housing supply in the 1950s, see David Halberstam, *The Fifties* (New York: Ballantine Books, 1993), chap. 9.

55. Irving Welfeld, *Where We Live: The American Home and the Social, Political, and Economic Landscape, from Slums to Suburbs* (New York: Simon and Schuster, 1988).

56. Edgar O. Olsen, "Fundamental Housing Policy Reform" (University of Virginia, Department of Economics, 2006), p. 6.

57. Louis Winnick, "The Triumph of Housing Allowance Programs: How a Fundamental Policy Conflict Was Resolved," *Cityscape* 1, no. 3 (1995).

58. Alex Kotlowitz, *There Are No Children Here: The Story of Two Boys Growing up in the Other America* (New York: Anchor Books, 1992).

59. House Committee on Ways and Means, *2008 Green Book*, pp. 15-21 to 15-22. Despite the widespread belief that public housing has been a disaster, one study suggests that children living in public housing, compared with other poor children, do slightly better in school. See Janet Currie and Aaron Yelowitz, "Are Public Housing Projects Good for Kids?" *Journal of Public Economics* 75 (2000).

60. For a review, see Olsen, "Fundamental Housing Policy Reform," pp. 9–17.

61. Edgar O. Olsen, "Housing Programs for Low-Income Households," in *Means-Tested Transfer Programs in the United States*, edited by Robert A. Moffitt (Chicago: University of Chicago, 2003), p. 437. See also U.S. Government Accountability Office, "Federal Housing Assistance: Comparing the Characteristics and Costs of Housing Programs," GAO-02-76 (2002).

62. Janet M. Currie, *The Invisible Safety Net: Protecting the Nation's Poor Children and Families* (Princeton University Press, 2006), p. 94.

63. U.S. Department of Housing and Urban Development, *Waiting in Vain: An Update on America's Rental Housing Crisis* (1999).

64. Many individuals and organizations support the Low-Income Housing Tax Credit. Based on data from HUD, for example, the AARP claims in a 2006 publication that, since its inception in 1986, the credit had subsidized the construction of more than 1.3 million apartments for the poor and the elderly. The credit or any other current housing program could be removed from our proposal, the major effect of which would be to reduce the size of the housing subsidy available to low-income families. See Kim Bright, "Low-Income Housing Tax Credits: Helping Meet the Demand for Affordable Rental Housing" (Washington: AARP, 2006; www.aarp.org/research/housing-mobility/affordability/fs74r_lihtc.html).

65. Edgar O. Olsen and Jeffrey M. Tebbs, "The Effect on Program Participation of Replacing Current Low-Income Housing Programs with an Entitlement Housing

Voucher Program" (University of Virginia, Department of Economics, 2006). This is the first paper of an ongoing project; some estimates may change as the model is improved and as new data become available.

66. Ira S. Lowry, ed., *Experimenting with Housing Allowances: The Final Report of the Housing Assistance Supply Experiment* (Cambridge, Mass.: Oelgeschlager, Gunn, and Hain, 1983).

67. Research shows that fair market rents in many areas are closer to the average rent for apartments with a given number of bedrooms rather than 40 percent of that rent. Research also shows that fair market rents exceed the minimum rents necessary to occupy a unit that meets HUD's minimum standards. Edgar O. Olsen and William Reeder, "Misdirected Rental Subsidies," *Journal of Policy Analysis and Management* 11 (1983).

68. Estimate from Olsen and Tebbs, "The Effect on Program Participation of Replacing Current Low-Income Housing Programs with an Entitlement Housing Voucher Program," extrapolating from the HASE results that around 18 million households in the nation would be eligible for federal housing subsidies under the parameters followed in HASE (which are roughly equivalent to those in current law). The HASE experiment finds that about 40 percent of eligible households accepted the subsidy offer. Using 40 percent of 18 million households as the percentage of households that would accept the subsidy under our proposal, we calculate that around 7.2 million households would receive a housing subsidy.

69. The median length of a stay in public housing is 4.7 years; the median length of receiving a voucher is 3.1 years. Only 20 percent of families with children live in public housing longer than 8.9 years. Margery Austin Turner and G. Thomas Kingsley, "Federal Program for Addressing Low-Income Housing Needs: A Policy Primer" (Washington: Urban Institute, 2008), p. 5.

70. The evidence that moving to better neighborhoods helps low-income families is mixed. Based on a random-assignment experiment called Moving to Opportunity, in which some families were given vouchers to move to better neighborhoods, Jeffrey Kling and his colleagues find that, although the families did live in safer neighborhoods with lower poverty rates, there were no effects on adult economic self-sufficiency or physical health. There were some mental health benefits for adults and female youth, but there were negative effects on male youth. Jeffrey R. Kling, Jens Ludwig, and Lawrence F. Katz, "Neighborhood Effects on Crime for Female and Male Youth: Evidence from a Randomized Housing Voucher Experiment," *Quarterly Journal of Economics* 120, no. 1 (2005); Jeffrey R. Kling, Jeffrey B. Liebman, and Lawrence F. Katz, "Experimental Analysis of Neighborhood Effects," *Econometrica* 75, no. 1 (2007).

71. Fredrik Andersson, Harry J. Holzer, and Julia I. Lane, *Moving Up or Moving On: Who Advances in the Low-Wage Labor Market?* (New York: Russell Sage, 2005).

72. Claudia Goldin and Lawrence F. Katz, *The Race between Education and Technology* (Cambridge, Mass.: Belknap, 2008).

73. Sandy Baum and Kathleen Payea, "Trends in Student Aid: 2008" (Washington: College Board, 2008), p. 6.

74. Ibid., p. 13.

75. Based on Brookings tabulations of PSID data. Ron Haskins, "Education and Economic Mobility," in *Getting Ahead or Losing Ground: Economic Mobility in America*, edited by Julia Isaacs, Isabel Sawhill, and Ron Haskins (Brookings and Economic Mobility Project, an Initiative of the Pew Charitable Trusts, 2008), p. 96.

76. Congressional Research Service, "Cash and Noncash Benefits for Persons with Limited Income: Eligibility Rules, Recipient and Expenditure Data, FY2002–FY2004," Rl33340 (2006), table 5.

77. Kelly S. Mikelson and Demetra Smith Nightingale, *Estimating Public and Private Expenditures on Occupational Training in the United States* (Washington: Urban Institute, 2004), p. iv. We computed the estimate by taking the midpoint of spending by the Labor Department and dividing by the estimate of 500,000 people who received training (ibid., p. v).

78. Robert I. Lerman, "Are Skills the Problem: Reforming the Education and Training System in the United States," in *A Future of Good Jobs? America's Challenge in the Global Economy*, edited by Timothy J. Bartik and Susan Houseman (Kalamazoo, Mich.: W.E. Upjohn Institute for Employment Research, 2008).

79. For reviews of this literature, see Paul Osterman, "Employment and Training Policies: New Directions for Less-Skilled Adults," in *Reshaping the American Workforce in a Changing Economy*, edited by Harry J. Holzer and Demetra Smith Nightingale (Washington: Urban Institute, 2007); Harry J. Holzer, "Better Workers for Better Jobs: Improving Worker Advancement in the Low-Wage Labor Market," Discussion Paper 2007-15 (Brookings, Hamilton Project, 2007); David H. Greenberg and others, "A Meta-Analysis of Government-Sponsored Training Programs," *Industrial and Labor Relations Review* 57, no. 1 (2003).

80. Howard Bloom and others, "The Benefits and Costs of FTPA Title II-A Programs: Key Findings from the National Job Training Partnership Act Study," *Journal of Human Resources* 32, no. 3 (1997).

81. Andersson, Holzer, and Lane, *Moving Up or Moving On.*

82. Bloom and others, "The Benefits and Costs of FTPA Title II-A Programs."

83. Greenberg, Michalopoulos, and Robins, "A Meta-Analysis of Government-Sponsored Training Programs," p. 50.

84. Ibid.

85. James J. Kemple, "Career Academies: Long-Term Impacts on Labor Market Outcomes, Educational Attainment, and Transitions to Adulthood" (New York: MDRC, 2008).

86. Ibid., p. 38.

87. Linda Gennetian, "The Long-Term Effects of the Minnesota Family Investment Program on Marriage and Divorce among Two-Parent Families," paper prepared for U.S. Department of Health and Human Services, Office of the Assistant Secretary for Planning and Evaluation (New York: MDRC, 2003).

88. Robert Lerman, "Career-Focused Education and Training for Youth," in *Reshaping the American Workforce in a Changing Economy*, edited by Harry Holzer and Demetra Nightingale (Washington: Urban Institute, 2007).

89. Workforce Training and Education Coordinating Board, "Workforce Training Results Report" (Olympia, Wash.: 2008; www.wtb.wa.gov/Documents/WTR_Apprenticeship.pdf).

90. Osterman, "Employment and Training Policies."

91. Holzer, "Better Workers for Better Jobs."

92. Osterman, "Employment and Training Policies."

93. Lawrence M. Mead, "Toward a Mandatory Work Policy for Men," *Future of Children* 17, no. 2 (2007), p. 51.

94. Orlando Patterson, "Jena, O.J., and the Jailing of Black America," *New York Times,* September 30, 2007, sec. 4, p. 13. Patterson also attributes high rates of incarceration to the "crisis in relations between [black] men and women of all classes."

95. Orlando Patterson, "A Poverty of Mind," *New York Times,* March 26, 2006, sec. 4, p. 13.

96. Mead, "Toward a Mandatory Work Policy for Men."

97. The EITC currently has a childless worker credit, but the maximum benefit is only around $450, not enough in the view of most analysts to lure low-wage males into the labor force.

98. Barack Obama, *The Audacity of Hope: Thoughts on Reclaiming the American Dream* (New York: Crown, 2006), pp. 332–34. Also see Gordon L. Berlin, "Rewarding the Work of Individuals: A Counterintuitive Approach to Reducing Poverty and Strengthening Families," *Future of Children* 17, no. 2 (2007); Aviva Aron-Dine and Arloc Sherman, *Ways and Means Committee Chairman Charles Rangel's Proposed Expansion of the EITC for Childless Workers: An Important Step to Make Work Pay* (Washington: Center on Budget and Policy Priorities, 2007).

99. Greg J. Duncan, Aletha C. Huston, and Thomas S. Weisner, *Higher Ground: New Hope for the Working Poor and Their Children* (New York: Russell Sage, 2007); Virginia Knox, Cynthia Miller, and Lisa A. Gennetian, "Reforming Welfare and Rewarding Work: Final Report on the Minnesota Family Investment Program" (New York: MDRC, 2000); Charles Michalopoulos and others, "Making Work Pay: Final Report on the Self-Sufficiency Project for Long-Term Welfare Recipients" (New York: MDRC, 2002). For a review of these studies, see Berlin, "Rewarding the Work of Individuals."

100. Becky Petit and Bruce Western, "Mass Imprisonment and the Life Course: Race and Class Inequality in U.S. Incarceration," *American Sociological Review* 69 (2004).

101. Bruce Western, *Punishment and Inequality in America* (New York: Russell Sage, 2006), chap. 7. Western deals with this issue in great detail and concludes that imprisonment probably accounts for about 10 percent of crime reduction during, roughly, the last three decades of the twentieth century. Others estimate that imprisonment could account for up to 40 percent of that reduction.

102. Ibid., pp. 136–39. Western uses data from the Surveys of Inmates of State and Federal Correctional Facilities and the Surveys of Inmates of Local Jails to show that, between 1980 and 2000, the number of children with fathers in prison increased from

about 350,000 to 2.1 million. About one of every eleven black children had a father in prison or jail in 2000.

103. Devah Pager, *Marked: Race, Crime, and Finding Work in an Era of Mass Incarceration* (University of Chicago Press, 2007).

104. "Direct Expenditures by Criminal Justice Function, 1982–2006" (www.ojp. usdoj.gov/ bjs/glance/sheets/exptyp.csv).

105. Bruce Western, "From Prison to Work: A Proposal for a National Prisoner Reentry Program," Discussion Paper 2008-16 (Brookings, Hamilton Project, 2008).

106. *Gall* v. *United States*, 128 S. Ct. 586 (2007); *Kimbrough* v. *United States*, 128 S. Ct. 558 (2007).

107. Linda Greenhouse, "Court Restores Sentencing Powers of Federal Judges," *New York Times*, December 11, 2007, p. A1; "Justice in Sentencing," *New York Times*, December 12, 2007, p. A34.

108. United States Sentencing Commission, *Cocaine and Federal Sentencing Policy: Report to Congress* (Government Printing Office, 2007), p. 9.

109. Ron Haskins, *Work over Welfare* (Brookings, 2006), appendix; U.S. Department of Health and Human Services, Administration for Children and Families, "Fiscal Year 2008 Federal Child Care and Related Appropriations" (www.acf.hhs.gov/ programs/ccb/ccdf/approp_2008.htm).

110. Gretchen Rowe and Mary Murphy, *The Welfare Rules Databook: State TANF Policies as of July 2006* (Washington: Urban Institute, 2006), pp. 154–59.

111. Jonathan Morancy, Congressional Budget Office, personal communication with author, August 25, 2008.

112. The value of the block grant in 1996 was approximately $16.5 billion; by 2008 inflation had eroded its value by nearly 40 percent, to $9.9 billion.

113. They are also allowed to use the funds to promote marriage and to reduce nonmarital births.

114. Anderson, Holzer, and Lane, *Moving Up or Moving On.*

115. Harry J. Holzer and Robert I. Lerman, "The Future of Middle-Skill Jobs," Brief 41 (Brookings, Center on Children and Families, 2009), fig. 2.

116. Rebecca Blank, "Improving the Safety Net for Single Mothers Who Face Serious Barriers to Work," *Future of Children* 17, no. 2 (2007).

117. The determination that these disconnected mothers and children are living in deep poverty is based on the distribution of household income. However, if instead of income we examine the distribution of household consumption, the group at the bottom of the distribution does not appear to be as poor. One would think that consumption data—the actual goods and services purchased by a household—would be a more direct measure of well-being than income. But it has long been known that poor and low-income households consume at a level far higher than their household income. Although the exact reason for this apparent contradiction is not clear, these households may use savings; may get money from friends or family; may receive in-kind welfare benefits such as food, medical care, and housing; and may have undeclared (perhaps illegal) income. Bruce D. Meyer and Francis X. Sullivan, "The Well-

Being of Single Mother Families after Welfare Reform," Policy Brief 33 (Brookings, Welfare Reform and Beyond, 2005); Kerwin Kofi Charles and Melvin Stephens Jr., "The Level and Composition of Consumption over the Business Cycle: The Role of 'Quasi-Fixed' Expenditures," in *Working and Poor: How Economic and Policy Changes Are Affecting Low-Wage Workers*, edited by Rebecca Blank, Sheldon Danziger, and Robert Schoeni (New York: Russell Sage, 2006).

118. House Committee on Ways and Means, *2008 Green Book,* sec. 9, pp. 9-30, 9-36, 15-21, 15-22. This cost does not include the $5.3 billion the Joint Tax Committee estimates was spent through the tax credit for low-income housing in 2007; Joint Committee on Taxation, *Estimates of Federal Tax Expenditures for Fiscal Years 2007–2011*.

119. Maggie McCarty and others, "Overview of Federal Housing Assistance Programs and Policy," RL34591 (Congressional Research Service, 2008), p. 28.

120. All individuals with earnings pay FICA taxes, beginning with the first dollar of income. Although Social Security benefits are somewhat progressive, in contrast to the federal income tax system FICA taxes are regressive. Virginia P. Reno and Melinda M. Upp, "Social Security and the Family," in *Taxing the Family*, edited by Rudolph G. Penner (Washington: American Enterprise Institute, 1983); Lily Batchelder, Fred Goldberg, and Peter Orszag, "Reforming Tax Incentives into Uniform Refundable Tax Credits," Policy Brief 156 (Brookings, 2006).

121. For a review of these programs, see James A. Riccio, "Subsidized Housing and Employment: Building Evidence of What Works," in *Revisiting Rental Housing: Policies, Programs, and Priorities*, edited by Nicolas P. Retsinas and Eric S. Belsky (Brookings, 2008), pp. 201–03.

122. In 1997 HUD also initiated a program called Moving to Work, which selected twenty-four local housing authorities on a competitive basis to try more or less anything they could think of to encourage employment. Local authorities were given extraordinary flexibility in using HUD money to promote work. Again, however, there has been no evaluation of this program. Nonetheless, its mere existence shows that HUD and a number of local housing authorities are trying to promote work. Sandra J. Newman, "From the Eye of the Housing Practitioner," in *The Home Front*, edited by Sandra J. Newman (Washington: Urban Institute, 1999).

123. Howard S. Bloom, James A. Riccio, and Nandita Verma, "Promoting Work in Public Housing: The Effectiveness of Jobs-Plus" (New York: MDRC, 2005), esp. p. ES-8. A follow-up report now being written by MDRC shows that the earnings effect persists for at least three years after the end of the program, for a total of more than seven years of earnings effect. James Riccio, personal communication with author, February 25, 2009.

124. Riccio, "Subsidized Housing and Employment." Because of turnover in housing programs, an effective work program could serve many more recipients than the number receiving aid at any given moment.

125. Ibid., pp. 191–224.

126. The welfare reform law of 1996 seems to show that, if states sanction welfare recipients who do not work, work rates go up substantially. See Haskins, *Work over Welfare*, chap. 15. Our thinking is that some, but not all, local housing authorities

should implement programs that use sanctions to determine whether these programs would significantly boost work rates. Even though the Jobs-Plus experiment shows that a voluntary work program increases work rates, a mandatory work programs might increase them even more. In any case, we should find out.

127. Bloom, Riccio, and Verma, "Promoting Work in Public Housing."

128. Blank, "Improving the Safety Net for Single Mothers."

129. Haskins, *Work over Welfare,* chap. 15.

130. MDRC spent about $1 million a year on the Jobs-Plus evaluation. Allowing for inflation, we estimate that a similar multisite evaluation could be conducted today for around $1.5 million a year. We would include more funds so the secretary could pay for additional studies. Jim Riccio, MDRC, personal communication with author, August 19, 2008.

131. Under the American Recovery and Reinvestment Act of 2009 (commonly called the stimulus bill), this work requirement was suspended between April 2009 and October 2009 unless a state elects to follow the requirement. The act appropriates $20 million for states to provide work activities.

132. In 2007 states had $90 million in federal money to conduct the general work program. This money required no state matching funds. However, if states used all their federal funds and then spent additional funds out of their own budget, the federal government matched these additional expenditures at the rate of fifty cents on the dollar. Twenty-five states in 2007 spent about $32 million in excess of their share of the nonmatched funds. In addition to these two streams of money for regular work requirements, states can also qualify for a share of $20 million each year allocated for the work program that applies to recipients with no dependents. Only twenty-five states claim this funding.

133. A mother with two children earning $16,640 a year from an $8-an-hour job, and working full time, would be eligible for an EITC of $4,450, a Child Tax Credit of $690, food stamps worth $1,500, child care worth around $2,900, and Medicaid valued at $10,900 (all figures approximate). Her total work support package would be worth $20,440; when combined with her earnings, the family's total income in cash and benefits would be $37,080. Housing benefits could easily add another $6,000 to this total, although most eligible families do not receive the housing benefit.

134. Duncan, Huston, and Weisner, *Higher Ground.*

135. The Department of Labor and several private and public funders are supporting a demonstration program, being conducted by MDRC, that is attempting to provide disadvantaged adults with assistance similar in many ways to that provided by New Hope. The program, called the Work Advancement and Support Center (WASC), attempts to coordinate the local welfare and work support systems and to help workers obtain all the work support benefits for which they qualify. The centers also provide advice to workers about how to obtain training and engage in other activities that would help them advance to better and higher-paying jobs. Betsy L. Tessler and David Seith, "From Getting by to Getting Ahead: Navigating Career Advancement for Low-Wage Workers" (New York: MDRC, 2007).

Chapter Ten

1. Emily Yoffe, an editorial writer for *Slate.com*, made this point in responding to an e-mail she received criticizing her for being out of touch in her blogging on marriage. Emily Yoffe, ". . . And Baby Makes Two," Slate.com, March 20, 2008.

2. Barbara Dafoe Whitehead and Marline Pearson, "Making a Love Connection: Teen Relationships, Pregnancy, and Marriage" (Washington: National Campaign to Prevent Teen and Unplanned Pregnancy, 2006); see also Charles Murray and Deborah Laren, "According to Age: Longitudinal Profiles of AFDC Recipients and the Poor by Age Group" (Washington: American Enterprise Institute, Working Seminar on the Family and American Welfare Policy, 1986).

3. Andrew J. Cherlin, *The Marriage-Go-Round: The State of Marriage and the Family in America Today* (New York: Knopf, 2009), p. 17.

4. Congressional Research Service, "Cash and Noncash Benefits for Persons with Limited Income: Eligibility Rules, Recipient and Expenditure Data, FY2002–FY2004," RL33340 (Washington; 2006).

5. Adam Thomas and Isabel Sawhill, "For Richer or for Poorer: Marriage as an Antipoverty Strategy," *Journal of Policy Analysis and Management* 21, no. 4 (2002); see also Ron Haskins and Isabel Sawhill, "Work and Marriage: The Way to End Poverty and Welfare," Brief 28 (Brookings, Welfare Reform and Beyond, 2003); Robert I. Lerman, "The Impact of the Changing US Family Structure on Child Poverty and Income Inequality," *Economica* 63, no. 250 (1996 supplement).

6. Bruce Western, *Punishment and Inequality in America* (New York: Russell Sage, 2006), esp. chap. 1.

7. E. Mavis Hetherington, "Divorce: A Child's Perspective," *American Psychologist* 34, no. 10 (1979).

8. Judith S. Wallerstein and Joan B. Kelly, *Surviving the Breakup: How Children and Parents Cope with Divorce* (New York: Basic Books, 1980).

9. Paul R. Amato and Bruce Keith, "Parental Divorce and Adult Well-Being: A Meta-Analysis," *Journal of Marriage and the Family* 53, no. 1 (1991), p. 54.

10. Sara McLanahan and Gary Sandefur, *Growing Up with a Single Parent: What Hurts, What Helps* (Harvard University Press, 1994), p. 61.

11. The authors of the statement includes scholars such as William Galston, James Q. Wilson, William Doherty, Leon Kass, Linda Waite, and Amitai Etzioni; public intellectuals like Sylvia Ann Hewlett, Maggie Gallagher, Barbara Dafoe Whitehead, and Francis Fukuyama; leaders and scholars in ethics and religion such as Don Browning, Father Richard John Neuhaus, Jean Bethke Elshtain, and Rabbi Michael Lerner; and community activists and political leaders such as Bill Hardiman, Diane Sollee, Jeff Kemp, John Leopold, Michael McManus, Mitchell Pearlstein, and Tom Rossin. Coalition for Marriage, Family, and Couples Education, *The Marriage Movement: A Statement of Principles* (University of Chicago, Institute for American Values, Religion, Culture, and Family, 2000).

12. Sara McLanahan, Elisabeth Donahue, and Ron Haskins, "Introducing the Issue," *Future of Children* 15, no. 2 (2005), p. 10.

13. Norval Glenn and Thomas Sylvester with Alex Roberts, "The Shift and the Denial: Scholarly Attitudes toward Family Change, 1977–2002," Research Brief 8 (New York: Institute for American Values, 2008).

14. Carolyn J. Hill, Harry J. Holzer, and Henry Chen, *Against the Tide: Household Structure, Opportunities, and Outcomes among White and Minority Youth* (Kalamazoo: W. E. Upjohn Institute for Employment Research, 2009), p. 23.

15. Not every researcher agrees that the evidence on nonmarital births and single parenting shows definitively that children are harmed. Arline T. Geronimus and Sanders Korenman, "The Socioeconomic Costs of Teenage Childbearing: Evidence and Interpretation," *Demography* 30, no. 2 (1993)) find that problems with the children of teen mothers are due mostly to the disadvantaged background of the teen mothers themselves and not single parenting per se. Joseph V. Hotz and his colleagues, "The Impacts of Teenage Childbearing on the Mothers and the Consequences of Those Impacts for Government," in *Kids Having Kids: Economic Costs and Social Consequences of Teen Pregnancy*, edited by Rebecca A. Maynard (Washington: Urban Institute, 1997), compares pregnant teens that gave birth with those that had miscarriages and finds only small negative effects.

16. Jonathan Rauch, "The Widening Marriage Gap: America's New Class Divide," *National Journal*, May 19, 2001, pp. 1471–72.

17. William Julius Wilson, *The Truly Disadvantaged: The Inner City, the Underclass, and Public Policy* (University of Chicago Press, 1987); Kathryn Edin and Maria Kefalas, *Promises I Can Keep: Why Poor Women Put Motherhood before Marriage* (University of California Press, 2005).

18. Nearly 75 percent of the pregnancies of unmarried women are unplanned. National Campaign to Prevent Teen and Unplanned Pregnancy, "DCR Report: Data/Charts/Research Report" (Washington). "Unwed mothers are roughly 30 percent less likely to marry in a given year than childless women": Andrea Kane and Daniel T. Lichter, "Reducing Unwed Childbearing: The Missing Link in Efforts to Promote Marriage," Brief 37 (Brookings, Center on Children and Families, 2006), p. 4.

19. David T. Ellwood and Christopher Jencks, "The Spread of Single-Parent Families in the United States since 1960," in *The Future of the Family*, edited by Daniel P. Moynihan, Timothy M. Smeeding, and Lee Rainwater (New York: Russell Sage, 2004), p. 25.

20. See sec. 404(a)(1) of the Social Security Act.

21. Twenty-four states and the District of Columbia spent at least some of their TANF money or state matching funds on activities designed to increase two-parent family formation and maintenance; see "Use of TANF and Maintenance of Effort (MOE) Funds in Fiscal Year 2006" (http://clasp.org/publications/state_moe_fy06_all_worksheets.xls). For details on the most extensive program, see Robin Dion and Timothy Silman, "Starting Early: How the Oklahoma Marriage Initiative Helps Prepare Young People for Healthy Marriages," research brief (U.S. Department of Health and Human Services, Office of the Assistant Secretary for Planning and Evaluation, 2008).

22. Charles Murray, *Losing Ground: American Social Policy, 1950–1980* (New York: Basic Books, 1984); see also Charles Murray, "The Coming White Underclass," *Wall Street Journal*, October 29, 1993, p. A14.

23. *Responsibility and Empowerment Support Program Providing Employment, Child Care, and Training Act,* 103 Cong. 1993–94, H.R. 3500.

24. Bob Herbert, "In America: Inflicting Pain on Children," *New York Times,* February 25, 1995, p. A23.

25. Ron Haskins, *Work over Welfare: The Inside Story of the 1996 Welfare Reform Law* (Brookings, 2006), p. 231.

26. Douglas J. Besharov and Peter Germanis, eds., *Preventing Subsequent Births to Welfare Mothers* (University of Maryland, Welfare Reform Academy, 1998; www.welfareacademy.org/pubs/teensex/eval/toc.shtml).

27. For an overview of the legislative battle on the under age eighteen and the family cap provisions, see Ron Haskins, *Work over Welfare: The Inside Story of the 1996 Welfare Reform Law* (Brookings, 2006), esp. chaps. 4, 8, 9.

28. Bill Alpert, "With One Voice 2007: America's Adults and Teens Sound off about Teen Pregnancy" (Washington: National Campaign to Prevent Teen and Unplanned Pregnancy, 2007).

29. Sec. 510(b)(2), Social Security Act, defines abstinence education as a program that "(A) has as its exclusive purpose, teaching the social, psychological, and health gains to be realized by abstaining from sexual activity; (B) teaches abstinence from sexual activity outside marriage as the expected standard for all school age children; (C) teaches that abstinence from sexual activity is the only certain way to avoid out-of-wedlock pregnancy, sexually transmitted diseases, and other associated health problems; (D) teaches that a mutually faithful monogamous relationship in the context of marriage is the expected standard of human sexual activity; (E) teaches that sexual activity outside of the context of marriage is likely to have harmful psychological and physical effects; (F) teaches that bearing children out-of-wedlock is likely to have harmful consequences for the child, the child's parents, and society; (G) teaches young people how to reject sexual advances and how alcohol and drug use increases vulnerability to sexual advances; and (H) teaches the importance of attaining self-sufficiency before engaging in sexual activity."

30. Thomas DeLeire and Leonard M. Lopoo, "Welfare Reform's Influence on Childbearing by 15- to 17-Year-Olds," *La Follette Policy Report* 17, no. 2 (2008).

31. Laura Meckler, "Poverty: The New Search for Solutions; The Matchmaker: How A U.S. Official Promotes Marriage to Help Poor Kids; To Encourage Couples to Wed, Wade Horn Plans to Spend $500 Million in Five Years; Mr. Cobb Starts a Family," *Wall Street Journal*, November 20, 2006, p. A1.

32. Although the reauthorization bill passed Congress in late 2005, because of a drafting error the House and Senate bills were not identical and therefore the bill could not become law. The error was not discovered until after Congress had left for its Christmas recess. Thus Congress repassed the bill in early 2006, and it was signed into law in February, nearly four years after its planned date of enactment.

33. There is one community-based initiative that has been in operation for many years and has been evaluated by a reasonable, though not gold-standard, design. Called Marriage Savers, the initiative works with as many churches as possible in a given community to convince clergy to insist on marriage preparation training; to have retreats for married couples; to train troubled couples through the use of mentor couples; and to conduct other activities. A sophisticated evaluation comparing divorce rates in communities that had the Marriage Savers program with similar communities that did not, finds that marriage rates in communities with Marriage Savers increased faster than in comparison communities. See Paul James Birch, Stan E. Weed, and Joseph Olsen, "Assessing the Impact of Community Marriage Policies® on County Divorce Rates," *Family Relations* 53, no. 5 (2004).

34. The Healthy Marriage Promotion and Responsible Fatherhood grants may be found in sec. 403(a)(2) of the Social Security Act. The grants provide $100 million for the marriage initiative and $50 million for the fatherhood initiative. Funds from the fatherhood grants can be used to promote responsible fatherhood through counseling, mentoring, disseminating information about the advantages to children of being involved with both parents, enhancing relationship skills, and a host of other activities.

35. Quoted in Whitehead and Pearson, "Making a Love Connection," p. 6.

36. Lawrence B. Finer and Stanley K. Henshaw, "Disparities in Rates of Unintended Pregnancy in the United States, 1994 and 2001," *Perspectives on Sexual and Reproductive Health* 38, no. 2 (2006); Anjani Chandra and others, "Fertility, Family Planning, and Reproductive Health of U.S. Women: Data from the 2002 National Survey of Family Growth," *Vital Health Statistics* 23, no. 25 (2005), table 21.

37. Isabel V. Sawhill, "What Can Be Done to Reduce Teen Pregnancy and Out-of-Wedlock Births?" Brief 8 (Brookings, Welfare Reform and Beyond, 2001).

38. In 2006 and 2007 the teen birthrate increased for the first time since 1991. For analysis of possible reasons for the increase, see Kristin Anderson Moore, "Teen Births: Examining the Recent Increase" (Washington: National Campaign to Prevent Teen and Unplanned Pregnancy, 2008).

39. Richard Bavier and Wendell Primus, "Estimating Child Poverty and Single-Mother Impacts of Declining Teen Birth Rates by State" (Washington: National Campaign to Prevent Teen and Unplanned Pregnancy, 2005).

40. John S. Santelli and others, "Explaining Recent Declines in Adolescent Pregnancy in the United States: The Contribution of Abstinence and Improved Contraceptive Use," *American Journal of Public Health* 97, no. 1 (2007).

41. Sawhill, "What Can Be Done to Reduce Teen Pregnancy and Out-of-Wedlock Births?"; Santelli and others, "Explaining Recent Declines in Adolescent Pregnancy in the United States."

42. Richard J. Bonnie, Kathleen Stratton, and Robert B. Wallace, eds., *Ending the Tobacco Problem: A Blueprint for the Nation* (Institute of Medicine, 2007); James C. Fell, and others, *Increasing Teen Safety Belt Use: A Program and Literature Review* (U.S. Department of Transportation, 2005).

43. Douglas Kirby, "Emerging Answers 2007: Research Findings on Programs to Reduce Teen Pregnancy and Sexually Transmitted Diseases" (Washington: National Campaign to Prevent Teen and Unplanned Pregnancy, 2007).

44. Carmen Solomon-Fears, "Scientific Evaluations of Approaches to Prevent Teen Pregnancy," RS22656 (Washington: Congressional Research Service, 2007), p. 4.

45. A few high-quality abstinence-only projects were asked to participate but refused. Perhaps the most notable is Elayne Bennett's Best Friends program in Washington. Her program was subsequently evaluated by Dr. Robert Lerner using a reasonable, but not gold standard, research design. Lerner finds evidence that the program reduced smoking, drinking, drug use, and the likelihood of having sex by disadvantaged girls from the inner city. Similar results are reported for a different version of Best Friends, called Diamond Girls. See Robert Lerner, "Can Abstinence Work? An Analysis of the Best Friends Program," *Adolescent and Family Health* 3, no. 4 (2004); for more about Best Friends, see www.bestfriendsfoundation.org.

46. Christopher Trenholm and others, "Impacts of Four Title V, Section 510, Abstinence Education Programs: Final Report" (Princeton, N.J.: Mathematica Policy Research, 2007).

47. Sawhill, "What Can Be Done to Reduce Teen Pregnancy and Out-of-Wedlock Births?" p. 6.

48. Sevgi O. Aral, Kevin A. Fenton, and King K. Holmes, "Sexually Transmitted Diseases in the U.S.A.: Temporal Trends," *Sexually Transmitted Infections* 83 (2007); Centers for Disease Control and Prevention, *Sexually Transmitted Disease Surveillance 2004* (U.S. Department of Health and Human Services, 2005).

49. Alpert, "With One Voice 2007," p. 3. The figures used here are from a survey conducted in 2006. See also Robert E. Rector, Melissa G. Pardue, and Shannan Martin, "What Do Parents Want Taught in Sex Education Programs," Backgrounder 1722 (Washington: Heritage Foundation, 2004). A random-digit dial survey of California parents conducted in 2006 found that 89 percent preferred comprehensive sex education, while only 11 percent preferred abstinence-only education; see Norman A. Constantine, Petra Jerman, and Alice X. Huang, "California Parents' Preferences and Beliefs Regarding School-Based Sex Education Policy," *Perspectives on Sexual and Reproductive Health* 39, no. 3 (2007).

50. Robert E. Rector, "The Effectiveness of Abstinence Education Programs in Reducing Sexual Activity among Youth," Backgrounder 1533 (Washington: Heritage Foundation, 2002); Christine C. Kim and Robert Rector, "Abstinence Education: Assessing the Evidence," Backgrounder 2126 (Washington: Heritage Foundation, 2008); Stan E. Weed and others, "An Abstinence Program's Impact on Cognitive Mediators and Sexual Initiation," *American Journal of Health Behavior* 32, no. 1 (2008); Andrew S. Doniger and others, "Impact Evaluation of the 'Not Me, Not Now' Abstinence-Oriented, Adolescent Pregnancy Prevention Communications Program, Monroe County, New York," *Journal of Health Communication* 6, no. 1 (2001); Lerner, "Can Abstinence Work?" A program conducted in Atlanta in the 1980s with eighth-grade,

black, inner-city students added an abstinence component to an existing and ineffective sex education program. The abstinence part of the curriculum was taught by older teenagers, who showed the students how to avoid peer pressure to have sex. Today we would call this program abstinence plus. After adding the abstinence component, students who had not had sex by the time the program began were only a fifth as likely to have had sex by the end of eighth grade compared to students who had not participated in the program. Interestingly, students who did initiate sex after participating in the program were more likely to use contraception than comparison students. Thus the abstinence-plus program decreased sexual activity and increased condom use for those who were sexually active; see Marion Howard and Judith Blamey McCabe, "Helping Teenagers Postpone Sexual Involvement," *Family Planning Perspectives* 22, no. 1 (1990).

51. Carmen Solomon-Fears, "Reducing Teen Pregnancy: Adolescent Family Life and Abstinence Education Programs," RS20873 (Washington: Congressional Research Service, 2008).

52. Laura Duberstein Lindberg, John S. Santelli, and Susheela Singh, "Changes in Formal Sex Education: 1995–2002," *Perspectives on Sexual and Reproductive Health* 38, no. 4 (2006).

53. Laura Beil, "Just Saying No to Abstinence Ed," *Newsweek*, October 27, 2008, p. 58.

54. Robert Rector and his colleagues at the Heritage Foundation show that nine frequently used comprehensive abstinence-plus curriculums, as compared with nine "true" abstinence curriculums, had little content related to abstinence. Rector and his colleagues examined every page in the curriculums and counted the pages that had abstinence content and the ones that had material that promoted contraception. Whereas the abstinence curriculums had abstinence content on 54 percent of their pages, the abstinence-plus curriculums had abstinence material on only 5 percent of their pages. In addition, the abstinence-plus curriculums had material promoting contraception on nearly 30 percent of their pages, while the abstinence curriculums had none. There were numerous other differences between the two types of curriculums, perhaps the most important of which is that the abstinence-plus curriculums had little or no content about the importance of teens delaying sexual activity. See Shannan Martin, Robert Rector, and Melissa G. Pardue, *Comprehensive Sex Education vs. Authentic Abstinence: A Study of Competing Curricula* (Washington: Heritage Foundation, 2004).

55. Melissa S. Kearney and Phillip B. Levine, "Reducing Unplanned Pregnancies through Medicaid Family Planning Services," Brief 39 (Brookings, Center on Children and Families, 2008).

56. The authors calculate that there were 1.5 fewer births per fifty-four additional women served, implying that 1.0 birth was avoided for every thirty-six additional recipients of family planning services.

57. Congressional Budget Office, *Budget Options,* vol. 1, *Health Care* (2008), p. 48. This estimate puts the savings at about $30 million a year. However, the provision that

was part of the 2009 stimulus bill passed by the Energy and Commerce Committee was broader than the provision in the budget volume and was scored by CBO as saving $100 billion a year.

58. Laura G. Knapp, Janice E. Kelly-Reid, and Roy W. Whitmore, "Enrollment in Postsecondary Institutions, Fall 2004; Graduation Rates, 1998 & 2001 Cohorts; and Financial Statistics, Fiscal Year 2004," NCES 2006-155 (U.S. Department of Education, National Center for Education Statistics, 2006; http://nces.ed.gov/pubs2006/2006155.pdf).

59. Ellen M. Bradburn, "Short-Term Enrollment in Postsecondary Education: Student Background and Institutional Differences in Reasons for Early Departure, 1996–98," NCES 2003-153 (U.S. Department of Education, National Center for Education Statistics, 2003); see also National Campaign to Prevent Teen and Unplanned Pregnancy, "Briefly . . . Unplanned Pregnancy: What Community Colleges Can Do" (Washington: 2008).

60. Adam Thomas and Emily Monea, "FamilyScape: A Simulation Model of Family Formation," unpublished manuscript (Brookings, 2009).

61. HHS officials in the Bush administration felt it was necessary to avoid the term "marriage promotion." They wanted to characterize the marriage initiative as giving people the relationship skills to allow them to have healthy relationships, including healthy marriage. Rather than promoting marriage, their objective was to help people achieve "relationship" goals they already had before entering the program. Our view is that the true hope of the administration, and of conservatives in general, was to reestablish the norm of marriage before childbearing in the most direct way possible—by promoting marriage.

62. Frank F. Furstenberg, "Should Government Promote Marriage?" *Journal of Policy Analysis and Management* 26, no. 4 (2007), p. 957.

63. Wendy Sigle-Rushton and Sara McLanahan, "For Richer or Poorer: Marriage as an Anti-Poverty Strategy in the United States?" *Population* 57, no. 3 (2002).

64. Richard H. Thaler and Cass R. Sunstein, *Nudge: Improving Decisions about Health, Wealth, and Happiness* (Yale University Press: Yale, 2008).

65. The Office of Management and Budget has established a system for evaluating government programs called the Program Assessment Rating Tool (PART) system. After several years of use, PART has shown that the overwhelming majority of government programs have little if any evidence of success, let alone reliable evidence from high-quality evaluation studies. Indeed, many government programs do not even have clear goals or a clear logic model of how the program is designed to achieve its goals.

66. Peter H. Rossi, Mark W. Lipsey, and Howard E. Freeman, *Evaluation: A Systematic Approach,* 7th ed. (Thousand Oaks, Calif.: Sage, 2004); Larry L. Orr, *Social Experiments: Evaluating Public Programs with Experimental Methods* (Thousand Oaks, Calif.: Sage, 1999).

67. Centers for Disease Control, "Percentage of Young Adults Who Were Current, Former or Never Smokers, Overall and by Sex, Race, and Education, 1965–2006" (www.cdc.gov/tobacco/data_statistics/tables/adult/table_12.htm).

68. James C. Fell and others, *Increasing Teen Safety Belt Use: A Program and Literature Review* (Washington: National Highway Traffic Safety Administration, 2005), p. 12.

69. J. Kruger, H. W. Kohn III, and I. J. Miles, "Prevalence of Regular Physical Activity among Adults—United States, 2001 and 2005," *Morbidity and Mortality Weekly Report,* November 23, 2007.

70. Barack Obama, *The Audacity of Hope: Thoughts on Reclaiming the American Dream* (New York: Crown, 2006), p. 334.

71. C. Eugene Steuerle, *Contemporary U.S. Tax Policy* (Washington: Urban Institute, 2004).

72. Administration for Children and Families, "New Calculator Illustrates Marriage Penalties," press release (U.S. Department of Health and Human Services, May 3, 2006; http://marriagecalculator.acf.hhs.gov/marriage/dd/prog_L_desc.php?prog=3).

73. Gregory Acs and Elaine Maag, "Irreconcilable Differences? The Conflict between Marriage Promotion Initiatives for Cohabiting Couples with Children and Marriage Penalties in Tax and Transfer Programs," Paper B-66 (Washington: Urban Institute, New Federalism: National Survey of America's Families Series B, 2005), table 2.

74. Will Marshall and Isabel V. Sawhill, "Progressive Family Policy in the Twenty-First Century," in *The Future of the Family,* edited by Daniel P. Moynihan, Timothy M. Smeeding, and Lee Rainwater (New York: Russell Sage, 2004).

75. Tax Policy Center, "Tax Stimulus Report Card: Senate Bill" (Brookings and Urban Institute, 2009; www.taxpolicycenter.org/taxtopics/senate_refundable_child. cfm). In the American Recovery and Reinvestment Act of 2009, Congress and the Obama administration expanded the Child Tax Credit substantially by reducing the threshold for computing the refundable credit to $3,000 from $12,550. President Obama proposed making the $3,000 threshold permanent in his 2010 budget proposal.

76. Alan Berube and others, "The Price of Paying Taxes: How Tax Preparation and Refund Loan Fees Erode the Benefits of the EITC," survey series (Brookings and Progressive Policy Institute, 2002).

77. Adam Carasso and C. Eugene Steuerle, "The Hefty Penalty on Marriage Facing Many Households with Children," *Future of Children* 15, no. 2 (2005).

78. Marshall and Sawhill, "Progressive Family Policy in the Twenty-First Century."

79. A recent Rand study finds that exposure to sexual content on TV, controlling for a large set of variables, predicts teen pregnancy. Teens at the 90th percentile of exposure to TV sexual programming are twice as likely to get pregnant in the following three years as teens at the 10th percentile of exposure. See Anita Chandra and others, "Does Watching Sex on Television Predict Teen Pregnancy? Findings from a National Longitudinal Survey of Youth," *Pediatrics* 122, no. 5 (2008).

80. Elisabeth Hirschhorn Donahue, Ron Haskins, and Marisa Nightingale, "Using the Media to Promote Adolescent Well-Being," policy brief (Brookings and Woodrow Wilson School of Public and International Affairs, Future of Children, 2008).

81. W. Douglas Evans, "Social Marketing Campaigns and Children's Media Use," *Future of Children* 18, no. 1 (2008).

82. Leslie B. Snyder and Mark A. Hamilton, "A Meta-Analysis of U.S. Health Campaign Effects on Behavior: Emphasize Enforcement, Exposure, and New Information, and Beware the Secular Trend," in *Public Health Communication: Evidence for Behavior Change*, edited by Robert C. Hornik (Mahwah, N.J.: Lawrence Erlbaum, 2002).

83. Matthew C. Farrelly and others, "Evidence of a Dose-Response Relationship between 'Truth' Antismoking Ads and Youth Smoking Prevalence," *American Journal of Public Health* 95, no. 3 (2005).

84. Bill Cosby and Alvin F. Poussaint, *Come on People: On the Path from Victims to Victors* (Nashville: Thomas Nelson, 2007); Juan Williams, *Enough: The Phony Leaders, Dead-End Movements, and Culture of Failure That Are Undermining Black America—and What We Can Do about It* (New York: Three Rivers Press, 2006).

Chapter Eleven

1. Here are some examples of egregious federal spending from the "2008 Pig Book" maintained on the website of Citizens Against Government Waste: $97,314 for maple research; $125,000 for music archives at the University of Mississippi; $148,950 for the Montana Sheep Institute; $172,782 for the National Wild Turkey Federation in Edgefield, S.C.; $188,000 for Maine's Lobster Institute; $1 million for the Puget Sound Navy Museum; and nearly $15 million for the International Fund for Ireland, an organization that promotes economic development and political dialogue in Ireland that, among other things, pays for Sesame Workshop (a children's TV show), a conference for chefs, and support for three-star hotels. See www.cagw.org/site/Doc Server/CAGW-Pig_Book_08.pdf?docID=3001.

2. Some of our products include Alice M. Rivlin and Isabel V. Sawhill, eds., *Restoring Fiscal Sanity: How to Balance the Budget* (Brookings, 2004); Alice M. Rivlin and Isabel Sawhill, eds., *Restoring Fiscal Sanity 2005: Meeting the Long-Run Challenge* (Brookings, Budgeting for National Priorities 2005); William Frenzel and others, "Taming the Deficit," paper (Brookings, Budgeting for National Priorities. 2007).

3. Isabel Sawhill and Ron Haskins, "The Politics of Deficit Reduction," in Rivlin and Sawhill, *Restoring Fiscal Sanity 2005*; Ron Haskins, Alice M. Rivlin, and Isabel V. Sawhill, "Getting to Balance: Three Alternative Plans," in Rivlin and Sawhill, *Restoring Fiscal Sanity*.

4. USBudgetWatch, "Stimulus Watch: Government Responses to the Financial and Economic Crisis" (www.usbudgetwatch.org/stimulus).

5. Alan J. Auerbach and William G. Gale, "The Economic Crisis and the Fiscal Crisis: 2009 and Beyond," Tax Policy Center (Brookings and Urban Institute, 2009).

6. The Social Security Trust Fund, which has been running surpluses every year since 1984 and now has a balance of around $2.2 trillion, actually has nothing more than IOUs from the federal government in its account. Thus it is somewhat misleading to say that the trust fund will "run out of money" because, given the overall deficit of the federal budget, when "money" is withdrawn from the trust fund in the future to pay benefits, each dollar withdrawn represents another dollar borrowed by the federal

government. See "Old Age and Survivors Insurance Trust Fund, 1937–2008" (www.ssa.gov/oact/stats/table4a1.html); *The 2008 Annual Report of the Board of Trustees of the Federal Old-Age and Survivors Insurance and Federal Disability Insurance Trust Funds* (www.ssa.gov/OACT/TR/TR08/trTOC.html).

7. See "A Summary of the 2008 Annual Reports" (www.ssa.gov/OACT/TRSUM/trsummary.html).

8. Bill Frenzel and Ron Haskins, "'What, Me Worry?' Ignoring the Entitlement Tsunami," *Washington Times*, April 7, 2008, p. A17.

9. Peter Orszag, "Foreign Holdings of U.S. Government Securities and the U.S. Current Account," testimony before the Committee on the Budget, U.S. House of Representatives, June 26, 2007, p. 2.

10. Congressional Budget Office, *The Budget and Economic Outlook: Fiscal Years 2009 to 2019* (2009), p. 16. The $249 billion interest payment in 2008 could turn out to be modest compared with future interest payments. For example, under reasonable assumptions, Auerbach and Gale estimate that the cumulative deficit over the period 2009–19 could be a much as $11.5 trillion. Let's assume the actual deficits cumulate to a more modest $10 trillion. Added to the current cumulative debt of $5.8 trillion held by the public, the nation could be paying interest on a cumulative debt of nearly $16 trillion after 2019. Under this scenario, interest payments of $249 billion will look good. See ibid. and Auerbach and Gale, "The Economic Crisis and the Fiscal Crisis: 2009 and Beyond," app. table 2.

11. Commission on Thrift, *For a New Thrift: Confronting the Debt Culture* (New York: 2008).

12. U.S. Budget Watch, "Stimulus Watch: Government Responses to the Financial and Economic Crisis" (www.usbudgetwatch.org/stimulus).

13. See polling data by Celinda Lake at Partnership for America's Economic Success/Invest in Kids Working Group (www.partnershipforsuccess.org/docs/ivk/iik meeting_slides200801lake.pdf).

14. Isabel Sawhill and Emily Monea, "Old News," *Democracy: A Journal of Ideas* 9 (Summer 2008).

15. For high dropout rates, see Paul E. Barton, "One-Third of a Nation: Rising Dropout Rates and Declining Opportunities" (Princeton, N.J.: Education Testing Service, 2005); Miles Corak, "Do Poor Children Become Poor Adults? Lessons from a Cross-Country Comparison of Generational Earnings Mobility," Discussion Paper 1993 (Bonn: IZA, 2006).

16. Spending on nonchild Social Security, Medicare and Medicaid, defense, international, and interest on the debt can be estimated to consume all federal revenues by about 2040; see Adam Carasso and others, *Kids' Share 2008: How Children Fare in the Federal Budget* (Washington: Urban Institute, 2008), figure 19. As we finish this volume, the nation is in the midst of a recession that appears to be getting worse. Spending to fight the financial crisis and to stimulate the economy has imposed trillion-dollar-plus deficits on the federal government for the next several years, and the prospects of more spending to continue fighting the crisis in the financial markets or

to stimulate the economy seems likely. At the least, the additional federal revenue estimated by Carasso and his colleagues will be lower for many years, making the problem of fighting among claimants on federal dollars even more intense.

17. Karlyn Bowman, "Public Opinion on Taxes" (Washington: American Enterprise Institute, 2008; www.aei.org/publications/pubID.16838/pub_detail.asp).

18. Office of Management and Budget, "FY 2008 Appropriations Earmarks" (www.earmarks.omb.gov).

19. U.S. Government Accountability Office, *High-Risk Series: An Update* (2009; www.gao.gov/new.items/d09271.pdf. GAO-09-271).

20. James J. Mongan, Timothy G. Ferris, and Thomas H. Lee, "Options for Slowing the Growth of Health Care Costs," *New England Journal of Medicine,* April 3, 2008; Henry J. Aaron, "The Rising Cost of Health Care: Is It a Problem?" remarks to the 2004 Annual Meeting, Institute of Medicine, October 19, 2004; Congressional Budget Office, "Evidence on the Costs and Benefits of Health Information Technology," Publication 2976 (2008).

21. Congressional Budget Office, "Research on the Comparative Effectiveness of Medical Treatments," Publication 2975 (2007).

22. Rachel Tolbert Kimbro and others, "Race, Ethnicity, and the Education Gradient in Health," *Health Affairs* 27, no. 2 (2008).

23. Congressional Budget Office, *The Budget and Economic Outlook: Fiscal Years 2008 to 2018* (2008).

24. Divided We Fail, "Savings, Pensions, and Work" (www.aarp.org/issues/divided wefail/about_issues/divided_we_fail_platform_savings_pensions_and_work.html).

25. Author's calculations from U.S. Census Bureau, "Age of Head of Household: All Races by Median and Mean Income, 1967 to 2007" (www.census.gov/hhes/www/income/histinc/h10AR.html), table H-10.

26. Carmen DeNavas-Walt, Bernadette D. Proctor, and Jessica C. Smith, *Income, Poverty, and Health Insurance Coverage in the United States: 2007,* Current Population Report P60-235 (U.S. Census Bureau, 2008), table B-2.

27. U.S. Bureau of Labor Statistics, *Consumer Expenditure Survey* (2007), table 47.

28. Diana Farrell and others, "Talkin' 'Bout My Generation: The Economic Impact of Aging U.S. Baby Boomers" (Washington: McKinsey Global Institute, 2008).

29. U.S. Census Bureau, *Current Population Survey, Annual Demographic Supplement* (2007), table PINC-01.

30. James F. Fries, "Measuring and Monitoring Success in Compressed Morbidity," *Annals of Internal Medicine*, September 2, 2003.

31. Edward B. Fiske, "A Nation at a Loss," *New York Times,* April 25, 2008, p. A27.

32. Julia B. Isaacs, "Economic Mobility of Men and Women," in *Getting Ahead or Losing Ground: Economic Mobility in America,* edited by Julia B. Isaacs, Isabel V. Sawhill, and Ron Haskins (Washington: Economic Mobility Project, an Initiative of the Pew Charitable Trusts, 2008).

33. Sandy Baum and Jennifer Ma, "Trends in College Pricing: 2008" (Washington: College Board, 2008), p. 9.

34. UNICEF, "Child Poverty in Perspective: An Overview of Child Well-Being in Rich Countries," Report Card 7 (Florence, Italy: UNICEF Innocenti Research Centre, 2007).

35. Orley Ashenfelter, Colm Harmon, and Hessel Oosterbeek, "A Review of Estimates of the Schooling/Earnings Relationship, with Tests for Publication Bias," Working Paper 7457 (Cambridge, Mass.: National Bureau of Economic Research, 2000); Barbara L. Wolfe and Robert H. Haveman, "Social and Nonmarket Benefits from Education in an Advanced Economy," *Education in the 21st Century: Meeting the Challenges of a Changing World,* edited by Yolanda K. Kodrzycki (Boston: Federal Reserve Bank of Boston, 2002).

36. James Heckman and Alan B. Krueger, *Inequality in America: What Role for Human Capital Policies?* (MIT Press, 2002).

37. "Benefits Planner: Taxes and Your Social Security Benefits" (www.socialsecurity.gov/planners/taxes.htm).

38. After a detailed study of this issue for the Center for Retirement Research at Boston College, John Turner concludes: "The question of whether more workers could work past age 62 has two parts. First, how have older workers' capabilities changed? Second, how have job requirements changed? Overall, individuals in their fifties and sixties are effectively younger than people the same age 25 years ago in terms of life expectancy, disability rates, and self-reported health. These findings are consistent across gender and racial/ethnic groups. Along with health, employment has become less physically demanding, except for those with relatively little education." John A. Turner, "Promoting Work: Implications of Raising Social Security's Early Retirement Age," Work Opportunities for Older Americans Series 12 (Boston College, Center for Retirement Research, 2007). Also see Gary Burtless and Joseph F. Quinn, "Is Working Longer the Answer for an Aging Workforce?" Issue in Brief 11 (Boston College, Center for Retirement Research, 2002).

39. Henry J. Aaron and Jeanne M. Lambrew, *Reforming Medicare: Options, Trade-Offs, and Opportunities* (Brookings, 2008).

Appendix A

1. In calculating eligibility for student aid, the Department of Education uses a formula that takes into account several factors, including parent income and assets, family size, and family members currently attending college, in determining whether a student is eligible for aid and, if so, for how much.

2. Sandy Baum and Kathleen Payea, "Trends in Student Aid: 2008" (Washington: College Board, 2008), p. 14.

3. Rethinking Student Aid Study Group Report, "Fulfilling the Commitment: Recommendations for Reforming Federal Student Aid" (Washington: College Board, 2008), p. 13.

4. Baum and Payea, "Trends in Student Aid: 2008," p. 14; David P. Smole and Shannon S. Loane, "A Brief History of Veterans' Education Benefits and Their Value," RL34549 (Washington: Congressional Research Service, 2008).

5. Smole and Loane, "A Brief History of Veterans' Education Benefits and Their Value," p. 17.

6. The U.S. Military Academy (West Point), the U.S. Naval Academy, and the U.S. Air Force Academy opened their doors in 1802, 1845, and 1954, respectively. A four-year education at one of the academies is worth approximately $400,000, including monthly pay, tuition, books, room and board, food, summer programs, dorm cleaning services, and operation and management of facilities (www.academyadmissions.com/admissions/obligations.php).

7. National Association of State Student Grant and Aid Programs, "38th Annual Survey Report on State-Sponsored Student Financial Aid: 2006–2007 Academic Year" (Washington: 2008; www.nassgap.org/viewrepository.aspx?categoryID=3#collapse_295).

8. State Higher Education Executive Officers, "State Higher Education Finance: Early Release FY 2008," (Boulder, Colo.: Author, 2008; www.sheeo.org/finance/shef/shef%20fy08%20early%20release%202pdf).

9. Robert Haveman and Timothy Smeeding, "The Role of Higher Education in Social Mobility," *The Future of Children* 16, no. 2 (2006).

10. Institute for Higher Education Policy, *Private Scholarships Count: Access to Higher Education and the Critical Role of the Private Sector* (Washington: 2005).

11. The National Defense Education Act of 1958 established the first federal loan program for postsecondary education.

12. These four-year costs were computed by multiplying one-year costs by four; the one-year costs are $13,589 for in-state public colleges, $24,044 for out-of-state public colleges, and $32,307 for private colleges. See Sandy Baum and Jennifer Ma, "Trends in College Pricing: 2007" (Washington: College Board, 2007), p. 2.

13. Thomas D. Snyder, Sally A. Dillow, and Charlene M. Hoffman, *Digest of Education Statistics 2006*, NCES 2007-017 (U.S. Department of Education, Institute of Education Sciences, 2007), chap. 3.

14. Baum and Payea, "Trends in Student Aid."

15. Under both the subsidized and unsubsidized Stafford programs, the federal government pays interest costs while students are in school and for six months after students graduate. In the subsidized program, students repay only the loan principal and interest that accrues after the grace period; in the unsubsidized program, students repay both principal and interest. Many students have both types of loans.

16. In his 2010 budget, President Obama proposes to provide $6 billion a year in new loan volume for up to 2.6 million students.

17. C. Eugene Steuerle, *Contemporary U.S. Tax Policy* (Washington: Urban Institute, 2004), chaps. 6, 7. All families pay Social Security and Medicare (FICA) taxes beginning with the first dollar of earnings.

18. Lily L. Batchelder, Fred T. Goldberg Jr., and Peter R. Orszag, "Reforming Tax Incentives into Uniform Refundable Tax Credits," Policy Brief 156 (Brookings, 2006). All individuals with earnings, however, pay FICA taxes beginning with the first dollar of income. Although Social Security benefits are somewhat progressive, by contrast

with the federal income tax system FICA taxes are regressive; see Virginia P. Reno and Melinda M. Upp, "Social Security and the Family," in *Taxing the Family*, edited by Rudolph G. Penner (Washington: American Enterprise Institute, 1983).

19. House Committee on Ways and Means, *2004 Green Book* (Government Printing Office, 2004), sec. 13, WMCP: 108-6.

20. Pamela J. Jackson, "Higher Education Tax Credits: An Economic Analysis," RL32507 (Washington: Congressional Research Service, 2007).

21. An above-the-line deduction is subtracted from a tax filer's income to arrive at adjusted gross income (AGI). A below-the-line deduction is subtracted from AGI. The former is generally more valuable because it will always reduce a filer's tax bill (assuming that filer has nonzero income taxes), but a below-the-line deduction may not. If filers simply claim the standard deduction, below-the-line deductions do not help them.

22. Jackson, "Higher Education Tax Credits."

23. Leonard E. Burman and others, "The Distributional Consequences of Federal Assistance for Higher Education: The Intersection of Tax and Spending Programs," Discussion Paper 26 (Washington: Urban Institute, Tax Policy Center, 2005).

24. See Gallup's annual personal finance poll, updated April 2–5, 2007, asking Americans to rate the concern they have about each of several financial problems. Lydia Saad, "Financial Anxiety Is Prevalent among Americans, Even Affluents," May 7, 2007 (www.gallup.com/poll/27505/financial-anxiety-prevalent-among-americans-even-affluents.aspx).

Appendix B

1. Jane Reardon-Anderson and others, "Systematic Review of the Impact of Marriage and Relationship Programs" (Washington: Urban Institute, 2005), p. 23.

2. See www.acf.hhs.gov/healthymarriage/pdf/june18_list_marriageedprograms.PDF.

3. "A Brief Snapshot of Funded Healthy Marriage Programs" (www.healthymarriageinfo.org).

4. Steven L. Nock, "Marriage as a Public Issue," *Future of Children* 15, no. 2 (2005); Theodora Ooms, Stacey Bouchet, and Mary Parke, "Beyond Marriage Licenses: Efforts in States to Strengthen Marriage and Two-Parent Families" (Washington: Center for Law and Social Policy, 2004).

5. Chris Mooney, *The Republican War on Science* (New York: Basic Books, 2006).

6. The sites are in Broward and Orange counties, Florida; Atlanta; Allen, Lake, Miami, and Marion counties, Indiana; Baton Rouge; Baltimore; Oklahoma City; and San Angelo and Houston, Texas.

7. Alan M. Hershey and M. Robin Dion, "Implementing a Large-Scale Test of Marriage and Relationship Skills Education: Building Strong Families" (Princeton, N.J.: Mathematica Policy Research, 2008).

8. M. Robin Dion and others, "Implementing Healthy Marriage Programs for Unmarried Couples with Children: Early Lessons from the Building Strong Families Report" (Princeton, N.J.: Mathematica Policy Research, 2006), p. 53. See also M. Robin Dion and others, "Implementation of the Building Strong Families Program" (Princeton, N.J.: Mathematica Policy Research, 2008).

9. M. Robin Dion and Barbara Devaney, "Strengthening Relationships and Supporting Healthy Marriage among Unwed Parents," Building Strong Families Brief 1 (Princeton, N.J.: Mathematica Policy Research, 2003); Barbara Devaney, Alan Hershey, and Debra Strong, "Supporting Healthy Marriage and Strengthening Relationships of Unwed Parents: Technical Assistance Available," Building Strong Families Brief 2 (Princeton, N.J.: Mathematica Policy Research, 2003).

10. The sites are in Orlando; Wichita; New York City; Oklahoma City; Bethlehem and Reading, Pennsylvania; El Paso and San Antonio, Texas; and Seattle (www.supportinghealthymarriage.org/description.html/).

11. MDRC, "Guidelines for Supporting Healthy Marriage Demonstration Programs" (New York: 2005).

12. M. Robin Dion and others, "Implementation of the Building Strong Families Program" (Washington: Mathematica Policy Research, 2008), p. 99.

13. Robert I. Lerman, "The Community Healthy Marriage Initiative: Early Lessons, Future Goals," Power Point presentation prepared for conference, "Healthy People, Healthy Families: Connecting Marriage Research to Practice," African American Healthy Marriage Initiative, Administration for Children and Families, Chapel Hill, N.C., June 19–21, 2007.

14. William J. Doherty and Jared R. Anderson, "Community Marriage Initiatives," *Family Relations* 53, no. 5 (2004).

15. See www.rti.org/page.cfm?objectid=5D34F7B2-15CA-4C89-AFCBDA490C670DF9.

16. Anupa Bir and others, "Piloting a Community Approach to Healthy Marriage Initiatives: Early Implementation of the Healthy Marriage Healthy Relationships Demonstration—Grand Rapids, Michigan" (Washington: RTI International, 2005).

17. Michael L. Gillette, *Launching the War on Poverty: An Oral History* (New York: Twayne, 1996).

Index